Radical Shakespeare

Routledge Studies in Shakespeare

Radical Shakespeare

Politics and Stagecraft in the Early Career

Chris Fitter

Routledge
Taylor & Francis Group
NEW YORK   LONDON

First published 2012
by Routledge
711 Third Avenue, New York, NY 10017

Simultaneously published in the UK
by Routledge
2 Park Square, Milton Park, Abingdon, Oxon OX14 4RN

*Routledge is an imprint of the Taylor & Francis Group,
an informa business*

Typeset in Sabon by IBT Global.
Printed and bound in the United States of America on acid-free paper by
IBT Global.

Library of Congress Cataloging-in-Publication Data
Fitter, Christopher.
    Radical Shakespeare : politics and stagecraft in the early career / Chris
Fitter.
        p. cm. — (Routledge studies in Shakespeare ; 6)
    Includes bibliographical references and index.
    1.   Shakespeare, William, 1564–1616—Political and social views.
    2.   Shakespeare, William, 1564–1616—Dramatic production.
    3.   Radicalism in literature.   I. Title.
    PR3017.F58 2011
    822.3'3—dc22
                                                            2011023099

ISBN13: 978-0-415-89793-8 (hbk)
ISBN13: 978-0-203-15367-3 (ebk)

For Catherine Lenore Parrish

For your love, your wisdom, your strength,

and matchless sweetness

It is strange that those who find in Cade's barbarity an indication of Shakespeare's horror of the mob should neglect to find in the barbarity of Queen Margaret or of my lords Clifford and York an indication of his horror of the nobility.

John Palmer, *Political Characters of Shakespeare* (London: Macmillan, 1948), 318–19

Edward Ellis a vagrant who died in the street.
A young man not known who died in a hay-loft.
A cripple that died in the street before John Awsten's door.
A poor woman, being vagrant, whose name was not known, she died in the street under the seat before Mr. Christian Shipman's house called the Crown . . . in the High Street.
A maid, a vagrant, unknown, who died in the street near the Postern.
Margaret, a deaf woman, who died in the street . . .
A young man vagrant having no abiding place . . . who died in the street before the door of Joseph Hayes, a brazier dwelling at the sign of Robin Hood in the High Street . . . He was about 18 years old. I could not learn his name

Burials in a London parish 1593–98, cit. A.L Beier, *Masterless Men*, 46

So distribution should undo excess,
And each man have enough.

King Lear, 4.1.67–71

Contents

Acknowledgements

I should like to thank David Norbrook for inviting me to voice my heterodoxies at a graduate seminar at Oxford; Katharine Goodland for the kind invitation to present a paper in the Columbia University Shakespeare Seminar series; and Harry Keyishian for warmth and encouragement to lead a session in one of the Fairleigh Dickinson Shakespeare Colloquia at Madison, New Jersey. James Holstun, Andy Wood, James Bednarz, Terry Eagleton, Curt Breight, Ivo Kamps and John Farquhar were each generous enough with their time to read some early chapters of this book, and all, irritatingly, supplied constructive criticism. (I should note for the record that each still feels, I darkly suspect, that there's plenty more where that criticism came from.) I am truly in their debt; and remaining misdemeanours are conspicuously my own.

Portions of this book were published as relatively brief, early drafts, and I should like to thank the following journals for republication permissions: *Shakespeare Studies* (vol. 32, 2004) for Chapter 3; *Medieval and Renaissance Drama in English* (vol. 23, 2010) for Chapter 9; *English Literary Renaissance* (vol. 30.2, Spring 2000) for Chapter 7; and *English Literary History* (vol. 72.1, Spring 2005) for Chapter 4.

All quotation of Shakespeare is given from *The Norton Shakespeare*, edited by Stephen Greenblatt, Walter Cohen, Jean E. Howard and Katharine Eisaman Maus (1997).

1 Historical Foundations

The Black Nineties and the Tudor Richesse of Political Dissidence

Inequalities of wealth and status ensured that social relations were politicised at every level in early modern England, and a reconstruction of these political realities both undermines the recent comfortable historiographical consensus on orderliness and stability and emphasises the severity of the problem of government.[1]

The largest category of popular disorder insurrections and riots which protested the administration of justice. This category includes symbolic acts such as rescuing prisoners from pillories and prisons, a riot at an execution, an assault upon constables, and violent demonstrations that directly challenged the authority of the mayor. Of the nine remaining instances of disorder during this period, four riots were directed against gentlemen and lawyers.[2]

Had these excesses [London riots] proceeded soley from the spirit of mischief and plunder, or even from the mere wantonness of youth and strength, the case would have been common enough; but they were often distinguished by a mixture of good though misguided feeling— by a wild notion of righting some imaginary wrong, of reaching some offence, of abating some nuisance untouched by law—which raised their authors above the level of vulgar rioters.[3]

(Orazio Busino, chaplain to the Venetian ambassador)

One of today's best known images of William Shakespeare is the bust in Holy Trinity Church, Stratford. There Shakespeare sits, chubby and stolid, memorably described by Dover Wilson as resembling "a self-satisfied pork butcher".[4] A sketch of the bust made in 1634, however, by the reliably accurate engraver William Dugdale for his later *Antiquities of Warwickshire Illustrated* (1656) records a lean-faced man, with long, drooping whiskers. He holds neither quill nor book. The effigy that we know today has been transformed beyond recognition from the original. It has even been argued recently that the bust does not depict William Shakespeare at all. More probably it represents the poet's father, who had held, unlike his son, several civic offices in Stratford, and was restored to the borough council by the time of his death in 1601. John Shakespeare had also been a substantial dealer in wool, which may explain why the original bust placed both hands upon a woolsack.[5] Repeatedly in the eighteenth and nineteenth centuries, 'renovations' and 'beautifications' then altered the image until the original, as Dugdale's sketch reminds us, was altogether effaced by the self-impositions of subsequent periods. It will be the argument of this book that something not dissimilar has happened in literary criticism's portraits of Shakespeare's politics. Due to the distortive self-projections of subsequent cultural history, and a perhaps insufficient concern to recover the originary circumstances of representation, we have lost the political face of William Shakespeare. In the light, I suggest, of modern historical scholarship, much of Shakespeare's original political profile may be recovered—and to rather startling effect.

Let me open with certain historical fundamentals, which are, in my view, usually insufficiently stressed when meditating the politics of the historically disfigured bard.

"EXPOSE THYSELF TO FEEL WHAT WRETCHES FEEL": THE BLACK NINETIES[6]

Literary criticism seldom links Shakespearean drama to the currents of radical thought in Tudor and Stuart England. This owes partly to historians' tendency to focus radicalism at its two most active points in that period: the eruptive years of the Reformation (mid-sixteenth century), and the successfully revolutionary decades of the Revolution and Republic (mid-seventeenth). The1590s are generally passed over, despite two attempted risings: Hacket's Rebellion of 1591 (which we will discuss as central to the design of *2 Henry VI*) and the Oxford Rising of 1596 (possibly hinted at, I have argued, in *Richard II*).[7] That decade saw also the largest outbreak of rioting between Bosworth and 1642: the Apprentices' Riot of 1595, when nearly two thousand Londoners took to the streets, tore down pillories, overwhelmed the watch, and tried to break into a prison (the Counter) in the first London food riots since the 1520s—events which I shall suggest were crucial to the original meaning of *Romeo and Juliet*. London subsequently established three Provost-Marshals—roving disciplinary officials empowered to apply on-the-spot martial law. One of them was ordered to patrol Southwark's south bank: home to the Rose theatre, and the Swan, and later the Globe.[8]

Some historians speak thus of a "crisis of order . . . in the sixty years before the civil war."[9] Literary critics, however, are not uncommonly found defining the England in which Shakespeare began his career—Shakespeare appears to have arrived in London by the late 1580s—as one characterised by a post-Armada euphoria of national unity and admiration for the gallant queen. Such postulates overlook the bitter chasm between rich and poor, deepening in the century's final decades, which victory over the Spanish could not long mask; indeed as Curtis Breight has powerfully demonstrated, symptomatically harsh governmental attitudes alienated England's Armada mariners themselves.[10] Even as they stood listening to Elizabeth's Tilbury speech, the nations' defenders were (in Susan Frye's words), "unpaid and ill-equipped and even hungry".[11] As soon as they were disbanded, they tried desperately to sell their armour—a recourse immediately criminalised, on pain of death. It is true that the city of London staged initial rejoicings: the triumphal bearing of captured Spanish banners about thoroughfares, the production of Armada medals, portraits and ballads, the gushing of ebullient sermons. But as Fernandez-Armesto—possibly the Armada's most authoritative historian—remarks, "such officially sponsored junkets are, of course, no genuine guide to popular feeling . . . The boost to English morale, such as it was, is impossible to calibrate."[12] In the very month that London's Victory procession took place (November 1588), English soldiers were executed, in their camp at Ostend, for having mutinied over lack of pay.[13] It remains, further, "a curious fact that disillusionment, recrimination, and mutual reproach were almost as rife on the English side after the Armada, amid celebrations of success, as on the Spanish side amid a consciousness of failure." Though both countries faced the need to pay off large numbers of servicemen and treat the multitudes of the sick, the irony emerges of "the victorious English dying in the gutter; the defeated Spaniards going home to hospital beds and embroidered counterpanes."[14] The month of the Armada itself (August 1588) saw the Lord Admiral Howard inform the Privy Council that his fleet was so "grievously infected" by "a very plague" that "many of the ships have hardly enough men to weigh their anchors." So poorly organised had provisioning been that, after many weeks afloat, "my Lord Admiral was driven to eat beans, and some to drink their own water [i.e., urine]." Any residue of patriotic loyalty in the fleet was corroded by the widespread conviction that the sailors had been poisoned through negligent government planning. "The mariners have a conceit," wrote Howard, "and I think it true and so do all the captains here, that sour drink hath been a great cause of this infection amongst us; and, Sir, for my own part I know not which way to deal with the mariners to make them rest contented with sour beer, for nothing doth displease them more."[15]

Worst of all, many Armada mariners were dying from malnutrition, because they were unpaid. The response, however, of Gloriana's regime was to launch the decade of brutal crackdowns. When a crowd of 500 discharged soldiers assembled the following summer (1589: Shakespeare was then twenty-five years old) near the royal palace in Westminster to protest their non-payment, Provost-Marshals hauled out four and hanged them, while calling out 2,000 men from the city's trained bands. Alarmed again in June 1591 by "unlawful great assemblies of multitudes of a popular sort of base condition" in London and by "wandering idle persons . . .

some coloring their wandering by the name of soldiers returned from the war", Elizabeth once more created a Provost-Marshal, given lethal authority "without delay to execute upon the gallows by order of martial law" vagabonds and anyone "unlawfully gathering themselves in companies".[16] Beier evokes them "Riding through the countryside with a clutch of deputies armed with pistols, carbines and staves": a sight surely terrifying to the poor.[17] Some lawyers and thinkers felt dismay at this authoritarian suspension of common law by diktat of central government: the Earl of Essex would note that "it does agree with her Majesty's merciful and excellent government not to let her subjects die *sans replique*, as the Frenchman terms it, while her kingdom is free both from invasion and rebellion."[18] November, however, saw the follow-up proclamation that ex-military men found wandering without "sufficient passport for their dismission" should be imprisoned as deserters; vagrants posing as ex-servicemen were to be summarily executed.[19] "This amounted", comments Breight, "to *carte blanche*, or open season on the dispossessed".[20] If, following the two greatest explosions of disorder in the summer of 1595, no further London riots followed, this may well owe, thinks Ian Archer, to "tightened control rather than restoration of social calm."[21]

As such policy makes clear, to Elizabeth's government the poor seemed as potentially alarming an enemy as the Spaniard. With the Armada on the high seas, the Privy Council had resolved *against* levying the nation's 100,000 plebeian auxiliaries, trusting national defence only to the trained bands drawn from the prosperous classes—"hardly enough to confront the sort of field force of over 20,000 seasoned veterans which the Armada might have landed."[22] However, "the presence of large numbers in arms from the lower orders always alarmed the gentry", for "a naked basis of force underlay social relations".[23] Indeed, under the Tudors, "In many English towns, between one-quarter and one-third of the population were destitute because they did not receive regular wages."[24] (In Shakespeare's Stratford, the poor would make up a quarter of the population by the close of the 1590s, and class anger, for example against grain-hoarders, ran high: a Stratford weaver hoped "to see them hanged on gibbets at their own doors.")[25] Unsurprisingly, Ralegh predicted that if the Spanish invaded, the poor would say "Let the rich fight for themselves."[26] The decision of England's authorities, however, suggested the greater fear that their own lower classes, once armed, might actually rise in revolt. The Council ordered the round-up of "vagabond rogues and other suspected persons", along with the internment of Catholics, as potential recruits for the Spanish.[27] The government's sense of class-enmity was reciprocated by many commoners. Henry Danyell, of Ash, in Kent, declared in the early 1590s that "the Spaniards . . . were better than the people of this land, and therefore he . . . had rather that they were here than the rich men of this country."[28] A Canterbury artisan lamented in 1596 "If the Spaniards did inhabit here it would be better for us . . . [for] we could not live worse unless we were starved."[29]

Bartholomew Steere, seeking popular insurrection in 1596, taught that England "would never be well untill some of the gentlemen were knockt downe", and that "the commons long sithens in Spaine did rise and kill all gentlemen . . . and sithens that time have lyved merrily there."[30] "Kinge Philipp", alleged one former soldier, "was a father to Ingland and did better love an Inglishe man than the quenes majestie did, for he would give them meete, drinke, and clothes." Numbers of the poor, notes Jim Sharpe, felt Philip to be rightful king of England.[31]

The Elizabethan regime would remain haunted, we shall see, by fear of underclass rebellion throughout the 1590s. The period was deeply stressed by accelerating social polarisation. Although it "saw the erection of grander mansions by landowners and urban patricians and the rebuilding and refurnishing of the homes of the yeomanry and master craftsmen, it also saw a mushroom growth of bare cottages for the poor in country parishes and the emergence of squalid overcrowded pauper suburbs in the towns."[32] And while the income of the gentry, the yeomanry and the urban 'middling sort' expanded, a permanent proletariat, rural and urban, had emerged by the late sixteenth century, alongside fearfully impoverished small farmers and artisans—all three of which groups saw their income decline further. "By the end of the sixteenth century . . . the poor were no longer the destitute victims of misfortune or old age, but a substantial proportion of the population living in constant danger of destitution, many of them full-time wage labourers."[33] It will be with the restive distress of the poorer commoners, and with Shakespeare's engagement of the violently defensive political climate with which central and local government reacted, that this book will be most concerned.

For few decades in English history have seemed as liable as were the Black Nineties (as we might call them) to generate, in their escalating intensity of concentrated distress, revolutionary upheaval.[34] Overall, the sixteenth century may have experienced an inflation rate of some four or five hundred per cent, with the price of grain rising 400 per cent during the period.[35] During the 1590s, real wages sank on average 22 per cent lower than in the preceding decade.[36] Between 1594 and 1598, they were just 57 per cent of what they had been in the 1560s.[37] Justices of the Peace fixed wages at the lowest possible rates, assuming (mostly wrongly, as we shall see in discussion of *As You Like It*) that the poor relief system would alleviate hunger where necessary.[38] They thus established a wage-freeze in the midst of a meteoric price rise, for the harvests of 1594–97 were perhaps the most catastrophic in English agrarian history. Ominously, London was still "filling out at the bottom."[39] "Thousands of new apprentices, discharged mariners and soldiers, deserters, and vagrants . . . arrived each year (adding) to the overcrowding and confusion of the city and its burgeoning suburbs."[40] "The extramural parishes were overwhelmed with immigrants crammed into the proliferating alleys whose insanitary conditions made them bastions of crisis mortality."[41] In the moiling crush of the metropolis, bubonic plague struck almost annually through the 1590s. Even without it, the average life-expectancy in England was thirty-five; less for the poor.[42]

Additionally, war sent taxes shooting upwards. Parliament in 1593 granted an anguishing, historically unprecedented triple subsidy. Further, although historians, debating the severity of the 1590s crisis relative to that of the 1540s,[43] differ over the extent of the 1590s fall in real wages, it is clear that given corrupt under-assessment of richer taxpayers—successive Parliaments acknowledged "the notable and evident abusing and diminucion of manie men's values . . . specially of men of the better state of livelihood and countenaunce"[44]—the effect was to deepen the desperation of the poor: "the relative burden on the poorer sections of society was increasing."[45] Francis Bacon in the 1593 Commons noted the "impossibility" of such taxation for some: "The poor mens Rent is such as they are not able to yield it".[46] C. S. L. Davies has suggested that the conditions of plague, war and famine inflicted in the 1590s "what may well have been the low point in the living standards of the mass of the European population, at any rate since the Black Death."[47]

It didn't take a William Shakespeare to sense the national mood, or to guess the magnitude of potential consequences. An anonymous libel in Norwich, 1595, declared

> For seven years the rich have fed on our flesh . . . There are 60,000 craftsmen in London and elsewhere, besides the poor country clown who can no longer bear, therefore their draft is in the cup of the Lord which they shall drink to the dregs, and some barbarous and unmerciful soldier shall lay open your hedges, reap your fields, rifle your coffers, and level your houses to the ground. Meantime give licence to the rich to set open shop to sell poor men's skins. Necessity hath no law.[48]

A Kentish worker declared in 1598 that he "hoped to see such warre in this realme to afflicte the rich men of this countrye to requite their hardness of heart towards the poore".[49] In the words of historian Andy Wood, "The gentry were constantly aware that their numbers were small, and that the commons had good cause for complaint: as Fulke Greville put it in 1593, 'if the feet knew their strength as well as we know their oppression, they would not bear as they do.'"[50] "What can riche men do against poore men yf poore men rise and hold toguither?" asked an Essex labourer in 1594.[51]

Amid this aggravated misery and desperation, the sixteenth century hatched the ideological conditions making gradually possible, as Lawrence Stone has argued, the Civil War of the 1640s, by plunging the ruling class and key state institutions into (what Habermas would call) a deepening legitimation crisis.[52] The aristocracy, for instance, lost greatly in prestige and moral authority. Its military function being long decayed, it now derelicted its traditional responsibility of extending 'hospitality' to the needy, preferring to flock to extravagant lifestyles in London; and the magnate household as an educational centre was becoming replaced by middle class schools.[53] Court and government were resented for a corruption that maintained exploitative monopolies and tolerated illegal enclosures,[54] as well as for hyper-taxation and endless military exactions. In religion, the nation's zigzagging left a "morally dilapidated" Church, with declining numbers entering the ministry, lay contempt for bishops, and deep-seated religious apathy.[55] It has been suggested that the Elizabethan period was "the age of the greatest religious indifference before the twentieth century".[56] In education, the spread of literacy militated against blind obedience to traditional power-structures, reinforcing the natural anti-traditionalism of market society; and since the very large increase in enrolments in Grammar Schools, Universities and the Inns of Court was unmatched by suitable employment opportunities, the result was a generation of alienated intellectuals, a tribe of 'malcontents'.[57]

The new "credibility gap"—the "growing crisis of confidence in the integrity and moral worth of the holders of high administrative office, whether courtiers or nobles or bishops or judges or even kings"[58]—made traditional double-standards in penal justice particularly resented. Flogging and branding were sentences imposed daily on the lower orders, but from these the gentry were excluded. Martial law tightened its lynch knots around the throats of the unpropertied only. The upper classes were likewise exempt from press-gang action, from which, as *I Henry IV* demonstrates, the prosperous middle orders could bribe their way out. Thanks to Benefit of Clergy, those who enjoyed the class privilege of literacy could—notes *2 Henry VI*—escape execution for murder. In early modern England, suggests Christopher Hill, "only the gentry and better-off merchants" seemed relatively satisfied with the legal system.[59] The later sixteenth century was in fact, Archer reminds us, "probably the bloodiest period in the history of the English criminal law."[60]

In Shakespeare's London, the heartbreaking sight of the destitute could be itself a provocation, as John Howes noted, complaining of the governors of Bridewell in 1587: "They see in the streates a nomber of poore, aged and lame in greate miserie, but that they can not remedie. They see in the streates a nomber of poore children lie under stalles all the yere long. They see divers poore woemen delivered of of [sic] childe in the streates, churches and cadges, and no provision for them. They have sene allso a greate number of poore men, which have died this sommer of the sicknes in the streates for wante of reliefe, and no place provided for them. These things are to to apparant in the eyes of the people, that heaven and earthe cryeth vengeance, and suerly god can not but be angrie with us, that will suffer our Christian Bretheren to die in the streates for wante of reliefe."[61] Burial lists in the London of the 1590s complete the picture:

> Edward Ellis a vagrant who died in the street.
> A young man not known who died in a hay-loft.
> A cripple that died in the street before John Awsten's door . . .

> A maid, a vagrant, unknown, who died in the street near the Postern.
> Margaret, a deaf woman, who died in the street . . .
> A young man vagrant having no abiding place . . . who died in the
>   street before the door of Joseph Hayes, a brazier dwelling at the
>   sign of Robin Hood in the High Street . . . He was about 18 years
>   old. I could not learn his name.[62]

The genteel might fulminate against vagabonds and restive peasants, but as Robert Crowley, the poet, printer and preacher, told the 1549 parliament, the gentry had no right to rebuke the poor for disobedience when they themselves broke the law by enclosing. "Unlesse, I saye, the possessioners of this realme wyll repent the violence don to the poore and nedy membres of the same . . . they shall, at the daye of theyr account, be bound hand and fote and cast into utter darkness . . . Nowe herken you possessioners, and you rich men lyfte up your ears."[63]

> They say we must,
> Their judgement trust,
> And obey theyr decrees,
> Although we see,
> Them for to bee,
> Against God's verities.[64]

Hunger could not but breed disaffection. As an anonymous treatise of the mid-century asked, "What Faith and allegiance will those men observe towards their prince and governor which have their children famished at home for want of meat?"[65] In this climate of popular desperation (one Mary Bunton was alleged to have stated in 1599 "I care not a turde for the Queene nor hir precepts"),[66] of accelerating class hatred, and of goaded intellectual scepticism, new political thinking arose, of a radicalism that might surprise traditionalist literary critics. "Men ought to have more respecte to their countrey, than to their prince: to the common wealthe, than to any one persone", wrote John Ponet, in his *Treatise* of 1556. "Common wealthes mai stande well ynough and florishe, albeit ther be no kinges . . . Common wealthes and realmes may live, whan the head is cut of, and may put on a newe head, that is, make them a newe governour, whan they see their olde head seke to muche his owne will and not the wealthe of the hole body, for the which he was only ordained."[67]

To counter subversion, Elizabeth's government mounted a sustained propaganda campaign to demonise popular restiveness and foes of the state church, tarring these, as Brents Stirling long ago documented, by association with Anabaptist atrocities and anarchic levelling.[68] The authorities also inflicted a wide range of penal horrors. The hand that wrote sedition could be hacked off; the ears that listened, nailed to the pillory or even sliced away. Conviction for treason could climax in deterrence's horror show, with the burning of human beings alive, or their torturing to a slow death through mutilation, castration, and living disembowelment. Elizabeth would issue some ninety warrants for torture. Tudor parliaments added altogether sixty-eight new treason statutes, including (from the 1534 Act on) the charge of treason for spoken words critical of the monarch.[69]

A tiny class-fraction—the gentry and aristocracy comprised around three per cent of the population—thus sought, with the aid of a self-serving magistracy and the prosperous middling sort who furnished oligarchic parish officers, to preserve an ideological control at times reinforced by traumatising public savagery, in maintenance of an order of brutal social inequity.[70] Sixteenth-century censorship makes our calculations speculative, but the proportion of Elizabethan dissidents of one type or another appears to have been immense. In religion, Elliot Rose suggested that if we include Catholics, Calvinists, and their silent supporters, it may well be that the majority of the nation were 'conscientious objectors' to the Crown and the Church of England (though as Peter Lake suggests, the complexities of category definition entail tentativeness in assessing religious alignments).[71] Added to these were the dislocated indigent (Elizabethan England produced at the very least 15,000 vagrants; Peter Clark thinks the number to have reached around 80,000 by the early seventeenth century);[72] the inescapably pauperised (between a third and a quarter of the rural population were trapped in a new agrarian proletariat by 1600),[73] the university malcontents, and the disaffected younger sons of the gentry (like Orlando in *As You Like It*) who risked impoverishment in a system of primogeniture harsher in England than anywhere else in Europe.[74] To these forces of disaffection we must add, of course, the impact of patriarchy and its discontents, recently problematised by Puritan teachings which elevated the status of women in marriage. Even the upper classes flirted with constitutional critique. Aristocratic dissidence was expressed not only in personal antagonisms but in philosophic questioning of the immunity of kingship to prosecution. The revolt of the Earl of Essex, whose career I will argue Shakespeare subjected to hostile focus in *2 Henry VI* (and later elsewhere) came extraordinarily close to ending Elizabeth's reign in a bloody *coup d'état*.[75]

The "permanent background of potential unrest" characterising social relations in the sixteenth century erupted in its last two decades into a virtual epidemic of disorder, when around 37 riots and unlawful assemblies took place in the London area.[76] Contemporaries noted that sometimes women, and even members of the gentry, figured among highway robbers; and local militias were often reluctant to suppress food riots in their area, from sympathy with the hungry.[77] Even "in time of peace", conceded Henrician publicist Richard Morison, "be not all men almost at war with them that be rich?"[78]

"HERE'S FINE REVOLUTION, AND WE HAD THE
TRICK TO SEE'T" (*HAMLET*, 5.1.83): TUDOR
TRADITIONS OF POLITICAL OPPOSITION

It has long been considered an historiographic truism that, bereft of mass literacy, a popular press, and party politics, pre-modern commoners were pre-political. Shakespeare's political thinking, by implication, must have aimed only at the court and a smattering of intellectuals. Recent historians, however, have demolished the former myth. A post-revisionist school of early modern political history has emerged, revealing the 'social depth' of the political nation, and establishing a new 'social history of politics'. Its contention, in the words of Andy Wood, is that "popular political culture in Tudor England was rich, sophisticated and vibrant and that it deserves to occupy an important place in the historical interpretation of the period."[79] Further, as innumerable archives reveal, plebeian political thinking, far from being irrecoverable as often stated, is anything but a lost Atlantis. "It was difficult to escape from the popular political voice in Tudor England, which impinged upon formal political discourse and drama just as it seethed within the alehouse environment. The main problem for the historian of popular political speech arises not from an absence of material, but from its excess."[80] Tim Harris summarises the findings that "Ordinary men and women did have opinions about how duly constituted authority was supposed to be exercised, and how those who governed—not just at the local but also the central level—were supposed to rule; that they often engaged in activity that was designed to influence how the political elite ruled over them; and that the ruling elite frequently found that they could not afford to ignore the political opinions and acts of the people they governed."[81] Spectacular examples included the crusading popular embrace of *politically congenial* elements of the evangelical platform in the 1540s, in a mass-movement which helped to co-create the English Reformation (as documented by Ethan Shagan), and to precipitate Protector Somerset's agrarian reforms with a wealth of pro-Somerset risings in 1549 (best documented by Andy Wood).[82] The commons likewise dethroned Lady Jane Grey in 1553 in favour of Mary Tudor, defying King Edward's will, the Privy Council, and the principal Judges; and this book will note the strategic courtship of the commons by the Earl of Essex in the early 1590s, evoked in the persona of York in *2 Henry VI*.

Tudor grammar schools sought to create active citizens through extensive education in rhetoric, a training "intensely political in character . . . schoolboys at the age of 12 or 15 were expected to speak regularly, and on both sides, about taxes, laws, foreign trade and foreign policy."[83] For adults, full citizenship in early modern England and Wales came not through parliamentary franchise, but participation in direct government of the local community, as Mark Goldie has argued. National government was dependent not just on county administration but on parish self-government, which operated through regular rotation of a large number of local offices among a community's menfolk. England had 9,000 parishes;[84] and so "astonishingly high" was the consequent extent of office-holding that at any one time some 50,000 men might be governing.[85] In London, Archer estimates, as many as one in three householders in a wealthy ward might expect to hold office in any one year.[86] England's body politic thus deserves reconceptualisation as "an unacknowledged republic", concludes Goldie: its concern with republican ideals derived not just from discussion by intellectuals of classical Rome and contemporary Italy, but from longstanding Saxon tradition.[87] Versed in power-sharing, with its rhetorics, realities and ruses, Englishmen of Shakespeare's time—like Shakespeare's own father, as Chief Alderman and Bailiff—were thoroughly political creatures.

Within the nation-wide subculture of the parochial executive, staffed by men of 'the middling sort', a multitude of fresh intrusions by central government, relentless through the 1590s, generated animating voltages of "political electricity".[88] Implementation of the blitz of government directives compelled local authorities, themselves hectored or monitored for compliance by circuit charges and articles of inquiry, into a direct and explicit deliberation of the crown's policy agenda.[89] Variously received with welcome as local empowerment, or resistance as overweening dictate, invasive multiplication of state mandate produced as one correlative the conditioning of a habit of dissent, expressed in mundane particulars of sly negation.[90] If "princes are the glass, the school, the book, / Where subjects' eyes do learn, do read, do look", as Lucrece warns Sextus Tarquinius, then those observant subjects, structurally politicized in a circuit of surveillance, may reciprocate critique: "O be remembered, no outrageous thing / From vassal actors can be wip'd away: / Then kings' misdeeds cannot be hid in clay."[91] That Shakespeare's plays commonly centre upon figures of power at the helm of state accordingly demonstrates not antipopulist snobbery (a literary critical indictment frequently imputed)—for the impact of policy, convulsing commoners' lives, is never far away—but reflects rather, I suggest, the enforced contemporary gaze of the hyperactive political nation, in late Tudor England's polymorphous state.

That scrutinised world of central power propagated the following official doctrines, widely recognised by scholars as ideologically foundational to Tudor rule. Investment of supreme authority in a monarch appointed by God and blessed with superior powers, whose sacred person as God's principal representative on earth made him (from the 1530s) rightful Head of the Church of England; governance of commoners by an appropriately privileged hereditary upper class of nobility and gentry, whose authority was both divinely ordained, and manifest in gifts of judgement and successful leadership exercised over centuries and honed by education; a hierarchic social system of inherited, permanent and inalterable class and rank ('degree'), whose verticality was ordered on the pattern of the cosmos itself; the imperative of submission to official authority, local and national, without right of active resistance no matter how egregious the misconduct of a social superior, the role of the commons being an unjudging and industrious obedience; the quiet submissiveness of women, as natural inferiors of men, to husbands and male heads of household, as commanded in *Genesis* 3 and as analogous to the deferential subjection of subject to monarch and mortal to deity.

In the nourishing climate we have just examined, however, of economic distress, ideological disaffection, delegitimation of traditional power, and compelled politicization, at least six traditions of Tudor oppositional thought developed, which assaulted or destabilised those core political principles. Often neglected in Shakespeare criticism, yet demonstrably surfacing in his drama, these varied intellectual sightlines raking fire across the official political doctrines of Tudor England merit review. Their brief conspectus may at least disprove, I hope, the groundless conservative myth, seeking derisive preclusion of analyses such as those of this book, that hostility to the class structure, antipathy to hereditary rule, and indictment of wealth for exploitation of the many, are reflex sentiments peculiar to modern democracy, foolish anachronisms in imputation to Shakespeare's world.

The Radical Humanism of the early century (particularly the Thomas More circle) frequently excoriated the institution of hereditary aristocracy. The traveller in *Utopia*, for instance (1516; translated into English in 1551) declares that in surveying the social organisation of contemporary nations, "God help me, I can perceive nothing but a certain conspiracy of rich men procuring their own commodities under the name and title of the commonwealth",[92] and vilifies the nobility as parasitic, greedy, violent, and frequently criminal idlers. The puncturing Ciceronian assertion that 'true nobility' lay in neither lineage nor wealth, but in virtue and civic contribution, became so revered a topos of Tudor humanism that it would be the debating theme for candidates for Oxford's M.A. in 1583. Combined with Puritan emphasis on the priority of godliness over birth, humanism's polemical redefinition of *vera nobilitas* helped erode aristocratic mystique and destabilize deference for hereditary class governance.[93] *Utopia*'s speakers demystify even kingship, as lazy, arrogant, and preoccupied with militarism: "the most part of all princes have more delight in warlike matters and feats of chivalry . . . than in the good feats of peace, and employ much more study how by right or by wrong to enlarge their dominions than how well and peaceably to rule and govern that they have already."[94] Sovereigns emerge from the actual historical record, argued Erasmus' *Adagia*, not as exalted Platonic philosopher-kings but as meriting "the terrible reproach that Achilles hurls at Agamemnon in Homer, 'people-devouring kings'". This position will be echoed perhaps in the Malcolm-Macduff dialogue of *Macbeth* (4.3.40–101). "They sweep the whole wealth of the community", declared Erasmus, "into their own treasury—which is like collecting it in a leaky barrel—and like the eagle cram themselves and their young with the entrails of innocent birds."[95] More's Latin poem, 'Quis optimus reipublicae status', argues the preference for Republicanism over monarchy, and memorably compares greedy kings to an anomalous species of leech, which will not drop from a body until the last drop of blood has been sucked.[96] Vives, writing in 1526, noted sympathetically that "The poor envy the rich and are incensed and indignant that they have abundance to lavish on jesters, dogs, harlots, asses, pack-horses, and elephants; that in truth they themselves have not the wherewithal to feed their little hungering children, while their fellow-citizens revel splendidly and insolently in the riches which have been wrung from them and others like them."[97] The interlude *Gentleness and Nobility* (c. 1525) probably written by an intimate of the More circle, John Rastell, staged a stormy debate between classes in which the hereditary nobility was arraigned by a Ploughman figure for insatiability of violent extortion. Remarkably, the disinterested Philosopher who closes the interlude concluded the need for the class of "governors" to be "brydelyd and therto compellyd / By some strayt laws for them devysyd", with officials subject to strict penalties for breach of law, and serving only limited terms of office.[98] In a scene notably absent from his sources, Shakespeare enunciates in the gardener's speech in *Richard II* similar misgivings about overmighty subjects that "look too lofty in our commonwealth", declaring the need to "trim and dress" the political garden, "Lest being overproud in sap and blood / With too much riches it confound itself" (3.4.36, 60–61). Shakespeare's presentation of catastrophic national violence as the eruption of an almost demented self-seeking by the hereditary aristocracy is endemic in his Histories. "A knot you are of damned bloodsuckers" (Grey's judgement on murderous courtly intriguers in *Richard III* 3.3.5) sums up the perspective, in possible echo of More.

A second oppositional tradition gained prominence, even notoriety, with the mid-century advent of the Commonwealthmen. This loose affiliation of highly educated men—including government administrator John Hales, Bishop Hugh Latimer, ex-friar Henry Brinklow, divines Thomas Lever and Thomas Becon, and protest poet Robert Crowley—were driven by the visionary energies of the Reformation to urge economic transformation of England. Sharing "undoubted elements of continuity"[99] with the earlier reforming circles of More's Erasmian Humanism, of Tyndale's radical Protestants, and of Thomas Cromwell's 'revolutionary' administration, these eminent churchmen and public figures fought unsparingly to instate economic and social improvements for the commons as the correlative of religious reform. The Reformation had inflicted "an intensification of the oppression of the poor", as the landed elite who purchased former church lands wrenched up rents and manorial dues to extortionate levels.[100] Consequently, in the case of many tenants, in Brinklow's words, "the pore man that laboryth and toyleth upon it, and is hys slave, is not able to lyve."[101] The commonwealth group, several of whom were close to Protector Somerset, angrily denounced the phenomenon of poverty in England as a direct consequence of unconscionable upper-class exploitation, to be eradicated in a purified nation. "The lordes be the only cause of all the dearth in the realme", declared Brinklow. "The comynaltye, is so oppressed . . . by wicked lawes, cruel tyrann[t]es, which be extorcionars and oppresors of the common welth."[102] "The 'godly commonwealth' thus provided", notes Shagan, "a point of entry where Protestant ideas could be insinuated into popular culture".[103] Scathingly affirming the moral equality of rich and poor, the Commonwealthmen demanded, as a Christian and political imperative, redistribution of wealth. This was to be voluntary—though Edward's government did consider establishing a maximum income.[104] "Hardly ever in English history has more devastating and caustic criticism of social conditions been voiced than in the time of the Commonwealthmen", notes one of the few historians to have examined the movement closely. "Not until the nineteenth century, not even in the pronouncements of the seventeenth-century Levellers or the English radicals of 1789, was the discourse of protest so sharp and uncompromising."[105] As Crowley put it in his *Infomacion and Petition*, addressed to Members of Parliament in 1549:

> If the impotent creatures perish for lacke of necessaries, you are the murderers, for you have theyr enheritaunce . . . If the sturdy fall to stealeyng, robbyng, & reveynge, then you are the causers thereof, for you . . . enclose, & wytholde from them the earth, out of the whych they should dygge and plowe theyr lyveynge."[106]

Symptomatically, the very existence of the Commonwealthmen has succumbed to mainstream nescience in Shakespeare criticism. Even the recent contextualization of the playwright's politics attempted by avowed professionals of political theory, the Cambridge School theorists of *Shakespeare and Early Modern Political Thought*, validates eclipse of the Commonwealthmen, allocating the movement precisely two sentences. In a paradoxically depoliticising introduction, Armitage *et al.* explain that "the mid-century Commonwealthmen", whom they leave unnamed, wrote in "relatively tranquil years", and followed a Ciceronian politics ("pursued the common good driven by a commitment to virtue and employing the tool of counsel"), thereby producing "idealistic images of England".[107] Yet contrary to this classic instance of empirically delusional conservative myth-spinning, the Commonwealthmen, like so many Tudor Isaiahs, thundered denunciation of England's wealthy, and proclaimed a vengeful God who was angrily championing the downtrodden poor: "you engrossers of fermes and teynements, beholde, I saye, the terrible threatynges of God . . . The voyce of the pore (whom you have . . . thruste out of house and home) is well accepted in the eares of the Lorde, and hath steared up hys wrathe agenyst you."[108] Exploitative landlords, charged Latimer, sought "plainly to make the yeomanry slavery".[109] Such teachings, moreover, conspicuously paralleled much in the spirit of Protector Somerset's agrarian reform policies, whose anti-enclosure commissioners sought increasingly to circumvent a hostile gentry by working directly with village governors.[110] Somerset himself "pursued a strategy of 'popularity' politics to compensate for his structurally weak position as Lord Protector."[111] Nonetheless, "The upstart aristocracy of the future had their teeth in the carcass, and, having tasted blood, they were not to be whipped off by a sermon."[112] Crusading denunciation of the unconscionable injustices of the hereditary ruling class thus contributed to the populist upsurge of the rebellions (including Kett's) of 1549. In its bloody aftermath, the rhetoric of commonwealth maldistribution was driven largely underground. The very term 'commonwealth', we shall see in *2 Henry VI*, acquired suspect, talismanic connotations. Nonetheless, such perspectives were not entirely suppressed. "Mightie men, gentlemen and all riche men", preached Bernard Gilpin in a sermon to the court of 1552, sought "to robbe and spoile the poore".[113] And as James Holstun has argued, as late as the 1550s, John Heywood, as a late Commonwealthman, dared to urge Queen Mary in his allegorical *The Spider and the Flie* to adopt the agrarian reforms which they had sought under Protector Somerset.[114]

The Commonwealthmen were rearticulating, in the self-rededicating spiritual climate of the Reformation in England, traditional Church teachings on wealth and ownership which went back to the Church Fathers: a body of radical thought all but *terra incognita* in modern contextualisation of Shakespeare. "This is robbery: not to share one's resources", had declared John Chrysostom. "Not only to rob others' property, but also not to share your own with others, is robbery and greediness and theft."[115] We should recall that in the medieval and Renaissance period, Chrysostom was the most authoritative of the Fathers after Augustine: with eleven English translations of his work before 1642, and at least seventeen Latin editions of his complete works on the continent between 1504–1614.[116] Chrysostom's chastisement of riches, furthermore, was no fleering *opusculum*, but urged a logic of incrimination expounded widely in the Greek Fathers, sometimes dubbed the 'Doctors of Poverty'. Humanity, they taught, sharing a common origin, common nature, and common destiny, had received from God the earth and its bounty likewise as *koina*: things made to be common to all. Accumulated private possessions, beyond necessities for self-sufficiency and human dignity, become in a world of beggary, *superfluities*: and as such must be redistributed to the needy. Thus, *autarkeia* (independence) once attained, the Christian imperative of *koinonia* must follow: that deep, divinely modelled fellowship of sharing, in the common inheritance of mankind. Accumulated private property was consequently theft. "Are you not a robber?" demands Basil of the rich. "You who make your own the things which you have received to distribute? . . . That bread which you keep, belongs to the hungry; that coat which you preserve in your wardrobe, to the naked".[117] Private wealth was unnatural, a religious offence, constituting dispossession. "Why do you cast out the fellow sharers of nature, and claim it all for yourselves? The earth was made in common for all" thundered Ambrose from the pulpit.[118] The Fathers, notes Charles Avila in his amply documented survey, "could think of the rich-poor cleavage only in terms of a relationship between exploiters and exploited, expropriators and dispossessed."[119] "Avarice must be the cause of our need", Ambrose told the poor.[120] It was aboriginal greed, the *prima avaritia*, that destroyed the original human communality created by God, taught Ambrose; a doctrine whose corollary was impugnment, as Lovejoy notes, of the free market, wherein profiteers gouged the poor. "Sharing is the way of nature".[121] Ambrose sought permanently to lash the consciences of the wealthy to large-scale redistribution. "You cover walls, but you leave men bare. Naked they cry out before your house, and you heed them not . . . the cost of the jewel in your ring would have sufficed to save the lives of a whole people. "[122] Fond as it is of brandishing theatrical metaphors for relations of power, today's Shakespearean scholarship has yet to alight on St. Basil's image for wealthy landowners: "You are like one occupying a place in a theatre, who prohibits others from entering, treating that as one's own which was designed for the common use of all."[123]

Echoing the Fathers, Medieval canon law would enshrine the doctrine that 'superfluities' belonged to the poor. Aquinas expounded natural law as entailing that in times of necessity, all things are common property. In consequence, when the hungry stole food or anything urgently needed to sustain life, their action, *ex auctoritate*, did not constitute theft.[124]

The compassionate distributivist ideals voiced in *King Lear* fit plainly with this accusatory commonwealth heritage. "Take physic, Pomp", cries Lear: "Expose thyself to feel what wretches feel, / That thou mayst shake the superflux to them, / And show the heavens more just" (3.4.34–37). Once precipitated into outcast poverty, Gloucester agrees. Were the establishment's "superfluous and lust-dieted man" himself to feel the lashings of material want, then "distribution should undo excess, / And each man have enough" (4.1.67–71). "What authority surfeits on would relieve us. If they would yield us but the superfluity while it were wholesome, we might guess they relieved us humanely", grieve the starving rebels opening *Coriolanus* (1.1.13–15). "Superfluous branches / We lop away, that bearing boughs may live" the gardener teaches in *Richard II* (3.4.64–65).[125]

"Tudor England was an arena of vigorous public debate and controversy . . . the age in which the protest pamphlet and tract came to the fore".[126] The Commonwealthmen, as Neal Wood demonstrates, were flanked by a sequence of Tudor political thinkers, who, though conservatives of deep faith in hierarchical society, feared the ideal of a virtuous co-operative polity to lie now under death-threat from both overmighty monarchy and relentless abuse of poorer commoners. Conscious, like Plato in the *Laws* and Augustine on humanity's *libido dominandi*, that power was intrinsically corruptive, and reacting to the gathering pace of Tudor centralisation of power, these reformers confronted the dangerous potential of royal absolutism.

Their forerunner Sir John Fortescue in *De laudibus legum Anglie* (composed c. 1470, but published in 1546 with large impact) extolled Crown subjection to the English law, within a 'mixed' constitution. Thomas More praised in his Utopia a mixed constitution of meritocratic rule to avoid tyranny and factionalism; and Thomas Starkey's *Dialogue between Pole and Lupset* (c. 1530) proposed revival of the medieval office of the Constable, to counterpoise Crown authority by heading a permanent Council of State, composed among others of leading clergymen, four judges, four citizens of London, and members nominated by parliament. All three thinkers deplored absolutism as liable to tyrannic destruction of state and kingship alike, emphasising that monarchic self-interest lay in fostering the self-interest of subjects. Another source of alarm for the reformers was the aristocracy. To Edmund Dudley, in *The Tree of Commonwealth* (1510), they recalled Nebuchadnezzar and Nero. In their insatiable appetites and overweening pride, England's nobility were "the worst brought up for the moste parte of any realme of christendom." Kings should take special care to end nobles' oppression of the people, Dudley argued; and perhaps only the combination of a university education with eloquent recrimination by a rededicated clergy could redeem the peerage from what he called their "ungracious delectation".[127] Thomas More, we have seen, berated them as turbulent, even criminal squanderers. Starkey's *Dialogue* argued that compulsory education, as well as military training, could alone rehabilitate so enfeebled and dissolute a warrior class.[128] To attribute to Shakespeare, then, a steadily negative representation of monarchy and peers is hardly to indulge, *pace* conservative dogma, in ideologically driven anachronism. By the 1590s, such perspective was established meliorist truism.

A final, and repeated, advocacy of the Tudor reformers was elimination of the sufferings of the poor. A fearsome ground of crime, unrest and insurrection, left unchecked it could destroy the state itself.[129] Detailed in their agendas for an economically restructured state, they redefined poverty, momentously, as "a distressing social aberration" rather than an eternal consequence of original sin.[130] Shakespeare's humane concern for *res plebeia*, the condition of the commons, and his plays' cannily polyvalent usage of the term 'commonwealth', thus derive not only from the popular orientation of the public theatres, but from a major intellectual current of the age.

As a number of historians have been concerned for some decades to demonstrate, medieval and Tudor underclasses were not ideologically quiescent in their servitude.[131] Although "Most subordinate classes throughout most of history have rarely been afforded the luxury of open, organised, political activity . . . such activity was dangerous, if not suicidal", nonetheless "the penetration of official platitudes by any subordinate class is to be expected", for a number of obvious reasons, observes anthropologist James C. Scott. "One can speak in an agrarian society of 'folk socialism' . . . just as one speaks of 'folk religion.'" "Every subordinate group", Scott suggests, "creates, out of its ordeal, a 'hidden transcript' that represents a critique of power spoken behind the back of the dominant."[132] ("The same man who touches his forelock to the squire by day and who goes down to history as an example of deference, may kill his sheep, snare his pheasants or poison his dogs at night.")[133] In Tudor England there existed precisely such a 'transcript' in the immemorial peasant contestation of the political order.

Outwardly, for much of the time, peasant and ruler shared a common political culture: a working agreement by which routine obedience was conditional upon upholding of customary rights and the enforcement of patriarchal obligations. "This did not mean blind obedience to authority, for when authority fell short of the expected standard of good rule resistance was easily provoked."[134] Pragmatic plebeian accord did not, however, preclude foundational underclass counter-definition of the governing system, as an unwarranted, even unnatural rule by oppressive hereditary overlords. Popular mythoi of suppressed popular liberty and prevailing injustice, emerging openly in times of crisis and class-conscious collective resistance, included the myth of the Norman Yoke: belief that Anglo-Saxon liberties were destroyed by the invasion of William the Bastard, whose regime imposed alien law, customs, and king upon 'the freeborn Englishman'. As "a rudimentary class theory of politics", this "may well have had a continuous history since 1066"; Christopher Hill traces its to the nineteenth century.[135] Asserting the origin of the state in organised violence, it "gave something concrete to set against the authority of bishops and Kings";[136] and revering the common law as embodiment of a cherished ancient constitution, it helps explain the striking phenomenon in medieval England of peasant legalism, seeking recourse against oppressive noblemen in courts of common law.[137]

But pan-European and supremely influential in peasant contestation of the political order was the indictment of social class *per se* on the basis of a natural egalitarianism: "When Adam delved and Eve span / Who was then the gentleman?"[138] Stoicism and Christianity both taught the grievous loss of an original egalitarian state of nature. Church orthodoxy qualified this inflammatory perspective by the doctrine that Original Sin introduced need of constraining hierarchic governance. Natural rights thus did not extend beyond the state of nature. Plebeian critical thinking, however, insisted that it was hierarchic authority itself that comprised the intrusion of Sin: providential equality had been shattered by criminal individuals elevating themselves as hereditary lords. Though the state of nature with its distributive justice was not wholly recoverable, Ambrose had preached "a virtually equalitarian and communistic ideal of a Christian society".[139] The sense of protective community fostered by its internal redistribution of resources had been a principle reason for the Church's survival, thinks Peter Brown.[140] For the Acts of the Apostles had itself commended communism as a unifying holy practice of the primitive church: "they had all things in common . . . for as many as were possessors of lands or houses sold them, and brought the prices of these things that were sold, and laid them down at the apostles' feet: and distribution was made unto every man according as he had need" (Acts 4.32–35; compare 2.44–45).

Such views sprang afresh in peasant anger and outright rebellion throughout the middle ages, to surface again with Kett's rebels, and later the Levellers.[141] John Ball asked in 1381 "If we are all descended from one father and one mother, Adam and Eve, how can the lords say or prove that they are more lords than we are—save that they make us dig and till the ground so that they can squander what we produce?"[142] The Plowman in Rastell's Humanist debate of the 1520s, *Gentleness and Nobility*, urges the demystification: "So possessyons began by extorcyon . . . So the law of inherytaunce was furst begon, / Whych is a thyng agayns all good reason".[143] Kett's men were likewise said to have demanded in 1549 "While we have the same forme, and the same condition of birth together with them, why should they have a life so unlike unto ours, and differ so farre from us in calling?"[144] In 1560–62 Bishop Pilkington noted the jingle "When Adam delved" to be a "common saying". Bishop Bancroft cited it in 1593 to tar Puritanism with the brush of 1381.[145] The "Christian radical tradition" as Rodney Hilton calls such insurrectionary doctrines, mingled easily with what Christopher Hill terms "plebeian sceptical materialism.[146]

The Mousehold articles drawn up in 1549 by Kett's rebels, parallelling much in the rebel demands in Germany's Peasants' War (1525), sought to abolish serfdom and establish an alternative social order, "Taking power from the lords and placing it instead within the village".[147] Though the agenda was tinged by oligarchic self-interest, and friction existed between the disciplinary village elites organizing the revolt and the more radical and violent anti-seigneurialism of poorer rebels—the hereditary elite were to be left uneradicated—the assault on class power was systematic. Gentry and lords were to be excluded from the local economy, the Church dispossessed of its wealth, clergy refocused on education and preaching alone, and the principle constructed of a maximal autonomy of village self-rule: all to shelter beneath the protective benevolence trustingly ascribed to the Crown and its laws. This last traditional component in medieval rebellion's 'monarcho-populism' (a valuable coinage of James Holstun) would elicit mockery from Shakespeare, I will argue, in *2 Henry VI*.[148]

Like Christianity, the Golden Age myth of Greco-Roman literature transmitted an egalitarian mythos, recalling, albeit as a poetic pose, nostalgia for an idyllic communitarian age preceding the iron regime of contemporary possessive cruelty, *meum* ever warring with *teum*.[149] For the poor, this was not necessarily a fanciful schema. Elyot's *Book Named the Governor* (published 1531) opens with denunciation of "fantastical fools" who would have all in common. The book's "whole political project", thinks Woodbridge, "was called forth by fear of social unrest and communism."[150] Crowley stated the upper classes to be certain the lower orders wished to terminate degree: to "have all men like themselves, they would have all things common".[151] Reformation volatility allowed possessive communality doctrinal potential, prompting anxious official repudiation in England's Forty-Two Articles of 1552, and later in the Thirty-Nine Articles of 1562: "The riches and goodes of Christians, are not common as touching the right, title, and possession of the same, as certaine Annabaptistes doe falselie boaste".[152] In 1591, Spenser's fable on contemporary abuses, *Mother Hubbard's Tale*, would demonise the egalitarian rhetoric of original collective possession, clearly simmering as a moral philosophy of penurious merit, by rendering it as high-toned guile in the mouths of lawless vagabonds.[153] Both Sidney's *Arcadia* and Spenser's *Faerie Queen* took populist egalitarian thinking seriously enough to vilify it in remarkably brutal terms.[154] "The ruling class had no doubt of its continued existence" from 1381 on, notes Charles Hobday, discussing "their terrified denunciations".[155]

Shakespeare's plays, however, are relentless in the sceptical ontology of rank. Tragedies such as *Hamlet* and *Troilus*, *Othello* and *Lear* are substantial explorations in such materialist unmaskings; and subversive assertion of class and rank as the betrayal of an essential human commonality is widely found in the Histories. Not even kingship is exempt. "Art thou aught but place, degree and form, / Creating awe and fear in other men?" asks Henry V of the "idol ceremony" (4.1.228–29, 222). "The King is but a man, as I am. The violet smells to him as it doth to me; the element shows to him as it doth to me. All his senses have but human conditions. His ceremonies laid by, in his nakedness he appears but a man" (4.1.99–102). Richard II, his divine right metaphysics crumbling before materialist realpolitik, cries out "Cover your heads, and mock not flesh and blood / With solemn reverence. Throw away respect, / Tradition, form, and ceremonious duty; / For you have but mistook me all this while. / I live with bread, like you, feel want, / Taste grief, need friends. Subjected thus, / How can you say to me I am a king?" (3.2.167–73). The theme recurs even in Comedies. "O place! O form!" declares Angelo in *Measure for Measure*, "How often dost thou with thy case, thy habit, / Wrench awe from fools, and tie the wiser souls / To thy false seeming! Blood, thou art blood." (2.4.12–15). The eloquence is Shakespeare's; the principle of contemptuous levelling from Parson Ball, Wat Tyler, and the alehouse in time of 'commotions'.

A fourth lineage of dissent in Tudor England, formidable in intellectual fire-power, was the Counter-Reformation. Peter Milward long ago demonstrated that Shakespeare's plays were denser by far in Catholic allusion than those of any other Tudor and Stuart playwright. Richard Wilson currently leads a set of scholars dedicated to researching the implications of Shakespeare having been very probably the theatrically invested 'William Shakeshafte', a young 'subseminarian' at Hoghton Tower in1581, brought there with other young Midlanders by the Jesuit Edmund Campion (soon after martyred) to undergo preliminary training for the Jesuit order prior to shipping out to Douai.[156] It is widely recognised that a number of Shakespeare's friends, family members and schoolmasters were Catholics. Antonia Fraser shows that "The town which lay at the center of [England's] recusant map was Stratford-on-Avon". Patrick Collinson believes that it was not until the mid-1580s that the town's Catholic culture was reformed.[157] Curtis Breight finds para-Catholic political perspectives and arguments dramatised in Marlowe and in Shakespeare's Henriad, suggesting the dramatists' familiarity with denunciations of English polity by Parsons and Verstegan smuggled into England.[158]

Yet whether or not 'Shakeshafte' reveals William Shakespeare caught in some Tudor papist moonlighting (and it is a speculative case, currently generating a firestorm), it seems hard to dispute that the dramatist was positioned from childhood, by geography, schooling and family bonds, for sympathetic familiarity with Roman Catholic perspectives on England's monarchy and conditions of rule. Though Elizabethan Catholic polemic was not always unambiguously damnatory, like Cardinal William Allen's *Admonition to the Nobility and People of England* that termed the queen "an incestuous bastard, begotten and born in sin, of an infamous courtesan", even the more compromising 'evil counsellor' polemics presented a monarch weak and vulnerable to the long-catastrophic misgovernance of machiavellian Protestant courtiers: a "sabre-toothed loyalism" as Michael Questier dubs it.[159] Richard Wilson emphasises that by the late century, many English Catholics were *politiques*. Private and quietist believers, confessing simultaneous allegiance to the old religion and Elizabethan sovereignty, they abhorred the fiery, charring logic of the Counter Reformation. Yet by their very commitment to the spirit of tolerance even these men and women must have felt horror, I would argue, towards Tudor history and the Elizabethan regime. English recusants were subject to harsh and escalating fines; their arms were seized and sold; they were subjected to crown surveillance and surprise raids; and with the Armada on the seas, they were interned in their hundreds.[160] "In their private life, Catholics were inevitably a prey to blackmail and intimidation . . . New prisons were established at Wisbech, Ely and Reading, and filled with Catholics."[161] Shakespeare would probably have known when very young how "the child of state", in a telling phrase "fears . . . policy, that heretic" (sonnet 124); and as a growing boy have learned instances, from his alderman father, of the agonies of apostasy and of partisan governance, across his own community and county—"purest faith unhappily forsworn, / And gilded honour shamefully misplaced / . . . And right perfection wrongfully disgraced" (sonnet 66). Between 1581 and 1603, Elizabeth would execute for their faith 131 priests and 60 lay-people. "England judicially murdered more Roman Catholics than any other country in Europe", notes Diarmaid MacCulloch, "which puts English pride in national tolerance in an interesting perspective."[162] Whether or not Shakespeare preserved into his playwriting days an intact religious faith (a speculation for which I see no evidence), or simply residual empathy with a menaced idealistic minority, it is clear that the radical transvaluation of English political ideology that we shall see him repeatedly effect is profoundly congruent with Catholic scepticism and propaganda under late Tudor rule. As Richard of Gloucester remarks, with staggering off-handedness, in Shakespeare's first History play, *2 Henry VI*, "Priests pray for enemies, but princes kill" (5.2.6). Presenting English national governance, as did Catholic polemic, in terms of a corrupt and faction-riven court, pursuing a policy of torture and grievously hyper-taxing its citizens,[163] the play, we shall see, further foregrounds as possible antidote the explosive principle of revocable monarchic allegiance. *Richard II* (as I have argued elsewhere) seeking in 1596 to discredit the Earl of Essex, England's foremost Protestant crusader, pursued a similar goal to the Jesuit Robert Parson's *Conference about the next succession*, published in 1594.[164]

A draft of the speech made by the commander of the Spanish Armada, Medina Sidonia, to his forces embarking against England in 1588, promised them the assistance of English saints. "We shall find waiting for us there the help of the Blessed John Fisher, Cardinal-bishop of Rochester, of Thomas More . . . There we shall be helped by Edmund Campion . . . Thomas Cotton and many other reverend priests, servants of our Lord, whom Elizabeth has torn in pieces with ferocious cruelty and nicely calculated tortures."[165] Thomas Cotton (or Cottam), who had set out to assist in Campion's Jesuit mission of 1580, was the brother of John Cottom: Stratford-on-Avon schoolmaster from 1579–81.[166]

Protestant counter-polemic under 'bloody Mary' likewise helped to normatize the treasonable, and could even drift close to levelling at times, merging with perspectives from Radical Humanism and peasant scepticism. "Whereof came the name of Nobilitie", asks Marian exile John Ponet "seeing all men came out of one man and one woman?". "Was it for their lustie hawking and hunting? For their nimble diceing and coning carding? For their fine singing and dancing? For their open bragging and swearing? For their false fliering and flattering? For their subtil piking and stealing? For their cruel poling and piking? For their merciless man murthering? For their unnatural destroing of their natural countreymen, and traiterous betraieng of their countrey?"[167] Official Tudor teaching of a class system sent from heaven was buckling under convergence of fire.

If the wars of religion submitted Tudor power to bitter transvaluation, a growing body of resistance theory pondered the rights and means of active intervention. At different junctures, both Calvinism and Catholicism, both Marian exiles and anti-Elizabethan Romanists, sought to enfilade the realm with incitements to rise against a God-forsaking monarchy. In this fifth tradition of oppositional political thinking, Protestants Christopher Goodman and John Ponet, John Knox and George Buchanan, ironically linked hands prepared to be bloody with Catholics such as Jean Boucher, Juan de Mariana and William Allen, to produce in the sixteenth century numerous, overlapping versions of justification of armed revolt against a reigning monarch.[168] Shakespeare narrates early in his career the successful rising to abolish kingship led by Brutus and honorably incensed kinsmen of

Lucrece: "For 'tis a meritorious fair design / To chase injustice with revengeful arms".[169] In *King Lear*, as Richard Strier has shown, Shakespeare would dramatise Renaissance resistance theory at its most radical, in heroizing a nameless servant for drawing lethal sword upon the Duke of Cornwall, in defence of the bound and tortured Gloucester.[170] Yet Shakespeare displayed, in fact, a career-long "propensity for representing disobedient but virtuous servants", honorably resisting wicked or foolish commands from their masters.[171] Further, by centralising (we shall see), as early as Parts Two and Three of *Henry VI*, the taboo issues of interrogable monarchic legitimacy and revocable subject allegiance, Shakespeare was making flagrantly explicit precisely the climate of problematised fealty heightened by decades of subterranean resistance theory. With *Richard III*, Shakespeare would exploit Tudor history's own aporia, the self-enthronement of Henry VII by bloody usurpation of Richard of Gloucester. Its resulting regicidal doublethink allowed as heroic, in Richmond, the rebel's cry that there is on

> England's chair, where he is falsely set,
> One that hath ever been God's enemy . . .
> Then if you fight against God's enemy,
> God will, in justice, ward you as his soldiers. (5.5.205–08)

Shakespeare thus flourishes in open playhouse proclamation and with contextually coerced sympathy precisely that incendiary principle of divinely endorsed tyrannicide which was repudiated, explicitly and with state-enforced regularity, in all English churches, in the *Homily Against Disobedience*.

Shakespeare in fact wrote more plays featuring "assassination of a malicious king" than did any other Renaissance dramatist, observes Andrew Hadfield.[172] Implied in such aggregation may not have been incorrigible institutional complacency (The King is dead; long live the King!), as assumed by generations of critics, but active complicity in a late Elizabethan climate of fascination by republican constitutionality. We have noted already Thomas More's radical humanist preference of republicanism over monarchy, expressed in 'Quis optimus reipublicae status', as well as the flourishing of "an unacknowledged republic" in English self-governance. That anti-absolutist theories of contractualist kingship, legitimate resistance, and republicanism were in fact circulating in European civic thought centuries prior to the English civil war has been the magisterial *demonstrandum* of Skinner and Pocock.[173] European feudalism was characterised by conditions of distinctively loose political coercion—the dispersed or "parcellized sovereignty" of which Perry Anderson writes—permitting townships to become historically unprecedented powerhouses of ambitious commercial wealth.[174] Consequently, Renaissance humanist recovery of classical culture, with its urban-republican ideals of citizenship structurally antagonistic to feudalism's hereditary governance, enjoyed extraordinary impact as expressing a political sensibility widespread beyond the halls of scholars. In Tudor England, such perspectives also infused Protestantism, and produced a radical literary tradition, revealed in the pathbreaking study of David Norbrook.[175] Seminal essays by Patrick Collinson observe that in late sixteenth century England "citizens were concealed within subjects", in a reconceptualisation of the 'kingdom' as the 'country' or 'commonweal' which was consolidated by such contingencies as the 1584 Bond of Association, and Burghley's surreptitious work "drafting the terms for an interregnum" or "acephalous commonwealth" upon the sudden death of Elizabeth.[176] Parliament debated juridical execution of Mary Queen of Scots in 1572, thereby conceiving monarchy "not as an indelible and sacred anointing but a public and localised office, like any other form of magistracy."[177]

Republics could transform human life, argued its most zealous advocates;[178] and a worried political nation fearing from Elizabeth's demise either civil war or the accession in James VI of a pro-Catholic despot, yearned for escape into a polity both just and stable. Venice, a stable republic for a thousand years, haunted contemporaries. Edmund Spenser provided a commendatory poem to Lewis Lewkenor's English translation of Contarini's laudatory *The Commonwealth and Government of Venice*; and Sidney, who visited no city but Venice in his trip to Italy, urged his brother Robert to study its constitution.[179] George Buchanan expressed "ferrent praise" in *De jure regni* for its rule by a *doge* who was elected, obeyed the laws, and did not enjoy the office for life.[180] Thomas Starkey advocated devolving monarchy onto an electoral basis, as "a wonderful stey of the pryncely state and stablyschyng of the true commyn wele".[181] In England, the House of Commons—*pace* longstanding historiographic deflation of Whig heroization of Tudor parliaments— was indeed increasingly seeking to assert its power and autonomy under Elizabeth, argues Oliver Arnold. Its strategy was precisely to emphasise its authentic popular representativeness, as a qualification counterpoising the authority of Lords and Crown. In the robust asseveration of Edward Coke, "[the] Commons though they were but inferior men, yet every one of them represented a thousand of men".[182]

Constrained by censorship, Elizabethan 'republican' thinking emerged as a loose ensemble of symptomatic topoi: "suggestive hints", argues Hadfield (51), rather than an enunciated program. Anti-tyrannical discourse, an emerging language of citizen rights and freedoms, call for educational reform, and an interest in histories of the Roman republic (especially those of Polybius, Livy and Lucan) were a subtextual republicanism's telltale motifs.[183] Primary imperative was "to control the powers of the crown" through "a coterie of virtuous advisors and servants" possessing "the constitutional right to counsel the monarch". Literature's voice was central: "most discussion of the succession question took place in literary and dramatic texts and not official political discourse".[184] Tudor political treatises and late Elizabethan dramas reveal the cumulative pressure of a republican climate of interest become loudly implicit. Though advocacy of a 'mixed constitution' could function as clichéd legitimation of the Tudor system, it could signify when pondering Polybius on popular inclusion, or the charismatic liberties of Venice, an indictment of the limited powers of the English parliament.[185]

Sidney's *Old Arcadia* would lament (in Basilius) "how great dissipations monarchal governments are subject unto",[186] and Norbrook demonstrates how this pastoral panorama aspired to be "a work that men like Languet and Buchanan could respect on political as well as literary grounds". "The political scenes seem to indicate Sidney's endorsement of the Huguenot theory of limited rebellion" against absolutism, though with "hesitations and ambiguities".[187]

Behind the monarchomach sentiment virulent in resistance theory might thus smoulder the case not just for a religious partisanship's monarchy of preference, but for constraint or abolition of the kingship *per se*. Lauding tyrannicide might encode the correlative that tyranny was monarchism's indefeasible immanence. Stratford-on-Avon's self-made man, narrating more of the Roman republican story than any contemporary dramatist, emerges "a highly politicized and radical thinker, interested in republicanism" argues Hadfield.[188] *The Rape of Lucrece* , dedicated, in Southampton, to a member of a disaffected aristocratic circle, narrates the monarchophobic foundation myth of Rome's Republic, wherein a rapist prince embodies kingship turned "Authority for sin, warrant for blame" (620); and a heroized Lucrece, despite formal acquiescence in divine descent of kingship (624), poses the fundamental philosophic objection—given circumspect displacement upon Helen of Troy—to unconstrained personal power: "Why should the private pleasure of some one / Become the public plague of many moe?" (1478–79). *Titus Andronicus* opens with the rallying cry of the humane Bassianus challenging hereditary succession of power: "But let desert in pure election shine!' (1.1.16). *Titus* consequently "stands out as a radical play", which "can be read as a courageous—or foolhardy— beginning [to Shakespeare's career], especially as *Titus* has no obvious sources."[189] *Hamlet*'s tyrant, Claudius, will be confronted by popular electoral demand—"Choose we!" (4.5.102)—and, agonizingly, will bamboozle its leader, Laertes, as to "Why to a public count I may not go" (4.7.17).

Given the Tudor flourishing of at least six lineages of critical political thought sketched above—Radical Humanism, Commonwealthmen preaching, peasant egalitarianism, Catholic polemic, resistance theory, and republicanism—the question becomes unavoidable as to why the breadth and depth of late Tudor political ferment is so little recognised in modern Shakespeare criticism. It is true that religion-based resistance theory has recently become a recognised context, and republican strains of thought are gaining acknowledgment. Yet in these the essential target of reformation was the executive apex of the system—securing a godly monarchy or constraining its suzerainty: a politics cramped in horizon in comparison with radicalism's foundational impugnments of economic inequity and hereditary class privilege: the impetus of the first three, and symptomatically neglected traditions.[190] Expositions of Shakespeare's outlook continue overwhelmingly to assume Elizabethan veneration of hereditary kingship and peerage, as God-given institutions of timeless beneficence. For the general public, Shakespeare's apotheosis as the highest reach of English literary genius has long enveloped both The Bard and his Queen in mystifying patriotic idealization. The Swan of Avon sings the decently moderate traditionalism of our peoples, and the greatness of our island story. Within the academy, Cold War tensions twinned loyal aversion to the discourse of class analysis with political euphemization.[191] Yet several more recent movements have sustained oblivion of the scalding political disaffection of Shakespeare's period. In historiography, the Revisionism led by Conrad Russell and Kevin Sharpe, denying the Civil War to derive from any large political or intellectual issues, comprising only the unintended flarc-up of serial contingencies, posits as corollary that pre-seventeenth century society was consensual and non-political.[192] The world of suffering commoners and reformist thinkers is likewise occluded by the nobiliary predilection of the New Historicism, confining its attentions largely to the politico-aesthetics of sovereign and courtiers.[193] Both movements seem currently in decline, but the authority of a third, the Cambridge School of political theory, still blindfolds contextualisations of Shakespeare, and so calls for some brief consideration.

Descended from the studies in political ideas between 1300 and 1700 of Quentin Skinner and J. G. A. Pocock, the Cambridge School addresses only published works, and takes for their social context only the 'vocabulary' of distinct historical moments. Within this narrative of disembodied intellectual history, as Ellen Meiksin Wood observes, there is "no substantive consideration of agriculture, the aristocracy and peasantry, land distribution and tenure, the social division of labour, social protest and conflict, population, urbanisation, trade, commerce, manufacture, and the burgher class."[194] In the resistance to history from below, notes Holstun, "Pocock reduces practice to discourse, discourse to elite discourse, and plebeian oppositional writing and speaking to silence."[195] The bland conservatism underlying the reductive methodology of canonical textualism emulsifies the fierce acidity of early radical humanism, and disregards the wide hinterlands of angry popular dissidence.[196] A symptomatic example is the epigonic recitation, by the editors of *Shakespeare and Early Modern Political Thought*, of Tudor political thought as merely the 'civic humanist' discourse of Ciceronian virtues and needful good counsel. Political thought is thereby bowdlerized, tastefully re-established as a gentleman's club: chastely neoclassical, it is silently expulsive not only of the riffraff with their oral tradition of "When Adam delved and Eve span", but of the prosperous yeomen's world with its written demands, formulated in the Mousehold articles and pressed by Kett's thousands of followers. It further ignores publications themselves that prove inconveniently populist, such as Brinklow's *Complaynt of Roderyk Mors* (1542), the anonymous *A ruful complaynt of the publyke weale to Englande*, or Crowley's *Way to Wealth* (both 1550).[197] Shrinking in wilful anorexia from neighbouring disciplines, the antipopulism of the Cambridge School is aversive both to realities routinely presented by mainstream Tudor history—for example John Guy, or Fletcher and MacCulloch, on Kett's rebellion[198]—and to the nutriments of a more encompassing school of political analysis, the discipline of 'political economy'. Though often associated with Hume, Mill and Marx, political economy is a legacy of political analysis born, ironically, in sixteenth century England itself. It substituted for classicizing ethical discourse an empirically detailed reconceptualisation of the state as economic in function and agenda, pondering relations of hereditary rulership to "civil society" (Sir Thomas Smith's term), and focusing poverty and class society in relation to revitalisation of an imperilled common interest. Contrast of Neal Wood's *Foundations of Political Economy* with Skinner's *The Foundations of Modern Political Thought* concretises the transforming inclusiveness of the earlier intellectual lineage, parlously neglected. Within the panelled chambers of the Cambridge School club, an allegedly upbeat political climate of 'Ciceronian' humanism of the early century becomes dissolved by a late Elizabethan, anti-courtly 'Tacitean' pessimism.[199] "By the time Shakespeare wrote, the political health of the court was in question"[200]—as if More's solution to scandalous national misgovernance were not an Ou-Topos, a Nowhere Land, and he had not likened kingship to an insatiable leech. Searing critiques of power had been generated, we have seen, through the entire century.

To present, then, as 'early modern political thought' merely the formal contemplation of civic humanism's repertoire of ethico-political motifs by a lineage of cherry-picked intellectuals is to occlude what is far more fundamental: in the first half of the century, the climate of steady political criticism and urging of reform, proceeding from deep anxiety over untrammelled monarchy, dissolute nobility and extortionate gentry; and in the last decades of the century, the apparency of a threatening disrespect for traditional authority *per se*, observable on every political level: from vengeful anti-injustice riots, through the demonizing prosecutory operations of paranoid local government (examined in our chapters on *As You Like It*), to decretal menacing by royal proclamation, impositions of Martial Law, and even redefinition of enclosure and food riots as treason.[201] Recurrently in Tudor England, basic structures of state and society were plunged into legitimation crisis, and throughout the anxiety-racked 1590s—characterised by Hindle as "a police state without police"[202]—there prevailed, for subjects and for governors, a sense of foundational political emergency.

> it will come to pass yt the people will shortly growe careless of lawes
> & maiestrates, and in thend fall to flat disobedience & open contempt
> whereof we do perceive & fynd to our greatte greafes a marvelous
> inclynacion & beginning already.[203]

"ANTIQUITY FORGOT, CUSTOM NOT KNOWN"? (*HAMLET*, 4.5.100)

Demonstrably insuppressible, proliferation of political critiques owed not only to local conditions but to a Western textuality incomparably more challenging than implied by the Cambridge School or Tillyardian conservatism. The armoury ultimately supplying so much of the fire-power for the multiple lines of oppositional discourse was housed, indestructibly, inside the hallowed temple complex of Judeo-Christian religion itself. Old Testament and New furnished myriad denunciations of power and privilege, with endless enjoinments to solidarity with the suffering poor.[204] ("O my people, they which lead thee cause thee to err . . . The Lord will enter into judgement with the ancients of his people, and the princes thereof: for ye have eaten up the vineyard; the spoil of the poor is in your houses. What mean ye that beat my people to pieces, and grind the faces of the poor? saith the Lord God of hosts." [Isaiah 3.12–15]) Anarchic yet unimpeachable, this vast textual matrix furnished plenipotentiary powers to numerous conflicting positions.[205]

The canon of Classical literature could prove likewise subversive to Tudor political dogma. The revered Aristotle taught that inequality, in all societies, breeds destabilising class-conflict, erupting periodically in revolution (*metabole*); and while preferring rule by cultivated gentlemen, he adduced a qualified defense of democracy as "safer and less liable to faction than oligarchy."[206] Indictments of despotism and encomia of political liberators resonated down the centuries in Greek tragic drama, classical historiography and political theory. Athens bequeathed the practice of *isonomia* (equality before the law), and Euripides placed enthusiastic championing of democracy, with equal justice available to rich and poor, into the mouth of the heroic Theseus in his play *The Suppliant Women* ("This is the call of freedom . . .", ll.405–55). Cicero, while preferring a 'composite' constitution to democracy, nonetheless taught the moral equality of rich and poor, championed tyrannicide, excoriated aristocratic corruption for perverting legal justice into farce, and meditated democratic sentiments. "Surely nothing can be sweeter than liberty; but if it is not the same for all, it does not deserve the name of liberty."[207] Republicanism was praised, in Polybius, Livy, and Tacitus, for a political balance, freedom and nourishment of virtue lost under monarchy. Lucan's *Pharsalia* became "one of the key republican literary works" for the early seventeenth century, and Hadfield has argued it a paradigm for Shakespeare's first tetralogy.[208] It is thus unsurprising to find Hobbes concluding the classical legacy to have been a leading cause of the English civil war, famously declaring that the learning of "the Greek and Latine tongues" in English universities had functioned "as the wooden horse was to the Trojans", teaching "Rebellion in particular against monarchy" and the virtues of "popular forme of government."[209] In summary, "Foundational ideas of citizenship and civic equality" did not disappear in political thought along with Greek democracy, but persisted, as Ellen Meiksins Wood has shown, paradoxically co-opted "to serve the cause of inequality and domination."[210]

Given the intense resultant ambiguity of Western culture's political magisterium, conceptions of wealth and poverty within *societas Christiana* were complex and slippery.[211] From the twelfth century on, the antinomies of poverty were reconciled for officialdom through distinction between the deserving poor and the wickedly shiftless: a disciplinary classification emphatic in Tudor England.[212] Yet countless medieval sermons "reserved their most virulent criticism for the rich and powerful", often characterising the Last Judgement as the day of vengeance of the poor. "All that was required to turn such a prophecy into revolutionary propaganda of the most explosive kind was to bring the Day of Judgement nearer", observes Norman Cohn.[213] "In the Christian West", concludes Debora Shuger, "orthodoxy itself is problematic and complex, fissured by a guilty disillusion over its own institutional bases, ambivalent about power, troubled by a bad conscience."[214] That the flourishing of opulence amidst pauperised heartbreak was a godless malignity, proved finally an ineliminable doctrine. The iniquity of inequity found its simplest formulation in a Tudor rebel: "why shulde oone manne have all and an other nothinge"?[215] "Christ himself", thundered Bishop Latimer, accused of subversive preaching, "was noted to be a stirrer up of the people against the emperor; and was contented to be called seditious."[216] Given the prolific interrogation of polarised power and privilege by both sacred and Classical legacies, canonically integral throughout the *longue durée* of exploitation of the many by the few, it is purblind ideology to proclaim the inexistence—in any Western society, let alone in Shakespeare's England—of foundational indictment of material inequality and human subjection.

"MY TONGUE WILL TELL THE ANGER OF MY HEART, / OR ELSE MY HEART CONCEALING IT WILL BREAK" [217]

Given the interweaving of religious, philosophic, economic, political and military unrest in the Black Nineties, it would have been remarkable indeed had a major genius like Shakespeare *not* engaged traditions of angry political demystification, speculated urgently on alterities.[218] Shakespeare's plays offer, as Holstun has demonstrated, "a virtual encyclopedia of the various forms of riot and rebellion in early modern England."[219] The political system was "astonishingly vulnerable to a concerted challenge from below", judges Archer, "and an awareness of that vulnerability shaped the panic-stricken rhetoric of 1590s."[220] The possessing classes responded by subordinating ideological frictions between themselves to the security of a defensive bloc: a *marriage de convenance* consolidated by structural commonality of wealth.[221] The majority of propertied Englishmen swallowed political grievances to support the status quo from terror of anarchy and levelling underclass rebellion: if "the ruder sort" were "privy to their own strength and liberty allowed them by the law", observed an MP in 1597, they "would be as unbridled and untamed beasts."[222] The authorities intelligently conceded to "the poorer sections of society" just enough material relief, argues Archer, "to ensure that popular attitudes to them remained ambiguous. It was recognised that elite action was wanting on some issues, but it was appreciated that little could be achieved without their support."[223] A combination of rewarded plebeian defeatism with the obsessively inculcated fear of arousing the many-headed monster thus helped pre-empt in late Tudor England any mass rising by overburdened commoners. Shakespeare's politics, by contrast, often reversed the perspective: in 2 *Henry VI* (as in *Coriolanus*), we shall find that these can be populist in perception, and radical in their scale of delegitimation of power, as well as appreciative of the practical gains that insurgence might achieve. Yet if, in the last resort, Shakespeare, too, seems to have remained sceptical about prospects for large-scale political transformation, this was due, I shall suggest, not to simplistic propertied anti-populism, so much as to realist pessimism about the unpropitious political conditions of the *fin de siècle*, recognising the absence of reforming agency. Shakespeare's political vision comprised, I will argue, the suffering, paradoxical position of a radical deconsecration of authority that was pragmatically resourceless, yet remained unreconciled to a morally untenable social and political order. Remarkably audacious in its topicality and allusiveness, Shakespeare's playwrighting stimulated his countrymen to intensive scepticism about the claims and nature of power, and it employed, we shall see, the special force of drama—often through a uniquely inventive political stagecraft of deixis, framing and doubling—to break spectators' incorporation in a range of state ideologies.

"MY WORDS EXPRESS MY PURPOSE"
(*MEASURE FOR MEASURE* 2.4.148)

Mine is not, of course, the first voice to suggest Shakespeare a radical. When, already far down these pathways of rather lonely conclusion, I was coming to suspect that I might have slipped unawares into irretrievable dementia, I was hugely relieved to engage at different points the pioneering works of Jan Kott, Annabel Patterson, Jonathan Dollimore and Curtis Breight.[224] From their learning and brilliance I have gained much insight, as ensuing pages acknowledge. That Shakespeare was in key respects a radical is a view, however, still confined to a handful of works, floating largely unregarded in the almost immeasurable ocean of Shakespeare studies. This book, I can but hope, will contribute to a sea-change.

My approach will be to marry original conjunctural meanings, recovered from detailed historical contextualisations, to a sustained concern for the original stagings of Shakespeare's scripts. Stagecraft examination discloses a variety of ideologically potent subtextual mechanisms, strongly hinted in the scripts themselves, including framing actions, doubling, expressive silences, and—above all—the workings of deixis: so transforming in theatrical impact yet so very rarely noted. This combination of close attentions opens up the canon in a striking way, I suggest, to reveal populist, at times even radical meaning at the heart of the drama. To recognise Shakespeare's allusiveness to 1590s controversies and dissident thought, and to recover the subtextual politics of Shakespeare's distinctive stagecraft, is to discover a largely novel, and I would argue more authentic 'Shakespeare'. Sustained and lengthy close readings have been compelled not only by the legendary complexity and subtlety of Shakespearean art, but by the aspiration to cogency in a revaluative project. Paradigm shift can occur only through the cumulative pressure of an evidentiary mass.

To enhance the cogency of these findings, I have positioned my critical analyses upon inauspicious terrain: four of Shakespeare's Elizabethan dramas which are widely assumed to indicate the dramatist's conservatism. A number of the early plays fairly bristle with radical political perception: it would be no tall order to demonstrate the cynicism towards absolute fealty in *Titus Andronicus*, Shakespeare's scepticism regarding the nature of monarchic succession in *Richard III*, or the diagrammatic demystification that exhibits divine right rhetoric foundering on the rocks of realpolitic in *Richard II*. Instead, I selected a tragedy, two comedies, and a history play each of which is regarded overwhelmingly by Shakespeare scholars as evidence of a Shakespeare who either 'transcends' the political, or emerges a proponent of official, hegemonic doctrines. *The Taming of the Shrew* stands accused of brutal sexism; *As You Like It* is allegedly a flight into blithe escapism; *Romeo and Juliet* is taken for a work of timeless romance; and *Henry VI Part Two* supposedly showcases Shakespeare's anti-populism and fear of the mob. That through these plays William Shakespeare was in fact steadily articulating in the public amphitheatres contemporary class angers, indictments of power, and sympathy for an oppressed commons is the counter-valuative case this book seeks to establish.

The contrast is sharp with twentieth century literary criticism's overwhelming interpretation of Shakespeare's political vision as one of thematically central, persistently crafted, irresolvable ambiguation. Claiming the bard for Liberal Humanism's traditional celebration of benign pluralism, A.P. Rossiter bestowed seminal praise upon a Shakespeare evincing "that extra degree-of-freedom which is given only by what I have called a constant 'Doubleness': a thoroughly English empiricism which recognises the coextancy and juxtaposition of opposites, without submitting to urges (philosophical, moral, etc.) to obliterate or annihilate the one in the theoretical interests of the other. That is what I have tried to express by the figure of 'two-eyedness'."[225] Yet generating much in Shakespearean plurality of perspective was the brute and bloodstained fact of state censorship. No interrogative dramatisation of power could hope to see performance if it lacked powerfully overt, countervailing statements of political orthodoxy. Further, the very interpolation of ambiguating perspective—even when tactically discredited through characterisation and formal closure—comprised in itself a daring and dissident intervention in an era of absolutist claims by official thought. In the period when Philip Stubbes lost his right hand to a meat cleaver for impugning Elizabeth's marital plans, and Thomas Kyd was put to tortures which hastened his death for having shared rooms with the 'atheist' Christopher Marlowe, 'ambiguity' on foundational issues was not, as today, a matter of quietist complexity, but of active political dissent, a conscious destabilisation of official narratives.

I have not sought to deny the self-evident architectural pluralism in Shakespearean drama, the competing codes of value and crafted counterpoise of perspectives. Always in Shakespeare we hear polyphony. A master-dramatist, however, may array a wealth of characters and beliefs without implying as automatic correlative that no subsuming framework of values should emerge through and beyond their particularities. We need not synonymise dramatised plurality with an intended endpoint of irresolvable ambiguation.

In the case of Shakespeare, I conclude that an identifiable personal politics emerges beyond both the innate multiplicity and openness of dramatic form, and his own bravura gift for dramatising contrastive points of view. For there are, one might theorise, at least five elements in Shakespearean dramaturgy from whose examination the deduction of an authorial politics looks possible. First, the nature of his source deviations. (Is there a consistent character to that political matter, extraneous to the sources, which Shakespeare interpolates?) Second, the issue of topical alignments. (Does repositioning of the plays in their year of composition reveal, through apparent reference to current events, a political scepticism towards the state, or conversely a sympathy for its actions and rhetoric?) Third, the manipulation of audience identification in performance. (Do stagecraft effects disambiguate the equipoise of contrary positions arrayed upon the textual surface? What political direction to the patterning of audience empathy and hostility, of 'bonding' and 'targeting', emerges as demonstrably engineered by the scripts for on-stage activation in the public theatres?) Fourth, the nature of the endings. (Are the moments of impugnment of power and tradition effectively repudiated, and grievances shown to have been remedied? Are emotionally forceful 'reconciliation effects', as we might dub them, supplied to rebuild allegiance to political institutions antagonised and exposed? Or is intellectual alienation from an interrogated or discredited polity commonly left strategically uncountered, save by official rhetorics themselves falsified in the dramatic action?). Finally, combining all these elements, is the question of paradigmatic coherence across his works. (Are thematics of demystification and delegitimation recurrent? Is there regularity to the Shakespearean foregrounding of topics and questions currently embarrassing to power? Is it significant that Shakespeare—as contemporaries noted—wrote no elegy at the death of Queen Elizabeth, and penned no poetry welcoming King James to the throne?)[226] We will see in this book that through all five categories—source deviation, topical reference, manipulation of audience identification, the political character of endings, and career-long coherence—Shakespeare emerges as a substantially radical writer.

2 Theatrical Foundations
Performance Criticism and Transgressive Overdetermination

> It must be borne in mind that, so far as the external abuses of theatres go, the complaints of their bitterest enemies are fairly well supported by independent evidence.
>
> (E. K. Chambers, *The Elizabethan Stage*, 1.264)

> Given the tremendous success of *Tamburlaine*, it is clear that aggressive subversion and an assault on received wisdom was a winning commercial formula, one that helped to define the nature of the English public stage.
>
> (Andrew Hadfield, *Shakespeare and Republicanism*, 60)

BEYOND TEXTUALISM

Interpretations of Shakespearean drama have been for centuries quite literally *readings*. Shakespearean meaning has been sought at the desk, through years of cerebration, of multiple rereadings, that gradually educe an abstract thematics, a flowering of intricate ideal form too fine for the vulgarity of the senses. The richly petalled rose of Shakespearean meaning has been an exquisite bloom, separated from the roaring playhouse, nurtured to maturity in the decontaminating preserve of the library, unfolding delicately in the pure oxygen of scholarly sensitivity and disciplined erudition. Such readings not only employ, but imply, the primacy of a 'textualist' hermeneutics, privileging deskbound lucubrations and the saturating focus of exhaustive conceptual attentions. Its verdicts are the mighty meditations of Gutenberg men, supersubtle intricacies of hypermeditated sophistication.

The following pages construe Shakespeare's plays alternatively, as scripts; and as scripts whose dialogues are crafted for placement into *further* dialogue: with a gathered crowd, in a certain locus, within a specific cultural milieu. The insistence that Shakespearean drama essentially comprised not verse narratives but a set of flexible playscripts, aiming at a self-unfolding through action on a stage, not the turning of the page, is inestimably important. It foregrounds for analysis such dimensions of original meaning as the impact of auditorium location, music, costuming, blocking (the onstage grouping of characters), gesture, intonation, and manipulated audience interaction. That the medium of Shakespearean meaning was live theatre entails our need to recover at least three vital elements customarily lost with textualism: the physical, the festal, the dialogical.

It is the last of these elements that has proven, I feel, most neglected in Shakespeare criticism, and this book will accordingly highlight that principle in its close readings.

It is true that acknowledgment of the need to understand Shakespeare in these ways has been made for the better part of a century now; but despite many welcome works on particular aspects of early modern theatricality, astonishingly little literary criticism has been published that reads individual plays *systematically* in their light. This owes partly, no doubt, to economic factors: lengthy books are expensive to publish, and at most half a dozen plays can be systematically reconstructed in original theatrical terms in a single book. Yet the greater problem is that the task looks so daunting: drama is inherently so plastic a medium, so very many factors are in play at any one moment in live theatrical performance, and so little survives in the way of original eye-witness accounts, that it may seem speculative folly to presume to recover the ephemeral proceedings of four centuries ago. Such pessimistic conclusions are further authorised by the current Post-Modernist climate, with its chic neo-Heraclitean dogmas of flux and indeterminacy, of epistemological undecidability and history as the irrecoverably contingent.

Against such premises, not the least reply is that it would be folly for scholarship laboriously to amass, across diligent centuries, knowledge of early modern theatrical practice, then forswear its attempted application. Moreover, if tentativeness is indubitably called for in the reconstructive project, defeatism is not. If it is, as is sometimes suggested, an impossibility to recover original tone and affect in Shakespearean drama, then we should, in all honesty, abandon the attempt to exposit it. For the sweeping logic of such hermeneutic hypochondria would allow us no recourse against the claims, for example, that *The Merry Wives of Windsor* is a tense, depressive work, and *Macbeth* a bouncing exercise in quotidian high spirits. The very concept of genre, and the seriousness with which it continues to be invested by literary criticism, contradict a stance of dismissiveness toward the recoverability of emotional valences in Shakespeare. Above all, the plays themselves are in fact rich in clues to their own emotional shifts and tones. As Ann Pasternak Slater long ago demonstrated, Shakespeare exerts directorial control over action not only through his stage directions but by inserting "continuous descriptive direction" into the dialogue, "internal directions . . . forcing us to see what he wants us to see".[1] The emotionally declarative gestures compelled by his language are sometimes formulaic—crossing one's arms and pulling a hat over one's brows, "in the stock attitude of melancholy", or strutting on tiptoe, to signify a braggart[2]—but the majority are naturalistic evocations of feeling, such as smiling, frowning, whispering, kneeling, stamping, taking by the hand, dabbing eyes, wiping a child's nose, shaking a sword, embracing, running, dancing, striking, etc. More subtly, Tiffany Stern likewise notes that the Elizabethan system of actors studying their own parts solo entailed authorial provision of emotive prompts within the language, such as transitions from prose to verse, or from 'you' to 'thou'.[3] Shakespeare may build such simple foundations into complex structures, of course, whose total effect may at points grow problematic. But knowledge of the parts brings understanding of the whole into the realm of feasibility, and underwrites the project of inferential reconstruction.

Speculative, probabilistic, and incomplete though it must necessarily be, the play-long tracing of theatrically produced meanings in original performance of Shakespeare's playscripts may prove to be at least as objective as most 'textualist' interpretation. This is not only because textualist criticism, habitually ignoring the very medium through which the language and action are articulated, stands at an unexamined remove from original dramatic meaning. It is also because theatrically centred studies may unearth supplemental or transformative dimensions of meaning disclosed only in enactment: dimensions which work to disambiguate uncertainties of the textual level, or to contravene the rhetoric of authority figures. The book will offer many examples of such mechanisms of subtextual enunciation built into the scripts—'constructed latencies' as I call them, in distinction from the generic plasticity of dramatic form—which were designed to lie invisible on the written page but became almost unavoidably activated in performance.

IDEOLOGY AND VENUE

Elizabethan plays were performed, of course, in a number of locations: not only in London's public theatres (or amphitheatres, as Andrew Gurr suggestively terms them), but at the Inns of Court; on improvised stages in small towns when on tour; in the homes of noblemen seeking private showings; in hall playhouses from 1599; and at court. This book will suggest that Shakespeare wrote primarily with the public amphitheatres in mind: these were easily the most remunerative venue for Shakespeare in financial terms, as well as supplying by far the largest audiences.[4] (Theatres could hold over two thousand spectators per performance. London supplied its theatres in 1595 with around 15,000 playgoers per week.)[5] Yet Shakespeare wrote simultaneously, I suggest, with an eye to easy adaptability for court performance: it was precisely the function of his constructed latencies to confer concealed ideological flexibility upon his playscripts. Whilst pronounced ideological rhetorics of the surface enabled scripts to pass the censor and to pleasure the court, the plays' stagecraft secrets harboured dissident subtextual dimensions that were readily triggered in the conditions specific to the public playhouse, with its distinctive horizons of expectation.

This process was assisted by the virtually polarised reception conditions respective to court and amphitheatre. By longstanding tradition, players and playgoers in the public theatre were buoyantly interactional, savouring moments of both deixis (when a play's language swerves suddenly outside the fiction to indicate the material context of utterance, i.e., the auditorium or members of the audience) and occasional *ad hominem* repartee (dramaturgic encodings whose actualisation would have proven intolerable temerity at the Court's audience of peers and statesmen). There is thus a vital dimension missing in performances of Shakespeare at court. Indeed, if the courtly audience at the close of *A Midsummer Night's Dream* is anything to go by, plays staged there were regarded as trivial amusements, and their reception characterised by interruptions and idle chatter. Above all, since the court was the epicentre of national affairs, courtiers' attention must have been colourfully diluted by their own dramas of collective self-spectating and self-display. Engrossment in perusing the current formation of cliques and enmities, in circulating political or amorous messages among one other, and in descrying the mood and health of Elizabeth, whose responses they would largely echo, must often have proven at least as compelling as heeding the declamations of common players in their ephemeral entertainment. The "primary interest", acknowledges Wikander, "is not the show itself, but the reaction of the monarch to the show."[6] In the amphitheatres, by contrast, audiences were all eyes to decipher the current politics of court and national events precisely from their encoding in the particulars of the drama. To the consternation of their social superiors, Elizabethan commoners were incorrigible in political avidity and presumptious commentation. "Nowadays there is no vulgar, but all Statesmen", was Francis Bacon's sneer.[7] "Which of you will stop / The vent of hearing when loud Rumour speaks?" Rumour taunts his "household", the theatre audience (Induction to *2 Henry VI*, 0.1–2, 22). Leah Marcus speaks of "the interpretive maelstrom" swirling around drama in performance.[8]

More important still, there prevailed in the amphitheatres a climate of moral and political irreverence, its deeply anti-authoritarian impulses the product, I suggest, of a wide confluence of factors.

First, the new urban theatres inherited the legacy of medieval carnival, with its "customary licence to flout and fleer at what on other days commanded respect".[9] Under assault by Puritanism and by 'vestry values' (as we shall analyse them in discussion of *As You Like It*), the spirit of Saturnalian revels delighted its crowds with its "clear cut gesture towards liberty . . . its accession of wanton vitality." Indeed, "'Game' and 'play', 'gamehouse' and 'playhouse' seemed to have been used interchangeably well into the sixteenth century."[10] Elizabethan theatre commonly concluded—even following tragedies—with a jig: a burst of vigorous song and dance which included not only clowning and bawdy but "legal parody" and "burlesque of religious forms".[11] With its anarchic revolt of the body against moral discipline, its pillorying of authority figures, its jubilation in the world turned upside down, carnival's spirit of festive misrule comprised "a naively rebellious expression of the common man's sense of the world and his position in it."[12] Indeed, ludic disruption of established order extended beyond prescribed seasonal merriments into organised acts of underclass resistance: protests against enclosures and food-profiteering could don ritual carnival form, of masquerade and cross-dressing. Such practice aimed to reassure authority that its insurgence targeted a strictly defined grievance and was not to be taken as a general rebellion; yet the behaviour makes clear to us that, far from being a matter merely of cathartic exuberance, in Tudor life as in Tudor theatre the carnivalesque was anchored in political transgression and oppositional critique.[13]

Transgressive orientation was consolidated by theatrical location. As Steven Mullancy has argued, London's theatres were built in the Liberties, zones of authorised cultural anomaly. The literal 'place of the stage' was "the margins of the city . . . places where forms of moral incontinence and pollution were granted license to exist."[14] To see a Shakespeare play at the Globe, one had to exit the walled city (Bankside was around a mile and a half from St Paul's), and, unless able to pay sixpence to a ferryman, to cross the Thames over London Bridge. Just before one turned right, to pass St. Mary Overbury and plunge into the suburbs, high and conspicuous on the bridge's tower was crafted a final message from officialdom, composed in Tudor neon. Overhead yet clearly visible, impaled on spikes rotted the severed heads and sliced body parts of the executed. (When Iago claimed [*Othello*, 1.1.64–65] that he scorned to display his heart, for jackdaws to peck at, he invoked an empiric image.) Arrived in Southwark, on Bankside—allocated, we recall, a Provost-Marshal of its own from 1595—one entered an outerworld, or underworld, of vice. The theatres were surrounded by gaming houses and by numerous brothels; and "Without a doubt, the London theater and the plays performed in them were populated by whores and their bawds, in fiction and fact."[15] As Gary Taylor remarks, theatres and stews had much in common. "Prostitution and playing are both service industries; both cater gainfully to the market for real fantasy . . . Players and prostitutes worked in the same buildings, lived off the same customers; both simulated passions they did not feel . . . Whorehouse and playhouse alike stood on the uncertain periphery of the city and the law: condemned but condoned, persecuted and permitted."[16] Near the Rose Theatre was a bear-baiting pit; and theatre stages themselves were sometimes temporarily dismantled to drive in a stake for animal baiting, or to allow fencing competitions—forbidden within the City.[17] Southwark was the location, too, of England's last leper house, of prisons, a madhouse, and scaffolding for the public execution of traitors and criminals. Though boasting fine homes and gardens in some places ("the slums were in the suburbs, but the suburbs were not the slums"),[18] it was nonetheless swelling fast, its tenements overcrowded with subsistence migrants flooding in from the countryside, desperate to make a living whether by honesty or by crime. Southwark's theatres bordered 'the Maze', an area of distressed and turbulent garment workers and sweatshops.[19] Southwark provided also Roman Catholic safe houses, and a secret printing press in St. Mary Overbury's Close. Within the gamehouses, alcohol was on sale (playwrights in the tiring house, listening apprehensively to audience reactions to their work, could blanch and grow jumpy through mistaking the uncorkings of ale bottles for hissings from the audience).[20] Since all playhouses sold ale, "whether they counted as taverns or playhouses was a matter of name rather than of function . . . The Globe and the Fortune both had taprooms."[21] Some spectators smoked pipes throughout performances: "and it makes them riotous and merry", remarked Thomas Platter in 1599, "and rather drowsy, just as if they were drunk".[22] Further, as Harbage recorded, "Two groups are mentioned again and again in contemporary allusions to the theatres—the students of the Inns of Court and the apprentices of London."[23] Both youth groups were noted for high spirits and irreverence. We thus need scarcely swallow the outlandish invective of Puritan antitheatricalists (that drama comprised schooling in moral depravity) or the protests of City Fathers (that theatres were lawless) to recognise that the amphitheatres were home-ground to a recognisably carnivalesque revelry, with its traditionally mingled appetites for the ludic and the iconoclastic, for both release and political contestation. The theatre's liberty was, in Mullaney's phrase, "at once moral, ideological, and topological."[24] "To go to the public playhouse', judges Louis Montrose, "was to visit the interstices of Elizabethan social and cognitive order."[25]

The gamehouses were implicitly subversive in further respects. Admission to the yard cost one penny. For the price of a few beers, that is, labourers and stable-boys, washerwomen and fruit vendors, common sailors and ex-soldiers, bricklayers and apprentices could survey, judge, and even vocally condemn government decisions and the behaviours of princes. The alarm (or exhilaration, depending on class perspective) generated for Elizabethans by this levelling effect of open admission can be gaged by contrast with official insistence that the political role of commoners was questionless submission to the diktats of authority. The *Homily Against Disobedience* (1570) declared

> What a perilous thing were it to commit unto the subjectes the judgement which prince is wyse and godly and his government good, and which is otherwise, as though the foote must judge of the head—an enterprise very heynous, and must needes breede rebellion.[26]

Archbishop Parker had asked rhetorically "what Lord of the Council shall ride quietly minded in the streets among desperate beasts", if it be "referred to the judgement of the subject, of the tenant, and of the servant, to discuss what is tyranny, and to discern whether his prince, his landlord, his master is a tyrant?"[27] Robert Cecil nervously warned the House of Commons in

1601 "I ffeare we are not secrett amonge ourselves. Then muste I needes give yow this for a ffuture caution, that whatsoever is subject to a publique expectacion cannot be good. Whie, Parlement matters are ordinarye talke in the streetes . . . I thincke those persones would be glad that all soveraignitye were converted into popularitye . . ."[28] Indeed, through the 1590s dramas increasingly disclosed, in Andrew Gurr's words, "a new expectation of critical alertness in the audience".[29] In their prologues and epilogues, plays written by men of professional brilliance and the University Wits were often submitted explicitly to the authority of the audience—composed of fee-paying commoners, not traditional ruling elites. These audiences "were asked to approve or disapprove a play by their cries of 'aye' or 'no' at the end of the initial performance, so determining whether the play would live or die".[30] "Your stinkard hath the self-same libertie to be there in his Tobacco Fumes, which your sweet Courtier hath", complained Thomas Dekker: "your Car-man and Tinker claime as strong a voice in their suffrage, and sit to give iudgement on the plaies life and death, as well as the prowdest Momus among the tribe of Critick."[31] "The iconoclastic potential of the theater", argues Jean E. Howard, lay in making audiences "spectators to and judges of—rather than ritual participants in—a highly self-conscious scene of representation."[32]

We should recall, I think, that with some two to three thousand people gathering in any one theatre, the product was a voluntary popular assembly, in which men moreover became temporarily 'masterless', which was the size, suggestively, of a small army. We tend to forget today, with our vast sports arenas, the Elizabethan impact of so huge a gathering of commoners—which nervous authorities constantly associated with riot— whose fearsome numbers dwarfed those of constables, of the watch, and of the Provost-Marshal's patrol, even combined. As Shakespeare's *Henry VIII* implied, linking the vast crowd in that narrative with the audience watching it, the giantism of massed commoners could establish them as king-makers. ("We may as well push against Paul's as stir 'em", report the Porter and his Man of the crowd they have failed to disperse, implacably determined to attend Elizabeth's state christening. "An army cannot rule 'em" [5.3.15, 71].) This was not news to authority. "The official censor", observes Gary Taylor, "demanded changes in *1 Henry IV* and *King Lear*, not because he expected each individual to interpret the text differently but because he feared that three thousand spectators would respond collectively to Shakespeare's dangerous irreverence and would thereby recognize their own subversive cohesion."[33]

Attracting such numbers—twenty-five thousand playgoers per week at its height—theatre could see itself as the preeminent representative of the commons, the truly popular voice and focal point of the community. Intellectual command of the popular assembly could thus carry large political responsibility. (In 1577, within a year of the opening of the Theatre in Shoreditch, John Northbrooke angrily reported people to be claiming "that playes are as good as sermons, and that they learne as much or more at a playe, than they do at God's worde being preached.")[34] With their essentially secular, ideologically variegated model of reality challenging "the dominant paradigm of agency and authority", religious and hierarchic, the playhouses constituted "a new kind of social and cognitive space" and developed their own independent cultural authority.[35] When, I suggest, Shakespeare has the Prologue of *Henry V* instruct spectators "Piece out our imperfections with your thoughts . . . For 'tis your thoughts that now must dress our kings" (Prologue 23, 28), his words, reaching beyond the passage's ostensible apology for defective verisimilitude, embrace an educative political project which lies, I will argue, at the heart of his drama.

At the Prologue's feet in "this wooden O" lay a wide sea of underclass spectators. The many hundreds (or more) of 'groundlings' formed a restless, undulating body, filling the yard, and lapping the unquiet apron stage on three sides. We shall find in following chapters that Shakespeare's plays frequently invoke and address this adjacent, fluvial mass, through imagery of wave, ocean and water. We should thus note from the outset the political suggestiveness of that inflowing, marine vastness of the poor, ever surging and buoyant, often hissing and roaring, fluid at the very edge of the actors' platform. I suggest that such volatile interclass proxemics conferred, for instance, an immediacy of insulting confrontationalism upon the apparent doctrinal abstraction of Richard II:

> Not all the water in the rough rude sea
> Can wash the balm from an anointed king. (3.2.50–51)

This auditorial *mare infidum* recurs throughout Shakespeare, so that we shall find, for example, Queen Margaret, snarling anti-populist, insulting the crowd at her feet in *2 Henry VI* by boasting her survival of hostility from England's "vaulting sea" and "unkind shore" (3.2.94, 87). Comprising calculated 'stagecraft secrets', such invocations of the audience were invisible, because impossible, at court.

Acknowledging the groundling ocean is critical to our reconstruction of playhouse reception dynamics. For I would further suggest that not the least contribution to the subversive impetus of the popular amphitheatres was a consequence unintended in their physical design: though protecting the twopenny and threepenny playgoers from rain and leaving the groundlings exposed, the auditorial architecture functioned paradoxically to invert customary class relations. Outside the Liberties, the severity of class society would largely enforce, by fines, stocks and bloodied whip, the sharp and silent subordination of the poor: "Theis folke may not grudge nor murmure to lyve in labor and pain, and the most parte of there tyme with the swete of ther face."[36] "Plebeian obedience was synonymous with silence", notes Andy Wood, and unabashed speech a clamour associated with disorder or rebellion.[37] Yet within the high walls of the gamehouse the lapping underclasses dominated, I would argue, mood and spectacle. Although the precise class gradations of those who habitually stood around the stage are unclear, it is sure that, of the broad cross-section of classes from poor labourers through citizens to gallants attending the amphitheatres, the yard housed the poorest.[38] Separation of the lower classes in the yard from their betters in the galleries was probably a matter of more than admission fee, for contemporaries record supercilious aversion to the bad breath and sticky clothing of the groundlings.[39] The division, like the polarising economics of the 1590s, must have produced a high level of class consciousness. Though the yard could probably hold but a little over 800 people, as against a maximum capacity of over two thousand in the galleries, at most performances, Gurr believes, the groundlings probably formed nearly half the audience, and he speaks of them as "the principal audience".[40] Through sheer proximity to the stage, I suggest, this groundling ocean must have enjoyed a kind of primary possession of the drama. It was the 'men of *under*standing' who were close enough to fully appreciate the changing nuances of facial expression that were part of the players' acclaimed art of 'personation' developing through the 1590s ("Now comes the wanton blood up in your cheeks. / They'll be in scarlet straight at any news." "Ghastly looks / Are at my service, like enforcèd smiles, / And both are ready in their offices . . .").[41] More importantly, many of them being close enough to cuff at the legs of passing clowns, it was they who were best placed to exchange eye-contact with the actors, and to bandy repartee. The galleried, dozens of feet back, must have gazed down upon a double spectacle: the interaction of onstage deeds with reaction from the oceanic surround of buoyant groundling heads.

> Then sir, below,
> The very floor, as 'twere, waves to and fro,
> And, like a floating island, seems to move
> Upon a sea bound in with shores above.[42]

Conversely, at the beginning of *The Merchant of Venice*, in what looks strongly like mischievous deixis, Salerio employs the marine image to evoke the actors' view of this split-level audience. "Your mind", he tells Antonio, "is tossing on the ocean, / *There* [a word commonly introducing deixis, and probably accompanied by a pointing finger; italics mine] where your argosies with portly sail, / Like signors and rich burghers on the flood, / Or as it were the pageants of the sea, / Do overpeer the petty traffickers" (1.1. 8–12). Gamesome Salerio appears to pointing upwards to the wealthy-costumed auditors in the galleries, who "overpeer" the groundlings: thus making comic capital out of the signors' and rich burghers' showy dress— "portly sail", and later, "woven wings" and "silks" (9, 14, 34)—in a way which resembles that teasing of the audience for violating sumptuary codes elaborated by Jaques, we shall see, in *As You Like It* at 2.7. Underlining the probability that Salerio references the theatre is his image of wealthy citizens as forming the "*pageants* of the sea"—for a pageant was a mobile stage used for plays and processions. Completing the jest here is Salerio's assurance that the petty traffickers "curtsy to them, do them reverence, / As they fly by them with their woven wings" (14): surely a sly and comical irony given the festal state of things in these opening minutes. (Contrast "What care these roarers for the name of king?" fifteen lines into *The Tempest*, 1.1.15.)

For, within this "cockpit", as *Henry V* 's courtly Prologue scornfully termed it (11), co-present masters and superiors were in effect subordinated, deprived of restraining agency. Sequestered above in their roofed booths, 'paled in' by oak boards and iron 'pykes',[43] they were placed overwhelmingly, and thus obscuringly, behind the groundlings' backs. From few positions in the yard would the more prosperous ranks loom, as the groundlings always did for the galleried, into the main sightlines of stage spectacle.[44] The design of the later amphitheatres (including the Globe) indeed hardened the separation of the two audiences into impermeable division: gallery entry, once effected from the yard, was now made through separate outer doorways.[45] In such conditions of segregated auditorium domination, of transgressively democratic impunity, delight in liberated expressiveness and populist priority must often have been dizzying for the groundlings.[46]

Yet I do not wish to suggest settled and active opposition between groundling and galleried. The elating freedoms of the yard must surely have conferred upon the entire auditorial community the excited apperception of a realm escaped from customary confinements. To readers of this book who feel that I overestimate the theatrical importance of imputed groundling response, I would add that it is also far from clear that the groundlings monopolised the generation of carnivalesque energy within the theatre. Students from the Inns of Court, presumably disinclined to the yard's lack of comfort, may have been just as given to demonstrative revelling and subversive humour. At the conclusion of a performance of Jonson's *Poetaster* staged in the Middle Temple in 1601, the law students hurled fruit, with such unrestraint that subsequent performances of the drama were banned. Plays were likewise banned at the Merchant Taylor's School from 1573 because of "the rowdyism of the audience."[47] It is also the case that, as Margot Heinemann noted, several of the plays struck down by censorship—*Eastward Ho!*, *The Isle of Gulls*, *Philotas*—were written for the private theatres.[48] Apprentices in the yard and youths in the galleries may have thus have enjoyed cross-class bonding in mischievous spirits, as they sometimes did, we shall see, in the alehouses. Yet it is specifically the groundling multitude that we shall find often and conspicuously invoked by Shakespeare. The plays' references to such actions of audience celebration as throwing caps in the air would seem to rule out the galleried, as do repeated reference to stinking breath and physical lowness. For we shall find the human relations obtaining here in literal theatrical space—the outlook over 'wave' and 'sea', or the contrast of 'lowly' or 'base' men against 'lofty' ones—to be deictically woven by Shakespeare into the scripts themselves, in politically critical moments of audience address.

The resultant climate of response in the amphitheatres, however, though carnivalesque and groundling-heightened, was not, I should stress, narrowly plebeian. Commercial necessity, contemporary records, and the ideological contents of the plays all suggest otherwise. William Shakespeare's dramas catered, I argue, to a broad spectatorship of the sceptical, the merry-making, and the disaffected. Its *vox populi* included not just an ocean of 'mechanicals' and artisans, servants and poor husbandmen: it appealed to youth culture, in a period when around half of England's population was under twenty;[49] it appealed to propertied young gallants at the Inns of Court, fashionably cynical; to well born younger brothers (nearly thirteen per cent of apprentices were the sons of knights, esquires and gentlemen)[50] and to women, the discontented of primogeniture and patriarchy; to many citizens and burgesses, worried by national policies and frustrated by the concept of hereditary aristocracy. The groundlings and their student allies, readily tumultuous and vocal, may often have dominated much of moment by moment response to the plays; but groundling-buoyed suspicion of authority and authoritarianism, in the carnivalesque cockpit, subsumed a large, varied and intelligent constituency.

That an appeal to a broad, binarist sense of underclass unity could prove popular in the socially mixed public theatre is endorsed, I suggest, by the elasticity of the discourse that historians of class have found in the sixteenth and seventeenth centuries. It is not simply that in periods of exceptional class tension, such as during the mid-century rebellions, there emerged "countless examples of deferential speech patterns among commoners giving way to demands for ridding England of all gentlemen": a tendency re-emerging in the last decade of the century.[51] It is further that documented protest in rebellions, and legal complaints in central courts, revealed a crucially ambiguous rhetoric, emotive yet demographically indeterminate, which juxtaposed beleaguered, honest community against 'traitorous' enemies. "It is notable that in the rebellions of 1536, 1537 and 1549, otherwise wealthy farmers identified themselves as part of a 'poor commons', a 'commonality', an 'estate of poorality', or simply as members of something they called 'The Povertie'. Likewise, labouring people often mobilised the language of community in defining social conflict."[52] Prosperous and office-holding villagers and townspeople might thus normally define themselves through opposition to their inferiors, but when resisting noble authority, present themselves as members of 'the poor' or the 'trewe comons'. Consequently, "Precisely who constituted 'the commons' or 'the rich' could vary greatly."[53] In the hungry, crisis-ridden 1590s, the anti-authoritarian conditions of the public amphitheatres, bonding financially insecure spectators in a fellowship of licensed holiday from official values, could thus capitalise on disaffection's ambiguous inclusiveness. In such economic and ideological conditions, the 'trewe comons' and the 'estate of poorality', groundlings and galleried, could become one in resistant community.

To engage Shakespearean drama *qua* drama, as performances upon the public stage, is to recognise a gravitation toward the transgressive on one final basis. Theatrical responsiveness *per se* thrives upon spectacle, and on literally spectacular inversion of customary social and moral reflexes. In normal life, entering a room of hurled chairs and fistfights would likely find us beating a swift prudential retreat. In the playhouse, however, the experience may promise joyous thrill to the least pugilistic. In consequence, the anarchic Iago who engineers fight scenes endears himself to the audience, while the noble Othello, for making his followers drop their arms, is in danger of being hooted in frustration. Yet generations of literary critics, as Thomas Cartelli notes in a work of unjustly neglected sophistication, have missed the appeal of theatre as seductive fantasy, placing instead upon the dramas an interpretive grid of policed, official, extra-theatrical responsiveness.[54] Critics have long assigned to Elizabethan audiences a "moral restraint and religious and political orthodoxy [that] fail to correspond to the general tenor of reports about audience behavior and to the picture of unrestraint, impiety, and occasional sedition assembled here."[55] Cartelli demonstrates by contrast in a series of brilliant readings of Marlowe and Shakespeare that the Elizabethan playhouse often "encouraged resistance to authority and vicarious participation in the enactment of transgressive fantasies . . . That the most performatively appealing characters in such plays are usually the most outrageous suggests a direct correlation between the audience's experience of pleasure and the enactment of transgressive and often violent fantasies."[56]

In summary, theatrical impetus to transgressive autonomy of official culture was overdetermined. Anthitheatricalist indictments of popular drama for "utteringe of popular busye and sedycious matters" cannot be simply dismissed.[57] As Harbage noted long ago, "The theater was a democratic institution in an intensely undemocratic age."[58] Since its subversive tendencies established a framing "politics of the playhouse" conditioning reception of any individual play, literary criticism needs, as Jean E. Howard suggests, "to take account of the potential consonance or conflict between the ideological import of a drama and of the material conditions of its production."[59] To this task we now turn.

3 2 Henry VI
Jack Cade, The Hacket Rising and Shakespeare's Vision of Popular Rebellion

This nobility of bloud is not onelie cause of pride, and ignorance, but of unsufferable evil, and inevitable losse.[1]

"AND DO NOT STAND ON QUILLETS HOW TO SLAY HIM . . ." (3.1.261)

Thus died the most dangerous firebrand of sedition, most detestable traitor, most hypocriticall seducer, and most execrable blasphemous helhound, that many ages ever sawe, or heard of, in this lande.[2]

These well-turned thunderclaps roll to a formulaic horror. This is the familiar rhetoric for impeachment of a rebel against the state, its piously nauseated hyperbole fusing arraignments of religious offence, moral sophistry and treason. Found commonly where Tudor governments seek to anathematize declared opponents, the discourse in this instance takes on particular suggestiveness for scholars of Shakespeare, given the dates concerned. These superlatives of Richard Cosin's *Conspiracie for Pretended Reformation*, vilifying the leader of the Hacket rising of July 1591, and emerging from the presses in late 1592, may bring to mind another hyperbolised 'helhound' of treachery, Jack Cade, 'dangerous firebrand of sedition' of *Henry VI Part Two*—for it appears that Shakespeare wrote that play, and fashioned his highly peculiar Cade, somewhere between just those two points in time.[3] Indeed, the two 'helhounds', William Hacket, the 'detestable traitor' of the 1591 rebellion, and the notorious Jack Cade, here become kindred figures, as the inflationary generic categories of official propaganda elevate Hacket (risibly) into a kind of towering demonic equivalence with the worst rebels of English history. Tudor accounts of riot and rebellion characteristically conflated rebels past and present, so that, in the official imagination at least, in a kind of ghastly inversion of eucharistic divine co-presence, arch-demons of 1381 and 1450 merged with contemporary firebrands of sedition. Summing up at Hacket's trial, in July 1591, the Solicitor-General himself explicitly compared Hacket with, *inter alia*, Jack Cade.[4]

But just as the figure of Cade, for the public prosecutor, loomed darkly into the essential significance of Hacket, so the 'meaning' of Shakespeare's Jack Cade, as construed by commons audiences of 1591–92, must have come redolent of the recent and sensational experience of William Hacket. For the Hacket insurgency remained lurid in memory and controversial in interpretation for both Londoners and authorities for years afterwards: hundreds had witnessed the bizarre Cheapside rising and thousands the freakishly horrible circumstances of Hacket's execution. Given immediate government attempts to associate the rising with a Puritan leadership it was seeking to destroy, the rebellion was kept alive and topical in a stream of publications indicting and defending prominent Puritan divines that continued into 1596.[5] Catholic pamphleteers, such as Verstegan, Parsons and Southwell, likewise took up the event, in attacks on religion in England in general.[6] References to the Hacket affair also recurred in the writings of Francis Bacon, and in Nashe's assays against Gabriel Harvey, in pamphlets published in 1592 and 1596.[7] Hacket's fanatical followers were remembered well into the seventeenth century, when they were compared with Antinomian sectarians.[8]

Remarkably, however, criticism of *Henry VI Part Two* has never connected the two risings. In consequence, if popular memory of Hacket's recent rebellion figured, inescapably, among primary reception conditions disposing Shakespeare's audience, then proper historical reconstruction of just what Shakespeare was doing with and through the figure of his Jack Cade requires that we exhume, from long oblivion, the grotesque and haunting tragi-comedy of William Hacket and his followers. This chapter, following a preliminary outline of the critical debate over the politics of the Shakespearean Cade, will accordingly sketch the Hacket revolt and its popular reception, and demonstrate the playwright's suggestive remodelings of Cade as Hacket. Paradoxically, the major *effects* of superimposing the Elizabethan charlatan upon the Lancastrian rebel turn out to project a surprisingly substantial sympathy for underclass sufferings and popular rebellion. This Shakespearean populism, nuanced and ultimately ambivalent, will be scrutinized, then demonstrated again in that further play of topical allusion, and of remarkable stagecraft stratagem, which craft the death of this most complex and protean Jack Cade.

"WHY, RUDE COMPANION, WHATSOE'ER THOU BE, / I KNOW THEE NOT" (4.9.28–29)

Long central to political interpretations of the Shakespearean Cade have been the playwright's deviations from the chroniclers' Cade. These divergences have been frequently interpreted in baldly negative terms, as the anti-populist animus of an allegedly conservative bard. Richard Helgerson, for instance, construing the play's representation of common people as both straightforwardly hostile and lamentably brief, concluded that "It is as though Shakespeare set out to cancel the popular ideology with which his cycle of history plays began, as though he wanted to efface, alienate, even demonize all signs of commoner participation in the political nation." The reason lay in the "infatuation with royal power" of Shakespeare the ambitious social climber, seeking refined personal distance from the tainting plebeian energies of his theatre.[9] Judging the politics of the play as "not qualitatively different" from that of the "unambiguously monarchical" *Jack Strawe*, Walter Cohen declares that Shakespeare "present[s] the rebels' position in the serene confidence that it will be contemptuously dismissed."[10] Even the more complex verdict of David Bevington concedes that the ridicule of Cade and egalitarian ideas "reinforces the point that 'justice' administered by private citizens will soon lead to anarchy", and that "the topical force of Shakespeare's political portraiture is non-progressive."[11] The "potentially subversive" rebellion scenes "seem finally designed to justify oppression", concludes Phyllis Rackin. "Dissident sentiments are first evoked, then discredited and demonized as sources of anxiety, and finally defused in comic ridicule and brutal comic violence".[12] William Carroll concurs: although "Cade's complaints were real ones", Cade is "demonized so as to invalidate, or at least qualify, his claims of social injustice."[13] Widely quoted is the dictum of Richard Wilson: Cade is "metamorphosed into a cruel, barbaric lout, whose slogan is 'kill and knock down', and whose story, as 'the architect of disorder', is one long orgy of scatological clowning, arson and homicide, fuelled by an infantile hatred of literacy and law." Shakespeare, insists Wilson, "used his professional debut to signal scorn for popular culture and identification with an urban elite . . . The ideological function of the 'wooden O' was less to give voice to the alien, outcast and dispossessed, than to allow their representatives the rope to hang."[14]

Such voices have not gone unopposed. Christopher Hill saluted the juridical accuracy, and authentic popular anger, concentrated in Cade's accusation, "because they could not read, thou hast hanged them" (4.7.37–38).[15] Thomas Cartelli, demonstrating the play's fidelity to the reciprocal class angers of 1590s England, has argued that Cade's war against literacy, far from projecting a demonized fanaticism, was brusquely cogent in branding literacy as nexus of resented privilege, scarcely definable by other criteria. "Although the attendant scorn directed at literacy itself may constitute a displaced (and arguably self-defeating) symptom of political dispossession, the indictment of its beneficiaries could not be more apt."[16] In a further acknowledgment of the shrewdness of insurgent popular reasonings, Annabel Patterson redirects attention to the play's earlier, and "morally authoritative" popular rising, which successfully protected the king from Suffolk by enforcing his exile.[17] Even the second popular rising of the play, it is argued by Stephen Longstaffe, may not have generated the unequivocal revulsion against Cade and rebellion that critics like Wilson have argued, as we recognize when we attend to the drama's performance values at that point. The modulation of the Cade sequence into knockabout, carnivalesque mode, not to mention the likely impersonation of clowning Cade by hilarious Will Kemp, would have unloosed a 'dialogic' of complex effects, establishing "not simply parody, but metaparody." Nor, Longstaffe speculates, would the rowdy audience appetite thereby inflamed necessarily be dissolved by the burgeoning violence.[18] Ellen C. Caldwell has sketched historical analogues between popular distress in 1450 and the 1590s, concluding a considerable sympathy for Cade (although her determination to find only political seriousness in Cade's carnivalesque proposals that the three-hooped pot shall have ten hoops and the pissing-conduit run claret for a year, suggests limited ear for dramatic tone).[19] Jean Howard emphasized the foundational principle of aristocratic culpability in this play, wherein, indisputably, Shakespeare lays the primary blame for war and suffering at the door not of Jack Cade, manifest tool of megalomaniac York, but of the "unspeakable selfishness of the English nobles".[20] In similar vein, Paola Pugliatti, tracing the systematic "degradation" and "levelling to the lowest plane" of *all* the play's main characters, high and low, that Shakespeare imposes through his deviations from the Chronicles, concludes that, although Cade and his followers are "grotesque and almost subhuman", "it was the abasement and disfiguring of the high sphere that determined a parallel and reflected process of degradation in the low sphere . . . The political lesson is there for those who want to see it."[21] As Victor Kiernan, in an unjustly neglected work, elaborates such perspective, "A certain miasma of the insane, of violence out of control, pervades all the earlier Histories, as the spiral of crime goes on mounting. Amid it all the old political order shows itself irretrievably bad, incapable of regeneration. Its animating spirit is an unreasoning, insatiable thirst for power."[22]

Where critics agree is the fact that Shakespeare's Cade is historically inauthentic: a complex and composite figure. The narrative outline of his major actions does broadly conform to the events of the historical Cade rebellion of 1450, as taken by Shakespeare from Hall and Holinshed.[23] The killing of the Stafford brothers by the rebel army camping on Blackheath, their incursion into Southwark and release of prisoners from its gaols, the flight of the King, and subsequent triumphal entry of Cade and rebels into London ("Now is Mortimer lord of this city"),[24] all derive from the Chronicles; as do the arraignment and execution of Lord Saye and Sir James Cromer, the placing of their heads on poles, whence they are made to "kiss", the death of Matthew Goffe in battle, and the abrupt dispersal of the rebel army when offered a pardon, thereby abandoning Cade to his later fate on the sword of one Alexander Iden of Kent.

Yet into this dizzy course of events Shakespeare infuses yet a headier brew. Cade and his followers had been motivated by limited political aims, essentially seeking deliverance from crushing taxation, and expressing themselves in a formal 'Complaint', articulating "the general grudge of the people for the universal smart that, through misgovernment, everywhere they suffered, who thus forwearied with the peise [weight] of burdens too heavy for them any longer to bear."[25] By contrast, the Peasants' Revolt of

1381 had fought for a fundamental transformation of the socio-political system. Aiming to relieve themselves and their families from injurious economic exploitation forever, Wat Tyler's rebels undertook the widespread burning of financial records, the execution of lawyers and justices, attack on the Inns of Court, and even the swearing of grammar school teachers to forbear instruction in literacy. Further, John Ball's sermons had urged the logic of full-scale egalitarian revolution. "They might destroy first the great lords of the realm, and after the judges and lawyers, questmongers, and all other whom they undertook to be against the commons; for so they might procure peace and surety to themselves in time to come, if, despatching out of the way the great men, there should be an equality in liberty, no difference in degrees of nobility, but a like dignity and equal authority in all things brought in among them."[26] As scholars have long recognised, Shakespeare pours this radical spirit of 1381 into his nominal account of 1450 at several points. "The first thing we do, let's kill all the lawyers" is the cry that stimulates Cade's meditation on the lamentable guilt of parchment, and precipitates the slaying of the Clerk of Chartham (4.2.68–98); while, "all the realm shall be in common" (4.2.60), and the address of his followers as "fellow kings" (4.2.148) are patent echoes of the egalitarian thematic. "We will not leave one lord, one gentleman—/ Spare none but such as go in clouted shoon" (4.2.167–68) is the headlong war-cry of a committed class-warfare distinctly at odds with the agenda and events of 1450.

The Shakespearean purpose behind such revisionism is variously explained. For some critics, this may be no more than that habit of Tudor authorities, already noted, of conflating popular historical rebellions: "What more odious smell to all true English hearts than the unhappy memory of Cade, Straw, Ket, Perry, and others of like deserts?" asked the author of *Caesar's Dialogue* (1601).[27] Yet such essentialization of rebellion is itself ideologically loaded, impatiently effacing the particularities of commons suffering and rebel grievance, for an absolutized reflex of malediction. The commons, as it were, are always (and utterly) revolting. "The people", gestured Archbishop Whitgift, "are commonly bent to novelties and to factions and most ready to receive that doctrine that seemeth to be contrary to the present state and that inclineth to liberty."[28] Even the chroniclers concede much to this patrician damnatory haze. The Kentish rebels of 1450, shrugs Hall, in a tautology betraying temporary slippage from mental attention, were "ever desirous of new chaung [*sic*], and new fangelnes."[29] Similarly, literary critics "convinced of the majority view that Shakespeare was always a law-and-order playwright" will construe the syncretistic drive here as evidence of a propertied dramatist's eagerness to tar all popular insurgency with the same, 'extremist' brush.[30] Yet quite the opposite construction is possible. Introduction of the 1381 material, with its conveniently radicalized Cade, permits Shakespeare to establish, I suggest, in the face of censorship, an at least fleeting critique of the social order at its most fundamental. After all, as Patterson notes, the Elizabethan collation of popular risings, past and present, implies a *continuing* "cultural tradition of popular protest", stubbornly egalitarian across centuries of suffering.[31] More specifically, as James Holstun has recently suggested, Shakespeare may be smuggling surreptitious echoes of Kett's rebellion into his play, activating subversive memories of that reforming, class-based rebellion of 1549 which haunted the later sixteenth century, and whose ending in "a gentleman's riot" of exterminatory savagery ensured a legacy of gentry paranoia and biding underclass bitterness.[32] If Shakespeare is allusively reviving the traumatized popular feelings left by Kett's rebellion (and memories of "the camping time" endured for three generations),[33] then he is indeed generating, in a phrase of Annabel Patterson's, "ethical and pathetic claims whose force may linger beyond [detraction's] powers of persuasion."[34]

To judge, however, among such polarized perspectives on Shakespearean intention, we must establish the fuller picture of his modeling of Cade; for Shakespeare's divergences from the chronicles extend well beyond the radicalising ahistorical supplement of the Peasants' Revolt. The core character of Jack Cade is transformed: indeed demonized, as critics like Wilson see it. For Hall, Cade had been 'A certayn yong man of a goodely stature, and pregnaunt wit" (Hall p. 220), just as for Holinshed, lords had found him "sober in talk, wise in reasoning" (Holinshed vol. 3, p. 224). And though Holinshed records that the same lords also (and inevitably) thought him, on demanding direct negotiation with the King, "arrogant in heart, and stiff in opinion", the impression remains not only of persuasive intelligence, but of a guiding restraint, tactical at the least, within rebellion. In Southwark, Cade "prohibited to all his retinue murder, rape, and robbery, by which colour of well meaning he the more allured to him the hearts of the common people". Hall even notes that Cade's discourse was so extraordinarily convincing to the commons that the King, "doubtyng as much his familiar servauntes, as his unknowen subjectes (which spared not to speake, that the capitaynes cause was profitable for the common wealth) departed in all haste to the castell of Kylyngworthe in Warwyckeshyre" (Holinshed vol. 3, p. 224). By contrast with Cade the model of a cool reasonableness that could compel the King's familiars from his side, the Cade of *Henry VI Part Two* revels in bloody cluster-bombs of anarchy. His followers a rabble rather than clear co-reasoners, his maxim is ebullient disorder: "then are we in order when we are / Most out of order" (4.2.172–73).

Yet this, too, may transpire to be something quite other than demonization.[35] Through this second pattern of divergence from the chronicles, to the composite rebel of 1450 and 1381 is added a further dimension, which guarantees much popular appeal: in this rowdiest incarnation, Jack Cade becomes that ancient delight, the carnival tradition's Lord of Misrule. From the very outset of the Cade sequence, with its lath swords and idled, wise-cracking labourers, Shakespeare transposes the fundamental mode of the drama, dislocating it at a snap from sharp and sombre realism, political and psychological, into a festive disruption of illusionism, and a fireworks of punning and pillorying. Since real, not prop, swords were normally used for the fight scenes, the dramaturgic 'subcoding' inherent in the switch to wood here would for a contemporary audience have instantly transformed the nature of the sequence's 'violence'. Thanks to the explosive release of energy in this medium, Cade billows into a crude giantism, gains the primal force of archetype; and through the carnivalesque's collapse of chronicle realism, his philosophic contradictions become *ludic* rather than ludicrous, naturalised into familiar shows of hilarity.

> There shall be in England seven halfpenny loaves sold for a penny, the three-hooped pot shall have ten hoops, and I will make it a felony to drink small beer. (4.2.58–60)

Slashing the price of bread, of course, was guaranteed to go down well with a commons facing endless inflation and mounting tax demands, yet the real relief here is festal. Francois Laroque is unquestionably right to recognise in Cade "the vein of parodic eloquence that a Lord of Misrule would favour . . . a Carnival king whose reign ushers in the era of a world set upside down." [36]

Yet Laroque curiously neglects the political effects. As the violence so terrible in a realist mode turns here into festal stage knockabout, the killings into Punch-and-Judy slapstick, the very medium, I suggest, becomes an accomplice of Cade. As on Shrove Tuesday, uproar, vice, and anti-authoritarian energies are licensed, appropriate, and welcomed. With moral norms inverted, and comic whim the driving dramatic principle, dealing out whacks is just hilarious stage feigning.

Cade: And now henceforward it shall be treason for any that calls me otherwise than Lord Mortimer.
        Enter a soldier running
Soldier: Jack Cade! Jack Cade!
Cade: Zounds, knock him down there!
        They kill him
Butcher: If this fellow be wise, he'll never call ye Jack Cade more; I think he hath a very warning. (4.6.4–8)

To interpret this Cade sequence solemnly as a political essay dispraising popular insurgency is to miss—as surely the Elizabethan censor was intended to miss—these crucial performance values, the gratification offered a commons audience by the outbreak of 'playing' in a 'playhouse'. Bonding through asides, sharing jubilant mischief against spluttering high seriousness, Cade revels with the commons in Saturnalian flouting.

Stafford:	And will ye credit this base drudge's words
	That speaks he knows not what?
All:	Ay, marry, will we—therefore get ye gone.
Stafford's Brother:	Jack Cade, the Duke of York hath taught you this.
Cade: (Aside):	He lies, for I invented it myself. (4.2.136–40)

As Lord of Misrule in the carnival world, what Cade conquers is audience hearts.

Only at a later point in the rebellion sequence will come the gradual return from playing to acting, from liberative stage topsy-turvy to morally serious illusionism—as reinstatement of historical portrayal necessitated—with the execution of Lord Saye, and in time for the slaying of Jack Cade: that crucial coda with which this chapter must close.

Neither should we miss, I suggest, the further force of joyous liberation here, that ensued when the underground language of class defiance suddenly dared speak itself publically. Successive parliamentary extensions of treason laws from 1534 to indict speech against state policies and personnel had built a higher wall of fear around political outspokenness, and established an intensive monitoring of popular speech. As a Suffolk commoner complained in 1537, "Wee are so used nowe a days at Bungay as was nev[er] sene affore this; for if ii or iii gud felows be walkyng togedr, the constables come to theyme and wolle knowe what communycacon they have or ellys they shalbe stokkyd." In 1597, two labourers strolling on a country road, grumbling of the failings of the aristocracy, found themselves forced before the Privy Council, reported by a servant hidden below a hedge as they had passed.[37] Consequently, as historian of popular ideology Andy Wood puts it, "There was something liberating about those moments when poor men and women spoke publicly against authority . . . To speak of politics became a moment of transgressive freedom."[38] That bursting free from discursive restraint, launched with the opening of the Cade sequence—"Well, I say it was never merry world in England since gentlemen came up" (4.2.6–7)—was clearly just such a liberative experience, I suggest; and its extended gratification, in the intense publicity of open, playhouse utterance, must have reached the dizzying maximum.

One further factor suggests that these scenes rendered subversiveness more attractive and immune to ideological containment than is usually surmised. Jonathan Dollimore has argued that "Jacobean tragedy does often effect some kind of closure, but it is usually a perfunctory rather than a profound reassertion of order (providential and political). We may feel that such closure was a kind of condition for subversive thought to be foregrounded at all. But we should recognise too that such a condition cannot control what it permits: closure could never retrospectively guarantee ideological erasure of what, for a while, existed prior to and independently of it."[39] Performance-based criticism strengthens the point, I think. Textualist criticism meditates drama as organic form, extrapolating theme and import from scannings of the whole design, and it thus attaches considerable weight to closure. Elizabethan playgoers, by contrast, appear to have responded more substantially to individual character performances. The private conning of their parts in an age of little group rehearsal disposed actors against seeing plays as a unity: players concentrated instead on launching their own set of dramatic performances. Plays could thus unfold as a chain of relatively isolated 'highs' from actors in competition for applause, with the result that audiences, as Tiffany Stern suggests, "had a tendency to watch in a part-focused way".[40] (The attainment of celebrity status by leading actors during the 1590s must have accentuated this phenomenon.) Thus, for the spectators witnessing Kemp's bravura enactment of political resistance in these scenes, one of the major 'meanings' of the play may well have lain, I suggest, in an exhilarated admiration for the spirited role: an experience in political fashioning far less diminished by the play's monitory statements of political orthodoxy or the impact of the drama's closure than textualist exposition suggests.

Excavation of this third and festal layer to Cade, exposing the reign of a Lord of Misrule, has hitherto completed literary critical stratigraphy of Shakespeare's composite Cade. History itself, however, had taken a hand in Shakespearean creativity with the announcement in Cheapside, at market time one busy summer morning, of the arrival of the Messiah.

"OUR ENEMIES SHALL FALL BEFORE US, INSPIRED WITH THE SPIRIT OF PUTTING DOWN KINGS AND PRINCES" (4.2.30–31)

At approximately eight o'clock on the morning of Friday July 16th 1591, the Angel of Mercy and the Angel of Judgement, mad with the mania of the Holy Spirit, met as planned, to launch the apocalypse, in the lodgings of the Messiah, near Broken Wharf, London. They found him still in bed. The Angel of Mercy, one Edmund Coppinger, a Suffolk gentleman and minor servant of the Queen, and the Angel of Judgement, Henry Arthington, a Yorkshire gentleman, fell to their knees and burst into prayer. Coppinger, thanking God for his mission despite his own unworthiness, joyously acknowledged the universal supremacy of William Hacket as King of Europe, whereupon Hacket, Northamptonshire yeoman and reincarnation of John the Baptist, dressed only in his shirt, leapt from the bed. He prayed fervently that the honour of Jesus Christ might be advanced, then climbed back under the bedclothes.

Coppinger resuming his former line of prayer, Hacket once more arose and pointedly prayed that God's prophets might fully honour Christ, thereafter returning to bed, whereon Arthington recognised the need to anoint the King of Europe. Both Angels now fell flat before the bed, the Angel of Mercy kissing three times the boards of the floor that had been touched by the King's feet. When Mercy then rose and moved toward the King, Hacket clasped hands with him and cried, "You shall not neede to annoynt mee, for I have bene alreadie annoynted in heaven by the holy Ghost himselfe." "Goe your ways both", he instructed them, "and tell them in the Citie, that Christ Iesus is comme with his Fanne in his hand to judge the earth. And if any man aske you where he is, tell them he lies at *Walker's* house by *Broken Wharfe*: & if they will not believe it, let them come & kill me, if they can: for as truely as Christ Iesus is in Heaven, so truely is he come to judge the world."[41] The Angel of Mercy then rushed from the chamber so swiftly that the Angel of Judgement had no time to put his gloves on. Nonetheless, he followed at once, and the two commenced crying out in the streets below, as startled crowds began to gather, that Christ Jesus was come.

The account is from Richard Cosin's work of government propaganda, and its details thus probably fictitious. Although it is closely matched in Arthington's own, subsequent testimonial in *Seduction of Arthington by Hacket* (1592), the latter pamphlet, written in prison to appease the authorities and appeal for release, doubtless sought to conciliate the government by endorsing its every position. Nonetheless, the accent in the government account here, upon hilarity and transparency of fraudulence, was a crucial feature of the entire event as presented by almost all commentators, and one we must bear in mind in consideration of Shakespeare's Cade.

What ensued was probably far better grounded in fact, for as Curtis Breight argues, "Most of the events were witnessed by hundreds of people, and so an official account filled with lies would have been liable to refutation" by those challenging the long-controversial conclusions to which the government put this case. [42] Coppinger and Arthington proceeded along Watling Street and Old Change to Cheapside—a route, suggests Breight, imitating that of official ceremonies such as the Lord mayor's Pageant—all the while crying "Repent, England, repent", and announcing the advent of the Messiah.[43] By the time they were close to their destination, Cheapside Cross, there had gathered such a "mightie concourse of the common multitude" that "the throng and preasse of people" prevented both further movement and proper audibility. They therefore mounted a convenient empty cart close by,

> and out of that choise pulpit . . . made their lewde and trayterous preachment unto the people: wherein they stoode not onely upon the wordes of their former crye, but (so neere as I could learne from so common an Auditorie, and in so confused an action) they reading something out of a paper, went more particularly over the office and calling of *Hacket*: how he represented *Christ*, by partaking a part of his glorified body . . . and by the office of severing the good from the bad with the fanne in his hands, and of establishing the Gospell in *Europe* . . . and of bringing in that *Discipline* which they so often bable of, and which they meane by the terme of *Reformation*.[44]

Coppinger, as Angel of Mercy, promised great comfort and unspeakable joys to all who repented, while Arthington, as Angel of Judgement, pronounced terrible punishments to engulf London and all who repented not.

> This judgement against *London* . . . was that, men should (there) kill and massacre one another (as Butchers do kill swyne) all the day long, and no man shoulde take compassion of them. There was then and there delivered by them, or by the one of them, that *Hacket* was King of *Europe*, and so ought to be obeyed and taken: and that all Kings must holde of him, and that the *Queenes Maiestie* had forfeited her Crowne, and was worthie to be deprived . . . Lastly, in very unmannerly and sawcy tearmes they prayed to God, to confound two great Lordes of her Maiesties Counsell: for these two (together with a certayne Knight) they then and there openly and most lewdely accused in generall tearmes of treason.[45]

Alas, the crowds responded to these apocalyptic prospects in likewise unmannerly and saucy terms, mobbing the Angels with cat-calling merriment. This embarrassment, combined with the increasing "preasse . . . of common people to gaze and woonder at them", obliged the pair at length to seek refuge in the Mermaid tavern. Coppinger finally sought to flee continuing uproar by returning home, and Arthington, who appears to have kept up his trayterous preachments somewhat longer than Coppinger, was followed as he fled Cheapside "by a great multitude of lads and young persons of the meaner sort."[46]

Seeking the Messiah at his Broken Wharfe lodgings, Arthington found him gone, but became forcibly detained there himself. When Hacket returned, finding all in hubbub, the Angel of Judgement cried out in relief "There cometh the king of the earth!" Hacket, however, told him grimly to shut up. Yet a number of alarmed citizens were now searching both men, and the chamber, and they found upon Arthington a letter to the Queen depriving her of office. "This strange accident", meanwhile, "being quickely blowen through the citie, all was in a buzz, and in a kinde of astonishment, what to thinke of the matter."[47] Word of it swiftly reaching the Queen at Greenwich, she dispatched two Privy Councillors to investigate, who at once arraigned the trayterous trio at the Lord Mayor's house. The rising was over.

The buzz and astonishment continued to feed, however, upon certain writings, put into circulation by the conspirators shortly before their annunciation of Hacket to the masses. A bundle of about a thousand pamphlets had been printed, for distribution to brethren in Northamptonshire, Essex and Hertfordshire, to explain "the reason for this course taken in reformation", and to urge assistance in this predestinate project. Some of these pamphlets, it was alleged at Hacket's trial, were "already abroad" before the rising.[48] Further, copies of some two hundred letters had been dispersed to certain brethren on the 13th July, three days before the rising, again requesting assistance in the "reformation" about to executed. These may or may not be the "certaine seditious letters" mentioned by Cosin, "that were purposely scattered five or six nights afore in many of the streetes of London, by some of the actors, or by their complices and favourers."[49] Also produced by the conspirators was another pamphlet, called *The Fool's Bolt*, this one aimed at the laity. Taking the form of a rhyming ballad, it contained the following:

> Yf you in youthe will learne
> A courtier for to be,
> Then must thou first come knowe
> Thy lessen true of me:
> A christian trew, althoughe he be a cloune,
> Shall teache a prince to wear his scepter and his crowne.[50]

Finally, according to the Attorney-General at Hacket's arraignment in Newgate, an order to the Privy Council had also been printed, in which the councillors were ordered not to leave their houses during the tumult until Hacket and his followers had taken possession of the city. (The printer of these materials died in prison—"for sorrow"—two days after his arrest.)[51] Throughout the week before the rising, Arthington had been working feverishly upon a final and culminating pamphlet, *A Prophecie of Judgements against England,* which explained the "extraordinary calling" of the three prophets, and the need to punish the city of London, the law-courts, and the Privy Council, for their failure "to bring in Reformation."[52] To this Coppinger had supplied an appendix, *Hacket's History*, sketching the persecution and physical torments suffered by Hacket in his preachings over previous years, as proofs of his Messianic status. Since, however, the *Prophecie* and the *History* were not completed until the night before the uprising, copies of these works presumably could not have been in circulation at the time. It seems likely that it was from his *History* that Coppinger read aloud to the crowd on the nature of Hacket's calling, as he testified, giddy and exalted, among the heckling masses upon his empty cart.[53]

All three were imprisoned at Bridewell, by this time (among other things) an equipped and notorious torture centre.[54] Under torment at Bridewell, and then on trial at Newgate on the 26th, Hacket pleaded guilty to the charge that he had denied the Queen's sovereignty, as well as to having defaced the royal arms in a lodgings house. He admitted that he had sought to displace certain members of the Privy Council, for their wickedness, and that he had claimed to be the anointed King of Europe, but he denied that he had ever wished to kill Elizabeth.[55] Sentenced to death, this strange, eventful history was now to end where it had begun, at Cheapside Cross.

The execution hour being set for "betwixt x and xi of the clock, when the market time is", Hacket was dragged forth on a hurdle from Newgate, on the morning of Wednesday 28th July.[56] He was at once lapped by an "incredible multitude (then in the streetes) but especially in *Chepside* from one end thereof unto the other (the like whereof at no assemblie in memorie hath bene seene)". The officers experienced great difficulty in making headway against the gigantic crowds, a task made no easier by Hacket's crying aloud, throughout, that the heavens were opening and Jehovah about to deliver him. Arrived at the gibbet, he "fell to rayling and cursing of the *Queenes Maiestie*", and prayed angrily to God to "send some miracle out of a cloude to convert the Infidels" and deliver him. "If not", he warned the Almighty, "I will fire the heavens, and teare thee from thy throne with my handes." As the executioner approached, he cried, "Ah thou bastards childe, wilt thou hange *William Hacket* thy king?" The officers "had much a doe" to get him up the ladder, and Hacket fought fiercely to avoid the encircling noose, jerking head and shoulders wildly from side to side. He was finally snared as he broke off the struggle to fire a final imprecation at the officers: "Have I this for my kingdome bestowed upon thee? I come to revenge thee, and plague thee." The crowd screaming with gratified fury at his blasphemies, Hacket was finally forced off the ladder, to swing high and violently above the sea of heads in Cheapside. When he was cut down, his heart was sliced out, and "shewed out openly to the people."

> Thus died the most dangerous firebrand of sedition, most detestable traitor, hypocriticall seducer, and most execrable blasphemous helhound, that ages ever sawe, or heard of, in this lande.[57]

As to Hacket's imprisoned fellow prophets, Coppinger apparently lost his mind under torture. Arthington, however, remained convinced that none could harm Hacket, as the Messiah. When the news came that Hacket had been successfully executed, Arthington finally broke down. Coppinger, who had refused food and drink, died. These spirits being melted into thin air, the baseless fabric of their vision quite dissolved, there was left but the rack behind.

They had been, however, such stuff as conspiracy theories are made on. The government publicized the contacts (overwhelmingly spurned) made by Hacket and his followers with the Puritan leadership in the months before their rising, and sought to associate both the Hacket affair and Puritanism with the infamous egalitarianism of Anabaptist Munster.[58] Catholic writers seized on the rising to discredit religion in England. But most people, it seems, just laughed. Hacket, noted Francis Bacon, "must needs be thought a very dangerous heretic, that could never get but two disciples; and those, as it should seem, perished in their brain . . . those two fellows the people rather laughed at as a may-game, than took any heed of what they said: so as it was very true that an honest poor woman said when she saw Hacket out of a window pass to his execution, 'It was foretold that in the latter days there should come those that have deceived many; but in faith thou hast deceived but few.'"⁵⁹

To exactly such a reception of self-pleasuring popular scoffing arrived soon another pretender-King, around the spring of 1592, who at once announced himself "inspired with the spirit of putting down kings and princes." To a jockeying crowd of heckling bystanders, 'Jack Cade' pointedly declared: "Your captain is brave, and vows reformation" (*Henry VI Part Two*, 4.1.30–31, 57).

"THIS DEVIL HERE SHALL BE MY SUBSTITUTE" (3.1.371)

The Cade of the chronicles had been so formidably compelling in rational argument that, according to Hall, his "perswasions" boded seduction of even the royal household servants (Hall, p. 220). Shakespeare, however, takes the extraordinary step of presenting Cade in terms of zero credibility as Mortimer, and as engulfed in boisterous popular ridicule. Referring to him from the outset as "Jack Cade the clothier" (Bevis,⁶⁰ 4.2.4), Shakespeare is at pains to emphasise that not only are the commons permanently undeceived as to Cade's real identity, but that his listeners are thrown into merriment by the manifest absurdity of his perswasions.

Cade: We, John Cade, so termed of our supposed father—
Butcher: [*to his fellows*] Or rather of stealing a cade of herrings.
Cade: For our enemies shall fall down before us, inspired with the spirit of putting down kings and princes—command silence!
Butcher: Silence!
Cade: My father was a Mortimer—
Butcher: [to his fellows] He was an honest man, and a good bricklayer.
Cade: My mother a Plantagenet—
Butcher: [to his fellows] I knew her well, she was a midwife.
Cade: My wife descended of the Lacys—
Butcher: [to his fellows] She was indeed a pedlar's daughter and sold many laces.
Weaver: [*to his fellows*] But now of late, not able to travel with her furred pack, she washes bucks here at home.
Cade: Therefore am I of an honourable house.
Butcher: [to his fellows] Ay, by my faith, the field is honourable, and there he was born, under a hedge; for his father had never a house but the cage. (4.2.28–46)

In contradiction of Bevis's statement that the rebels "have been up these two days" (2.4.2), Shakespeare chooses, for his introduction of Cade, not to introduce the rebel *in medias res*, accompanied by believing followers. Instead Shakespeare presents him at a vulnerable *originary* moment, crafted as a laughable self-annunciation. The entire model of presentation here, with its hilariously transparent impostor structure, the abrupt announcement of grand claims ("We, Jack Cade") to a heckling lower-class crowd, the raucous laughter as the vulgar identity is skewered beneath the swelling pretensions, and the commoners who choose to stay with the uproar despite disbelief in the declamatory nonsense, surely recalls in unmistakable terms the scene in Cheapside, only months previously, when Hacket's 'Angels' fulsomely proclaimed, to mirthful crowd reactions. The tone of uproarious comedy and hyperbolical excess is thus due not only, on a general plane, to carnival's Lord of Misrule, but more specifically to July's Hacket rising and its farcically naive apocalyptic grandstanding. All commentators on the rebellion recorded the risibility of the pretenders (Cosin uses words like absurd, childish, ridiculous), and the resultant hilarity of the crowds; many of whom, recorded Cosin, could not tear themselves away from these revels of the preposterous. ("All the way that Arthington went, hee was followed by a great multitude of lads and young persons of the meaner sort.")[61] Cosin relates how an alleged "Gentleman in a white doublet" so "plucked at Coppinger whiles hee was in the Carte, and rebuked him for his strange and lewde demeanour and speeches" that the badgered prophets were eventually forced to flee catcalling disparagements for shelter in the Mermaid tavern.[62] Bacon, we have seen, was appropriately reminded of carnival behaviour ("those two fellows the people rather laughed at as a may game, than took any heed what was said"); and Nashe, lacerating Gabriel Harvey in the same year as the play, picks up the tonality: "The tickling and stirring invective vaine, the puffing and swelling Satiricall spirit came upon him, as it came on Coppinger and Arthington, when they mounted into the pease-cart in Cheape-side and preacht."[63] A letter, possibly by Phelippes, in the *Calendar of State Papers* confides that most people thought the Hacket trio mere fanatics, "which is very likely", and that the Queen was "more troubled with it than it is worth."[64] Even the Attorney-General at the Newgate arraignment conceded that "in all appearancie Hacket was franticke":[65] an antic disposition feigned, somewhat Hamlet-like, to escape prosecution, as the government purported to believe.[66] Vastly amused, the desire of the mob in *2 Henry VI* to move with Cade is due not to deceit, but to gloating in the outrageous, to political anger, and to the possibility of gain:

> 2 Messenger: The rascal people, thirsting after prey,
> Join with the traitor; and they jointly swear
> To spoil the city and your royal court. (4.4.50–53)

This 'hilariously transparent impostor structure' is perhaps the most obvious of a set of five major parallels through which Shakespeare grafts Hacket onto Cade. The second is the projection upon Cade of religious idiom and context. Given, like Hacket, to a reflex religious or even Puritan diction, the Shakespearean Cade affects to see himself as a champion embroiled in cosmic battle, warring against demons and passionately accountable to the heavens. The chroniclers' Cade, by contrast, had been entirely free of religious concern or phrase. Shakespeare's Cade thus introduces himself as one whose enemies will fall down because he is "*inspired with the spirit* of putting down kings and princes" (emphasis added). Echoing *Isaiah* 14.23 ("and I will sweep it with the besom of destruction"),[67] he promises his followers, "I am the besom that must sweep the court clean of such filth" (4.7.26–27). Condemning Lord Saye, he declares "he has a familiar under his tongue; he speaks not a [in] God's name" (4.2.30–31; 4.7.98–99). Abandoned by his followers, he cries, with paranoid grandeur, "In despite of the devils and hell, have through the very middest of you! And heavens and honour be my witness . . ." (4.7.201–02). Slain by Iden, he swears, "Let ten thousand devils come against me, and give me but the ten meals I have lost, and I'd defy them all" (4.9.59–60). Above all, in his opening self-revelation, he promises the crowd: "Your captain is brave, and *vows reformation*" (4.2.57; emphasis added).

'Reformation' was the supercharged term, constantly bandied about by Hacket and his followers, and derided by the government prosecutors, that summed up that sublime project of ecclesiastical transformation sought by the Hacket rebels, as by more sane Puritan opposition to the Anglican *via media*. Only when spelled with a capital 'R', records O.E.D., did its sixteenth century meaning narrow to the purely religious referent. Spoken aloud on the stage, however, its spelling would be conjectural, and its signified will thus have embraced both secular and religious possibilities. Arthington's pamphlet, *A Prophecie of Iudgement against England*, had been peppered with excited promise of 'Reformation'. Cosin's counterblast suspends the term in disdainful revulsion between finger and thumb at innumerable points. His very title took aim at the seditious potentiality of the word: *Conspiracie for Pretended Reformation*. Moreover, Reformation radicalism had insisted, from the beginnings in the 1520s, that "Reformation meant much more than changes in devotional practices and ecclesiastical institutions; public life as a whole was urgently in need of Christianization."[68] In Kett's Rebellion of 1549, captured gentlemen, according to the Sotherton account, were led by the rebels to judgement at their 'Tree of Reformacion'.[69] As late as the 1590s, in London the term was clearly shading the religious with political meaning, as when Richard Bancroft, in a pamphlet of 1593, written to exculpate himself of subversive association with Hacket's followers, recorded that Hacket had declared in early July "that if the Magistrates did not governe well, the people might draw themselves together and see a reformation."[70] In 'vowing Reformation', Shakespeare's Cade reeked of Hacket and of radical Puritan insurgency.

But there is more to this 'Cade' than a generally reforming, religious character. Crucially, 'Reformation', for Hacket, Coppinger, and Arthington, was entwined with the idea of revengeful 'Judgement', happily anticipating the prospect of punishing opposed magistrates and councillors in the potentially violent transformation of government needful for true theocracy. The third parallel between Hacket and the Shakespearean Cade lies in just this pronounced and megalomaniac arrogation of Judgement claims—something from which the Puritan opposition was desperate to dissociate itself. Arthington's *Iudgement against England* had declared that *"the fearefull iudgements of God shall be sure to fall on the reprobate: being already prepared, and put into the handes of the Mightie Messenger of the Almightie God,* William Hacket, *to be powred out upon this great Citie of London, and upon all places, where repentance followeth not this publication"* [italics in the original].[71] Arthington and Coppinger, we have seen, had been designated by Hacket, and introduced themselves to the doubting vulgar of Cheapside, as God's Angels of Judgment and Mercy respectively: "ordained to separate the Lambes from the Goates."[72] Cade, confronted with the unfortunate Clerk of Chartham, thus solemnly enunciates his prerogative of mercy or condemnation: "The man is a proper man, of my honour. Unless I find him guilty, he shall not die. Come hither, sirrah, I must examine thee" (4.2.83–85). Like Hacket, oracular apostle of vengeance, Cade will command the kingdom: "My mouth shall be the Parliament of England" (4.7.12). Lord Saye is loftily condemned on grounds of religious authority: "he speaks not a [in] God's name. Go, take him away" (4.7.99). The Jack Cade of the Chronicles, though he ordered the same executions as Shakespeare's character, had exercised mere *ad hoc* authority by force of arms: he had never insinuated religious mandate.

The Shakespearean Cade, moreover, pretends to kingship. Introducing the claim from his first word (*"We,* John Cade . . .", 4.2.28), its iteration is one of his delights: "It is to you, good people, that I speak, / Over whom, in time to come, I hope to reign—/ For I am rightful heir unto the crown" (4.2.116–18). Shakespeare has fun with a Cade bumblingly incorrigible in his regal prerogatives: "What canst thou answer to my Majesty?" he demands of Saye (4.7.23). "There shall not a maid be married but she shall pay to me her maidenhead" (4.7.111–12). Contradictorily, faced with *Sir* Humphrey Stafford, Cade makes good his own claim that Stafford will be encountered with as good a man as himself by exercising a little impromptu ennoblement:

Cade: To equal him, I will make myself a knight presently.
        [He kneels and knights himself]
        Rise up, Sir John Mortimer.
        [He rises]
        Now have at him! (4.2.106–08)

Once again, any such claims are foreign to the chronicler's Cade, who had never gone beyond the high water mark of "Lord of this city". Predictably, however, they everywhere adorn the epical delirium of Hacket. Anointed by the Almighty, Hacket would "not onely establish the Gospell in all kingdomes, but all *Kings* and *Princes* should also yeelde their scepters unto him, and hee shoulde bee established chiefe king over all *Europe*."[73]

Unfortunately, since Mr. Hacket was, as of July 16th, King of Europe and "above all the princes in the world" (Cosin 36), a certain delicate ambiguity ensued as to proper relations with *Her* Majesty. One can well imagine that this unsubtle constitutional point was not lost on the interested citizens of Cheapside. The same solution to the dilemma is thus found in both the Hacket declamations and in *2 Henry VI*: by gracious permission, the national monarch will be allowed to retain the crown, but will rule henceforth under the true king as their Protector. "Shee may not raigne as *Soveraigne*", adjudged Hacket, as Cosin narrates his conversation with Arthington, "and yet shee shall live better than ever shee did, albeit shee must bee governed by another, thereby also meaning *Hacket*" (Cosin 37). Kings of the earth would henceforth "holde their scepters of him, and be governed by such lawes and orders, as he should appoynt" (Cosin, 99). "Go to, sirrah—tell the king from me", commands the Cade unknown to history, "that for his father's sake, Henry the Fifth, in whose time boys went to span-counter for French crowns, I am content he shall reign; but I'll be Protector over him" (4.2.141–44).

Finally, there is one last twist with which Shakespeare tugs the antic cloak of Hacket firmly down over the quasi-historical torso of Cade. In the opening boasts of his grand self-annunciation, Cade's only argument for his fitness to rule (following his caricatured dynastic claim) is curiously framed by Shakespeare, through both Cade and his auditors, in terms of a proven capacity for suffering.

Cade: Valiant I am—...
Cade: I am able to endure much—
Butcher: [to his fellows] No question of that, for I have seen him whipped three market days together.
Cade: I fear neither sword not fire.
Weaver: [to his fellows] He need not fear the sword, for his coat is of proof.
Butcher: [to his fellows] But methinks he should stand in fear of fire, being burned i'th' hand for stealing of sheep.
Cade: Be brave then, for your captain is brave and vows reformation" (4.2.47,49–58).

Coppinger had advanced for Hacket just such an endurance qualification. In his appendix, *Hackets Historie,* to Arthington's pamphlet, Coppinger had recounted Hacket's gruesome torments and many humiliating public punishments as proof of Hacket's "extraordinary calling"; and it appears that he recapitulated these in Cheapside, going, as Cosin records, "more particularly over the office and calling of Hacket". Ejected from York and driven out of Lincoln, imprisoned for twenty days in Hampshire, bastinadoed, chained in Hertfordshire "in a sincke hole of a seller", where he was beaten, and "his eies were fallen downe, and his tongue thrust out of his head, so as he could not pull it in againe one Barley cornes breadth", thrown into Northampton gaol for seventeen weeks, Hacket had doggedly persevered in apocalyptic preachings, sustained throughout by heavenly visions.[74] For Coppinger and Arthington, monied gentlemen, protected by their class against whipping and branding, the survival of so savage a saga testified irrefutably to soaring prophetic status. For the common multitudes on market streets, however, the story of Hacket's accumulated stripes, breathlessly announced by the Angels from the cart, allowed, as Shakespeare shows us, of more jovial interpretation.

Reformation radicals, too, subscribed to a doctrine of preparatory suffering. Hans Hut, for example, who escaped the slaughter of the Peasant's War to continue preaching radical ideas until his arrest at Augsburg in 1527, and whose tracts circulated in manuscript over a wide area, taught that through sustained suffering "authentic faith will be revealed" and "a person [will be] consoled again in the holy spirit. Then he will ready for the Lord and useful for every good work. It cannot happen to a person otherwise."[75] As Michael Baylor notes, "Hut's view, that the authentic message of the gospel is one of suffering, offered consolation in the aftermath of the Peasants' War."[76] Persecution was naturally to nurture such a doctrine.

Further parallels between 'Cade' and Hacket can perhaps be adduced. The egalitarian motif may derive not only from the 1381 Peasant's Revolt, but from the Hacket insurgence, and its tradition of Reformation radicalism, though there is some uncertainty here. The rhyming ballad that Hacket's followers had printed, with its refrain

> A Christian trew, althoughe he be a cloune,
> Shall teache a prince to wear his scepter and his crown

was quoted at his prosecution in evidence against Hacket; and Cosin makes clear the authorities' fear of "popular tumult" when "so many soldiers were about the Citie" (Cosin 35, 57). Behind Hacket's religious fervor lay, at a now unspecifiable distance, the original Reformation 'exaltation of the common man', a perspective so central to the Reformation in Germany that some historians have re-entitled 'the Peasants War' of 1525, 'the Revolution of the Common Man.' Within such reforming perspectives, the commoner, simple, hard-working and pious, was better able to expound the scriptures than pedantic and gluttonous monks or priests; and it is perhaps such self-righteous anti-clericalism, rather than just the anti-literacy efforts of Wat Tylers' fourteenth century rebels, that is being parodied in the arraignment of the Clerk of Chartham. ("Hast thou a mark to thyself like an honest plain-dealing man?" 4.2.90.) Although in reality, Hacket and his Angels seem to have been more concerned with aggrandizing themselves than with transvaluating the masses, the Solicitor-General insisted at Newgate that

Hacket's company sought Munster-like egalitarian revolution. "Yf a noble-man rebell, his meaninge ys onlie to usurpe the Crowne, not impayringe the governmente; but ther can be no means to these peasants to accomplishe ther purpose, excepte by the absolute extirpation of all governmente, mag-istracy, nobility and gentrye."[77] This line of reasoning, resumed enthusiasti-cally by Cosin in the last twenty pages of his own work, seems tendentious, however. The authorities' concern was here less to explore the intentions of the Hacket trio than to accommodate their opportune nonsense to the government case that Puritan enthusiasm, left unchecked, could but follow a short road to Munster.

Shakespeare's two references to Cheapside in the Cade section might also be enlisted as reminders of the beloved Hacket fiasco. Since Cheap-side was the place where the King of Europe had been proclaimed, "In Cheapside shall my palfrey go to grass" (4.2.61) may have elicited knowing groundling cheers. The butcher's question, "My lord, when shall we go to Cheapside and take up commodities upon our bills?" (4.7.132–33) appears, for no particular reason, to have selected Cheapside for its chuckling venal agenda, from among the variety of main commercial thoroughfares of cen-tral London. This argument is unquestionably weakened by the facts that Cheapside was also the location, as the Chronicles tell us, of the execution of Lord Saye by the historical Cade, of rebel executions by Wat Tyler, and of many royal executions and proclamations. Nonetheless, Shakespeare's two references to Cheapside make no such historical connection, failing to mention it, for instance, in relation to Cade's execution of Saye. Rather, both references have an abruptness, a contextual gratuitousness, and both form part of an instant and obvious appeal to mirth: characteristics which leave Hacketian connotation a real possibility.

In reviewing the entire body of evidence,[78] we can see that at numerous textual points, Shakespeare lassoes his Cade to the Cheapside captain of reformation, whom the authorities feared enough (or so they pretended) to execute briskly and incriminate voluminously in one hundred and two pages of nervous derision and determined inflation. Shakespeare 'Hacketizes' Cade through a number of otherwise bizarre features of his presentation: his introduction through the hilariously transparent impostor structure; his reflex and somewhat paranoid religiosity; his self-advertised arrogation of Judgement function; his claim to kingship, carelessly mitigated by permit-ting the reigning monarch to retain the crown under his Protectorate; and his leadership qualification by proven endurance of sufferings. It is impor-tant, moreover, to recall that these parallels drew not on privy particulars available only with Cosin's account in September 1592, but were rather the stuff of common knowledge, disseminated to the London multitudes on the day of the rising. Indeed, Cosin himself professed reliance on public knowledge in narrating the events of that day ("so neere as I could learne from so common an Auditorie, and in so confused an action).[79] It is hard to believe, therefore, that their significance would not have been instantly apparent to the early audiences of *Henry VI Part Two*. Thanks to the art of William Shakespeare, William Hacket, religious megalomaniac, achieved immortality after all.

To contemporary audiences, fully as visible in the Shakespearean 'Cade' as William Hacket was the pious countenance of radical Puritanism: a reforming tradition whose values Hacket and his prophets largely shared, and within which government prosecutors were at pains to contextualize and execute him, despite his self-evident lunacy. 'Cade', as we have seen, comes crafted in a kind of burlesque halo of key motifs—preparatory suffering, egalitarianism, anti-clericalism, and (through his Judgement function) apocalypticism, not to mention the very term 'reformation'—each of which ties him clearly to the reforming radicals. Imprisoned in the Fleet since October 1590, and facing Star Chamber examination from May 1591, Thomas Cartwright must have encountered such creatures of caricature coursing through his nightmares.[80]

"AND WILL YOU CREDIT THIS BASE DRUDGE'S WORDS?" (4.2.136)

To what purpose, precisely, does Shakespeare so liberally douse the historical actions of Jack Cade in the comedic gasoline of the Hacket rising? A conservative response might be that Shakespeare, *qua* law-and-order dramatist, vilifies Cade and rebellion all the more thoroughly through association with the craziest of a long line of turbulent maniacs. Such a view runs into trouble, however, with that dramatic *endearment* of Cade that we have noted, generated alike by the carnivalesque mode, and the ambivalent fondness for Hacket the buffoon. It conflicts, too, with much in the play that appears to establish sympathy for the rebel's views of the state: a consideration to which I shall return. Why, moreover, would a dramatist demonizing rebellion to a London audience so alter the chronicles as not only to suppress history's pitched battle between Londoners and rebels, but actually to claim their joining forces (4.4.48–52)? And why would a conservative Shakespeare present as ethical and successful the play's first armed rising by the commons?

What follows, then, from the Shakespearean morphing of Cade into Hacket is not heightened denigration of rebellion, but four, rather more complex effects to the contrary.

First, the consequence of these substitution effects, graphically remodeling Cade as William Hacket, lunatic Puritan radical, is to mount a merely *ad hominem* repudiation, rather than a condemnation of popular insurgency *per se*. To 'anomalize' Cade as Hacket is immediately to invalidate this Cade's credentials as an authentic representative of popular political consciousness. The more obviously he becomes Hacket, or the voice of religious Reformation, the less he is to be taken seriously as the stuff of genuine leadership of an oppressed and mutinous commons. Hilariously delegitimated, 'Cade' warps into a figure of opportune farce and fun on the margins of hard political grievance. The last thing he can stand for, as Shakespeare is at pains to show us, is the authentic vision of the masses, who revel, rather, in his exposé.

An authentic populist rebel leader, persuasive to the commons like the historical Cade, could not, of course, have been objectively presented under the gaze of Elizabethan censorship, which demanded demonization of state rebels as the condition of their presentation. Consequently, where Shakespeare has been compelled to demonize, he has artfully nullified the force of indictment, demonstrating the target never to have been the genuine article at all. What roasts, by command, in the government bonfire is not the serious embodiment of popular revolutionary consciousness, but a mannequin, smuggled in to trick the eye. It is last year's buffoon, the Messiah of Cheapside, London's favorite political idiot.

Second, we must accordingly recognize the ensuing *differential class construction* of the Cade figure that Shakespeare has contrived here. Cade's demonization would have been entirely pleasing to the censor, and the government ideology he subserved. Not only did the Cade sequence appear to ridicule rebellion as product of a preposterous megalomania, and illustrate the doctrine of the *Homily Against Disobedience* that rebellions contained within themselves all seven deadly sins.[81] In its adumbration of Hacket, it also promised apparent popular support to the ongoing Star Chamber prosecution of the Puritan leadership for sedition. Indeed, one might say that in the shameless hypocritical capering of the Shakespearean Jack Cade, the savagely parodic spirit of Martin Marprelate was flipped back against the godly. (This was much what the anti-Martinist tracts of 1589–90 had done, with a comic acumen Shakespeare would reprise in Falstaff.)[82] Such serviceability, I suggest, may well explain why the presentation of rebellious demagoguery and initially successful popular uprising were here permitted on the public stage, in sharp contrast to the censor's suppression of the uprising passage in *Sir Thomas More*, composed not long afterwards (probably 1592–94).[83]

But 'Cade', as we have seen, was as false in his pretension to credible radicalism as he was in his claim to the throne. To the eyes of the commoners in the public amphitheatre, Cade was manifestly pseudo-populist. Though certain of his declarations—"because they could not read, thou hast hanged them" (4.7.37–38)—were keen shafts piercing hated institutions, this Cade will have been essentially delegitimated as a representative of popular consciousness as far as the commons themselves were concerned, on at least three grounds. In the London of the 1590s, a greatly higher percentage of commoners than in 1381 were literate; and the acquisition of literacy— whose unaffordability to the poor was bitterly lamented by the Commonwealthmen[84]—appears to have been esteemed and desired rather denigrated than by the commons.[85] Kett's rebels, for instance, called for beneficed clerics to "teche pore mens chyldren of ther paryshe the boke called the cathakysme and the prymer."[86] Yet the economic crises of the 1590s must have impacted the costs of schooling, almost certainly producing a decline in school attendance and dwindling literacy levels.[87] In such conditions, Cade's anti-literacy crusade actively contradicted the popular will: particularly, one assumes, that of commoners paying to savour the sophistications of literate language in a professional theatre. Moreover, since Puritans were traditional enemies of theatre and the carnivalesque, the bloodshot eyes of Hacket protruding through Cade, and his rasp of apocalyptic Puritan self-righteousness, disclosed a fool and a foe for mockery. (The spectacle of a Puritan plunging into carnivalesque behaviour figured just that laughable compromise of ostensible high principle by transparently naive egoism that would wreak further damage in Malvolio.) Finally, Cade was clearly accountable to goals and constituencies other than the commoners he incited: to the Duke of York, within the plot, and to continental Reform, as Puritan reformer. In sum, that Shakespeare demonized in this 'Cade' a rising that was at key points adversarial to popular aspiration rather than embodying authentic radical populism, was a fact that could hardly have been lost upon a contemporary common audience. Modern literary critics who deny Shakespeare's populism, for associating the commons with such a Cade, miss this *dissociation* of Cade. The mindset, however, of the Elizabethan governing classes that we noted earlier—contemptuously, even hysterically indiscriminating in its fury toward all revolt—will have prevented the registering of any such distinction.[88]

Disqualification of this Cade as ideological spokesman of popular radicalism must displace the play's assessment of rebellion onto the commons as a whole, and onto the conditions that had motivated them. The third effect of 'Hacketizing' Cade is thus to relocate agency and analysis in the play. Such deflection becomes theatrically graphic in the spectacle of a Cade paradoxically directed by his followers. Spark, not spokesman of commons revolt, a fantasist commandeered by focused discontent, Shakespeare's Cade is a man more instrumentalized than instrumentalizing. When Cade effuses doggerel daydreams (seven halfpenny loaves for a penny, himself as king and everyone in livery, his palfrey going to grass in Cheapside), the Butcher injects strategy: "The first thing we do let's kill all the lawyers." "Nay, that I mean to do", concurs Cade (4.2.57–69), as though he had already thought of it. When the Clerk of Chartham, still under examination by Cade, is condemned by the mob ('All Cade's followers': 4.2.94), Cade, who has just laid it down that "Unless I find him guilty, he shall not die", instantly complies, and tries to make it sound like his own decision: "Away with him, *I say*" (4.2.84, 96: emphasis added). Confronting Stafford and his forces, Cade again babbles happy megalomania (himself as king, but the sovereign may retain nominal rule), and it is the Butcher who intervenes to proclaim the intended execution of Lord Saye, for selling the dukedom of Maine. ("And good reason", adds Cade (4.2.141–147). When the Staffords are slain in battle, Cade gives himself to appareling himself in their armour and ordering self-aggrandizing ceremony; and it is once more the Butcher who breaks in with practicality: "If we mean to thrive and do good, break open the jails and let out the prisoners." "Fear not that, I warrant thee", acquiesces the nominal leader (4.3.10–15). Victorious in London, Cade executes Saye as promised, then plunges again into tyrannical self-exaltation (all peers must pay him tribute, all brides their maidenhead), when a rebel interrupts: "My Lord, when shall we go to Cheapside and take up commodities upon our bills?" "Marry, presently", indulges Cade (4.7.110–15, 133–35). With so ductile a leader, it is little wonder that the Butcher, justified in a rape (4.7.121–131), requests Cade that "the laws of England may come out of your mouth" (4.7.5). Lost without the commons' cues, Cade customarily has difficulty not only in maintaining any dignity, surrounded by hecklers as he is—the Butcher himself enjoys ridiculing him in asides (4.2.29, 33, 39, 44, 50, 55)—but even in making himself heard: he has to call for silence in his first speech; and this is achieved only when commanded by the butcher (4.2.32). Interrupted or jostled when interrogating the Clerk of Chartham, he is reduced to calling out weakly "Let me alone" (4.2.89). The stage direction opening 4.3 suggests that Cade is likewise no crucial agent in battle: 'Alarums . . . wherein both the Staffords are slain. Enter Jack Cade, and the rest.' Cade, it is clear, is *not* the killer of Strafford; and it is the Butcher who is immediately praised for deeds of arms (4.3.3–7). Deft though he may prove in rhetorical elaboration of clues supplied by others (lawyers and parchment at 4.2.67–73, the indictment of Saye at 4.7.17–24), Cade is repeatedly reduced to a directionless zany pirouetting in the footsteps of his nominal followers. Puppet or tool, not leader or thinker, he is a figurehead whom Shakespeare divorces from, and renders inferior to, authentic popular consciousness.[89]

If, therefore, we seek Shakespeare's real assessment of the character and morality of popular rebellion, we must seek it in his sketch of the words and deeds of the body of the commons itself, not in the travesty of a topical lunatic himself a travesty. And here we find, surely, a nuanced and complex vision. Sympathy with popular grievances, and some limited endorsement of armed resistance, mix with the recoil from anarchy of a larger political pessimism.

Scattered past the censor's hand, several lucid fragments of glimpsed critique suggest Shakespeare's sympathy for the rebels' complaints. Protest of the legal double-standard implicit in 'neck-verses', and the complaint to Lord Saye that his very horse is dressed better than many commoners [90] (4.7.34–42), expressed standing class resentments escalating throughout the 1590s: a decade described by one historian as "what may well have been the low point of in the living standards of the mass of the European population, at any rate since the Black Death."[91] In Cade's curse of his deserting followers—"Let them break your backs with burdens, take your houses over your heads, ravish your wives and daughters before your faces"

(4.7.170–72)—Shakespeare lends cogency to such class critique, for Cade's words echo an earlier petition for redress by a poor man whose wife and land had, indeed, been illegally taken from him by a nobleman's retainer: a petition torn brusquely in pieces by the Queen (1.3.18–20,43). "It is worth remembering the useful generalization of Yves-Marie Bercé", note recent historians of Tudor revolt: "'The trigger of revolt is not destitution, but injustice—and not objective injustice, but the conviction of it.'"[92] Thomas Cartelli seems therefore correct to note "a politically astute reckoning with a long list of social grievances whose inarticulate and violent expression does not invalidate their demand for resolution."[93] Christopher Hill draws similar conclusions:

> "Kill all the lawyers." "Burn all the records of the realm." "The King's Council are no good workers." "Let the magistrates be labouring men." "There shall be no money." "It was never merry world since gentlemen came up." Yet many of these apparently extreme sentiments were to be considered seriously by legal reformers in the sixteen-forties, and others were lower class complaints of long standing . . . When Cade said of Lord Saye and Sele, "he can speak French, and therefore he is a traitor", he was drawing on the popular myth of the Norman Yoke . . . It is difficult to think that Shakespeare was not conscious of what he was doing when he so frequently opened up questions which were to lead to revolutionary actions thirty years after his death.[94]

As to Shakespeare's endorsement of popular revolt, the commons, we recall, had risen already in the play, long before the appearance of Cade, when, outraged by the murder of Gloucester, it compelled the king to exile the Duke of Suffolk. Since Shakespeare represented the insurgency as morally motivated, politically astute, and swiftly successful, it is hard not to infer some endorsement of popular rising, *pace* the Elizabethan *Homily against Disobedience*. Furthermore, Shakespeare takes pains to show us other rebels pardoned: those of the second rising (like those of the first) go unpunished for their actions. In a departure from Hall (where the king had "punished the stubburne heddes", when he "delivered" some five hundred others),[95] the dramatist shows penitent rebels, "with halters about their necks", gain a universal pardon (4.8.15–21). Dressing oneself in a nightshirt or wearing a halter was a traditional appeasement tactic of the commons, a language of visible deference eagerly sought by the ruling class, who often felt that public repentance better served their hegemony than physical punishment. (In 1525, Henry VIII had pardoned, with great ceremony, some four hundred convicted rioters paraded before him in halters.)[96] Shakespeare's deviation again suggests populist sympathies: this unhistorical scene would scarcely serve to terrify commoners from future revolt. Shakespeare will likewise pen play after play, from *Titus Andronicus* and *Richard III* through *Hamlet* to *Macbeth*, in which regicide itself offers satisfying rough justice, as a goal the audience is manipulated to desire. *Henry VI Part Two* thus appears to exhibit that conditional endorsement of armed revolt which would be reaffirmed throughout his career.

The position was hardly unique in the sixteenth century. "If a prince robbe and spoile his subjectes, it is thefte, and as a thefte ought to be punished . . . God himself gave thexample [*sic*] of punishmente of evil governours", John Ponet had argued. [97] It was, he claimed, a Christian duty to disobey the demands of princes if they contravened the laws of God and nature, and to resort even to insurrection and tyrannicide if necessary. Thomas Starkey's *Dialogue between Pole and Lupset* had Pole explicitly denying that tyranny was God's punishment for subjects' sin, arguing that since man and not God was responsible for tyranny, men have the right to depose tyrants.[98] Sir Thomas Smith, secular analyst of state power and function, would neither justify rebellion nor condemn it. With Machiavelli and Cicero perhaps in mind, he judged it pragmatically, commenting that "learned men" assessed uprisings in terms of the motivations of their leadership, and the circumstances that provoked the rising.[99] Shakespeare's position, we shall see, was similarly circumstantial and realist.

The prevailing tones of Cade's revolt—liberating carnivalesque slapstick mingled with cogent political barbs—change emphatically, however, with the watershed-execution of Lord Saye, whose visible fear restores a moving psychological realism which renders the rebels sadistic.

Butcher: Why dost thou quiver, man?
Saye: The palsy, and not fear, provokes me.
Cade: Nay, he nods at us as who should say 'I'll be even with you'. I'll see if his head stand steadier on a pole. (4.7.83–86)

Saye's superbly articulate innocence prompts guilt from even Cade ("I feel remorse in myself with his words" [4.7.96]). The ensuing waving of freshly severed heads on poles then consolidates this alienating re-establishment of the realist mode: not only through the doubtlessly gory special effects made possible here to a theatre of few props, but because such sights were an empirical Tudor reality, glimpsed even en route to Southwark theatres atop poles on London Bridge. Thereafter ensues unqualified degeneration into mob frenzy, with its significantly *mirthless* crudity in "Kill and knock down! Throw them into the Thames!" (4.7.145–56). Shakespeare's strategic use of London patriotism drives home the point. When the rebels had first invaded London, Shakespeare carefully omitted that prolonged battle between the rebels and London citizens which featured large in the chronicles; but following the pivotal slaying of Saye, he newly foregrounds a brutal opposition of rebel and citizen: "Up Fish Street! Down Saint Magnus Corner! Kill and knock down!" (4.7.145).

This downturn into simplified denunciation of rebellion is very short: it lasts, to be precise, just fifty lines, after which the rebels relent, to "follow the King and Clifford!" (line 196). The brevity of this dark final phase in the play's extended representation of rebellion is itself highly suggestive. Telling, too, is that the same pattern holds true of the play's Quarto variant, *The First Part of the Contention betwixt the two Famous Houses of York and Lancaster* (1594), in which a far shorter text (the Folio version is one-third longer), probably cut for performance acceleration on tour in the provinces, produces a simplified, more brutal Cade: largely apparent, however, only from the Saye trial onward.[100] (The Quarto omits Cade's twinge of remorse in condemning Saye, and his act five soliloquy on hunger; it also adds Cade's horrific 'punishment' of the sergeant whose wife had been raped [4.7.116–31], and makes the rebels all the more ignorant in misrecognising Saye's Latin as Dutch, French or Italian at 4.7.49–51). Nothing in the variants disturbs the attractive exuberance of the Punch-and-Judy slapstick of the preceding actions, which form the majority of the rebellion section; and the only pre-Saye cut that 'downwardly' revises Cade, York's lines on Cade as fighting bravely in Ireland (3.1.360–373), can be attributed to the revisions' concern for a faster-paced production.

Nonetheless, terminating as it does in barbarity and an abrupt desertion of Cade and the cause, this failed rebellion clearly underlines Shakespearean pessimism about the possibilities of popular political revolt when moving beyond such limited interventions as the play's first rising. That the breakdown of public order, whether due to commons rebellion or patrician ambition, *may* escalate into sprees of murderous anarchy, as here and in *Julius Caesar*, is an obvious and widely drawn cautionary conclusion. The directionless violence of the rebel commons in *Henry VI Part Two*, however, deserves closer inspection and some historicization.

We have seen that the Shakespearean Cade, doused in Hacket, was no authentic representative of the discontented commons, but offered a mere leadership of convenience: swiftly and superficially taken, then swiftly and superficially dropped. The fourth conclusion to be drawn from the 'Hacketization' of Cade is precisely the *leaderless* populism of the 1590s.

The Tudor period had seen four successful rebellions, but no rebellion had prevailed beyond the first half of the century.[101] Despite the deepening of poverty and underclass desperation in the 1590s, the three attempted rebellions of the decade—Hacket's in 1591, the Oxford Rising of 1596, and the Essex revolt of 1601—all failed miserably, through the striking absence of popular support. This absence was due, however, not to the sustained campaign by nervous authorities throughout the 1590s and beyond to demonize popular revolt as the most evil imaginable ("of all other seditions and rebellions none doth bring such infinite waste and desolation upon a kingdom or state as these popular insurrections").[102] Rather, as Fletcher and MacCulloch recognize, the powerful support underlying the success of the earlier rebellions had derived from a vanished alliance of 'high' and 'low' politics: the combination of aristocratic disaffection with a commons rising mobilized by what loosely can be termed the 'middling sort'. Through the later sixteenth century, by contrast, the lifestyle of the middling "came closer to that of their gentry superiors", in terms of wealth, literacy, culture, and even pronunciation, so that their grievances became channeled through law-suits and parliamentary interests rather than leadership of popular rebellion.[103] Thus, in simplified terms, after the risings of 1549, the natural leadership of popular Tudor rebellions turned to alternative arenas for self-advancement. Consequently, by the late sixteenth century the language of plebeian protest incorporated wealthy farmers, 'cornmongers', and 'merchants' alongside the traditional targets of gentry and "rich men".[104] It is precisely this tragically leaderless condition to contemporary popular discontent that Shakespeare presents, in the spectacle of a citizenry whose simmering anger against pervasive injustice can find no organized outlet, no organic commons leadership. In the words of a report on prisoners interrogated in the Marshalsea following the Southwark feltmakers' riot of 1592, "When the apprentices were unruly, and would have broke up the Marshalsea, Rich. Webster, another prisoner there, said they could not agree because they had no head, and that if they had one, all the commons would rise, for they all disliked the State and Government."[105]

This objective historical reality of English political life in the 1590s helps explain that degeneration of the rebels into an apparently fickle mob, which is so often construed as a timeless wisdom with which to admonish Progressives.[106] For the political consciousness of Cade's rebels in *Henry VI Part Two* is not 'fickle', I would argue, so much as manipulable through this circumstantial volatility. Given the lack of leadership and of institutions that could give explicit, synthesized and durable form to the insurgent instincts and perceptions of the commons, rebel consciousness was perforce ideologically labile and disunitary. The systemic ideological coherence lacking in the 1590s would emerge in the very different circumstances of the mid-seventeenth century, in the writings of Gerard Winstanley, for instance, just as cross-class alliances would resume in the anti-Buckingham organizing of the 1620s, and the early 1640s emergence of alliance between the Parliamentary anti-absolutist faction and the London crowds.[107] But in the late sixteenth century, tightening censorship, fear of local informers, espionage networks, the gallows, increased use of torture, and ultimately royal armies, along with the 'defection' of the commons' natural managerial class, prevented the emergence of any stable discursive formation to cohere a mutinous commons. Torn, thus, between explosive levels of dissidence, and customary, pragmatic quietism,[108] as well as between conflicting internal elements within lower-class ideology (hatred of the aristocracy and Privy Council versus patriotism and monarchism), a disaffected 'low politics' was now chronically open to divisiveness: a liability ably exploited by the rhetoric of Buckingham and Old Clifford, whose calculated appeals to pragmatism (promise of pardon), patriotism (the French threat), and monarchical greatness (Henry V) rapidly seduce the rebels from Cade's side (4.7.154–195).

As a posturing puppet rather than organic leader, Cade had been able neither to direct the commons fruitfully, nor to lift them above a passing mood of vengeful anger and transcend the volatile status of a mob. Misleading justified protest into mania and mayhem, Hacketized Cade was a 'spoiler' figure, terminal emblem of that politically paralysed conjuncture. To read Shakespeare historically is thus not to impute to him a damnation, *sub specie aeternitatis*, of democratic-populist sentiments, fated forever to gullibility and misdirection. It is rather to recognise a master dramatist's acute reading of the dilemma of a contemporary political ideology, accurately pinpointing the volatile contradictions within populist attitudes in the leaderless 1590s: a cocktail that could lead to a bang, as authorities feared, or more likely a whimper, as in the Hacket and the Oxford Risings. What pessimism resides here mirrors contingent impasse.[109]

Historically grounded comparison of the play's two risings may consolidate the point. Medieval and early sixteenth century rebellions tended to frictive internal division, notes historian Andy Wood, between their leadership by office-holding 'middle men' and their following by more violent and angry men, poor and often younger. Occasionally the latter would rise, only to have their community superiors, partly in defence of their own propertied interests, opt to collaborate with them with a view to retaking control, establishing an articulated agenda and disciplined limitation of violence. Kett's rebellion revealed this pattern.[110] Shakespeare's drama, I suggest, through its contrasted risings, foregrounds the defining loss of such alliance by the 1590s. The first commons commotion—orderly, contained, sharply focused on a specific grievance (expelling Suffolk)—embodied the kind of initiative managed by Tudor rebellion's natural leaders. The second— gloatingly violent, aimlessly anarchic beyond massacre of the hereditary elite, and propelled by a butcher, a weaver and a sawyer with their clueless demagogue—depicts the freebooting footsoldiers bereft of oligarchic command. Further, while the first rising shrewdly diagnosed an incompetent sovereign in need of an arm-twisting, the second rebellion, effortlessly dispersed at the very name of Henry V, displayed a naive monarcho-populism: an ideology discredited for many Elizabethans by the demystifying climate of the Counter-Reformation and resistance theory. It is this latter form of insurrection, a directionless eruption of the unorganised poor, indiscriminately violent, and still addled by sentimental medieval monarchism, that radical Shakespeare would appear to indict; and even here, as we have seen, the judgement by no means lacks sympathy and qualification.

The tragic betrayal of a rising by its leadership becomes a theme, in fact, suggestively pervasive in Shakespeare. At precisely the moment in *Hamlet* that he wins political control through popular force of arms, Laertes, agonizingly, is sweet-talked into gross misdirection by the murderer, Claudius. The risen commons in *Julius Caesar* is at once dispossessed of its legacy by a tyrannical Octavius and Mark Anthony. Nominated by the people to cast their vote, Titus Andronicus instates, catastrophically, the antipopulist Saturninus, rather than Bassianus whose principle is "Let desert in pure election shine" (1.1.16). Bolingbroke's rebellion in *Richard II*, hoped by its supporters to "shake off our slavish yoke, / Imp out our drooping country's broken wing, / Redeem from broking pawn the blemished crown" (2.1.293–95) replaces a tyrant merely with another. The Lear restored by armed invasion (though not in this case by specifically popular forces), having repented the dereliction of his people's needs ("Oh, I have ta'en / Too little heed of this! Take physic, pomp!" 3.4.33–34) turns politically amnesiac in the face of domestic calamity in the form of Cordelia's death. Malcolm's Machiavellian dialogue with MacDuff at 4.3.14–140 suggests that the successor to a Macbeth driven from his throne by invasion and the mass desertion of his people may prove scant improvement. Even Caliban, giddily insurgent against insult, stripes, and servitude, is ridiculously betrayed by his supposed betters and deliverers, Trinculo and Stephano ("What a thrice-double ass / Was I", 5.1.299–300). *Henry VI Part Two* inaugurates, it would seem, popular insurrection's tragic pattern: a recurrent configuration whose indictment is not the phenomenon of the commons in arms, but its betrayal by self-interested leadership when once empowered. Shakespeare's complex and often generous vision of popular rebellion, though touched by sympathy and some conditional endorsement, thus terminates repeatedly in a final pessimism centering on the ineluctable treachery of power. It may have been, I suggest, the hard tenacity of that outlook, the reflex despair over rebellions stillborn, that elicited the repellent refusal of an "ungentle Shakespeare" to assist popular opposition to William Combe's violent enclosures at Stratford in the last years of the playwright's life.[111] Old Clifford's words on Cade, "Nor knows he how to live but by the spoil—/ Unless by robbing of your friends and us" (4.7.181–82), seemed to William Shakespeare but the way of all rulers: bitterly close to immitigable.

"SUCH QUIET WALKS AS THESE" (4.9.15)

Closing the rebellion sequence, a Cade appears who has ceased to be Hacket. Clinching the argument for a populist Shakespeare sympathetically alive to commons sufferings, act four scene nine garbs Cade in a fresh persona, and supports him with some remarkably innovative stagecraft invoking further class-injustice.

In a reprise of carnival clowning to be extinguished by genteel butchery, Cade bobs back up, starved but unconquerably merry, to bond with the audience through witty soliloquy.

> I think this word 'sallet' was born to do me good; for many a time, but for a sallet, my brain-pan had been cleft with a brown bill; and many a time, when I have dry, and bravely marching, it hath served me instead

of a quart pot to drink in; and now the word 'sallet' must serve me to feed on. (4.9.8–13)

Cade is here no erstwhile rebel leader (nothing beyond "Fie on ambition!" glances at this past), but an apparently rank-and-file ex-soldier, hungry and on the run. The accent on mundane particulars of foot-soldiering experience would bond Cade to many in his commons audience; and the accumulating subtle overtones of a veteran status ("many a time . . . and many a time") that produced only hunger, must have struck a note of shared grievance for many, given the longstanding complaints over lack of pay that had stimulated a march on London in 1589 by unpaid troops who had survived the Armada and the disastrous Portugal expedition. So many soldiers had gone unpaid that two royal proclamations had to be issued, unsuccessfully, to forbid their "disordered and undutiful" approach to London; whereafter in London itself, riots broke out.[112] "We must eat. Having no money, how can we pay and content our hosts?"[113] Denounced by proclamations, suppressed by trained bands, and intimidated by summary executions under declaration of Martial Law, such hungry veteran soldiers, reviled and slain by gentlemanly forces, may well, I suggest, be glanced at in this scene.[114] When Shakespeare's play opened, probably in the spring of 1592, such events would scarcely have been lost to memory for the London underclasses.[115] Desertion was in practice encouraged by the fact that Elizabethan soldiers would not be paid until the end of a campaign, being obliged in the interim to steal their food or run up credit with the militias' sutlers. When finally paid, they would be fortunate to receive seventy-five per cent of what they were owed by the state. A soldier thus "had every reason to decamp without settling his debts and every reason to forage, scavenge, and outright pillage as he went."[116] "We shall never know how many ex-soldiers and poor civilians were summarily hanged by provost marshals in quiet areas of the countryside . . . If one imagines them [provost marshals and their men] mounted and well armed with pistols, sweeping up and down the countryside and looking for anyone on the move, their coercive power becomes . . . even more terrifying from the vagabond's perspective."[117] Throughout 1591–93, we shall see in the following chapter, English soldiers were deserting in considerable numbers from the calamitous French expeditions supporting Henri IV in Brittany and Normandy. Hiding out and hungry in the English and French countryside, hundreds of such men knew miserably well what it was to fear sudden death, yet yearn for a sallet.

> These five days have I hid me in these woods and durst not peep out, for the country is laid for me. But now am I so hungry that if I might have a lease of my life for a thousand years, I could stay no longer.(4.9.2–5)

Nothing in the chronicles had suggested a Cade famished at his death: the condition is pure Shakespearean invention. There is, moreover, almost nothing of William Hackett here: for it is now, at precisely the moment that he becomes, through fear and starvation, a true member of a suffering commons, finally established at his death as the genuine representative that he had never been during his revolt, that Cade is given sympathy by Shakespeare. Politically, nothing in his life became him like the leaving of it—a paradox Shakespeare will transfer onto another rebel, to trouble another king, in *Macbeth* (1.4.7–8). It is, I think, the Jack Cade of this final incarnation—'unaccommodated' Cade—who will ratify Thomas Cartelli's judgement of him as "the most realized example in Shakespeare's works of a character who is able to transform his political subjection into something amounting to our modern sense of class-based resistance"; and who will give the lie to the conviction that in the first tetralogy, the plebeian characters "can rebel against their oppression, but can never finally transcend the conventions of comic representation that keep them in their social place and mark their separation from the serious historical world of their betters."[118]

As Cade falls to the ground, where he lies eating grass (perhaps literally provided for him on the rush-strewn stage floor), Alexander Iden strolls the stage perimeter with a soliloquy of his own. Stage-directions in the Quarto make it clear that the two had entered by different doors, simultaneously; and that Iden is accompanied by no fewer than five followers. This simultaneity works, I think, not only to generate fear for a hopelessly outnumbered fugitive, but to undermine Iden from the moment he begins speaking.

> Lord, who would live turmoilèd in the court
> And may enjoy such quiet walks as these?

becomes laughable, since the Iden extolling peaceable immunity fails to see the state's arch-demon, just feet away from him. If the groundlings lapping the stage are in any way audible at this point—calling out in warning to Cade, perhaps, or hissing the complacent gentleman and his henchmen (and at whom are these five looking? What does their body-language consist in?)—then Iden's words on "such quiet walks as these" become a pratfall, hilariously rendering him at once an 'outsider', decisively estranged from audience mood and consciousness.[119]

Such stagecraft-generated satiric effects escalate, I suggest, in his next speech, as he reproaches Cade for trespass:

> Is't not enough to break into my garden,
> And, like a thief, to come to rob my grounds,
> Climbing my walls in spite of me, the owner,
> But thou wilt brave me with these saucy terms? (4.9.30–33)

A properly righteous indignation here swells swiftly into an alienatingly pompous self-importance, established by the obsessive reiteration of personal pronoun and self-reference: *my* garden, *my* grounds, *my* walls, *me* the owner, brave *me*: a landed-gentlemanly arrogance that perfectly fulfils Cade's shrewdly sarcastic "here's the lord of the soil" (22). Further, by building deixis into these lines, as he surely is doing, Shakespeare hoists Iden skywards with a petard hidden to censorship. For as Iden gesticulates largely about him—my gardens, my grounds, my walls— his possessive gestures almost inescapably indicate the *theatre* walls, the *theatre*'s ground, along with its "rude companion[s]" whom he "knows not" (28–29). Thus the heavy-handed proprietorial aggression enacts an unwitting arrogation of all around, its abrupt exclusionism backfiring into a comic and devastating deictic 'targeting' of this blindly possessive country gentleman.

In these moments of ingenious Shakespearean stagecraft, then, Iden, by sweepingly claiming the surroundings for his own even as he ignores the commoners in 'true' possession of them, *performs* in live theatrical space that very process of arrogant dispossession so widely detested in contemporary landowners by the less affluent commons. For as Cartelli has perceived, the Quarto makes it clear that the original had enveloped Iden in the hated tones of an *encloser*: "Thou hast broke my hedges."[120] Both the illegal enclosure of common lands, and the new legal doctrine of possessive, 'quiritary' ownership, by which a landlord might legally, in the teeth of all traditional usage, moral obligations to tenants, and customary rent-levels, do whatever he fancied with inherited estate, were generating intense levels of class anger in the countryside throughout the early modern period.[121] Robert Crowley, like other Commonwealthmen, had protested to parliament against the new mentality:

> If the possessioners woulde consyder them selues to be but stuardes, and not Lordes ouer theyr possessions, thys oppression woulde sone be redressed. But so long as thys perswasion styketh in theyr myndes,—"It is myne owne; whoe shall warne me to do wyth myne owne as me selfe lysteth?"—it shall not bee possible to have any redresse at all. For if I may do wyth myne owne as me lysteth, then maye I suffer my brother, hys wyfe, and hys chyldrene to lye in the strete, excepte he wyll gyve me more rent for myne house then euer he shal be able to paye. Then may I take his goods for that he owth me, and kepe his body in prison, tournynge out his wyfe and chyldren to perishe, if God wyll not moue some mans herte to pittie them, and yet kepe my coffers full of goulde and syluer.[122]

The converse tradition, that "man's relation to his property was one of temporary stewardship rather than absolute ownership" was, indeed, one of "a common fund of ideas . . . which approached the status of moral orthodoxy" among not only the poor, but the parish officers of town and village under Elizabeth.[123] The new possessive absolutism in ownership ideology made a mockery of the poetic fashion for Penshurst-style encomium of contented and paternalist rural retreat:[124] just as Shakespeare does here, exposing the hypocrisies of an Iden who had claimed to "send the poor well pleased from [his] gate" (l.21).[125] For Iden, despite his professions, will precisely "wax great by others' waning" (l.18): on slaying Cade, he promptly forswears his boasted rustic contentment and hastens to court rewards. There, he will gladly accept knighthood and the king's offer of courtiership (4.9.80; 5.1.77–82).

The chronicles had supplied no information on Iden beyond his identity as a gentleman of Kent, who (in Hall only) slew Cade in self-defense in a garden. Shakespeare's representation of Iden has thus been entirely his own creation; and he concludes it with a bully's taunt, and slaughter.

> Set limb to limb, and thou art far the lesser—
> Thy hand is but a finger to my fist,
> Thy leg a stick comparèd with this truncheon.
> My fist shall fight with all the strength thou hast,
> And if mine arm be heavèd in the air,
> Thy grave is digged already in the earth. (4.9.44–49)

Cade's responses have themselves been impudently threatening. Yet they continue to be leavened by humour, as he holds up his sword and direly threatens to remould it into hobnails should it fail to sliver the "burly-boned clown" (54–57). Dramatic sympathy thus appears still strongly weighted in his favour as, a small, starved, undaunted man, he is done to death by a huge, unpitying, well-fed one, visibly reinforced by the menacing encirclement of no less than five henchmen. In his dying words, Cade, despite undiminished vanity ("Tell Kent from me she hath lost her best man") is not discourteous: "Iden, farewell, and be proud of thy victory"(69–70). It is the gentleman slayer who turns to savagery. Repeatedly, he stabs Cade's bleeding corpse, before dragging it to decapitation and—in contradiction of the chronicles—to a dunghill.[126]

> And as I thrust thy body in with my sword,
> So wish I I might thrust thy soul to hell. (75–76)

Tellingly, the action is paralleled in the sequel play, when its hunchbacked "murderous Machiavel" (3.2.193) gratuitously re-stabs the corpse of Henry VI, in order to revel in the vileness of the deed: "I that have neither pity, love, nor fear" (5.6.68). Closing the Cade sequence in *Henry VI Part Two* is thus the unmistakable image of a gentlemanly class-hatred turned mutilatory: a reflex still bloodily at work in the post-Kett world, as 1590s England sank deeper into polarization and paranoia.

Pace volumes of criticism claiming Shakespeare for conservatism, close examination of the entire Cade sequence, restitutive of contemporary contexts, alert to shifts both in tone and mode, discloses a quite contrary political creature. Dextrous already in strategic skills to free an art made tongue-tied art by authority—sly allusiveness in topicality, selective reconstruction of chronicle materials, controlled suspension of sober stage illusionism—Shakespeare makes his debut, audacious and committed, as a nuanced and powerful protest playwright.

4   *2 Henry VI*

Contexts and Allusion

Anjou and Maine are given to the French,
Paris is lost, the state of Normandy
Stands on a tickle point now they are gone . . .

(1.1.213–15)

If, as I have suggested, behind capering Cade there looms manic Hacket, then *Henry VI Part Two* must have been composed somewhere between the latter half of 1591 and early 1592: produced, that is, when Shakespeare was some twenty-seven years old. Penned so very early in his career, it is a gateway play: an eye-catching construction through which a young actor paraded his ambitious new identity as a metropolitan playwright, and signalled a distinct dramaturgical identity. To demonstrate, therefore, as I hope to, that already his politics are radical, that from his very entry into drama Shakespeare seeks to destabilize establishment ideology, is to challenge fundamentally that traditional conception of a 'genteel' bard which has so confidently underlain expositions of Shakespeare from Coleridge to Eagleton.

FEALTY'S BARD

That this play could thus deceive is no surprise. On its surface, the work wears the apparency of a loyalist drama, fitting topical realities into a pattern of orthodox, if beleaguered, political loyalties, royalist and hierarchical. Such reassuring fidelities were the condition, however, of evading censorship's proscription: for the drama's public context was a period of (literally) racking anxiety for the Elizabethan authorities.

Worries about the vulnerability of the childless queen were nothing new. Orders from Cecil, over two decades before, had seen to it, among other precautions, that perfumed gloves and sleeves were banned near Elizabeth, since they might conceal poison, unless "corrected by some other fume"; that the back doors of waiting women's chambers were made secure lest assassins slipped in; and that even the royal underwear was "circumspectly looked to", to prevent the insinuation of lethal substance into the regal epidermis.[1] Events of the 1580s, however, greatly intensified the climate of personal threat to Elizabeth, little allayed by the symptomatic Bond of Association (1584): a solemn oath by which thousands of Englishmen voluntarily swore vengeance upon any who might kill the Queen, or (like Mary, Queen of Scots) benefit by the assassination. "I am not", Elizabeth coolly informed representatives of Parliament in 1586, "so carelesse, as not to weigh that my life dayly is in hazard".[2] The execution of Mary (1587), prompting attempted invasion by the Spanish Armada (1588), made only more graphic the dynastic menace. In his speech at the opening of Parliament in 1589, Sir Christopher Hatton summed up the heightened fears of domestic and international Catholic threat, noting the campaign of Jesuit infiltration of England, several assassination attempts on the Queen, a second papal bull excommunicating Elizabeth (1587), this one by Sixtus V, and the blessing of this Pope ("exceeding all that went before him in tyranny and cruelty") upon attempts to murder Elizabeth.[3] Terrorist acts against national leaders were no mere speculation: William of Orange had been fatally wounded in his town house by a serving man in July 1584; the Duke and Cardinal of Guise were assassinated by agents of Henri III in December 1588; and Henri III of France was murdered, in August 1589, by a Capuchin monk. In the terms of Erasmus' fable, the royal eagle, incorrigible predator, was ever menaced by the vengeful hatred of the lowly dung-beetle.[4] England's secret service was expanded, and its expenditure increased, throughout the decade.[5]

For there was also the threat from below. Popular restiveness at home soared in the face of ongoing military levies, ferocious taxation, and the disastrous casualty rates of the English expeditions sent to support Henri IV in his war against the Catholic League. When unpaid troops marched on London in 1589, they were greeted with executions, and the unleashing of Martial Law. Hacket's revolt, in the summer of 1591, had seemed dangerous precisely because "so many souldiers were about the Citie", as Cosin noted, deepening the probability of "tumult and sedition".[6] In such conditions, Shakespeare's play, as illustrating the horrors loosed by dynastic destabilization, and the brutality of popular revolt, seemingly gave implicit support to an imperilled Elizabeth and a panicky traditional order. Jack Cade's plummet, for instance, from insurrectionary joy into regretful starvation—the latter (4.9.1–5) a fiction invented by Shakespeare—worked at one level, I suggest, toward pointed reassurance, as an exemplary monitory orthodoxy. "Who seeth not" urged the *Homilie against Disobedience*, conveniently placed in churches next to the Bible and *The Book of Common Prayer*, and read monthly from the pulpit, "that extreme famine and hunger must needs shortly ensue and follow rebellion?"[7] No wonder that one critic has (momentarily) mused "One may wonder whether there was some governmental impulse behind the Henry VI plays. They may have been felt to make a contribution to the official propaganda."[8]

The play's thrust is thus largely read as irreproachably conservative: typical product of that law-and-order priority with which Shakespeare long has been identified. The loyalties, however, are of the surface. The subtext of *2 Henry VI*, I shall argue, seethes with topical political angers, foregrounds resistance theory, and inflames contempt of court authority. More subtly, through brilliant stagecraft, we will see in Chapter 5, the drama's deixis extends excited mobilization of popular retaliation into audience behaviour itself.

THE ART OF TOXIC PARALLEL

This is not just a dark, but an angry play. For Elizabethan commoners, it must have been an experience smarting at every point with contemporary grievance, a thesaurus of political indictments. Equally attuned to popular protest and its commercial payoff, the ambitious actor–author emergent through it deftly selected numerous elements from chronicle sources whose contemporary parallels effectively articulated political furies close to boiling point in 1591–92. That Shakespeare made Cade a clothier, thereby glancing at the Midsummer Riots of 1592, has been widely recognised;[9] and that he further modelled Cade to suggest Puritan angers and voice a spectrum of resentments, I have suggested already. These, however, are but the more egregious instances of Shakespeare's gloved adeptness in explosive source manipulation.

The very medium of popular Elizabethan drama generated topical resonance. "Not many objects in the foreground of literature", notes Andrew Gurr of English Renaissance drama, "have been as dependent on their background to give them form and identity . . . Except for a few of the poets, nobody gave a thought to posterity. The companies that bought the plays were actively hostile to the idea of printing them. The players were there to give entertainment and to take money. There was no need to make the product durable or to record it for future generations . . . Plays by their nature were thoroughly occasional productions."[10] Since deeply occasional in character, they were frequently topical in implication and reference. Supplying rumour and arch-allusion in an era before newspapers, "Dramatists acted as intelligencers to the nation", suggests Michael Hattaway, "not only seeing through the cult of monarchical magnificence . . . but also subjecting the whole institution of the court to a more radical critique."[11] Gurr's illuminating essay on the London theatres as "the first great market for daily journalism" records how in 1599, for instance, Sir Robert Sidney learned that his recent military adventures against the Spanish had just been staged, replete with suitable beard and accurate costumes.[12] At such points, we can practically hear Hamlet, observing drily "The players cannot keep counsel, they'll tell all" (*Hamlet* 3.2.127–28). Plays such as *The Isle of Dogs, Eastward Ho!, Isle of Gulls, A New Way to Pay Old Debts, Hog Hath Lost His Pearl* and *A Game At Chess* clearly lampooned well-known individuals, including James I.[13] Elizabeth's government itself, of course, commissioned plays to ridicule Martinists.

2 Henry VI, I suggest, unfolds at moments almost like a newsreel, in the wealth and specificity of its reportage.

> Anjou and Maine are given to the French,
> Paris is lost, the state of Normandy
> Stands on a tickle point now they are gone (1.1.213–15)

Arraigning Saye, the pirate lieutenant charges:

> By thee Anjou and Maine were sold to France,
> The false revolting Normans thorough thee,
> Disdain to call us lord, and Picardy
> Hath slain their governors, surpris'd our forts,
> And sent the ragged soldiers, wounded, home. (4.1.86–90)

The loss of French territories and English life are felt not as sorrows but as trauma. Reading aloud the marriage articles awarding Anjou and Maine to the French, Gloucester lets fall the paper, paralysed, and cannot read on. The facts thereby receive a second reading, now by the Cardinal. Salisbury thunders at the horror, and Warwick weeps (1.1.109–19). York's soliloquy reprises the lament; which is later renewed by the pirates, then finally Cade (4.7.18, 24, 58, 140–41), in their summary trials and executions of alleged noble traitors. The nation is transfixed; the trauma persists and will not be repressed; someone must pay a penalty.

The conditions, of course, were contemporary. Shakespeare had found a period in the Chronicles which neatly paralleled much in contemporary national crisis; and he stretched his scorching parallelism to the point of blatant anachronism where necessary. Literary criticism has done little hitherto in the tracing of theses parallels, so their recovery and function become important.

The conscript soldier, recorded William Lambarde in 1589, "comes as willingly to serve his unknown captain as does the beggar to the stocks or the dog to hanging".[14] Nonetheless, the Willoughby Expedition had dispatched 3,600 men in September 1589 to the aid of the new Protestant king Henri IV, desperately battling the Catholic League. When the French king called off their failing siege of Paris ("Paris is lost", 1.1.216; compare 1.3.176), they trawled Normandy and Maine for months in great hardship fighting sporadic actions. Shoeless, unpaid, compelled to live off the land, and drenched by wet weather, many died of sickness. Of the three thousand ragged soldiers come wounded home in December, only eight hundred remained fit for service.[15] But like the French King in the play, "whose large style / Agrees not with the leanness of his purse" (1.1.107–08), Henri IV was impecunious, and controlled less than half of France. Urgently in need of funds and troops as he confronted not only the Leaguers, but, from October, three thousand Spanish soldiers landed in Brittany, Henri's situation worsened as many of the Norman towns he had regained in the autumn of 1589 now reverted ("false revolting Normans") to the Leaguers. Elizabeth aided him with a further ten thousand pounds in 1590 (bringing his total 'loans' from her since 1587 to some eighty thousand pounds)[16] and dispatched in the spring of 1591 two further expeditionary forces. In April, Sir Roger Williams landed in Dieppe with six hundred men, and in May Sir John Norris arrived in Brittany with three thousand foot.[17]

Norris' force, though soon reinforced by a further six hundred men, dwindled rapidly from desertion and illness; and proving too small for independent survival, was compelled to follow French troops into the interior to the borders of Anjou, skirmishing futiley. By November, they were down to two thousand, and in December 1591, the French abandoned them, to survive miserably as best they could by living off the land. By February, only seventeen hundred men were left, most of them sick; yet "Norris' stream of requests for reinforcements, supply, and money went largely unanswered."[18] In April, joining the French to besiege the town of Craon, they suffered disastrous casualties: just eight hundred English soldiers survived, of whom only six hundred were able to serve. In the same month, at Rouen, where Williams' forces, reinforced by Essex and total influxes of several thousand men, had camped for long months, Henri abandoned the siege. Angered but optionless, Elizabeth began, in the summer of 1592, discussing with the French ambassador the raising of another English army of four to six thousand soldiers to aid the Protestant ally.

Nothing had been gained, no end was in sight. "The League was still in full control of the strategic centers of Normandy. Some 6,000 to 8,000 English soldiers had been committed to the struggle; the bulk of them were dead or had been invalided home. Thousands of pounds of the Queen's scanty funds had been effectually wasted. And besides the human and material losses there was the intangible damage to Elizabeth's role in her partnership with Henri."[19] These were the abominated circumstances of ruinous 'generosity' to the French king, ensuing military catastrophe, humiliating territorial erosion, and deepening domestic fury in the period when Shakespeare wrote *2 Henry VI*.

That Shakespeare's primary concern was political engagement of his contemporary moment, rather than reconstruction of the mid-fifteenth century, is clear in his recurrent departures from the Chronicles: a process varying from the subtle to the blatant. The reference to Picardy (which "Hath slain their governors, surprised our forts, / And sent the ragged soldiers, wounded, home", 4.1.89–90) is glossed haplessly in the Second Arden edition with "source unidentified", and in the Third, with the speculation that Shakespeare had somehow confused Picardy with Pontoise.[20] Yet the derivation is manifestly historical: by late 1590, Henri was begging Elizabeth for help in Normandy and Picardy; and by September 1591, Gournay, which commanded the approach roads from revolted Picardy, had been beseiged.[21] The region is referenced again early in the play's 'prequel', *1*

Henry VI, at 2.1.10, as among the areas currently loyal to England—a situation changed with Burgundy's defection in 3.3. Rather less subtly, "The wilde Onele [O'Neill] my Lords, is up in arms" (Q1, 1124) was shamelessly anachronistic; and it became one of the lines prudently cut in the Folio.[22] Most obviously, Old Clifford's inflammation of patriotic fear in the commons through the spectre of invasion—"I see them lording it in London streets, / Crying '*Villiago!*' unto all they meet" (4.7.187–88; emphasis added)—designedly turns the invaders, I suggest, from medieval Frenchmen into contemporary Spaniards, by recalling their cry at their notorious sack of Antwerp in 1576.[23] Some months later, *I Henry VI* would owe its economic success to imitating this art of topical allusiveness, 'updating' war coverage with repeated suggestions (as critics have long recognised) of the siege of Rouen (December 1591–April 1592).[24]

Such merging of 'Tudor' conditions with 'medieval' should not surprise us. We saw, with Hacket, how contemporary official rhetoric subsumed history's diverse risings and rebels into timeless typology. We should recall, also, that neither 'Tudor' nor 'medieval' were terms or categories current in Shakespeare's day. As C. S. L. Davies has argued, the word and concept 'Tudor' seems to have been established to demarcate that period from the 'Middle Ages' by David Hume in 1757. The monarchs we label Tudor emphasised rather their Plantaganet continuity, "their membership of the medieval royal line . . . There was little sense of a break with what we, again anachronistically, call 'the Middle Ages'".[25] The significant rupture for contemporaries was not Henry VII's dynastic victory but Henry VIII's break with Rome: whose complex, warring relations with the Continent were freighted with their own 'medieval' continuities, as Shakespeare's *King John* makes clear. Though 'Tudor' is indispensable to our own historiography, we must note that its designees did not place themselves mentally in a sharply different world from the England of Henry VI.

Contrasting with both bitter Elizabethan mistrust of a French king who insultingly abandoned English troops at will—compelling the Council to an agonized "debating to and fro, / How France and French men might be kept in awe" (*2 Henry VI* 1.1.87–88)—and the popular anger that English armies had "so often lodge[d] in open field / In winter's cold and summer's parching heat" only to have "received deep scars in France and Normandy" (1.1.76–77, 83), was English enthusiasm for hitting back at the foe on a smaller, private level, and even turning a profit: through piracy. Kenneth Andrews estimates that one-to-two hundred privateering vessels set sail every year after 1585, producing an annual value of some 150,000–300,000 pounds; while MacCaffrey notes that between 1589 and 1591 at least 236 vessels were operating off the Spanish coast or in corridors to the New World, and that their 299 prizes brought in around 400,000 pounds in those three, "unusually profitable years".[26] Their backers, moreover, were substantially London merchants, a constituency not without impact upon mood and theatre in the nation's capital. 1591 saw also the flaming destruction of Grenville and *The Revenge* under the massed cannon of fifty-five Spanish ships, a 'martyrdom' passing rapidly into national hagiography; and in July 1592 privateers captured the *Madre de Dios*. Its jewels, spices and silks, worth some half-a-million pounds, pilfered by the victorious crews, were soon swirling through Plymouth. In these circumstances, Shakespeare transforms the captors of Suffolk from the Chronicles' crew of a "ship of war" owned by the Earl of Exeter, into pirates, debarked from a marauding pinnace. Given the glamour of privateering in 1591–92, as "Protestantism, patriotism and [sea-] plunder became virtually synonymous",[27] the recasting will have helped generate popular approval, initially at least, of this intensely subversive presentation of a Duke coolly executed by commoners. Pirates, it is true, were distinct from privateers—whose vessels were authorized by state commission to attack foreign ships and ports, in contrast to the freebooting enterprise of piracy—but the distinction easily became blurred.[28] "Ordinary indiscriminate piracy remained a serious social evil", notes Andrews, "and the government's attempts to suppress it were unavailing. But in times of crisis pirates could be useful, provided they concentrated on the right prey."[29] Shakespeare, I suggest, capitalizes on just this ambiguity, as the pirates pour eloquently forth thirty-three lines of patriotic indictment of Suffolk (4.1.71–104), even echoing the *Homily Against Disobedience*, as spokesmen of the national military angers;[30] and in their grimly efficient avenging of English betrayal, the pirates' actions contrast sharply the three years of humiliating bungling by English armies.[31]

Pirates were to become "class-conscious and justice-seeking", write Linebaugh and Rediker in their pathbreaking study of the 'hidden history of the revolutionary Atlantic.' By the late seventeenth century, "The pirate ship was egalitarian in a hierarchical age." Not only would pirates elect their officers, institute a ship's council enfranchising every man aboard, and distribute booty evenly; having captured a prize vessel, they would even impose a 'Distribution of Justice', inquiring as to how the ship's officers had treated their crew, then flogging or executing any found to have maltreated their sailors.[32] At the close of the sixteenth century, however, pirate vessels tended to be controlled by figures higher-born than was the case a century later, having normally "some connection with the minor gentry."[33] We might note that Walter Whitmore—a character invented by Shakespeare, sociologically astute as ever—is apparently an impoverished gentleman, touchily insistent on his possession of family honor and a coat-of-arms (4.1.40–44), and that the Captain (likewise the author's creation) had been formerly a court retainer sufficiently senior for Suffolk to have written on his behalf (53–65). Nonetheless, it was noted as early as the Elizabethan period that seamen preferred the harsher, more uncertain conditions of privateering to working in the royal navy: "Nothing breeds this but the liberty they find in the one, and the punishment they fear in the other."[34] "There was", records Andrews, "an element of democracy in [Elizabethan] privateering", where skill enjoyed pragmatic primacy over rank, gentlemen often had to labour with the rest of the crew, and brawling over division of spoils could prove hard to control. Consequently, even in privateering it was normal "to consult the crew in any important matter."[35] Fascinatingly, Andrews records two instances from 1591, of "great turmoil" reported from the decks of the *Swallow* and the *Examiner*, as captain and crew fought over prizes:[36] ferocious insurrections whose distant echoes we are possibly hearing in our play.[37] Certainly, anti-hierarchic sea-dog sentiment was already crystallizing in the writings of Henry Roberts, the Elizabethan sailor-poet, whose work boasted "conscious pride in the deeds of citizens other than 'cavaliers.'" "This is the literature of the Elizabethan ground-lings", notes Andrews percipiently (though with no literary specification), "and it is significant that its subject is privateering."[38] In Shakespeare's play, the oppositional, proletarian order of the pirates—the 'hydrarchy' in Linebaugh and Rediker's coinage—is expressed in flaunted contempt for gentlemen: an itching disrespect established from the opening of the scene, through both taunting—

Cap.:   What, think you much to pay two thousand crowns,
           And bear the name and port of gentlemen?
Whit.:   Cut both the villains' throats . . .

—and the suggestion that pirates' lives are of great (or greater) value:

Whit.:   The lives of those which we have lost in fight
           [ ]
           Be counterpoised with such a petty sum![39] (4.1.18–23)

Suffolk's confrontation with Whitmore and the Captain is then dramatised as one of raging class-conflict ("Obscure and lousy swain" versus "proud, encroaching tyranny", ll.51 and 96). Further, the reciprocated hatred of landed wealth for the carnivalesque[40] ways of pirates had already been exhibited in York:

Pirates may make cheap pennyworths of their pillage,
And purchase friends, and give to courtesans,
Still revelling like lords till all be gone,
Whileas the seely owner of the goods
Weeps over them, and wrings his hapless hands,
And shakes his head, and trembling, stands aloof,
While all is shared, and all is borne away. (1.1.221–27)

What does seem clear is that Shakespeare, ever receptive to oppositional thought and experience—the proletarian radicalism of Cade's followers, the regicidal indictments in *Hamlet* and *Macbeth*, the resistance theory behind

King Lear, the outlaw greenwoods of *As You Like It*—has here tapped another source, the early stirrings of the maritime radical tradition.[41]

Shakespeare presses his play's subversively cumulative contemporary parallels well beyond particulars of military fiasco, into turbulent domestic repercussion. Astride a white steed, clad in a silver breastplate over her white velvet dress, Elizabeth at Tilbury, addressing her troops on August 8th 1588 as the country awaited the first Spanish Armada, had allegedly proclaimed her love of her people and preparedness to die among them. "I myself shall be your general, judge, and rewarder of every one of your virtues in the field. I know already for your forwardness, you have deserved rewards and crowns; and we do assure you, in the word of a Prince, they shall be duly paid you."[42] The following day, however, the Armada, Queen Elizabeth, and indications of payment, disappeared together. The Lord Admiral Howard was obliged to write to Walsingham begging for funds. "The maryners ther kry owt for Money. and they know not wher to be payed." A day later, Howard implored Burghley for money, as sick and penniless military men were dying in the streets: "It wold greave anie mannes hart to see them that have served soe valiantlie to die soe miserablye." He requested also basic clothing for the fleet, "for they have bin soe longe at sea and have so litle shifte of aparell" that "in verie shorte time I looke to see moste of the mariners goe naked." Burghley, however, suspicious that money was disappearing into the pockets of corrupt captains, and worried by the crown's dire financial straits, refused to disburse funds. Desperately, Howard wrote again on August 22nd, warning of the "unfurnishinge of the realme of such needfull and moste necesarie men in a comon welthe", and noting the ideological mood. The men, he said, finding their pay "to com but thus scantlie unto them it breades a mervailouse alteratione amongste them." "It were too pitiful", he wrote to Walsingham, "to have men starve after such a service."[43] In Shakespeare's play, the Lord Protector stands twice accused (3.1.60–62, 105) that he "stayed the soldiers' pay", with disastrous military consequences. This allegation he smartly rejects: "I never robbed the soldiers of their pay" (3.1.108). In Hall, however, the charge of pocketing soldiers' pay had been levelled at Somerset;[44] and Shakespeare's transfer of the black charge onto Gloucester is one, we shall see, of numerous departures suggesting identification of Protector Gloucester with Elizabeth's principal statesman. It is hard to see that audiences of *2 Henry VI* would not have perceived and responded darkly to such parallels, deeply concerned by unfolding military events as commoners were given the looming probability of further levies and the terrors of impressment—especially since theatres, like fairs and alehouses, were locations potentially subject to press-gang action. Audiences may indeed have caught, in the words of the play's fellow-mariners (the pirates) on the sending of "the ragged soldiers, wounded, home" (4.1.90) an echo of the notorious raggedness of the payless Armada mariners.

"The figure of the starving, often lame sailor in the seaport town", Linebaugh and Rediker note, "became a permanent feature of European civilization."[45] Indeed, as Carroll records in his study of Tudor demonisation of vagrants as idle tricksters, "The destitute mariner is another of the traditional beggar's roles."[46] Patricia Fumerton has recently enlarged on the theme, examining how "peripatetic types" such as "seaman, soldier, and vagrant" were "intimately intertwined".[47] In consequence, as Roger Manning observes, "late-Elizabethan and early-Caroline epidemics of disorder in the metropolis coincided with periods of military and naval mobilization. The experience of impressment, military service (sometimes overseas), and discharge, often without pay, did much to give veterans a sense of shared discontent and made them more disposed to take collective political action than most Englishmen . . . the problem was especially acute in the metropolis."[48]

Protesting veterans and "wandering idle persons" were greeted through 1589–91, we saw in Chapter 1, with the impromptu noose, swinging high at the hands of Provost-Marshals. In this climate, Shakespeare broke quite consciously with the chronicles to transform the murder of Lord Saye, I suggest, into a kind of martial law from below.[49] "Now art thou within point-blank of our jurisdiction regal", Cade crowingly informs Saye (4.7.22). He indicts Saye for unjust execution of "poor men": "because they could not read, thou hast hanged them" (4.7.35, 37). Departing from Hall's *Chronicle*, which recounted Cade arraigning Saye before Justices in the Guild Hall, before removing him to Cheapside for execution, Shakespeare gives us an open-air, summary trial and execution, in vengeful parody of Provost-Marshal proceedings. Likewise, the peremptory indictment and execution of Suffolk by the pirates takes on the aspect of contemporary martial law. In contrast once more with Hall's version, formal charges are levelled, and the tone assumed of mandated authority, with royal overtone ("The commons here in Kent are up in arms / . . . reproach and beggary / Is crept into the palace of the king"), before brisk dispatch is imposed ("Hale him away, and let him talk no more") [4.1.100–02, 133]. The Elizabethan underclasses, traumatized by arbitrary execution in city and country, are thus provided in the play with a tailored spectacle of popular vengeance.

In such mimetic reprisal, moreover, Shakespeare gives us an authentic picture of Tudor popular politics, insofar as the rituals of popular rebellion commonly appropriated the mechanisms of state process, from bell-ringing, oath-taking and militia-style organisation to establishing courts and meting execution. Such appropriation was symbolic: "In plebeian rebels' bottom-up vision of the late medieval and early modern English state, the commons were considered to represent the foundation of legitimate authority."[50] Kett's rebels created a shadow government, which they believed acceptable to the Protector.[51] In his lethal instances of populist counterstrike, then, Shakespeare presents a commons whose actions are not hoarse blood-lust, but rather a bitter class retaliation that works, initially at least, through the familiar mechanism of impromptu application of official process.[52]

Such actions might nonetheless, of course, incur the death penalty for commoners. In the context of Tudor state terror inflicted by summary executions, the very clemency of Henry VI towards his rebels takes on subversive dimension. Buckingham had offered the commons, on behalf of the king, "free pardon to them all / That will forsake [Cade] and go home in peace" (4.7.152–53): a promise that, upon their desertion of Cade, vanished along with the rebellion. Replacing it is but a vague hopefulness on Buckingham's part: "we'll devise a mean / To reconcile you all unto the king" 94.7.209–10). Though no literary critic has noted the mysteriously dissolving royal promise here, it is hard to feel that Elizabethans were so comfortably indifferent to a history of slaughterous betrayal of promise. Violated pardons lingered long in underclass memory. Assurances of a full and free pardon from Henry VIII to the men on the Pilgrimage of Grace (1536) conduced to royal treachery: both Robert Aske and close to two hundred of his pilgrims were executed following their trusting dispersal. More recently, when Warwick's herald had offered, in August 1549, a pardon to Kett's followers in Norwich if they would lay down their arms, many cried "that pardon in appearance seemed good and liberall, but in truth would prove in the ende lamentable & deadly, as that which would be nothing else but Barrels filled with Ropes and Halters."[53] Kett's rebels at Bury and Melton were promised, like the play's rebels, a king's general pardon, only to witness subsequent executions. Twenty years later, popular bitterness toward the royal betrayal still ran deep. "We wyll not be deceyved as we were at the laste rysinge" declared a prospective rebel at Lavenham, "for then we were promised ynoughe and more then ynoughe. But the more was an halter."[54]

Many in the Elizabethan audience of this play must thus have entertained great scepticism toward the outcome when its rebels were herded before the king. The contrast with Tudor policy, however, was shocking. "God forbid so many simple souls / Should perish by the sword" worries this monarch. In what may have been received as pointed contrast to Elizabeth's prompt execution of leaders of 1589's protesting soldiers at Westminster, Henry agrees at once to hear the rebels' supplication (4.4.7–10). He then honours his word in breathtaking fashion.

> Soldiers, this day have you redeemed your lives,
> And showed how well you love your prince and country.
> Continue still in this so good a mind,
> And Henry, though he be infortunate,
> Assure yourselves will never be unkind.
> And so, with thanks and pardon to you all,
> I do dismiss you to your several countries. (4.8.15–21)

The tonality borders on the miraculous, and Henry's lenience is open to pragmatic question; yet the contrast is powerful between, on the one hand, the graphic spectacle of a sincerely loving king, who in choosing to mete out "doom of life or death" (4.8.12) to shackled men kneeling before him, bestows a summer of warmth and forgiveness, and on the other, the punitive violence repeatedly launched by Elizabeth against the poor. ("Despite Elizabeth's personal preference for summary punishment, the Crown's policy was to use martial law only against the propertyless.")[55] Further, both action and effect here notably transgressed the ferocious absolutism of the government's *Homily against Disobedience*. God "dothe shewe that he alloweth neither the dignitie of any person, nor the multitude of any people, nor the weight of any cause as sufficient for the which the subjectes may move rebellion against their princes" declared the homily.[56] "Turne over and reade the histories of all nations, looke over the chronicles of our owne countrey, call to mynde so many rebellions of olde tyme, and some yet freshe in memorie, ye shall not finde that God ever prospered any rebellion . . . but contrarywyse that the rebelles were overthrowen and slaine, and such as were taken prysoners dreadfully executed."[57] To create this subversive effect, moreover, Shakespeare had once again transgressed his source material. Hall had specified that while most rebels were pardoned, the "stubburne heddes" were "justely put to execucion", and the 1587 Holinshed (227) related royal commissioners executing in town after named town.[58] Successful rebellion as historical fact—shown in Shakespeare's play, indeed, defeating royalist armies, capturing London, executing unpopular councillors, yet emerging happily in free and universal pardon—was a phenomenon which so worried the authorities in its implication of divine approval, that James VI took care to refute such interpretation in his *Trew Law* of *Free Monarchies*, published 1598.[59]

Shakespeare may have been hinting at the one successful popular rising against another King Henry (VIII) in 1525, recorded in Hall's Chronicle, when the leaders of four thousand Suffolk men refusing to pay the 'Amicable Grant' came submissively before the Dukes sent to enforce royal will, with halters round their necks, explaining that their non-payment rose only from poverty. They were pardoned, and the grant repealed.[60] Rebellion, *2 Henry VI* makes clear, might actually pay off. (One cannot but speculate, therefore, whether this aspect of *2 Henry VI* might not have influenced the Southwark feltmakers, who apparently resolved in June 1592—probably not long after this play came into performance—to break into the Marshalsea prison on the anniversary of the day [June 11] it had been broken into by Jack Cade in 1450, and set afire by Wat Tyler in 1381: an action generating a bloody Elizabethan riot.)[61] Lenience towards rebels, insisted Sir William Paget in a letter to Protector Somerset of July 1549, would encourage further "boldenes."[62] This, it appears, was Shakespeare's point precisely.

Crushing taxation was another smouldering grievance Shakespeare ventriloquised in his play. In the face of colossal war-costs, the government took 75,000 pounds in forced loans from wealthy subjects in 1588, and two successive loans, totalling 56,000, from the City. The 1589 parliament took the extraordinary step of granting two subsidies, which brought in 280,000 pounds. (In 1593, they would take the unprecedented step of granting three subsidies.)[63] Parliament's measure was the harsher for the poor, since the final instalment of the 1587 subsidy was still being gathered at the close of 1588; and one new member of the 1589 parliament warned against a second subsidy given "the suits, exclamations, complaints and lamentations of the commons of this realm, well known to the most part of this house."[64] Burghley, too, was worried: "I see a general murmur of people, and malcontented people will increase it to the comfort of the enemy."[65]

Incorporating precisely such concerns into his narrative, Shakespeare establishes an intelligible and serious ground of complaint for the commons: a moral logic consolidated by the vignette he creates of commoners whose petitions are torn up with contumely by the queen and Suffolk (1.3.1–44). "The commonwealth hath daily run to rack", allege the Protector's enemies in Shakespeare's drama; and driving home the point, "The commons hath thou racked" (1.3.128, 132). "And did he not, in his Protectorship, / Levy great sums of money through the realm / For soldiers' pay in France, and never sent it?" (3.1.60–62). "No: many a pound of mine own proper store," Gloucester protests, "Because I would not tax the needy commons / Have I dispersed to the garrisons" (3.1.115–17). The insurrectionary commons declare the commonwealth "threadbare"; and the rebel announcing Saye's capture is triumphant that "Here's the Lord Saye . . . He that made us pay one-and-twenty fifteens and one shilling to the pound the last subsidy" (4.2.6; 4.7.17–18). Significantly, Shakespeare has again departed from his sources, here to inflate and transpose the Chronicles' account of financial accusation. In Hall, Cade had indeed promised his followers no more fifteenths, nor any further taxes, for *Suffolk* had obtained from parliament a subsidy of one-fifteenth. Suffolk had further been accused by the commons of swallowing up the king's treasure.[66] Shakespeare notably transfers these accusations onto Gloucester, whom in Hall had been accused merely—and apparently maliciously—of advancing "his awne private thinges and peculier estate" above "common wealth and publique utilitie"[67] Concentrating these accusations upon Gloucester, and emphasising the grievance of taxation more than the private peculation, Shakespeare appears again to suggest, as he had in transposing from Somerset onto Gloucester the accusation of witholding troop payments, some identification of Henry's ageing Lord Protector with Elizabeth's elderly premier statesman.

Yet a third line of indictment of Gloucester sounds overtones of Burghley. "Thy cruelty in execution / Upon offenders has exceeded law" (1.3.136–37) charges Buckingham. "Did he not, contrary to form of law, / Devise strange deaths for small offenses done?" echoes the cardinal (3.1.58–59). "In your protectorship", hammers York, "you did devise / Strange tortures for offenders, never heard of / *That England was defamed by tyranny*" (3.1.121–23; emphasis added). It is true that the charge against Gloucester of torture, unlike the others, does occur in the chronicles (though few audience members would be likely to know this). The imputed consequent 'defamation' of England, however, did not: for the denunciations of Gloucester in the chronicles had been but fabrications encouraged by Queen Margaret (Hall, 209). It was *Elizabeth's* England which was experiencing international scandal for its widespread use of torture, and Elizabeth's Lord Treasurer who was closely associated with the charge.

Putting priests to the torture had shocked feeling within the country; and in 1581, the year that witnessed the Jesuit Edmund Campion, along with two fellow priests, hanged, drawn, and disembowelled, protest ballads appeared on the streets. In 1583, the Clerk of the Council himself, Robert Beale, published a condemnation of torture not only for cruelty, but as contrary to English law and liberties: a tract spawning government counterattacks, one of which, *The Execution of Justice in England*, published in 1584, was written by the worried Lord Burghley himself—with an eye, clearly, upon international perspectives. Babington's disembowelling in 1586 caused further public revulsion; Hacket and his followers were tortured for confession in 1591 (driving Coppinger, as we have seen, insane); and when the Jesuit Robert Southwell claimed angrily from the dock, in 1592, that he had been tortured, Topcliffe shouted denial in embarrassed fury.[68] The Catholic propagandist, Richard Verstegan, accompanied his detailed reports of the torture of loyal Catholics, published in 1587, with illustrations.[69] The period 1580–1603 has indeed been characterised by a modern authority as the "heyday" of English torture.[70] It was in this climate that Shakespeare not only made his characters allude three times to the grievance, but signally departed from the chronicles: first to remark the international scandal resulting, and next, to make Gloucester plead guilty to the accusation, proceeding to justify its selective use: "Murder, indeed—that bloody sin—I tortured / Above the felon or what trespass else" (3.1.132–33). Shakespeare departed twice more from his sources to *demonstrate* a Gloucester who juridically inflicted corporal pain: in the whipping of Simpcox ("You go about to torture me in vain": 2.1.148), and his unflinching commitment of Peter to trial by ordeal against the armourer:

Gloucester:　Let these have a day appointed them
　　　　　　　For single combat in convenient place . . .
Peter:　　　O Lord, have mercy upon me—I shall never be able to fight a
　　　　　　　blow! . . .
Gloucester:　Sirrah, or you must fight or else be hanged. (1.3.211–12,
　　　　　　　222–23, 224)

(In Hall, 207, resolution by combat had been requested by the Armourer himself.) It is consequently hard to imagine a contemporary audience not associating Lord Protector with the Lord Treasurer: piously decent torturers, both.[71]

COMMONWEALTHMEN AND RESISTANCE THEORY

The spectre of Christian socialism was haunting Shakespeare's England. "Dangerously ambiguous in troubled times", write historians of Tudor rebellion, "was the cliché of 'commonwealth' . . . It was difficult to defuse this explosive idea's power to arouse popular feeling and crystallize indignation."[72] "Nature hath poured forth all things for all men, to be held in common", St Ambrose had written in the fourth century, expressing a view prevalent in the early church: "but use and habit created private right."[73] This doctrine, we saw, became one foundation of peasant egalitarianism. Less radical, yet easily elided with it, was the Christian call for distributive justice. God created wealth as a medium for material provision for all of God's children, not for the luxuriation of a minority while others hunger. The incalculably influential Commonwealth ideal was enacted in *The Acts of the Apostles*, preached consensually by the Church Fathers, projected into monasticism, active on the fringes of medieval millenarian movements, asserted by Lollardy, watchword to numerous peasant revolts, and received lip service from authority throughout the Middle Ages. Articulating the economic ground for true Christian amity—a nation where all, freed from want and misery, could find gainful employment and enjoy the fruits of their work—the Commonwealthmen denounced creation of poverty through the pursuit of 'private commodity' (personal enrichment and power) by a minority of wealthy lords and gentlemen. "It is not agreeable with the Gospel", insisted the anonymous *Pyers Plowmans exhortation unto the lordes, knightes and burgoysses* (circa early1549) "that a few persons shall live in so great abundance of wealth and suffer so many [of] their Christian brothers to live in extreme poverty."[74] "The poorest ploughman is in Christ equal with the greatest prince that is", thundered Latimer. A rich man was but "God's treasurer", steward rather than owner of his riches.

The daring hopes raised by the Reformation and Commonwealthmen roused the resolve of an oppressed peasantry, suggested to many the sympathy of Protector Somerset[75] (who allegedly "hath conceived a wonderful hate against the gentlemen and taketh them all as his enemies")[76], and helped produce the conditions of Kett's Rebellion in 1549: "the closest thing Tudor England saw to a class war."[77] The 1549 risings in Sussex, Kent and Surrey were all led by a 'Captain Commonwealth', and their followers called by contemporaries 'commonwealths'. They "were remembered by this name by later generations."[78] These 'rebels' consequently anticipated government approval of their destruction of illegal enclosures, punishment of offending gentry, and remedying of local grievances. The rebellion's aftermath, however, with its pitched battles against royal forces sent to crush them, and the eventual massacre of some three thousand commoners at Dussindale, burned bone-deep into traumatized popular memory. As late as 1596 the 'camping time' would be invoked, when men in Kent talked of establishing a 'camp' to settle agrarian grievances.[79]

The magnitude of the rebellion (16,000 rebels were camped outside Norwich in August, whilst other encampments sprang up near Bury St. Edmunds and Ipswich), not to mention its efficient plebeian self-organization and orderly financial management, terrified the governing classes for decades to come, creating hysterical harshness toward underclass perspectives. "Ye pretende a commonwealth. Now a mende ye it, by killinge of gentilmen, by spoilinge of gentilmenne, by emprisononge of gentylmen. A marvelous tanned commonwealth", snarled Sir John Cheke in his account of the rebellion.[80] As Whitney Jones records, "All those who would check the unbridled operation of private profit to the common hurt were denounced as rabble-rousing Anabaptists by those who felt their interests to be opposed". Protector Somerset was typically admonished, as by Sir Anthony Aucher, that "under the pretence of simplicity and poverty there may rest much mischief. So do I fear there doth in these men called Common Wealths and their adherents."[81] Latimer's plea for hungry men driven to desperation— "for God's love restore their sufficient unto them, and search no more what is the cause of rebellion"[82]—fell on deaf ears. Crowley summarized the lock-jawed response of the leisured and well-fed, in *The Way to Wealth*, 1551: "We will teach them to know their betters. And because they would have all common, we will leave them nothing. And if they once stir again, or do but once cluster together, we will hang them at their own doors!"[83] Alarmed again by the 1569 rising, *Gorboduc*'s courtiers, in Sackville's ireful conclusion, likewise convey the standing brutal backlash against the semi-official radicalism of Somerset's day:

> Give once sway unto the peoples' lusts
> To rush forth on and stay them not in time,
> And as the stream that rolleth down the hill,
> So will they headlong run with raging thoughts
> From blood to blood, from mischief unto moe,
> To ruin of the realm, themselves, and all. (5.1.66–71)

> Those traitorous hearts that dare rebel,
> Let them behold the wide and hugy fields
> With blood and bodies spread of rebels slain,
> The lofty trees clothed with the corpses dead
> That, strangled with the cord, do hang thereon.[84] (5.2.60–64)

Sidney's 'New' *Arcadia* of the early 1580s stripped rebellious peasants of any vestige of humanity, striving to present the spectacle of patrician swordsmen slashing bumpkins into gushing slices as hilarious entertainment.[85]

As a watchword of rebellions in 1450 and 1549, 'commonwealth' thus could prove poisonous handling for the upper classes, slithering uncontrollably from innocuous equivalence to 'body politic' into seditious implications of equality at law, entitlement to rights and benefits, even a ground of impeachment of axiomatic human hierarchy. Sir Thomas Elyot refused in *The Book Named the Governor* to render *res publica* as 'commonwealth' (preferring 'public weal'), as it signified for him false identification "of *res publica* with *res plebeia* or weal of the commoner or multitude."[86] However, a posthumous edition of Elyot's Latin-English *Dictionary* (1548) revised by Thomas Cooper, carried a preface lauding precisely such priorities. "The advauncement of the commonweale", it informed the king, " . . . is, truely to minister justice, to restreigne extortion and oppression: to set up tillage and good husbandrie, whereby the people maie increase and be mainteined. Your godly herte wolde not have . . . grounde so enclosed up that your people shoulde lacke foode and sustinaunce: one man shuttyng in of fieldes and pastures to be made, and an hundred thereby to be destroid."[87] Anne McLaren, who argues "signal continuities between the political culture of Edward VI's and Elizabeth's reigns, especially the influence in both of commonwealth values and beliefs",[88] has documented the accentuation, in the later and more troubled decades of Elizabeth's reign, of both Protestant-elect and Republican dimensions to the term. 'Commonwealth' values could thus supply a framework of thought within which anti-absolutist ideals could be publicly articulated, the 'commonwealth' implication of "spiritual and potentially political equality among the godly" suggesting a leading role in the state for men "normally excluded from political affairs."[89] McLaren links the conception with such developments as the Bond of Association (1584) and Burghley's plan for a *Magnum Consilium* to elect a successor in the case of Elizabeth's sudden death without heir. At times, "we can see commonwealth ideology eliding into a potentially radical oppositional stance."[90]

But the term, I would recall, had also a proletarian currency, concomitant with the high tide of class antagonism rising through the mid- and later sixteenth century. "In the language of late medieval and early modern popular protest . . . The interests of the 'poorality' were synonymous with those of the 'commonwealth'" notes Andy Wood.[91] The word implied that "a viable political order rests on the collective wealth of the people", glosses political theorist Neal Wood.[92] "A commonwealth", cautioned Raleigh, " . . . is the government by the common and baser sort without respect of the other orders."[93] When a crowd of demonstrators surged up the stairs and into the Lobby of the House of Commons in November 1601 to protest against the mass suffering inflicted by monopolies, they identified themselves as "Commonwealth men".[94] In this polarized semantic climate, Shakespeare elected to pepper his plays with references to the 'commonwealth'. When demanded, for instance, in 2 *Henry IV* to justify his opening "the lawless bloody book / Of forged rebellion", the Archbishop of York replies "the commonwealth / I make my quarrel in particular" (4.1.91–94): thereby sounding, as James Holstun recognises, "the classic populist trope of Tudor rebellion."[95] Gadshill brags in *1 Henry IV* of hard-drinking alehouse thieves ('Trojans') who "pray continually to their saint, the commonwealth" (2.1.73–74): the term here, as a kind of code for under-class economic grievance, euphemises theft as the retaliatory prerogative of the oppressed commons. Hotspur bitterly derides the King in the same play that, having taken "on him to reform / Some certain edicts and some strait decrees / That lie too heavy on the common wealth", he won "The hearts of all that he did angle for" (4.3.80–82, 86)."Go thou", bids *Richard II's* gardener, following the King's defeat, "and like an executioner, / Cut off the heads of too fast-growing sprays / That look too lofty in our common-wealth. / All must be even in our government" (3.4.34–3). In disdainful recoil, the term may render aristocratic condescension to proletarian clods: "Here comes a member of the commonwealth", sniffs Boyet, as Costard plods into the courtly circle in *Love's Labour's Lost* (4.1.41–42). ("God dig-you-de'en, all" . . .)[96]

In *2 Henry VI*, the word occurs more frequently than in any other play. 'Commonwealth' becomes the iterated keyword, saturated in connotation of violated preciousness, of what is decently owed the people: now deployed as the most virulent ground of arraignment. Seeking to hurl from power Protector Gloucester, Suffolk charges:

> Since thou wert king—as who is king but thou?—
> The commonwealth hath daily run to wrack. (1.3.127–28)

Arresting Dame Eleanor in the midst of infernal seance, York's barb of choice is "The King and common weal / Are deep indebted for this piece of pains" (1.4.41–42). Having flung out, enraged, from the chamber upon "spiteful false objections" against his rule, Gloucester on return showcases a dignified calm, and establishes an exalted, statesmanlike tone for his rebuttal, by invoking the talismanic term:

> Now, lords, my choler being overblown
> With walking once about the quadrangle
> I come to talk of commonwealth affairs. (1.3.156–58)

"To heaven I do appeal", he cries, in final self-defence, "How I have loved my King and common weal" (2.1.200–01). Almost inevitably, the usage culminates in the word's brandished appropriation, knowingly jubilant, by popular insurgence:

> I tell thee, Jack Cade the clothier means to dress the commonwealth, and turn it, and set a new nap upon it. [97] (4.2.4–5)

A commonwealth run to wrack was arguable cause of rightful resis-tance: and discussion of such prerogative is not the least subversive of the drama's darings. "Whether there were limits to the obedience that inferiors owed their social and political superiors was one of the great questions of

Renaissance and Reformation political thinking", noted Richard Strier in a classic discussion of Shakespeare's dramatization of resistance theory in *Lear*.[98] As both Tudor and Stuart political theorizing demonstrated, "The key question in the minds of contemporaries was not so much the right to vote, as the right to revolt . . . The crucial question was not whether power originated with the people, but whether and under what circumstances they or their representatives could reclaim it."[99] "Obedience is due", declared Bishop Gardiner in 1553, "but how far the limits requiring obedience extend, that is the whole question to be demanded."[100] Shakespeare would virtually make a career from supplying the answer anathematized by the crown, relentlessly penning dramas of resistance to monarchy: whether apparently justified—*Titus, Richard III, Hamlet, Lear, Macbeth*—or problematic: *Richard II, King John, 1 Henry IV, 2 Henry IV, Julius Caesar, The Tempest.* In *2 Henry VI*, he makes a point of not only providing three, separate actions of popularly initiated violent resistance (the insurgence into the palace to expel Suffolk; the pirates' execution of Suffolk; Cade's rebellion), but of handling nakedly upon stage the radioactive question of absolute allegiance.

Shakespeare's treatment of popular rising in this play, as argued in Chapter 3, reveals a generous and complex vision, which, though conditioned by awareness of possible anarchic degeneration, and by pessimism about its larger transformative possibilities given the phenomenon of leadership betrayal, nonetheless includes conditional endorsement of armed uprising. Sympathy for the plight of the poor, whose petitions are shown supercility shredded, and the shared moral anger that places moments of penetrating critique in the mouth of Cade, are complemented by remarkably positive rendition of the first uprising. Joining hands in their pact on Gloucester's murder, Suffolk, the queen and York concluded, in careless superbia, "And now we three have spoke it, / It skills not greatly who impugns our doom" (3.1.280–81). To this homicidal insouciance, the people in arms prove heroic nemesis. Swift, shrewd, and successful, the commons' intervention to drive murderous Suffolk from a dithering court seems to glow with authorial approval. Contrasts between this insurgency and Cade's appear crafted, in Annabel Patterson's words, to offer "an opportunity for discrimination . . . between socially useful or abusive styles" of "the popular voice protesting".[101] Tudor England was, after all, in the words of a major historian, "pockmarked with minor disorders", urban craftsmen refusing lower wage rates, and "self-confident manorial communities" responding with "truculent resistance" to "fend off any encroachment upon [their] customary rights".[102]

Shakespeare's explicit and extended meditation of resistance rights thus sprang from a climate of beleaguered popular prerogative, becoming dramatic in calculated sedition when extended to monarchy. It is, in the words of Michael Hattaway, "a demonstration of Shakespeare's radicalism . . . that he is asking the kind of question that princes did not want to be asked."[103]

Official Elizabethan prohibition of resistance, as in the *Homily against Disobedience*, was crisply absolute. The example not only of Old Testament sages but of Christ himself teaches that "it foloweth unavoydably that such as do disobey or rebell agaynst their owne naturall gratious soveraignes . . . [are] in deede no true Christians, but worse than Jewes, worse then heathens, and such as shall never enjoy the kingdome of heaven".[104] Yet opposing the official *diktat*, an alternative piety of convenience, variously Catholic or Protestant as the crown's denomination *du jour* necessitated, declared in its most radical (Calvinist) form that "When the Magistrates and other officers cease to do their duety . . . then God geveth the sworde in to the peoples hande, and he himself is become immediatly their head."[105] Legitimation of tyrannicide infiltrated even Renaissance English Bibles, notes Patrick Collinson, through printed marginal notes that on occasion seemed to contradict Biblical meaning to impose their point. The Geneva Bible, Bishops Bible, and even the Authorized Version, all *condemned* King Asa's sparing of his usurping mother in 2 Chronicles 15.16; and likewise the comment of the Geneva Bible and the Bishops, on David's sparing of Saul as the Lord's anointed, is that regicide would have been lawful since Saul was a tyrant.[106]

The Catholic regime under Mary, and the Protestant under Elizabeth, sought to distance themselves, of course, from such perspectives, which naturally morphed, with their own accession to power, from spiritual imperative to anathematised menace. Nonetheless, "Nobody writing in the 1590s could have had an unproblematic faith in the Tudors as a legitimate dynasty chosen by God to rule England."[107] Elizabeth's own claim was "arguably as problematic as that of Henry VI", since it descended from her grandfather's victory in battle, since she had been declared a bastard at one point by Henry VIII, and since she had been excommunicated [twice] by papal bull.[108] Throughout the 1590s, as Elizabeth in her sixties looked increasingly feeble yet refused to announce a successor from the many candidates, and the prospect seemed imminent of civil war along dynastic and religious lines as in France, to pose questions of legitimacy and succession became all the more explosive. The context makes Shakespeare's relentless evocations of questionable legitimacy in hereditary rulers, and of revocable allegiance, all the more outspoken. Nonetheless, his presentation of hereditary monarchy as a destabilizing institution—undermined by problematic legitimacy, and responsible for plunging the nation into bloody vicissitudes—would recur in all his history plays.

"For shame! In duty bend thy knee to me" thunders an appalled King Henry, as Salisbury transfers allegiance to York. Yet Shakespeare makes breathtakingly explicit—and leaves resonantly unanswered—precisely the question which the *Homily against Disobedience* was designed to bury from all view, thereby foregrounding a glaring aporia in the logic of monarchical discourse:

King: Hast thou not sworn allegiance unto me?
*Salisbury:*I have.
King: Canst thou dispense with heaven for such an oath?
*Salisbury:*It is a great sin to swear unto a sin,
        But greater sin to keep a sinful oath.
        Who can be bound by any solemn vow
        To do a murd'rous deed, to rob a man,
        To force a spotless virgin's chastity,
        To reave the orphan of his patrimony,
        To wring the widow from her customed right,
        And have no other reason for this wrong
        But that he was bound by a solemn oath?
Queen: A subtle traitor needs no sophister. (5.1.177–189)

Salisbury, moreover, is the noble with whom a commons audience was perhaps most likely to bond. Not only has he proven, while others "do labour for their own preferment", uniquely concerned (with the exception of Gloucester) "to labour for the realm", his priorities resolutely paternalist ("We . . . cherish Duke Humphrey's deeds / While they do tend the profit of the land" (1.1.178–79, 203–04). When confronting the first popular rising, though his son spurned the crowd as "the rude multitude", Salisbury had presented the people's demands to the court with such respectful and eloquent articulation that Suffolk accused him of complicity: "Tis like the commons, rude unpolished hinds / Could send such message to their sovereign" (3.2.135, 245–71, 273–74). Shakespeare now deploys Salisbury once more to dignify underclass perspective—to become, in Suffolk's frightened jibe, "Lord Ambassador / Sent from a sort of tinkers to the King" (278–79)—for it is a distinctively 'commonwealth' language of concern (the lexicon of forced virgin, wronged widow and reaved orphan) that Salisbury employs to argue a moral ground for dissolving fealty. Shakespeare's choice of speaker and rhetoric here thus works not only to maximize the popular appeal of a seditiously conditional theory of citizen allegiance, but to sympathetically reconnect commonwealth language with resistance rights in a syllogism Kett might have admired.

Most strikingly of all, this passage must have generated a truly electrifying level of seditious suggestion in late 1591/early 1592, as we discover when we reposition the drama, once again, in its immediate historical context. Believing (accurately) that, preparatory to another invasion by Philip of Spain, a fresh wave of Jesuits was infiltrating the nation to reason English Catholics out of their loyalty to the Crown, Burghley in October 1591 caused a remarkable royal proclamation to be issued. Confessing fear of the "underminings of our good subjects under a false color and face of holiness to make breaches in men's and women's consciences and so train them to treasons", it commanded all heads of household, "of what degree soever", to institute "a present due and particular inquisition of all manner of persons" who had eaten or lived with them during the last year: probing their loyalty and profiling their movements and attendance of church, with a view to uncovering both Jesuits in disguise and persons "weak of understanding" who might succumb to seditious argument.[109] Written records were to be kept for inspection, and commissioners created in every county for oversight and the interrogation of recusants. A national witch-hunt was thus launched, projected from the secret files on Burghley's tireless desk outward into almost every domestic chamber in the kingdom, in a campaign which Burghley's principal biographer characterises as "savagery."[110] "Great men", we recall Lord Saye bragging, minutes before execution by a vengeful populace, "have reaching hands. Oft have I struck / Those that I never saw, and struck them dead" (4.7.73–74).

Had Shakespeare been questioned by the authorities on his presentation of Salisbury, legitimating rightful transference of sworn loyalty from the crown, he could have answered in defence that the peer's secession was mere chronicle history, and demonstrably a treason whose monstrous consequence was civil war. Nonetheless, the fact remains that, in this climate of fresh, high-surveillance hysteria over potential disloyalty to the English monarch, Shakespeare opted not only to dramatize a successful suborning of royal allegiance, but to supply it with steadfast justification, on grounds of principle, by a beloved and noble character, in populist terms, that go unrefuted. Shakespeare's behaviour here reveals extraordinary political daring; and it surely implies remarkably tenacious sympathy with dissident perspectives.

In *3 Henry VI*, the playwright would further undercut the absoluteness of solemn oaths to monarchy by universalizing their violation. The forswearing of oaths in a changing world becomes here so routinely pragmatic that inflexible fealty seems in danger of constituting—as in *Titus Andronicus*—grotesque fanaticism. Demystification of absolutised obedience to hereditary ruler links all parts of *Henry VI* with *Titus*.[111]

That fretting proclamation of October 1591, combatting "the underminings of our good subjects under a false color", recalls us to the historical figure Shakespeare limned in 'Gloucester': Her Majesty's Lord Treasurer, Lord Burghley.

PATER PATRIAE, AND THE DOG THAT REACHED AT THE MOON

"Unanimously", the Tudor chroniclers had presented Gloucester as 'the good Duke Humphrey', loyal servant of the realm and beloved of the commons.[112] Shakespeare emphatically reproduces the popular gratitude for justice (see 1.1.155–59; 1.3.4–5; 3.1.28; 3.2.125–27, 250), and underlines the Duke's unswerving, impeccable loyalty to the crown (1.2.17–21). He also, however, introduces a range of further characteristics that must, in

the minds of many in the audience, have rendered identification of Gloucester with Burghley entirely inescapable at many significant moments.

At the pinnacle of national power, subordinate only to Elizabeth, in official estimation Burghley was the most respected man in the kingdom; and
his record suggests that, at one time at least, he had commanded considerable respect from the commons. Francis Bacon dubbed him "the Atlas of
the commonwealth"; yet in a tribute, "circulated widely in manuscript" following its composition in 1592, Atlas is conceded to have grown unpopular.
Burghley is "worthily celebrated as pater patriae in England; and though
he be libelled against by fugitives, yet he is prayed for by a multitude of
good subjects."¹¹³ As a former member of the Edwardian circle of commonwealthmen, the dedicatee of the first translation of Thomas More's
Utopia (by Ralph Robinson in 1551), and longtime friend of Sir Thomas
Smith in particular, whose promotion he doggedly sought under Elizabeth
despite her dislike,¹¹⁴ Burghley had sought implementation throughout the
reign of principled, paternalist policy: "to content the people", as he put
it, "with justice and favourable government which is not to exact frequent
payments nor molest them with innovations."¹¹⁵ Revering Cicero, carrying
De Officiis about with him, and ordering Cicero's works from France in
portably sized volumes, ¹¹⁶ Burghley established, conclude modern historians Heal and Holmes, economic policies that translated "the language of
commonwealth" into pragmatic modern ventures for generating wealth for
all: whether fen drainage, protection of fisheries and immigrant labor, or
sustaining of grain levels and strategic commodities.¹¹⁷ In London (as may
have been known to Shakespearean audiences) Burghley "cut a distinctive
figure in St. Margaret's parish by instituting a yearly personal dole sufficient to pay for bread and beef to feed seventy-two poor parishioners."¹¹⁸ In
true commonwealthman fashion, he condemned courtiers motivated only
by private profit as "cankers of the commonwealth."¹¹⁹ Like Gloucester
again, his loyalty to crown and state was unimpeachable.¹²⁰

Both men enjoyed a reputation for shrewd justice as judges. Shakespeare
shows us a group of "poor petitioner(s)" awaiting Gloucester (1.3.26), just
as Burghley, according to an early biographer, "drew upon him such multitudes of suits as was incredible . . . there was not a day . . . wherein he
received not threescore, fourscore and a hundred petitions."¹²¹ In trials,
records Beckingsale, "His skilled examination rather than any rough handling of the defendant proved lethal";¹²² and Shakespeare's interpolation
of the Simpcox episode (from Grafton or Foxe: not present in Hall and
Holinshed) showcases the devastating sceptical realism. That Shakespeare
invents Simpcox's feigned lameness, thereby introducing a Gloucester who,
effectively, conducts interrogation with a whip, of a sweating subject who
cries in terror "You go about *to torture* me in vain" (2.1.148; emphasis
added), makes memorably concrete the accusations of torture levelled
against both men. Shakespeare indeed makes the judgement more severe
than does his source. Simpcox and wife are sentenced not to the stocks, but

to be "whipped through every market-town / Till they come to Berwick, from whence they came" (158–59): a punishment, perhaps, once more suggesting Burghley—author of the Poor Law reforms which introduced the flogging of vagabonds and their compulsory return to town of origin.

Unquestionably smacking more of Burghley than of Gloucester, however, was Shakespeare's version of the accusation, in Hall (209), that the Duke "had not so muche advaunced & preferred the common wealth and publique utilitie, as his awne private things & peculier estate." Shakespeare rearticulates the charge as expending "public treasury" upon "sumptuous buildings" (1.3.134). The Lord Treasurer's well-indulged taste for architectural splendour was legendary. Theobalds, completed around 1585, was "the most admired and visited grand mansion of its day." Its lavishness, scale and novelty "inevitably gave rise to obloquy."[123]

Indeed, Edmund Spenser had just attacked Burghley precisely for pious self-enrichment in Mother Hubbard's Tale, in 1591: "And when he aught not pleasing would put by, / The cloke was care of thrift, and husbandry, / For to encrease the common treasures store; / But his owne treasure he encreased more."[124]

Quite absent from the Chronicles, moreover, and entirely peculiar to Burghley, were further key traits. First, notably long hours of work. Gloucester recounts how he "Studied so long, sat in the Council House / Early and late, debating to and fro", and later, how he long had "watched the night, / Ay, night by night, in studying good for England" (1.1.86–87, 3.1.110–11), just as Burghley's exceptionally "diligent and industrious course of life", in the words of an early biographer, "caused all his friends to pity him, and his very servants to admire him."[125] Second, the desire for retirement. "I beseech your Majesty, give me leave to go. / Sorrow would solace, and mine age would ease" Gloucester implores the crown. "Here, noble Henry, is my staff. / As willingly do I the same resign / As erst they father made it mine" (2.3.20–21, 32–34). "In 1590 the seventy-year-old William Cecil, Lord Burghley, began to dream of retirement", records James Sutton.[126] Health failing—in October 1591 we hear that both hands are so badly taken by gout that he is unable to write[127]—and saddened by bereavements, he withdrew to semi-retirement at Theobalds, where in 1591 he greeted the arrival of queen and court with an entertainment wherein a 'hermit' recounted how Burghley had lived there due to "excessive grief" for two years. Playing along with the fiction, Elizabeth had a Mock Charter issued to "the hermit of Theobalds", permitting retirement to the delights of his home, yet warning him to "abiure desalacon & moourning" as prejudicial to age. (In fact she kept him busy, despite protests, until his death in 1598.)[128]

A third 'Cecilian' characterization of Gloucester introduced by Shakespeare was his recent change of temperament. "The barriers of bland benignity and studied moderation which controlled the inner tides of feeling generally held", observes Beckingsale of Cecil; but the acute sufferings of his last few years produced, according to his earliest biographer, unaccustomed "morosity." [129] Whether Gloucester's two occasions of abrupt withdrawal—dropping the scroll with the royal marriage articles at 1.1.50–52, and exiting upon accusations of treason at 1.3. 141—be taken as evidence of irascibility, or as working instances of the famous reputation for emotional control, is perhaps open to question; but Queen Margaret refers pointedly, across sixteen lines, to "The strangeness of his altered countenance . . . how proud, peremptory, and unlike himself" he has become. Once "all the court admired him for submission", whereas now, at every meeting, "He knits his brow, and shows an angry eye" (3.1.4–20).

A fourth key similarity was a cluster of parallels centering upon the peers' wives. "Art thou not second woman of the realm" demands Gloucester of Dame Eleanor: a position in some ways that of Burghley's wife, Mildred. Mildred knew that "the status of her husband" demanded her "visibility at the centre of power", and was a regular attender at court. [130] Duchess Eleanor's rivalry with her queen was invented by Shakespeare, so perhaps reflects Elizabethan reality, since Mildred was also a nationally revered scholar who participated in the 1572 revision of the Bishop's Bible. [131] What is certain is that Gloucester's conspicuous pain over a 'lost' wife ("sorrow and grief have vanquished all my powers", 2.1.193) echoed Burghley's: Mildred had recently died (1589), and Burghley's spirit was left, in his own words, "oppressed with the greatest grief." [132] "Unprecedentedly absent from privy council meetings for a month", [133] he deserted court for Theobalds, whence Elizabeth was ever after able to extract him only with difficulty. Burghley's recent bereavement was public knowledge: given the absence of royal burials between 1558 and 1603, the magnificent funeral ceremonies taking Mildred (like her daughter, and later Burghley) to a spectacular funerary monument in Westminster Abbey, "must have constituted the grandest series of processions" of the period. [134] On Mildred's tomb, Burghley's inscription, "the longest surviving epitaph on a female monument", describes himself as "This old man, grey-haired, venerable" declaring love for a wife "dearest above all", who had lived with him harmoniously for 43 years. [135] She had long been a figure well-known to the educated: a standard Latin primer in English history was dedicated to her, and "generations of English schoolboys must have translated the dedication." [136] In this context, it becomes clear, I suggest, not only why Shakespeare departed from the chronicles ("the duke of Gloucester, toke all these thynges paciently, and saied litle", Hall 202) to articulate in Gloucester a very public and tender heartbreak over his wife's fate—"Mine eyes are full of tears, my heart of grief . . . I beseech your majesty, give me leave to go" (2.3.17, 20)—but also why act two scene four is structured as elegiac, the couple's exchange functioning as an intimate final farewell ("Sweet Nell . . . I'll prepare my tear-stained eyes to see her miseries ", 2.4.11, 16–17), despite the fact that Eleanor's punishment is not execution, but merely to "live in your country here in banishment / With Sir John Stanley in the Isle of Man" while her "scandal" is "wiped away" (2.3.12–13, 66). "Art thou gone too? All comfort go with thee" laments the Duchess. "My joy is death—/ Death, at whose name I oft have been afeared . . ." (ll.88–90). Burghley's "emphasis on the secrecy of Mildred's benefactions"[137] may suggest that she had been, like Dame Eleanor, an unpopular figure: owing, perhaps, to her high prices for influence-peddling,[138] or to a personality which her portraits suggest to have been haughtily dour.[139]

The last of Shakespeare's Cecilian remodellings include the invention of close affective relations with the monarch, tearing from the Crown at Gloucester's death one of play's most moving laments (3.1.198–222); and the creation of a primary court antagonism between solitary veteran counsellor and a set of younger courtiers united in hungry opposition ("the welfare of us all / Hangs on the cutting short that fraudful man", 3.1.80–81). Leicester had died in 1588, Mildmay in 1589, Walsingham, Croft, and Warwick in 1590, and finally Hatton in 1591. "As the last fully active survivor of his generation, old Lord Burghley no longer had any equals . . . this was clearly a body in desperate need of new blood."[140] Enemies spoke bitterly of a *regnum Cecilianum*[141] ("Since thou wert king—as who is king but thou? . . ." 1.3.127); noblemen resented the rule of a relative commoner ("duty that to us belongs", 3.1.17); and within these embittered conditions, Shakespeare transposed onto Gloucester, as we have seen, the accusations against Cecil of excessive taxation and non-payment of troops.

Though differences necessarily remained between the two figures, contemporary censorship always necessitating, in Annabel Patterson's words, a "scattershot approach" rather than seamless identification,[142] the unbroken series of 'Burghleyan' indictments levelled at Gloucester at 1.3.127–39—*de facto* kingship, subjection of the nobility, economic and military disaster, lavish expenditure on private buildings, an overdressed wife, the torture of prisoners—must cumulatively have become unmistakable as they rang across the stage. Fledgling Shakespeare was taking large political risks. Though Burghley himself took little interest in contemporary literature, his "reaching hands" were everywhere: *Mother Hubbard* had been immediately called in by the authorities, and Spenser's prompt exile to administration in Ireland indicates prudent flight or Burghley's punishment.[143] The poet's thinly veiled reference to Burghley in 'The Ruines of Time' (1591) in fact lamented precisely that fall in age from exemplary virtue embodied in Shakespeare's ambiguating portrait of 'the good Duke'.

> O griefe of griefes, O gall of all good heartes,
> To see that vertue should dispised bee
> Of him, that first was raisde for vertuous parts,
> And now broad spreading like an aged tree,
> Lets none shoot up, that nigh him planted bee. (449–53)

The potential dangers to such portrayal perhaps helped determine the playwright's hedged presentation of Eleanor. If Dame Eleanor's sumptuous dress (she "bears a Duke's revenues on her back", 1.3.84, 134) had further hinted at Mildred Cecil, whose "splendid garb", worn from the earliest days of her marriage and reflecting "personal pleasure not a necessary uniform", has been remarked on by biographers and displayed in portraits,[144] it must more strongly have invoked, at least for privileged audiences, a very different creature—the beautiful Countess of Leicester, née Lettice Knollys: Elizabeth's second cousin, mother of Essex, and widow of Elizabeth's former favourite, the Earl of Leicester.[145] "Ostentatious and extravagant", the Countess had taken not only to riding to court in a dazzling procession followed by knights, thirty gentlemen, and other coaches, so that crowds would gather and cheer, thinking her the Queen or some foreign prince; she had even "deliberately started wearing in the royal presence dresses that were finer than the Queen's own garments" (compare "Strangers in court do take her for the queen" etc, 1.3.79–84). Inevitably, Elizabeth exploded: boxing her ears, and shrieking that she would have but one Queen in England, she expelled the Countess permanently from court.[146] The play's similar outburst—the Queen's insult of Dame Eleanor as a "minion", followed by her blow, some shouting, and the humiliated exit of Eleanor at 1.3.141–51—clearly echoed the notorious incident for all interested in court gossip. As with the composite Cade, Shakespeare had prudently pluralized the allusiveness of a major character: thereby simultaneously securing defence against possible prosecution, and milking topicality.

The exit from power of the aged and crippled Lord Treasurer looked imminent. This was just the point when the rocket-thrust of the Essex take-off magnetized the court. It was precisely in late 1591/1592 that Burghley's own nephews, Francis and Anthony Bacon, concluded that "the earl of Essex' rare virtues and perfections and the interest he had worthily in my sovereign's favour" logically dictated their defection to the circle of this rising young nobleman.[147] The dramatist, however, glanced less than favourably at Essex, too, I suggest: in the turbulent profile of the Duke of York.

Essex had returned to England from the siege of Rouen in January 1592: and it was at just this point, Read remarks, that his rivalry commenced with his former guardian, Burghley, for supremacy with court and queen. During Essex's campaigning in France, "it had been part of Burghley's business to transmit royal rebukes", and the earl blamed his fruitless military endeavours on Burghley.[148] In a number of cases of "friction between Essex and 'old Saturnus' . . . Essex's reported impatience at the continuing sway of Burghley and Hatton in 1591 clearly implied he wished to supplant them," suggests Essex's latest biographer.[149] Returned recently, like "Brave York", from the French wars, Essex had publicly shown dashing heroism also in the Portugal Expedition (1589), where he had leapt, sword in hand, into shoulder-deep water at Peniche to lead the first wave of troops against the Spanish troops awaiting them on the beach. At the siege of Lisbon, he had hurled his lance into the city gate, and challenged Spanish officers (without success) to single combat: a deed celebrated in ballad even after

his death, and contributing to a hero's welcome in England, where George
Peele anointed him Sir Philip Sidney's heir in his *Eclogue Gratulatorie*[150]
At Rouen likewise, Essex had recently challenged the French governor.[151] In
the 1588 Accession Day tilts he had both opened and ended the jousts; and
in 1589 led them once more, "to the publique view of so many thousand
Citizens which usually flocked to see him, and made within the reach of his
own ears large reclamations in his praise."[152] Delighting to claim superior
qualifications, as a man of action, over mere *noblesse de robe*, York may
thus well remind spectators of Essex as he boasts his military experience
and personal wounds, hotly defending his soaring honour:

> I rather would have lost my life betimes
> Than bring a burden of dishonour home . . .
> Show me one scar charactered on thy skin.
> Men's flesh preserved so whole do seldom win. (3.1.297–98, 300–01)

Gloucester, denouncing his enemies, notes that he has had to "pluck back"
York's "overweening arm"—an echo of his restraints of the intemperate
earl's continental adventures?—and characterises him as "dogged York,
that reaches at the moon" (3.1.158–59). That the moon was one of Elizabeth's favourite personal symbols, and that the vociferously ambitious
young earl flirted hopefully with Cynthia, were common knowledge.[153]

The furious court atmosphere of the drama, with its duelling challenges,
may echo the fiery feuding of Essex with Ralegh (and other rival favourites)
from 1588, when Essex challenged Ralegh to a duel and the queen angrily
intervened. Through 1590 the two courtiers poured out hostile verse against
one another, and the rivalry "rumbled on for all to see."[154] It is even possible
that York's boasted design of deploying Jack Cade as an intelligence instrument, "a minister of my intent" (3.1.355), may hint at Essex's new role as
spymaster, having taken over Walsingham's surveillance network, from the
early months of 1591, following the latter's death.[155] For like other spy-
masters, Essex deployed *agents provocateurs* (a technique the Elizabethans
called 'projection'[156]) in the way that York uses Cade: for depth-soundings
and detections within selected seas of potential conspiracy. ("By this I shall
perceive the commons' mind", 3.1.374.)

In summary, many in the earliest commons audiences of *2 Henry VI* must
have found their own contemporary grievances, military, political, and economic, channelled with eloquent anger into the play; must have noted with
drawn breath the imbrication of radically inflected Commonwealth ideals
with resistance theory; and must further have decoded Burghley and Essex
in the terminally feuding figures of Gloucester and York. Given the decay
of Burghley and the soaring of Essex's star, in 1592 the drama must have
functioned on one level as a kind of terrifying essay on a potential future
for England: the veteran statesman gone, the monarch sunk in vacillation,
and the nation fragmenting into popular risings and baronial warfare. The

play's wildly successful 'prequel', *1 Henry VI*, though a clumsy patchwork by different hands, would noisily echo the catastrophe of court factionalism, and even (briefly) the two views of Gloucester, despite the otherwise amateurish monochrome of his characterisation. ("Gloucester, a foe to citizens . . . O'ercharging your free purses with his fines" at 1.4.61, 63, opposes a follower's panegyric on "So kind a father of the commonweal", 3.1.97–104.)

Yet *2 Henry VI* does more, I will argue, than speculate. Like some modern political poll, it actively takes findings among the commons, compelling audience members into positional alignments, as key characters reach out from the fiction to make deictic appeals for political support. Shakespeare's final assessment of the ambiguated figures of Gloucester / Burghley and York / Essex is therefore to be found, as we now shall see, in a complex patterning not of abstract sympathy and critique, but of declared, live audience responses, solicited through bonding and repudiation.

5　2 Henry VI
Political Stagecraft

York:　　I cannot blame them all: what is it to them?
　　　　'Tis thine they give away, and not their own.

(1.1.219–20)

Cade:　　And you that love the commons, follow me!
　　　　Now show yourselves men—'tis for liberty.
　　　　We will not leave one lord, one gentleman—
　　　　Spare none but such as go in clouted shoon,
　　　　For they are thrifty honest men, and such
　　　　As would, but that they dare not, take our parts.

(4.2.165–70)

York:　　Would'st have me kneel? First let me ask of these
　　　　If they can brook I bow a knee to man . . .

(5.1.109–10)[1]

Messenger:The rebels are in Southwark—fly, my lord!

(4.4.26)

Elizabethan class-conflict, we have seen, is no wanton anachronism, but was a bitter reality escalating through the post-Armada years. Increasingly it yielded, Keith Wrightson has noted, "a dichotomous perception of society", a "language of 'sorts'" which, in disregard of "the fine-grained (and highly contested) distinctions of the hierarchy of degrees" generated a language that "regroup[ed] the English into two broad camps . . . cleaving society into the haves and have nots, the respected and the contemned". We need, agrees Andy Wood, to recognise "the continuing willingness of contemporaries to conceive of a simple division between 'rich' and 'poor' . . . Plebeian definitions of social conflict worked within a dualistic perception of society".[2] "What whoresones were we that we had not killed the gentlemen" lamented the jailed Captain Cobbler, following the collapse of the Lincolnshire rising of 1536, "for I thought allwayes that they would be traytors."[3] William Poynet was prosecuted in 1549 for the claim that "Gents and Richemen have all catell and wolles & suche like things in ther hands nowe a days & the pore pe[o]ple are now Famysshed but C of us wyll rise one daye agenst them & I wylbe one."[4] 'The rich', as a hate-category, indeed expanded in the last decades of the sixteenth century, notes Wood, to encompass merchants and wealthy farmers.[5] Plebeian class critique was frequently convinced that its superiors were conspiring to destroy working men. As Somerset food rioters expressed it in 1596, "the ritche men have gotten all into their hands and will starve the poore."[6] Popular anger might even prove ignorant of that dazzled reverence for courtliness primly mandated by New Historicism: "Shyte uppon your Queene", responded a labourer to magistrates in 1585: "I woulde to god she were dead that I might shytt on her face."[7]

The public theatres—carnivalesque, scandal-ridden and demoticizing—were notorious foci, we have noted, of popular anger; and Thomas Cartelli has well illustrated the generation of simplistically polarised class hatreds into the reciprocal insults in which 2 *Henry VI* welters. Indeed Cade's command

> We will not leave one lord, one gentleman—
> Spare none but such as go in clouted shoon,
> For they are thrifty honest men, and such
> As would, but that they dare not, take our parts (4.2.167–70)

"demarcates that pivotal moment when a class 'in itself' become[s] a class 'for itself'."[8]

Yet to measure this play's mediation of that principle, we must relearn appreciation of Shakespeare's astonishingly precocious manipulation of the potentialities of audience interaction within the Elizabethan O. Traditional Shakespeare criticism, acknowledging somewhat abstractly the ludic and vocal dimensions to audience receptivity, rarely attempts systemic rethinking of the scripts in terms of their design, by a practised actor, for performance specifically within the interactional, carnivalesque playhouse. Yet fashioned for celebration as well as cerebration, the plays come replete with cues for spectator response, just as for actors'. They are scripts for audible exasperation, collective inflammation, comradely bonding and shocks of recoil. It is through such auditorium dialectics that Shakespeare designed his drama to accrue and generate their meanings.

Theatrical illusionism was intermittent: players, recalls Andrew Gurr, "performed in daylight, and their audiences were never expected to forget where they were, in daylight amongst thousands of other Londoners, standing in the rain to watch a game of obvious pretence."[9] Within these conditions, characterization, I hope to demonstrate, was often the product of a genuine dialogic: spectator assessment of onstage characters could be conditioned by the regard which those characters reciprocally bestowed upon spectators, a cognizance exhibited in differing forms of acknowledgment and degrees of proximity. It is vital to recover the workings of this principle of reciprocity: yet to the best of my knowledge, no Shakespeare critic has ever noted the scale and centrality of the dramatist's deixis, or charted its half-concealed patterns of political articulation. This chapter will consequently seek to argue an intelligible primary pattern to such dialogic as it evolves through 2 *Henry VI*.

In the opening scene, I suggest, crucial distinctions were created through performance which were quite at odds with the chroniclers' simple picture of 'good Duke' versus 'ambitious' York. Though the busied throng of onstage nobles apparently ignore the existence of the audience, Shakespeare's Gloucester ambiguously *addresses* it; and he is trumped by a York who will establish exclusive audience address. Deixis, I will argue, was a primary shibboleth of Elizabethan performance, inherited from the medieval tradition of the 'Vice' who exuberantly buttonholes the audience behind other characters' backs in soliloquies that are in fact moments of what we will dub carnival bonding. Through deictic language, York will establish himself as the primary figure of audience identification—'our man' on stage—whilst displacing Gloucester to an ambiguous remove from us. The entire remainder of the nobility onstage, wholly non-cognizant of the spectators, are rendered thereby remote: faces in profile, as it were, not eyes that seek us out. The affective ranking here was doubtless reinforced by stage blocking or *figurenposition*. York will have hovered or strolled on the stage periphery (Robert Weimann's *platea*), the shared zone where characters doubled fictive role with audience interaction, whereas the other peers will have remained further upstage, sightlessly immured within the *locus* (or realm of the fiction), with its throne and other symbolic props. Gloucester, whose 'Burghleyan' political ambiguation by Shakespeare we just studied, will logically have moved between the two zones, objectifying in *figurenposition* and audience relations his ambiguity as putative commonwealth hero. His convulsive dropping of the scroll at line forty-eight may have precipitated a movement away from the throne-group, and a resultant restlessness, perhaps allowing delivery of his "Brave peers of England" speech (from line seventy-one) from a location closer to the audience.

Such reconstructions will doubtless initially strike the reader as hopelessly speculative and quaintly idiosyncratic; yet the logic of affective and spatial positioning, I hope to show, is inherent in the script, and is objectively deducible by a close reading that is informed by knowledge of topical issues, and guided by what we know of the carnivalesque orientation of the Elizabethan amphitheatres. In the contexts of what I have called Shakespeare's 'art of toxic parallel', and of the intrinsically iconoclastic impetus of what Jean Howard terms "the politics of the playhouse",[10] what must have stood out politically in the opening scene, for instance, was response to the French calamities, as narrated by the nobles on the royal departure. Gloucester opens the outcry, with twenty-eight lines of passionate indignation (71–99), to be shared by Salisbury, Warwick and York. Unlike these, however, Gloucester launches into open-ended address. "Brave peers of England", he cries; and again, with "O peers of England, shameful is this league . . .", he invokes "the *common* grief of all the land" (71, 94, 73, italics added). The sweeping vocatives here (with accompanying hand movement?) strongly suggest extension to the audience; and that Gloucester is appealing to the people is further supported by his language, which through contrast with Suffolk's opening pomp and the royal archaisms ("alder liefest", "Y-clad with wisdom's majesty", 29.5, 31), combines simplicity with proverbial diction ("Suffolk, the new-made Duke that rules the roast", 105;[11] compare 3.1.170–71). Exiting the scene, Gloucester refers to the nobles in scornful diminutive as "lordings" (142) as he prophecies catastrophe. Departed, the very language in which his popularity is decried suggests playhouse behaviour: "What though the common people favour him, / . . . Clapping their hands and crying with loud voice . . ." (1.1.155, 157). Audience-aware, he is for the most part, however, audience-aloof: only intermittently will he bond, through acknowledgment, with the community of spectators, as in his final words before death, complaining of the peers that his life "is made the prologue to their play, / For thousands more that yet suspect no peril / Will not conclude their plotted tragedy" (3.1.151–53).

Capping the populism of Gloucester, York, alone on stage, appeals directly to the audience. Drawing the commons into political affairs as potential supporters was, after all, "a strategy characteristic of a late medieval populist nobleman", and pursued, for example, by Protector Somerset.[12] Working up once more the inflammatory grievances ("Anjou and Maine are given to the French, / Paris is lost, the state of Normandy / Stands on a tickle point now they are gone", 213–15), York makes his pitch with shameless political hucksterism, deftly fusing class-contempt with deictic solidarity with the commons. "The peers agreed, and Henry was well pleased / To change two dukedoms for a duke's fair daughter. / I cannot blame them all—what is't to them? / 'Tis thine they give away, and not their own" (217–20). Gesticulating downwards from the stage-edge above the commoners' upturned heads, and compelling response though direct address and an emotive question ("What is't to them?"), York is effectively canvassing the audience for support; and through his metaphor of the commons as a victim of robbery, who is "Ready to starve and dare not touch his own", he has probably gained it from many. Lords, he urges, "pillage", like pirates, "revelling . . . till all be gone, / Whileas the seelly owner of the goods / Weeps over them, and wrings his hapless hands, / And shakes his head, and trembling stands aloof, / While all is shared and all is borne away" (221–227). The juxtaposition of distressed commoner and predatory lord cunningly echoed that bitterly "dichotomous perception of society" we have seen historians observe as product of economic polarisation. Given the notorious expressiveness of popular audiences, exercised in carnival tradition—hissing, answering back, cheering, hurling caps skyward—the groundlings at least, and maybe many in the galleries, will have actively responded to York's patent solicitation. His ensuing confession of seeking to unthrone an incompetent concludes with another calculated populism, disparaging Henry's "bookish rule" (258). A "full-blown reptilian narcissus"[13] turns out winningly congenial when deixis is restored.

The stagecraft is breathtaking. Though drawing on the direct address tradition of the medieval popular stage, it places the device within a play as highly wrought as any academic drama, and its angry appeal to commoners breaks suddenly outward from a lavishly courtly setting. There had been nothing quite like this sustained combination in English drama before Shakespeare; and generations of Shakespeare scholars, meditating texts rather than scripts, have missed it.[14] *Titus Andronicus*, written probably a year or so previously (c.1590–91), had premiered, I think, the device of political deixis in Shakespearean dramaturgy. The opening of *Titus* had stationed rival princes, competing onstage for the imperial throne itself, *below* their electors, the senators and tribunes, who were positioned, significantly and unnecessarily, to spectate princely appeals from 'aloft'. Since the stage gallery in which these electors were emplaced completed the circle of theatre galleries, paying spectators, co-elevated in adjacent galleries, could effectively have found themselves, too, invoked and apostrophized: collectively subsumed into the place of judgement, as Saturninus and Bassianus craned their necks, and addressed their arms and their speeches upwards in political beseeching. In performance, the address by the imperial heir—"Noble patricians, patrons of my right, / Defend the justice of my cause with arms"—could effortlessly have solicited in its sweep a number (or multitude) of wealthier commoners in the galleries: an effect invisible on the page, but exerting a powerful frisson of political suggestion. These flanking rows of auditing commoners, set into the position of determining authority over supreme state power, would be usurping (literally) over-mighty place: a presumption treasonable in the world of Tudor ideology beyond the walls. ("Choose we!" would be the rebels' cry, as they burst into the palace in *Hamlet*). Further, if the would-be emperor addresses the galleried as "Noble patricians", his balancing appeal, moving from patricians to plebeians—"And countrymen, my loving followers, / Plead my successive title with your swords"—would logically have embraced the groundling pit (1.1.1–4). This centrifugal *figurenposition* thus projected above and beyond the boundaries of the stage an electioneering dynamic, supplying in live space much of that tantalizing Republican prerogative of popular choice with which the fiction opens; and it is hard to see why Shakespeare set his knot of critical arbiters aloft in a gallery if the subversive enfranchisement effect was not his intention. Such stagecraft, acknowledging the massed commons as potential king-makers, precisely matched the notable radicalism of the rhetoric: "Let desert in pure election shine" urged Bassianus, explicitly repudiating the principle of hereditary rule: "And Romans, fight for freedom in your choice" (1.1.16–17).[15] Regicidal rebels demanding enfranchisement in *Hamlet* would press the demand in curiously theatrical terms: "Caps, hands, and tongues applaud it to the clouds!" (4.5.103).

2 Henry VI will systematically sustain such stagecraft. What York has achieved with his solicitation is not merely a working of the crowd, in order (like Jack Cade) to "perceive the common's mind" (3.1.374); he has triggered the indignant watchers, vocally interactive, into a kind of a plebiscite, a show of alignment in the coming struggle: and activated their bitter political judgement into complicity with what turns out to be planned insurgence. Crucially, Shakespearean drama will work by such deictic outreach, shredding the possibility of that even-handed, readerly detachment imputed to audiences by centuries of Shakespeare criticism, and replacing it by a fuelled participation, which interpenetrates the unfolding fiction with what we might term 'playhouse action'. Repeatedly needling a discontented commons, then providing cheered spectacles of popular retaliation, we will see that Shakespeare stage-manages in microcosm that national political temptation so feared by contemporary authorities. *2 Henry VI* thus conscripts disaffected Elizabethans into a kind of shadow politics, challenging spectators to a kind of declarative para-activism. Less than action on the streets, it was subversively more than passively inward, imaginary experience. In the context of the national sufferings outlined earlier, of fears for the future, and of a half century of draconian punishment for 'seditious' complaints, the 'virtual' politics of Shakespeare's interactional playhouse must have been sensational.

When York demagogically inflamed the national military and economic angers to foment audience insurgence, he provided the inaugurating instance of the play's political and tonal master-movement: the process that will five times move, with instructive inexorability, from audience goading, into gratifying retaliation, then horror. York, Eleanor, Queen Margaret, Suffolk and Cade will all prove subject to the same fated rhythmic formula.

The play's second scene opens with an action prudently undisclosed by directions in Quarto or Folio.

> *Duchess:* Why droops my lord, like over-ripened corn
> Hanging the head at Cere's plenteous load?
> Why doth the great Duke Humphrey knit his brows,
> As frowning at the favours of the world?
> Why are thine eyes fixed to the sullen earth,
> Gazing on that which seems to dim thy sight?
> What seest thou there? (1.2.1–7)

That seven lines are here allocated to a mere posture of pensiveness may itself alert us to the presence of further theatrical business. The deictic "there", accompanied by references to "the world", "sullen earth", and a fixity of downward stare, suggest, if we seek to reconstruct Gloucester's physical placement on the stage unquietly lapped by groundlings (York has just prowled off, contemning English government), that the duke's absorption transpires as he paces or stands on the platea: his downturned "frowning" at "the world", a gaze over the goaded audience. Gloomily, Gloucester "hang[s] the head" as he takes in—and shares—the angers of the commons: an ire through which York has just deictically won support. Yet unlike York, "the good duke" does not seek retaliatory address, remaining immobilized, "Gazing on that which seems to dim [his] sight." As in scene one, his state remains paradoxical: demotically audience-conscious, yet not directly deictic, Commonwealthman yet officer of state. It is a condition his ambitious wife perceives. That the commons may prove a king-maker, she knows as well as York; and like Lady Macbeth she seeks to rouse her over-principled husband.

> What seest thou there? King Henry's diadem,
> Enchased with all the honours of the world?
> If so, gaze on, and grovel on thy face
> Until thy head be circled with the same. (7–10)

"Grovel" introduces her contempt of the crowd, despite her eagerness to instrumentalize them.

Standing by her husband's side, Eleanor then embarks on a remarkable political dumb-show:

> Put forth thy hand, reach at the glorious gold.
> What, is't too short? I'll lengthen it with mine;
> And having both together heaved it up,
> We'll both together lift our heads to heaven
> And never more abase our sight so low
> As to vouchsafe one glance unto the ground. (11–16)

Hauling up the imagined crown from the commons at their feet, Eleanor mimes her political strategy; and she is ruthlessly clear, as York is not, about the dispensability of the people.

Eleanor's word "abase", which will return in deictic usage throughout the play, often varied as "base" and "abject," embodies in a traditional enough way the inherited medieval world of correspondences, fusing political with spatial meanings of 'high' and 'low'. Though literary critics have long been alert to that material symbolicity of the theatre by which the zone below the trapdoor was associated with the infernal, and elevated space (like Juliet's balcony) signified 'higher' existence, critical recognition of deictic referencing of the poorer audience members—sneeringly dubbed 'groundlings' by Hamlet—has been confined to appreciation of comedic references, jests on "men of *under*standing". We shall see, however, that throughout his career and for a range of purposes, Shakespeare will invoke, like Eleanor, the palpable realm of spectators at the feet of the actors through a deictic tropology of 'ground', 'earth', 'lowliness', 'baseness', and so forth.

Her dream of an ascent assisted 'from below' spurned by her husband, Eleanor recurs to her bitter deixis upon Gloucester's disapproving departure. Impotence renewing her scorn of the commoners even as she disparages Gloucester, a raging Eleanor provokes from the upturned heads below a likely outbreak of carnival targeting:

Follow I must; I cannot go before
While Gloucester bears this base and humble mind.
Were I a man, a duke, and next of blood,
I would remove these tedious stumbling blocks
And smooth my way upon their headless necks. (61–65)

Ebullient in her stage role as popular enemy, Eleanor next switches her wickedness delightedly into comic mode as she invites Hume out upon a raucously ringed stage:

Where are you there! Sir John! Nay, fear not, man.
We are alone. Here's none but thee and I. (68–69)

The combination of malevolence with a grinning wit, that winks the audience into a moment of bonding, was also medieval, a hallmark of the 'Vice': whose legacy would romp on in Richard III, Iago, and others.[16]

Yet to the goading of Eleanor's murderous contumely ("headless necks"), the pleasure of retaliation was swiftly provided. Hume provides it first, with his gloating, clownish exposition of aristocratic plottings, distinctively populist in tone and proverb (100) as he anticipates the Duchess' "wrack" (105): a word whose spoken meaning doubtless doubled as 'rack'. Retaliation by the threatened, insulted groundlings is granted with Eleanor's subsequent exhibition in humiliating criminal uniform (2.4). "Sweet Nell", dreads her husband, "ill can thy noble mind abrook / The abject people gazing on thy face / With envious looks, laughing at thy shame" (11–13). Class-vengeance is in then in full playhouse swing, as the Duchess, barefoot in a white sheet, verses pinned on her back, and surrounded by officers, must undefended cross the hostile boards.

Look how they gaze,
See how the giddy multitude do point
And nod their heads, and throw their eyes on thee.
Ah, Gloucester, hide thee from their hateful looks. (2.4.21–24)

Tenderly counselling "Be patient, Nell; forget this grief" (27), Gloucester, characteristically, acknowledges audience behaviour whilst remaining outside deictic relations. Lamenting, however, that she is "followed with a rabble that rejoice / To see my tears and hear my deep-fet groans", that the people laugh to see her sliced feet (33–37), Eleanor knows herself now "made a wonder and a pointing stock / To every idle rascal follower" (47–48). Yet the Duchess's goading has incurred a retaliation which comes to envelop all in grief. For Shakespeare, consummately confident it seems in his powers of alchemy, now so elaborates the sufferings of the distressed aristocrat, intensifying them through refraction in a helpless husband's agonized eyes, that, by stripping Eleanor down to a suffering common humanity—"To think upon my pomp shall be my hell" (42)—she becomes, *Lear*-like, "the thing itself": the unaccommodated Duchess is no more but such a poor, bare, forked animal as we all are. As husband and wife forever part, he choked with tears (87), she welcoming death (89–93), playhouse vengeance slowly subsides, falters into compassion, falls silent. Lust for retaliation parts with them. It is another form of what we could dub carnival repudiation; and its humane if paradoxical politics comprise, we shall see, in their tutelary iteration, the telos of both the drama and the dramatist.

The identity of Queen Margaret, like that of Dame Eleanor, is centrally constituted by active antagonisation of the groundlings. The play's third scene presents her, along with Suffolk, tearing up supplications from oppressed commoners: among whom is Peter, the Armourer's man, imprinted on audience memory by his comic role (33–36). The queen's scorn of the commons is unappeased even by rending the desperate petitions of the poor, for she caps it with class invective: "Away, base cullions!" (44). The deictic hint in "base" is confirmed by a stream of demonstrative pronouns, whose sweep surely embraced and ironized the populace below as she berates the commoners' petitionary prerogative.

> My Lord of Suffolk, say, *is this* the guise?
> *Is this* the fashions in the court of England?
> *Is this* the government of Britain's isle,
> *And this* the royalty of Albion's king? (46–49; emphasis added)

Her superciliousness hurtles on elsewhere, to focus in particular Dame Eleanor; and it is when that enemy has been brought low, with celebration from the queen in imagery of torture (2.3.40–42), that popular counterstrike is granted, intruding into the palace itself. Peter the prentice is reintroduced, and his ensuing mortal combat becomes the first of two scenes in the play—both invented by Shakespeare—in which a servant slays his master.[17] In violent alteration of his sources, Shakespeare makes the master guilty, and awards to the servant, Peter, innocence, victory and royal praise. Further, stagecraft once again loads the scene politically in a fashion quite lost when the play is merely read: for Peter's opposition to his master amplifies into a conflict of classes, as one group, of several apprentices (added by Shakespeare) confronts another of four well-to-do citizens (the Armourer and three 'neighbours') who can afford to swill charneco (a Portugese wine). If, as seems probable, the two actors with speaking parts flanking Peter are the same pair who had vocally petitioned with him earlier, only to receive laceration of their appeals, then the pattern of class retaliation becomes graphically concretised. Assuredly, "Fear not thy master. Fight for the credit of the prentices!" (74–75) invoked a class antagonism frequently violent on London streets; while reference to heady "double beer"[18] (65), and Salisbury's "see that thou thump thy master well"

(88), introduced insurrectionary and carnival associations into the palace itself (not Smithfield, as in the sources). Peter's comic histrionics (76–82, 99–100), whether or not played by the hilarious Kemp, would presumably attract the sympathy even of audience members in the galleries. Before the watching queen and Suffolk, in prolepsis of Cade's rebellion, lower class violence then wins the day.

Gloucester's murder, successfully plotted by the queen and Suffolk along with the cardinal and York, proves an explosion that drives the king reeling from his palimpsest of denial, leaves him tottering in blasted hostility. Embarking desperately upon the almost fifty lines of the second longest speech in the play (73–121), the queen therefore pitches the rhetorical fight of her life to rescue her own standing and her lover's from the monarch's shell-shocked morosity. Her speech "constitutes", as its most recent editor confesses, "the greatest puzzle in the play, since its dramatic purpose is far from clear. Perhaps it is simply a miscalculation by an inexperienced dramatist."[19] Urging her sufferings in travelling to England, the queen deploys however what we saw in Chapter 2 to be favourite Shakespearean figures for evoking the groundlings: the tropology of sea and wind. The passage thus yields its mystery if we recognise its function as elaborated deictic contrast between the enmity of the 'sea' of commons below her and the even greater cruelty of Henry. The sneering sarcasm of "Make my image but an alehouse sign" (81) launches the provocative anti-populism, continued as she develops the imagery—surely enacted in her stage location—of herself as standing looking out over a hostile turbulence. Complaining she has been "nigh wrecked upon the sea", driven "by awkward wind from England's bank", she notes its "unkind shore" (compare the low-lying imagery of 'abject' people, 'baseness' etc). The 'winds' threaten her not to seek a scorpion's nest by coming closer or setting foot upon this shore; and in response she has "cursed the gentle gusts". Yet out of spite, she claims, "the pretty [petty?] vaulting sea refused to drown me",[20] whilst the rocks, with "their ragged sides", perversely "cowered in the sinking sands." The sea will not kill her, but "left that hateful office unto thee" (83–100), she tells Henry.

At the close of this rousing tour-de-force of deictic *superbia*, there comes a "noise within"—and in a graphic reciprocation of hostility, a wrathful tide of "many commons" washes onstage. "The commons, like an angry hive of bees / That want their leader, scatter up and down / And care not who they sting in his revenge" (125–27). The guiding theatrical logic repaying deictic inflammation with crowd incursion is more streamlined in the quarto, where Margaret's lines are a mere seven, which contain the deictic essence ("wrackt upon the sea", "by awkward winds driven back", "scorpion's nest"), then jump at once to "The Commons like an angrie hive", omitting the folio's three intervening lines (122–24) on "the good Duke's" murder.[21] In the drama's sequel, Richard of Gloucester, contemplating a crown out of reach, will reprise the goading, marine deixis. Unpopular

Richard knows himself "Like one that stands upon a promontory / And spies a far-off shore where he would tread", and "chides the sea that sunders him from thence". The soliloquy's fearsome climax threatens "I'll slay more gazers than the basilisk".[22]

At the close of the queen's speech Henry is silent, immobilized: it is the commoners, demanding Suffolk's exile, who introduce activity and justice. If the little group earlier snubbed as petitioners were prominent among the rebels, retributory justice would again be visually underlined. Either way, thanks to the commons' pressure ("An answer from the King, or we will break all in", 280), thanked by the king (281–82), the queen's sweetheart is exiled: and her heart is broken.

The ensuing parting between Margaret and her love is a sub-scene running to over one hundred and ten lines (302–415). Free of deixis (unless there be hints in the accumulating references to rejecting "the world", ll.364–65, 382), it creates a polar change in tone. Jubilatory revenge yields once more to horror and tragedy, political personae to the vulnerability of private love, as the lovers first seek execrations so terrible as to fix one's hair on end (320), then break down, lamenting frenziedly the loss of their "heart's treasure" (384). By the scene's closure, Shakespeare has so thwarted insurrectionary delight that a music of heartbreak plays, whose tender turns repeatedly prefigure the aching and sublime self-transcendence of parting love in *Romeo and Juliet*. "Banishèd I am, if but from thee" moans Margaret (353). "For where thou art, there is the world itself" echoes desperate Suffolk (364).

Margaret: Go, speak not to me; even now be gone!
　　　　　 O, go not yet . . . (3.2.354–55)

Much anticipates Romeo's balcony scene, and the absolute fidelities of the Capulet tomb:

Now get thee hence. The king, thou know'st, is coming.
If thou be found by me, thou art but dead.

Suffolk: If I depart from thee, I cannot live . . .
　　　　　O, let me stay, befall what may befall! (388–90, 404)

Suffolk's closing words on Margaret's heart—

A jewel, locked into the woefull'st cask
That ever did contain a thing of worth.
Even as a splitted barque, so sunder we—
This way I fall to death (3.2.411–14)

—reprises precisely the imagery of precious jewel and "splitting" shipwreck (97, 414) with which the queen had goaded the audience, recalling the angry commons' responsibility for her grief. That tempest has now been stilled.[23]

Suffolk, however, is made of sterner stuff than Margaret. Following Suffolk's exile, the cardinal dies, in a raving Henry does his best to coat with piety (3.3.31–33); but the pirates, striding armed, and hauling gentry prisoners, into the succeeding scene, will have none of this penitential blather:

> The gaudy, blabbing, and remorseful day
> Is crept into the bosom of the sea;
> And now loud-howling wolves arouse the jades
> That drag the tragic melancholy night;
> Who, with their drowsy, slow, and flagging wings
> Clip dead men's graves, and from their misty jaws
> Breathe foul contagious darkness in the air. (4.1.1–7)

The hard men are here. "Gaudy, blabbing, and remorseful" contemptuously picks up the courtly tones, now to yield to proletarian revenge: the "sea" will bury such genteel histrionics. The marine metaphor here neatly links the groundlings, as goaded by the queen, with the onstage seamen as surrogate avengers. Action now passes to "loud-howling" creatures bringing tragedy, and to "jades" associated with foul contagious breath. 'Dragon' might be a more natural choice for the nocturnal creature of slow and flagging wings than 'jade': but "jade" is a common term of class contempt in Shakespeare—Suffolk will shortly spurn his commoner executioner as a "jady groom" (53).[24] And bad breath ("Breathe foul contagious darkness in the air"), is, we have seen, a frequent deictic signifier for groundlings. The tone of the passage, its conscious, louring menace, engineers a pivotal turn in the play, for this act inaugurates bloody lower-class vengeance, its 'wolves' and 'jades' moving from the sadistic killing of Suffolk to Jack Cade's full-scale revolt. Thus, like Queen Margaret's 'hostile sea' speech, this passage which has attracted critical bafflement and disapproval as elaborate pictorial excrescence reveals ingenious dramaturgical design as a deictically heightened music.

Suffolk of course has been habitual in scorn of "the commons, rude unpolished hinds" (3.2.273), tearing up their petitions, ridiculing their embassy to the king, and trusts here to his birth for ransom from the pirates: "Look on my George—I am a gentleman" (4.1.30). His survival strategy is the blazoning of his place, to shrivel the pirate lieutenant, he thinks, with the terrible heat of his class exaltation: "Obscure and lowly swain, King Henry's blood, / The honourable blood of Lancaster, / Must not be shed by such a jady groom. / Hast thou not kissed thy hand and held my stirrup? / Bare-headed plodded by my foot-cloth mule?" (51–55). Meeting only resolved hatred, he bursts into a rage of class insult, suggestive of audience indication in the usual spatial metaphors: "O that I were a god, to shoot forth thunder / Upon *these* paltry, servile, *abject* drudges. /

Small things make *base* men proud . . . It is impossible that I should die / By such a *lowly* vassal as thyself" (104–06, 110–111, emphases added). As the ghastly converse sinks in, Whitmore's goading presses the thematic: "Now will ye stoop?" (121). But Suffolk is absolute for death in class vilification.

> Suffolk's imperial tongue is stern and rough,
> Used to command, untaught to plead for favour.
> Far be it we should honour *such as these*
> With humble suit. No, rather let my head
> *Stoop* to the block than these knees *bow* to any . . .
> [or] stand uncovered to the vulgar groom." (123–27, 130; emphases added)

A minute later, Whitmore strews his head and body on the stage: two separate places.

That a scene of screaming class-conflict climaxing in the cold-blooded murder of an unarmed member of the royal family could make it past the censor was remarkable; more remarkable still was the skill through which Shakespeare made this possible. It helped that the chronicles supported it, and that the death-blow fell off-stage. More subtle was the textual camouflage of the class-dimension. The executory commoners, notably, do not reciprocate Suffolk's seigneurial invective with underclass vitriol: Suffolk is arraigned, rather, on the lengthy charge of betraying England ("By thee Anjou and Maine were sold to France" etc (86–104), and executed in ostensible defence of traditional order and patriotism. It is *Suffolk's* language—a language surely 'natural' enough to the courtly Master of the Revels—that pushes the scope and tenor of the scene, for an audience of commons, beyond loyal requital of crimes against England into a *class*-punishment of aristocratic arrogance, transmuting it from patriotism into rebellion. Further, the performance values in the commons amphitheatre must have flamboyantly re-centralized class animus, for Suffolk's sneers on 'base' men and 'lowly' grooms extended his contempt to the audience beneath him, thus conscripting its insulted partisanship. The deictic process would have been imperceptible to the censor, however, who reviewed the text, not the playhouse performance. Shakespeare's scene was a triumph for rebellion on more than one level.

The action then modulates, in the now familiar pattern, from goading to retaliation into horror. The manner of the pirates, aside from the superb patriotic arraignment (71–103)—which actually draws on indictments of Suffolk drawn up in the contemporary House of Commons [25]—is savage and debased; their affect in the coming murder not righteous indignation or the audience's buoyant animosity, but a close-in gloating, an intimacy of sadism (note the different tones behind 'thee'), which seeks to twist the knife.

Suffolk: I charge thee, waft me safely cross the Channel.
Whitmore: Come, Suffolk, I must waft thee to thy death. (115–16)

Whitmore's mutilated appearance, bleeding from a bandaged eye-socket (26), could only heighten the effect.

Conversely, Suffolk near death grows admirable in courage—"More can I bear than you dare execute" (132). He even begins to attract pathos before the end. The "we" in "Far be it we should honour such as these" (125), as he trembles, alone of all his class before implacable killers ("It is thee I fear", he has just confessed, 119), underlines not just a farcically inappropriate hubris but his ironic, desperate solitariness. His closing lines

> Come 'soldiers', show what cruelty ye can,
> That this my death may never be forgot (134–35)

transcends class arrogance for heroic personal magnificence: unsettling any hooting simplicity of revenging delight.

In the Jack Cade section succeeding Suffolk's murder, the rhythm of goading, retaliation and horror is sufficiently clear to require little demonstration: particularly as Chapter 3 tracks the shifting tonalities in some detail. The long outbreak of exuberant class revenge followed cumulative goading through the first three acts: the murder of Gloucester, the catalogue of crimes against commonwealth examined in Chapter 4 (military fiasco, overtaxation, unpaid troops, torture and Martial Law), the fecklessness of a cowardly monarch among 'noblemen' who resembled almost butchers in an abattoir.[26] As rebellion breaks out, stagecraft again supplies payback, as the sudden skip out of grisly realism into carnival mode wins the audience through festivity of wit amid play-world violence. Buttressing pro-rebel feeling is Shakespeare's deployment of 'tactical echo': Suffolk's screeches of class-abuse—"groom", "base' and "drudge" (53, 105)—are just minutes later hurled by Stafford at Cade's followers in demanding their surrender: "Rebellious hinds, the filth and scum of Kent . . . / forsake this groom"; "will you credit this base drudge's words . . ." (4.2.109, 111, 136). Cade then pitches a clearly deictic appeal: "It is to you, good people, that I speak"; and following some merriment, Stafford and his ilk are jeered off: "And will you credit this base drudge's words?" "Ay, marry, will we— therefore get ye gone" (116, 136,137). It is tempting to construe as similarly deictic appeal Cade's "And you that love the commons, follow me! . . . Spare none but such as go in clouted shoon, / For *they* are thrifty, honest men, and such / As would, but that they dare not, take our parts" (165, 168–70, emphasis added). The deictic dimension must have been hard to miss in the suddenly hilarious alarm of the messenger, bursting upon the king: "The rebels are in Southwark—fly, my lord!" (4.4.26).[27]

Return from the carefree carnivalesque to sombre naturalism, the repudiation of hilarity for horror, was produced, we saw, with the trial of Saye, and once more works through the personal touch: "Why dost thou quiver, man?" "The palsy, and not fear, provokes me" (4.7.83–84). When our revels are all ended, cold vengeance repels: Saye is executed despite Cade's confession of the injustice (96–97); Saye's bleeding head, and Cromer's, are brought on atop poles and made to "kiss"; and Cade now dwindles to that simple barbarian status so often remarked by critics ignoring all else: "Kill and knock down!" (4.7.145). Furthering audience alienation, indiscriminate assault commences against the London commons: "Up Fish Street! Down St. Magnus Corner! . . . Throw them into the Thames!" (145–46).

Audience-rebel relations being now reversed from bonding with companion revellers to dissociation from an ugly mob, the spectators watch, with new objectivity, a fresh appeal with deictic overtone: this one from the king's ambassador, Old Clifford.

Clifford:　What say ye, countrymen? Will ye relent
　　　　　　And yield to mercy while 'tis offered you,
　　　　　　Or let a rebel lead you to your deaths?
　　　　　　Who loves the king and will embrace his pardon,
　　　　　　Fling up his cap, and say "God save his majesty."
　　　　　　Who hateth him and honours not his father,
　　　　　　Henry the Fifth, that made all France to quake,
　　　　　　Shake he his weapon at us, and pass by.
All:　　　God save the king! God save the king! (4.7.154–62)

Pressing the point, Clifford urges "To France! To France! And get what you have lost!", whereon the rebels whoop their new loyalty: "A Clifford! A Clifford! We'll follow the King and Clifford!" (191, 195–96). The rapidity of the *volte face*, coupled with the summons to warfare overseas—which was surely just what many playgoers were currently *fearing*—further distances an already alienated audience; and Clifford's use of terms suggesting audience behaviour ("What say ye? . . . Who loves the king . . . Fling up his cap") could crystallize within the round O the spectators' refusal so to do. Indeed, that a blood-soaked mob waving heads on poles responds so enthusiastically to the call to invade France, carries that implication of militarism as murder articulated by Williams in *Henry V*. Cade's comment to the audience, "Was ever feather so lightly blown to and fro as this multitude? The name of Henry the Fifth hales them to an hundred mischiefs" (197–99) would heighten audience apperception of their rejection of the appeal.

Within the interactional world of simulated political action that is Shakespeare's playhouse, the mechanism of deictic triggering has here achieved an important goal. Manipulating self-awareness in group-dissent—these commoners do *not* throw up their caps—it has provided a salutary instance of education against manipulability, establishing the experience of critical self-detachment from official political rhetoric. The rebels are still in Southwark: but their secession is on a shrewder plane. The process offered, in short, a fine instance of that "thinking above the action" which was the goal of Bertolt Brecht: and which increasingly he discovered in Shakespeare's plays, producing them with demystifying effects in view. "Couldn't one do it just as it is, only with skilful direction?" is his last recorded entry in his working diary.[28]

Final horror of the Cade revolt is another butchery: his own. Chapter 3 argued the audience identification with Cade as fugitive soldier, hungry commoner, and clown, as well as Shakespeare's targeting of Iden, through what we might call 'deictic blunder': the booming of his audience-ignorant ownership claims to the locality. We may here note Shakespeare's reinforcement of sympathy for Cade through structural contrast with the Peter Thump scene. As before, a comical, populist little man (see 4.9.44–49) confronts a prosperous superior; and almost certainly the same actor (possibly Kemp) reprised the underdog role, with its Chaplinesque moments of winking to the audience, and threatening his sword. The Big Man has once more his group of supporters, here five henchmen (36): but the Little Man now has no-one. The 'replay', so easily underlined by performance echo, sets up an ominous abandonment effect.[29] A visual echo preserved in the script further heightens the pathos. The armourer, overthrown, had cried "Hold, Peter, hold—I confess": and hold it seems the little man did. He appears to have lowered his weapon, which then was then taken from him, at York's command (2.3.96). When small Cade, however, sprawls onto his back in death, gentleman Iden drives his weapon in fury repeatedly into the body: "as I thrust thy body in with my sword, / So wish I I might thrust thy soul to hell" (75–76). What the asymmetry drives in, along with Iden's sword, is the drama's master theme: the untenable brutality of political revenge.

In the wake of accumulated horrors, Shakespeare's art returns us, in the play's final act, to a kind of deictic coda, which counterpoints act one. As the insurgence he had secretly confided to the audience materialises, York launches the climax of a final deictic appeal.

York's fortunes with the audience already have fluctuated. Following his earnest early bonding with the commons ("'tis thine they give away"), he has kept up the special relationship through asides, as at 3.1.87–92. No-one else but Cade addresses us through asides.[30] York has also offered a little deictic jest. Leading two deictically 'sightless' peers onstage into full hearing of the audience, York opens the scene with "Now, my good lords of Salisbury and Warwick, / Our simple supper ended, give me leave / In *this close walk* to satisfy myself / In craving your opinion of my title" (2.2.1–4, emphasis added). It is the same deictic pratfall to which Dame Eleanor had summoned Hume (1.2.69), and through which Shakespeare had undone Iden (4.9.15, 30–33); and Shakespeare now renders Warwick 'naive' and York winkingly knowing as the former unwittingly perpetuates the joke.[31] "Then, father Salisbury, kneel we together, / And in this *private plot* be we the first / That shall salute our rightful sovereign" (59–61, emphasis added). York's role in the conspiracy against Gloucester, however, begins to dissolve commons sympathy, as does the murderous hubris of his articulation, when—like the Earl of Essex, Bullingbrooke, Henry V and Hamlet in their bi-polar class-swings—he treacherously slips gear from the demotic into the seigneurial ("now we three have spoke it, / It skills not greatly who impugns our doom", 3.1.280–81). Tellingly, his next soliloquy (3.1.331–383) is the drama's longest speech, and it is practically deixis-free. "Let pale-faced fear keep with the mean-born man" (335) only consolidates the alienation. He remains thereafter a backgrounded figure. It is much the same process that Shakespeare will employ in 'carnival repudiation' of central characters like Richard III, Falstaff, Toby Belch, Thersites, and Iago, who early in a play will 'bond' through asides and plebeian humour, only to have their creator phase out their sparkling wit to leave cruel behaviour stark in chilled moral distantiation.[32]

When act five, therefore, finds York sweeping back onstage at the head of a rebel army, an estranged audience is already out of sympathy with him. Shakespeare's manipulation, however, must be 'over-determined' to ensure its efficacy with audiences both heterogenous and volatile; and so, abetting the disidentification with York, comes careful dramaturgic timing. In the deep-seated mythopoeia of the Middle Ages and Renaissance, the ending of carnival should inaugurate Lent: cooled season of virtuous social discipline. When, however, Cade's rebellion terminates in executed leader and yoked-neck rebels, no sooner is Cade thrust through than another rebel army swarms onstage, its leader commanding further carnival behaviour ("Ring, bells, aloud; burn bonfires, clear and bright", 5.1.3), [33] and spouting the same crude ambition with naked megalomaniac gloating: "Let them obey that knows not how to rule; / This hand was made to handle naught but gold" (6–7). His imagery of hewing sheep and oxen directly echoes Cade (5.1.27; 4.3.3). Such sequencing in Shakespeare's very free handling of the chronicles in 5.1 establishes powerful subliminal aversion to York's insurrection. Catastrophically violating ancient social rhythm, it thrusts maniacally upward at the very point when carnival energies have been expended, we have supped full with horrors, and a fresh season should relieve surfeit. The invading army confronting the English is moreover Irish: a scalp-lifting image straight from a centuries-long nightmare.[34] Their presumable appearance will underscore the infamy: unlike Cade's rebels, they enter with drum and colours, and the 'galloglasses' and 'kerns' are said to be wearing "proud array" (4.8.27–28). The former perhaps bear their characteristic axes. Contrast is sharp with the "ragged staves" [35] and homely, even slapstick appearance of the English rebels ("Come and get thee a sword, though made of a lath": 4.2. 1–2).

The imminent confrontation between York and king is postponed briefly by Iden's entry with the severed head of Cade. Inspected by Henry, who underlines its significance through three lines of description in Quarto (a passage [H1r] perhaps reflecting Shakespeare's minor revision of foul papers),[36] the bloody object remains presumably visible throughout the scene, in the hands of the newly knighted Iden. Only at this point does York "unloose [his] long imprisoned thoughts" (88) with a grotesque Cadeian hauteur ("False king, why hast thou broken faith with me?"

[91])—underlined in Henry's astonishment by his "bedlam and ambitious humour" (130). The rebellion York had long since secretly promised the audience has finally arrived: "Give place! By heaven, thou shalt rule no more" (104). As Somerset strides forward to arrest him ("Obey, audacious traitor; kneel for grace" [108]), York flourishes his trump card:

> Would'st have me kneel? First let me ask of *these*
> If they can brook I bow a knee to man. (Arden editions, 109–10;
>   italics mine)

Given the absence of any clear referent within the fiction—York has neither troops nor kinsmen on stage—the cry flings out across the auditorium to embrace and activate the massed spectators. This is, literally, a plebiscite: as terminus of the drama's virtual politics, and telos of York's practised demoticism, popular forces are invited to break, yet again, into national politics. At this traumatic moment, Henry and his nobles may turn, like Simpcox, suddenly 'sighted', abruptly cognizant of two thousand people or more surrounding them: a brusquely revealed private army.

Failing to find sense in these lines, the Oxford *Complete Works* and the derivative Norton edition omit them entirely (though all others preserve them, including Roger Warren's more recent Oxford edition of the drama). The lines, however, are not a sloppy Shakespeare's forgetfulness that York's sons are not onstage, but a brilliant Shakespeare's deployment of deixis, as climax to the political stagecraft closely governing audience sympathies. Prudentially camouflaging the deixis with an *ensuing* command, "Sirrah, call in my sons to be my bail" (Norton 109), the playwright's art has built into his script a performance-activated 'stagecraft secret', contriving that York's appeal rings outs, once again, to the audience.

And the appeal falls—given York's vicissitudes with the audience, the arhythmic reprise of carnival, and the threatfulness of York's Irish army—upon hostile ears. "Call in my *sons* to be my bail. / I know, ere *they* will have me go to ward, / *They'll* pawn their swords" (110–11, emphases added) indeed suggests wounded overtones of deafening audience silence, the plebeian imagery hinting deictic rebuke. If York's opening plebiscite (1. 1.217–20) had been a referendum, this one proves a recall.

Somewhere in the background still hangs Cade's severed head: in the hands, presumably, of the tellingly silent Iden.[37] As Cade's slayer looks on, and as Cade's head dangles, or even drips, the court degenerates into open baronial mutiny and chaos ("He is arrested, but will not obey", 134). The visible juxtaposition created between the inert head of the rebel commoner and the duke's violent magnitude of anarchy is charged with political suggestion, retrospectively diminishing Cade's crimes before the eclipsing, true source of maniacal anarchy. The body-language of the inevitably appalled Iden—holding up the rebel's head, perhaps, to gaze bewilderedly into its suddenly insignificant face, then back, aghast, at York—could prove, like

Alexander Court's motions in *Henry V*, a silent but devastating framing device: redirecting indictment.[38] Commentary projected through silent framing actions would have been loud and clear under Elizabethan acting conditions: since players were trained in a repertoire of conventional expressive gestures to accompany every passion, silence could speak. ("There was speech in their dumbness, / Language in their very gesture.")[39]

The drama then closes in confused irresolution, as neither clueless Henry nor bedlam York, neither "holy Harry" the distant king dithering in the *locus*,[40] nor the repudiated demagogue decamped from the *platea*, attract our sympathies. Wit and deixis withdrawn, universal distantiation reigns; only slaughter and horror remain to engage the spectators: "York not our old men spares; / No more will I their babes" (5.3.51–52). The demystified vision is well summed up in Richard of Gloucester's cheerfully malevolent "Priests pray for enemies, but princes kill" (5.2.6): itself preceded by an anti-populist jibe ("So lie thou there—/ . . . underneath an alehouse' paltry sign", 1–2). It is in this bleak condition, as fractious court turns feral jungle, that Salisbury urges the right to cancel fealty ("It is great sin to swear unto a sin, / But greater sin to keep a sinful oath", 5.1.180–81): a conjuncture which, counterposing the strong appeal of its sentiment and speaker, just discussed, forces the daring moment into an overdetermined microcosm of terminal ambivalence.

One last deictic suggestion underscores the audience's political alienation. Directly the queen propels Henry, with "We shall to London get where you are loved" (5.4.10), Young Clifford bursts in to declare "Fly you must; uncurable discomfit / Reigns in the hearts of all our present parts" (15–16).

NEGATIVE DIALECTICS

With brooding historical acuity, the drama has throughout recognised an angry commons as formidable political agency, potential king-making powers in its feared grasp: "By flattery hath he won the commons' hearts, / And when he please to make commotion, / 'Tis to be feared they all will follow him" (3.1.28–30; compare 3.1.240). Eleanor's mime of stooping low to the groundlings to pull up the crown (1.2.1–17) gave the principle graphic emblematic definition. Indeed the play's folio version, judging by its cuts, was well aware of the play's seditious preoccupation with successful insurgence, and prudently excised, for instance, both Warwick's confidence he could raise "ten thousand Ragged-staves" (Q1, TLN 792), and Cade's execution of a sergeant (ibid., 1834–53). Rebellion, the nightmare of the Tudor state, was released in *2 Henry VI* from historical narrative into playhouse reality by an order of deictic language and manipulation, inflaming the spectators and compelling them to judgement, to the rousing or refusal of allegiance. Bristling with anti-courtly angers, the first three acts confronted spectators with topical national disasters and administrative mismanagement, along with a gallery of sneering or murderous courtiers, then elevated the commons (3.2) as heroic negation of court malfeasance. Act four, however, swung in pendular reaction *against* commons agency, as the pirate scene and Cade's revolt descended ultimately into atrocity. Manifestly schooled in Hegel, Shakespeare patterned a negation of the negation. In the absence of creative sublation, however, Shakespeare's ends as a sterile dialectic. Warwick's summary that closes the play—"Now by my hand, lords, 'twas a glorious day" (5.5.34)—is bitterly risible.

Even before the rebellions of act four, disaffection, inflamed by goading (Eleanor, Margaret and Suffolk), had been granted retaliation, only to find itself rapidly undermined: compelled by repulsion or compassion to wilt, shame-faced, into ambivalence. Shakespeare's telos of humanitarian clemency here, admirable at any point in history, is the more noble in his fanatical age of religious and political mutilation and disembowellment; yet generalised into a guiding principle, the logic would perhaps effect political paralysis. (Sparing the life of a Suffolk, for instance, would itself guarantee civil war.) The worst characteristics of the aristocracy, furthermore—mutiny, religious trickery, summary execution, fickleness, naive pietism, megalomania, revenge killing—were all matched by commoners, generalised into a network of pessimistic class parallelisms that conclude a common humanity virtually bereft of political hope.[41] To borrow a fine phrase of Ronald Knowles, "We confront not the farce of subplot but the possible farce of history."[42] The drama thus presents a kind of sustained review of contemporary political consciousness, featuring 'plebiscites' and popular insurgency effects, that moves within thoroughgoing demystification of both courtly and popular revolt to an endpoint mistrust of political involvement *per se*.[43] "Trust nobody, for fear you be betrayed" (4.4.57).

In the modern academy, so gloomily Derridean a procedure, purging away the last particle of positivity in a remorseless display of mandarin *kenosis*, may well represent a prosperous bourgeois *trahison des clercs*, a rationale of the well-fed for a life spent politically supine; and Shakespeare's absence of revolutionary confidence has sometimes so been read. But in the conditions of the 1590s, this political vision was radical. *2 Henry VI* closes with no theatrical reconciliation to the incompetent court it so lucidly exhibits, replete with vacillating monarch, corrupt senior statesman, and anarchic nobility. Nor has it truck with aristocratic reformism. It has educated spectators, to the contrary, against manipulation by the national elite: taught them *not* to fling their caps in the air when the honed rhetoric of ambitious lord or the monarchy's men—of the Earl of Essex, or Queen Elizabeth seeking troops—attempts their flattered seduction. Clinched in the compelled audience frigidity toward York's climactic appeal in act five, Elizabethan theatregoers have learned a clear-eyed class-skepticism. Limited commons revolt may have its rewards, but trust in noblemen is naivety; and vengeful slaughter breeds only horror. In *2 Henry VI* Shakespeare was already at work propagating the pregnant radical stance of humane political estrangement.

6 Carnival Dynamics and *The Taming Of The Shrew*

> Why should a man whose blood is warm within
> Sit like his grandsire cut in alabaster?
> > (*Merchant of Venice*, 1.1.83–84)

> The rabblement hooted, and clapped their chapped hands, and threw
> up their sweaty nightcaps, and uttered such a deal of stinking breath
> . . . If the tag-rag people did not clap him and hiss him, according as
> he pleased and displeased them, as they use to do the players in the
> theatre, I am no true man.
> > (*Julius Caesar*, 1.2.243–45, 256–58)

Shakespeare's plays, we have seen, did not unfold within the neutral atmosphere of polite expectancy prevailing in theatres today: our quiet, respectable audiences induced into passivity by fixed seating, into anonymity by the darkening of the auditorium, and into silence by the raising of the curtain. Neither were the intellective conditions intended for the plays' decipherment those of the scholar's solitary desk. For Elizabethan drama, opening action supervened upon a loudly predisposed world: upon a sea of spirited spectators, restless and gusty, buoyed by emancipation from customary restraints of class and ideology. If the performance was delayed, they might pelt the tiring house curtain with fruit.[1] It was upon that massing groundswell of festal energy, I would argue, that much in Shakespeare's plays moved; and it is by analysis of Shakespeare's manipulations of such in-house momentum that we can perceive his dramaturgy achieving many of its political special effects. Yet Shakespeare, Christ-like, could swiftly still the roaring waves. The boisterous sea mutated, under the spell of controlling genius, between the tone and manner of a holiday-making crowd and that of a rapt and silenced audience. Where the previous chapter emphasised Shakespeare's strategic activation of the interactional principle, the following will focus his politicised inflammation, channelling, or obstruction of the ready carnival surge. Shakespeare's scripts reveal, I suggest, a distinctive repertoire of master principles of energy manipulation—carnival dynamics as I will term them—grounded in dramatic confrontation of those free waves of jubilant high spirits and truant antipathy to authority. Astonishingly, Shakespeare seems to have mastered an entire range of such manipulations of the carnivalesque as early as *The Taming of the Shrew* (seemingly written c. 1590–91); and brief survey of these techniques will allow us, in effect, to chart much basic structure in that play. Such was Shakespeare's skill, I shall argue, in turning festive auditorium responsiveness against the ideological enunciations of that play's textual surface that generations of modern critics, raised to the page, have missed the radicalism of the stage.

CARNIVAL BONDING

Most easily identifiable among these dynamics is the process we might term carnival bonding, whereby the audience identifies with characters stimulating its buoyancy of gleeful release and holiday licence. Such spontaneous bonding with figures of jest and misrule would have been virtually inevitable in the opening minutes of any Elizabethan drama playing in the amphitheatres, before audience mood quietened towards the pleasures of percipience through absorption in Shakespeare's narrative complexities. In *Shrew*, as drunken Christopher Sly capers, hoots, and defies the threats of order—

Sly: I'll feeze you in faith!
Hostess: A pair of stocks, you rogue!
Sly: You're a baggage! . . .
Hostess: I know my remedy, I must go fetch the headborough
Sly: Third or fourth or fifth borough, I'll answer him by law! I'll not budge an inch, boy! (*Taming of the Shrew*, Induction, 1–3, 9–11)[2]

—the uproarious, visceral vitality in execrating authority, the exuberance of disinhibition, come straight from the world of carnival. Effortlessly effected in these early moments, such bonding is easily recuperable at later dramatic conjunctures, as revellers, jesters and transgressors conscript foundational in-house energies to precipitate them against structures of political and patriarchal authority. Lewd and ludic, disreputably incontinent, they embody and satisfy a theatrical orientation ebullient, iconoclastic and demystifying in mood, location and appetite.

The powerful appeal of such characters has been widely noted, of course, and Spivack's discussion of the emergence of many such from the Vice figure in medieval Morality plays—"his residual emotion is a limitless, amoral merriment, heightened by his jubilation over the success of his intrigue"—remains an indispensable study.[3] Yet the seditious *politics* of carnival bonding require underscoring. David Scott Kastan, for example, has well observed Falstaff to be "the sign of the play's resistance to the totalizations of power", his charisma threatening the primacy of kingship's narrative, and problematizing the play's very genre. "His exuberance and excess will not be incorporated into the stabilizing hierarchies of the body politic."[4] From Robert Weimann has come a landmark advance— its resonances still unincorporated in most critical discussion of individual dramas—in demonstrating the in-building of populist, anti-authoritarian perspective at the very structural level in Tudor dramaturgy through stage-craft convention. Weimann argues the medieval transmission of theatrical representation through a crucially class-nuanced spatial duality. The *locus* of any scene (the fictive location, symbolized by stool, throne, soldiers, etc., established upstage, or in a discovery space or upper gallery) is counter-pointed by a *platea*, into which the *locus* shades downstage in Tudor the-atre: a broad common zone or "unlocalized place" wherein plot merges with the here and now, and characters interact with the audience. "Shake-speare's theatre," argues Weimann, "did take on and expand some of the *platea*'s basic functions", establishing "a flexible relationship between the play world and the real world", with "deliberately varied degrees of dissoci-ation from illusionistic action". Establishing "the most intense interplay" of fictiveness and actuality, of mimesis and self-expression, the presentational duality entailed, argues Weimann, "the absence of a structural division between monologue and dialogue."[5] My own readings of Shakespearean drama uncover precisely this latter principle, traced in the extraordinarily recurrent and transformative workings of deixis. "An awareness of the the-atrical dimensions of this drama", declares Weimann in a tantalizing aside extended into brilliant but only fragmentary dramatic applications, "can best illuminate those deeper ambiguities which undermine the supposed orthodoxy of some of those plays."[6]

In medieval dramaturgy, it was on the *platea* that festive action took place; and in the *figurenposition* of Tudor drama, characters stationed there assume "a special relationship" with the audience, "even when direct address has been abandoned." Within a deeply encoded semantics of stage placement, these figures (Weimann instances Falstaff, Thersites, Apemantus, Richard III, Feste, Belch, Iago, Lear's Fool, and Hamlet at moments) "exist outside of the heroic, courtly, or romantic ethos of the main or state action". They are identifiable to us, and endeared themselves to contemporary popular audi-ences massed at hand, not only by sportiveness, jest, and wordplay but by demotic diction, everyday reference and proverbial speech, "rooted in the common experience and inherited traditions of the people."[7]

CARNIVAL TARGETING

Less self-evident than carnival bonding in Shakespeare's political drama-turgy is a companion process we can term carnival targeting. It was not only through a complicity of laughter, bonding with the bearers of carnival, that anti-authoritarian feeling was transmitted, but through the drama-tist's engineering of repulsion ("I'll so offend to make offence a skill"),[8] produced in a kind of graphic aristocratism of oppression. Dukes, lords and patricians will thus at key moments antagonise the community of revelry through an exercise of power variously displaying draconian threatening, brusque suppression of pleasure, or denigrative class arrogance. As with bonding, targeting effects were particularly potent in the earliest moments of any drama, and a number of plays open with figures alienating in their manner of authority. Seigneurial threatening of innocence, for instance, will have triggered audience hostility. In *A Midsummer Night's Dream*, a coldly hierarchical Duke Theseus overrules passionate young love ("either prepare to die / For disobedience to your father's will, / . . . Or on Diana's altar to protest / For aye austerity and single life", 1.1.86–87, 89–90), just as Duke Solinus commences *A Comedy of Errors* with stony pronouncement of death, declaiming that "rigorous statutes" and "solemn synods" "Exclude[s] all pity from our threat'ning looks" (1.1.9–10, 13). Both Dukes, having frigidly claimed immitigability of law, change their minds when the mood takes them, waiving the law in act five. Such capricious partiality "turn(s) preordinance and first decree / Into the law of children", in Julius Caesar's phrasing (3.1.38–39).

Alternatively, carnival targeting may proceed through class vituperation. The predictable impact upon commoners is explicit in the counselling of Hotspur against "Pride, haughtiness, opinion, and disdain, / The least of which haunting a nobleman / Loseth men's hearts, and leaves behind a stain" (*I Henry IV* 3.1.181–83). *The Tempest*'s opening is one of the clearest theatrical examples, as common sailors working to preserve all on board from shipwreck are interrupted by courtly passengers, requiring, amidst the mariners' frantic efforts, their observance of customary hierarchic decorum. The irritated response of the boatswain is manifestly deictic, invoking the unquiet waves of the audience: "What care these roarers for the name of king?" Inviting a councillor, in hilarious taunt, "Use your authority" (1.1.15–16, 20), the desperately busy Boatswain is then assaulted by his social superiors with a volley of class abuse ("you bawling, blasphemous, incharitable dog" etc, 36–43).

Targeting could be effected, too, by what we might call carnival suppression, the authoritarian squelching of theatrical gratification. It is for attempting precisely this that Malvolio is targeted in *Twelfth Night*, as he fails, to audience delight, to quell the songful roistering of Belch and Aguecheek: yet critics have overlooked Shakespeare's application of the same punitive technique to heads of state. In *Measure*, for instance, at the very approach of Duke Vincentio, one of the most enchanting songs in Shakespeare—"Take, O take those lips away / That so sweetly were forsworn . . ." (4.1.1–6)—is interrupted, and its singer bundled offstage ("Break off thy song, and haste thee quick away"), with profuse apologies to authority for such indulgence ("[I] well could wish / You had not found me here so musical"). The duke concurs with both dismissal and dismissiveness: "music oft hath such a charm / To make bad good, and good provoke to harm" (7, 10–11,14–15). Yet one of the great delights for commoners in attending the amphitheatres was, of course, precisely that there they might hear professional musicians who performed on occasion even for Queen Elizabeth; so that banishing and disparaging an exquisitely rendered "concord of sweet sounds" (*Merchant*, 5.1.83) must have struck an ugly dissonance with audience mood.

Twelfth Night opens with much the same stagecraft tactic, producing from one of the most beautiful and widely anthologised poetic passages in Shakespeare—"If music be the food of love, play on"—a political alienation invisible on the page. The spell of music begins, the stage direction suggests, before lord and retinue enter ("Music. Enter Orsino" etc.). Since played for a ducal court, and designed for the delight of an extravagantly aesthetic nobleman addicted to "sweet beds of flowers" (1.1.39), there can be no question that this music is delicious. For how long does this rapture, which comes "o'er [the] ear like the sweet sound / That breathes upon a bank of violets", caress the audience? It may be just for seconds; but it may be for several minutes. What is clear is that when Duke Orsino enters, ravished by esteem of his own sensibility, our pleasure in this spell is immediately imperilled, as the duke imposes his ownership of it—effectively dispossessing the audience—through capricious, controlling orders. As soon as he enters, Orsino waves ducal permission for continuance ("play on"). Another imperative immediately follows—"Give me excess of it"— only to be followed almost at once by a peremptory dismissal snapped out: "Enough, no more, / Tis not so sweet now as it was before" (1.1.1–2, 7–8). The politics of the killjoy effect here has never, to the best of my knowledge, been remarked. Possibly literary responsiveness has been unconsciously lulled by broad parallel of imagery and mood with Keats' 'Ode to a Nightingale'; but the gorgeous music in this sequence does not fade by nature, or cease upon a midnight with no pain. Suppressed at lordly whim, its brusque elimination surely kindles annoyance in the audience from whom it has been stolen: filliping that hostility toward dictatorial authority which was regularly to hand in the gamehouse in a play's opening minutes.

It may even be that Orsino's succeeding exclamation, "O spirit of love, how quick and fresh art thou", is a comic response to audience frustration, as just expressed in a swell of irritated groundling gestures or even frustrated outcry. That Shakespeare may be scripting here a deictic goading of the close-packed auditors is a conjecture the likelier for Orsino's imagery: he addresses, after all, a degrading "*sea*"; and he claims that "naught enters" this sea "But *falls* into abatement and *low price* / Even in a minute!" (9–14; italics mine).

Interpreting the opening of *Twelfth Night* in this fashion may strike the reader as simply perverse ingenuity. Conditioned as we are, however, by our centuries-old conventions of the proscenium stage, of fixed-feature auditorium proxemics, and of theatre as a sociofugal rather than sociopetal space (i.e. as a spatiality that keeps individuals sequestered in privacy, like executive offices or waiting rooms, as opposed to bringing them, like a French café or pop concert, into cohesion and sensed community),[9] we are today disablingly remote from the interactional subcodes of Elizabethan dramaturgy. Accordingly, convincing the modern reader of such Shakespearean encodings can result only from demonstrating the myriad examples of such constructed latency, recurrent as a central feature of Shakespearean playwrighting.

If, in the light of the pattern of carnival dynamics, we return now to *The Taming of the Shrew*, we can appreciate what may be Shakespeare's pioneering of carnival targeting, for hard upon the hilarity of Sly's exuberant defiance enters the very prototype of the antagonising peremptory autocrat, mingling insult with brusque command. Announced before entry by hunting horns—and hunting, we shall see in *As You Like It*, was the very embodiment of fiercely resented aristocratic privilege—this lord strides onstage with a hail of commands: "Huntsman, I charge thee, tender well my hounds. / Breathe Merriman . . . And couple Clowder with the deep-mouthed brach" (Induction 1.11–13). Since many in the egalitarian gamehouse will be temporary escapees, as servants, apprentices or women, from precisely such household dragooning, it is not hard to deduce majority responsiveness here. This lord, moreover, makes it clear that he cares more for the dogs than for the commoners at his command, for he rattles off the names of no less than five of his hounds (lines 13–22) but never names his listening huntsmen or servingmen. He then proves unable to recall the names of the players: "I have forgot your name" (82). Such values were precisely the target of contemporary underclass complaint: that the wealthy showed more concern for horses and hounds than for their servingmen is an accusation made in More's *Utopia*, and echoed by Shakespeare in both Jack Cade and Orlando. The comparison of poor men and dogs ("Ay, in the catalogue ye go for men, / As hounds and greyhounds, mongrels, spaniels, curs, / Shoughs, water-rugs, and demi-wolves are clept / All by the name of dogs" etc.) recurs in *Macbeth*, again in the context of overlord contumely (3.1. 93–96). Coriolanus, endlessly denigrating Rome's plebeians in bestial terms, will likewise praise a commoner and then prominently forget his name (1.10.81–91). *King John* lends the theme comic modulation, in the newly knighted Faulconbridge: "if his name be George I'll call him Peter, / For new-made honour doth forget men's names; / 'Tis too respective and too sociable" (*King John*, 1.1.186–88).

Shrew's lord, proceeding briskly to class insult ("the beggar, 37"), explicitly animalises Sly ("O monstrous beast! How like a swine he lies", 30), and exploits him for personal amusement as if he were indeed a beast ("I will practise on this drunken man", 32). Sneering at drunkenness in the carnivalesque amphitheatre ("how foul and loathsome is thine image", 31) would of course further antagonise the surrounding pleasure-bound audience, many of whose members would be themselves at that point swilling the ale on sale within the theatre.

Historical contextualisation makes the targeting effect of such super-ciliousness still clearer. As Patrick Collinson has noted, "In this society, downward deference was an important principle, almost a way of life, like upward deference . . . the gentry and professional intelligentsia of the six-teenth century were perfectly capable of pronouncing 'received English' but chose to 'condescend' in their speech to the rustic vernacular of meaner persons."[10] The queen herself, of course, "was so great a courter of her people, yea, of the commons" that courtiers said they never knew another "that stooped and descended lower in presenting her person to the public view as she passed in her progresses and perambulations."[11] The Earl of Essex was perhaps even more assiduously deferential. For the poor were quick to construe the rich as consciously gloating over their daily humili-ations. Patrician *schadenfreude* grows pleasuringly calibrative, plebeians feel in *Coriolanus*: "The leanness that afflicts us, the object of our mis-ery, is as an inventory to particularize their abundance; our sufferance is a gain to them" (1.1.16–18). In *As You Like It*, Rosalind rebukes tyran-nizing Phebe that "you insult, exult, and all at once, / Over the wretched" (3.5.37–38). "England is growne to such a passe of late, / That rich men triumph to see the poore beg at their gate" declares Parson Ball in *Jack Straw* (c. 1594).[12] Kett's rebels were said to have alleged that "their miser-able condition, is a laughing stocke to most proud and insolent men."[13] It is precisely as "a laughing stocke", or for a "triumph", that Sly is casually appropriated by *Shrew*'s lord, relishing his helpless indignity as an oppor-tunity for amusement.

We might recall as salient Elizabethan context that when a gentleman, notoriously, had amused himself at the expense of another poor man asleep in public, performing a mocking pirouette upon the belly of an apprentice asleep outside the Theatre in 1584, the result of this derisive upper-class "turn upon the toe" with accompanying class insult ("prentizes were but the skumme of the worlde") was the explosion known as the Apprentices' Insurrection, in which almost a thousand people participated in a week of angry riot and prison break-ins.[14] The Elizabethan cry of "prentices against gentlemen", comments Barbara Freedman, demonstrates not the aimless youth violence long assumed by theatre historians, but "ample proof of class-solidarity built upon common workers' concerns."[15]

Shrew's nobleman proceeds to issue orders for the sexual arousal and pairing of Christopher Sly ("with kind embracements, tempting kisses", 116), exactly as he supervises the mating of his hounds ("couple Chowder with the deep-mouthed brach", 14).[16] The parallel serves not only to heighten aversion, but to help establish the dominant parallel set up by the Induction: that between the lord's domineering over Sly, and Petruccio's over Kather-ine. Petruccio's whimsical and loveless commandeering of Katherine's per-son and sexual future ("I come to wive it wealthily in Padua; / If wealthily, then happily in Padua", 1.2.72–73; "will you, nill you, I will marry you", 2.1.263) matches the lord's instrumentation of Sly. The twinning of these figures of abusive authoritarian manipulation—pointed in the play's final speech, in Katherine's "Thy husband is thy lord" (5.2.150)—would have been underlined on the visual level, I suspect, at Katherine's wedding. The battered and unkempt wedding gear of Petruccio and his man—horse, boots and old jerkin are specified—most probably evoked the bespattered riding apparel logically sported by the lord and his huntsmen in the Induction, freshly returned from a hard hunt with 'embossed' and 'breathed' hounds. The same actor surely played both roles.

The converse parallel of Katherine with Sly establishes a correlation recurrent in Shakespeare's imagination: the suggestive affinity of beleaguered daughter with plebeian victim, kindred in subjection. *Lucrece* had associated its heroine's lonely agony with underclass oppression—"When wilt thou be the humble suppliant's friend . . . The poor, lame, blind, halt, creep, cry out for thee, / But they ne'er meet with opportunity . . . The orphan pines while the oppressor feeds", etc. (lines 897, 902–03, 905). The poem's spirited denial that women are "authors of their ill" (1244), instead the suffering products of overlord iniquity, carried like connotation of proletarian exculpation ("The weak oppress'd", "proud lords to blame", "tenants to their shame" etc: *Lucrece*, 1242, 1259–60). Sympathetic association of domineered maiden with pauper will be structural to *As You Like It*, as Celia and Rosaline embrace vagabondage and pastoral poverty; and we shall examine its recurrence in *Romeo*, where Shakespeare gives 'Juliet's rebellion' underclass connotations. Injurious captivity linked class and gender in these plays as in Elizabethan social practice. Like servants and the poor, women were required in their servitude, whatever their suffering, to maintain always the deference of silence. Venting—"My tongue will tell the anger of my heart, / Or else my heart concealing it will break" (4.3.77–78)—could incur legal prosecution.[17] Men could be clamped into the stocks for such unseemliness, and women carapaced in a scold's bridle.[18] Within the gamehouse, there must thus have prevailed an endearing homology between the groundlings' delicious access of free speech and Katherine's insurrectionary outspokenness. Indeed, the linkage found in *Shrew* of an exploited proletarian figure to a notably unruly woman was a frequent feature of insurgencies. "The prominence of women in enclosure and grain riots is well known and is one more sign of rejection of the submissive ideal. Female rioters were often joined by men disguised in women's clothes."[19] Twenty-seven armed women threw down an enclosure in Enfield, Middlesex in 1589. At Wye in Kent, 1595, twenty women commandeered corn being transported to Ashford market, to sell it at a 'fair price'. 'Captain Dorothy' led the attack on enclosing walls on Thorpe moor in 1602.[20]

A final targeting effect in *Shrew*'s opening lay in the remarkably extended passages on the lord's lifestyle: "Wrapp'd in sweet clothes, rings put upon his fingers, / A most delicious banquet by his bed, / And brave attendants near him when he wakes". We learn of a lavish world, adorned with music "To make a dulcet and a heavenly sound", and with the burning of "sweet wood to make the lodging sweet". It is equipped with "a silver basin / Full of rose-water and bestrewed with flowers", that pours "warm distilled waters". The luxurious existence is replete with "wanton pictures", horse and hounds, and loving lady (36–60). In the financially ruinous 1590s, when Francis Bacon warned in parliament that rising taxation levels meant gentlemen selling their plate and farmers their brass pots, the impact upon most commoners of this mouth-watering evocation of the sybaritic lifestyle of hereditary wealth would have worked, I suggest, as what we might term a tantalization effect. Agonisingly desirable, and seemingly so close at hand, such flaunted embodiments of a daily privilege forever unattainable were an embittering mirage, inflaming consciousness, already running high, of harrowing class inequity. We shall see arresting, glittering tantalization effects returning in many forms throughout Shakespearean drama.

ANOMALOUS PETRUCCIO

Notwithstanding *Shrew*'s opening juxtaposition of upper class targeting to an underclass bonding, the play's primary figure of misrule is respectably born Petruccio. Indeed, Shakespeare's most prominent bearers of carnival are customarily not paupers and nonentities, mere boozers and quipsters like Sly, the porter in *Macbeth* or the clown in *Anthony and Cleopatra*, but figures of some influence and position—*Sir* John Falstaff, *Sir* Toby Belch, Iago the aide to a supreme military commander, Edmund the son of a leading nobleman—if not outright royals, like Richard III and Prince Hal. As men of some consequence transgressing against figures of still higher authority, the wide field of their antics can thus both unmask and exemplify heartless typicalities sustaining the social and political order—the ideologies of the class system, the ruthless mechanisms of court realpolitik, the baseless propaganda of patriarchy. Yet true to their dramatic origins in the medieval Vice, these figures are also virtuosi of abusive endeavour, exploiting others callously or criminally for personal gain across a spectrum from calculating parasitism (Belch, Prince Hal) to regicide. Pitilessly self-seeking, their anti-authoritarianism, however charismatic, thus incurs inevitable audience ambivalence. Producing exhilarated politico-moral release through compelling ruse and ideological exposé, carnival bonding's dehumanisations set a primacy of comic attraction against a shadowing ethical disquiet.

These mixed feelings are all the sharper where anomalous Petruccio is concerned. Though it is his own Saturnalian antics that propel the play's comic momentum, crowing Petruccio is never, paradoxically, an oppositional figure: he is, precisely, a *master*-spirit. Nowhere does he dissent from the enclosing system of rank and privilege. His gloating exemplification of marital motivation as avaricious commodification may amount in the eyes of the audience, fond of romantic comedies of true-love triumphant, to an arresting exposé of the boorish truth behind patriarchal rhetoric; but Petruccio himself—like the play's opening lord—revels only against propriety: not (like Iago or Edmund, Thersites or Hamlet) against hierarchic power. Never subverting or impugning the social and political order in his own affirmations, as will Falstaff on "grinning honour" at Shrewsbury field, Petruccio's gamesmanship functions conservatively to consolidate patriarchal subordination of the victim. Directing hilarious misbehaviours toward authoritarian coercion, Petruccio thus shades into his doppelganger lord. It is no accident that Petruccio is also a servant-beater.

For much of the drama Petruccio's career seems essentially winning in its dazzling comedics, as through act two he out-jests Katherine in a carnivalesque tournament of wit, then, as her husband, perpetrates brutalities—authorised by patriarchy only in male heads of household—which remain consistently ingenious and entertaining. As Katherine, sleep-deprived, half starved and publically humiliated, is compelled to address the aged and startled Vincentio as "Young budding virgin, fair, and fresh, and sweet" (4.6. 38), the cruelty seems more than half-submerged in riotous mirth. Petruccio indeed sustains the precarious upper hand of his merriment by stepping out onto the platea and charming the audience by direct appeal. Just as Iago will tease his auditors with "And what's he then that says I play the villain, / When this advice is free I give, and honest . . . How am I then a villain?" (2.3.310–11, 322), so Petruccio demands jovially of his spectators "He that knows better how to tame a shrew, / Now let him speak. 'Tis charity to show" (4.1.191–92). We observed Shakespeare designing in *2 Henry VI* a competitive multiplicity to just such attempts to woo the audience through deixis and direct address, as the jockeying of political rivals.

CARNIVAL REPUDIATION

Finally, however, Shakespeare engineers a decisive turn against Petruccio. In the routing of mirth by pathos, we encounter a third dynamic, carnival repudiation. In this dramaturgic master- pattern, Shakespeare commonly enforces renunciation of audience complicity with carnivalesque mischief by a strategic fraying of the comic bond until, following a distinct and final snap, laughter dies in the gravity of horror and compassion. Such repudiation is often effected by repulsive violence. Othello's abrupt, ferocious slap of Desdemona at 4.1.235, and her helpless flood of tears, place Iago's scheming, displayed in his ensuing pretense of tender concern for her, in the light of subhuman cruelty. Richard III is divested by Shakespeare of his former charisma, following his murder of the princes in the Tower, as Falstaff is in Part Two of *Henry IV*, when his enabling heartlessness is exposed on sentencing helpless commoners, individually exhibited onstage, to cannon-fodder for his personal gain. In both cases, Shakespeare shuts off supply of virtuoso jest, replacing captivating belly-laughs with jokes of poor quality: sometimes indeed comprising failed, grey versions of those made early in the play. (Compare Richard III's irresistible merry mordancy on winning Lady Anne, capering across thirty lines at 1.2.215–50—"Was ever woman in this humour wooed?" etc.— with its reprise in a single, flat line at 4.4.362: "Relenting fool, and shallow, changing woman.")[21] Likewise Thersites, coldly wisecracking in the midst of Troilus' agony as he beholds Cressida's betrayal, induces nausea not delight. Romping fun with Jack Cade, we saw in chapter three, disappears abruptly, at the cold-blooded, conscious injustice of executing Lord Saye. In *Twelfth Night*, our bonding with Toby Belch is sundered by his lacerating viciousness to Andrew Aguecheek (5.1.199–200). We will find a similar turn against Jaques in *As You Like It*. Carnival repudiation destroys ambivalence, lifting us out of an almost slapstick perception of manipulation into a sobered theatrical realism, wherein a rising tide of pain and pathos floods out carnival perspective.

CARNIVAL FRUSTRATION

In *Shrew*, the dissolving of ambivalence towards Petruccio necessary for outright repudiation of his reign is produced, I suggest, by a final dramaturgic trick played by Shakespeare upon the audience. Driven by a welter of mutual insult between Katherine and a scarcely known character, the widow, the play's final scene builds excitingly towards promise of magnificent rhetorical massacre by Katherine.

Petruccio: To her, Kate!
Hortensio: To her, widow! (5 2.33–35)

Katherine's prodigious gifts of annihilating invective, and her constant goading by Petruccio through scene after scene, cue us to an elating climax of sensational fury. Katherine's electrifying powers of execration, charismatically paraded across act two, have established a standard of comic delight that haunts the play and promises a finale of intoxicating hilarity. The women's rapid exit denies us this pleasure, but the climax of fire-breathing uproar and dazzling contumely seems assured as Petruccio has the angry Katherine rudely ordered to reappear, then publically demeans her: "That cap of yours becomes you not. / Off with that bauble, throw it underfoot" (5.2.125–26). As Katherine throws down her cap, wordlessly, two thousand people must have held their breath. Petruccio—speaking *of* Katherine in the third person, rather than addressing her or offering affection ("I say she shall: and first begin with her")—demands she praise "lords and husbands". But the forty lines that follow collapse into spiritless docility. The expectation of sulphurous tongue-lashing we have been guyed to expect, which would have swept the scene's merriment to a peak of soaring theatrical energy, is shockingly thwarted. "But now I see our lances are but straws, / Our strength as weak, our weakness past compare" (5.2.177–78). The technique—carnival frustration—compels by its anti-climax a galled antipathy towards this sermon of hegemonic propaganda. Artfully stoked festal anticipation is hurled against blighting meekness. Where the game-house sought to climax in the spirit of carnival, it found its anguishing terminus was the dour privation of Lent.

"It is better to be a shrew than a sheep", remarked a contemporary proverb.[22] It will be left to the post-performance jig to restore hilarity and high spirits, commercially imperative, to smarting customers by departure time.[23]

With remarkable daring, the hostility generated through this wrenching disappointment by broken servility is generalised by Shakespeare to a perspective on the entire political system: for Katherine explicitly identifies foundational Tudor principles at the heart of these self-destructing homiletics. Her mortifying discourse affirms a husband "thy lord, thy king, thy governor", and insists "Such duty as the subject owes the prince, / Even such a woman oweth to her husband, / . . . And not obedient to his honest will, / What is she but a foul contending rebel / And graceless traitor" (5.1.142, 159–60, 162–65). Festal recoil from Katherine's kill-joy sermon thus interrogates, in this late Tudor era of dark political ferment, medieval fealty to magnate and crown. The world in which *Shrew* thus terminates, with its heartbreak, inhumanity, and compelled disgust toward hierarchic subjection as spirit-crushing oppression, is recognisably kindred to that of *Titus Andronicus*, written in just this period—the allegedly blithe aftermath of the Armada debacle.

To the same end, Katherine's concluding emblematic gesture of placing her hand beneath Petruccio's foot—in this version of the story, unrebuked by Petruccio[24]—constructs a disturbing aporia, figuring the liability of subservience to effortless brutality. Further, the image once more links female with underclass subjugation: the boot poised on her soft fingers had kicked out at servants who had failed to prize it off to Petruccio's satisfaction ("Off with my boots, you rogues, you villains . . . Take that!" [4.1.125, 129]).

As a kind of versified homily, Katherine's praise of husbandly overlord-ship has graphically supplied a dramatic resolution piously reassuring to state censorship; yet its theoretic enunciations comprise a tissue of falsehoods, its theses comprehensively falsified by the staged action—a characteristic form of sly Shakespearean subversion.[25] To pick from her speech a single example from many, "one that cares for thee, / And for thy maintenance commits his body / To painful labour both by sea and land" is rendered nonsense by the contexts of Petrucccio's lovelessly avaricious marital drive, and his fat satisfaction in idleness, announced only minutes before: "Nothing but sit, and sit, and eat, and eat" (5.2.151–53, 13).

Shakespeare will deploy frustration effects elsewhere to varied purposes. In *Twelfth Night*, frustration of promised theatrical gratification serves to problematise audience identification with character. "I can sing",

Viola had assured the sea captain and audience, as she urged her presentation to Orsino, "And speak to him in many sorts of music" (1.2.53–54). Yet when Orsino specifically requests music of her—"Give me some music ... Now good Cesario ... Come, but one verse"—she violates her promise, in a moment of awkward silence. "He is not here, so please your lordship, that should sing it", apologises Curio (2.4.1–2, 7). Viola's audience appeal is tactically diminished, and Feste's star rises. In *Henry V*, however, the function will again be political. By denying his audience even a single scene of armed combat at the legendary battle of Agincourt, the shortfall hobbles chauvinist jingoism, estranging spectating into clear-eyed judgement of the English monarch's conduct ("'Tis your thoughts that now must deck our kings").

In an inspired suggestion, Tiffany Stern has argued that, in a period where players spent most of their rehearsal time in solitary memorisation of their lines and cues, Shakespeare's scripting would sometimes supply 'trick' cues to an actor, by having his dialogue partner speak to him the phrase predesignated to elicit his own responding lines, yet then press on without due permissive pause into further speech. (The cue would then be given again, some lines later.) The result, Stern suggests, was to anger the listening actor by this frustration: a technique which then heightened the realism of his acting, as the thwarted player modelled all the more authentically the desired state of longing to fire back irked response.[26] If Shakespeare did indeed preserve fellow-actors in hapless ignorance of occasional 'premature cues', then he was, I suggest, applying to the individual player much the same mechanism that he imposed on whole audiences in what we dubbed carnival frustration. In both cases, the crafting of thwarted expectation produced a textually 'invisible' anger, maximising frustrated attention to the ensuing enunciations of dialogue: a technique brilliantly critical to the finale of *The Taming of the Shrew*.

SHAKESPEARE THE DIRECTOR

The recurrence in Shakespearean dramaturgy of these carnival dynamics—bonding and targeting, repudiation and frustration—underscores that festive ground, that relish in anti-authoritarian impulse, deeply innate to dramatic reception in the amphitheatres. Without a working acknowledgment of that ground, attempts to construe Shakespeare's political values are liable to disastrous misreading. *Shrew*, for instance, is repeatedly read either as "unredeemedly sexist", its ending "the perfect climax of a masculine fantasy", or else its cruelties are denied.[27] These theatrical dynamics suggest a directorial presence, probably Shakespeare's: and this is precisely what recent studies of the evolution of Elizabethan scripts suggest. Tiffany Stern demonstrates that 'attached' authors (contracted to a company) wrote with a specific ensemble and venue in mind; gave probably an introductory reading of the drama to the assembled company; were "given the first shot at casting the play"'; rehearsed the major actors with detailed instruction, including "a complete performance of the pronunciation and gestures required by the part, to be imitated by the actor"; and "took over practical aspects of the performance, accepting the role otherwise held by the manager." "Shakespeare and Jonson", she concludes, "in all probability, oversaw whatever collective rehearsal there was": thus taking charge of the music, clothes and properties for the production.[28] The sustained dramaturgic involvement of authors, from implementing the censor's revisions, through working with company emendations, to responding to first-performance audience reactions, is the theme of Grace Ioppolo's recent work. "Authors returned to their texts, or texts were returned to their authors, at any or all stages after composition . . . In essence, dramatists supported their plays throughout their transmission."[29]

Where court performance was concerned, the system, I submit, could hardly have worked better to Shakespeare's advantage. The censor's acquaintance was with page, not stage. The Master of the Revels usually satisfied himself, notes Stern, by inspecting a manuscript, seeking "generally, a silent reading that did not require the presence of actors." If 'performed' for him at all, a recitation of the play would take place in a private room. "Courtly rehearsals were about words and scripts, not performance."[30] Securing the *de facto* absence of a commons audience with its crucial co-creation of dramatic tone and meaning through anti-authoritarian mood and responsive interactions, private audition, I suggest, would transform a play's politics. Further, a period of rehearsal specifically for court production would often then take place, without the presence of the Master of the Revels.[31] In such rehearsals, it is not hard to see, the various inbuilt shibboleths or forms of 'constructed latency' whose operation we observe in this book—deictic address, framing actions, eloquent silences—could easily be suppressed or doctored, radically transforming any drama into a vehicle of innocent orthodoxy.

7 "The Quarrel is Between Our Masters and us their Men"
Romeo And Juliet, Dearth and the London Riots

If any trecherous insinuater goe about to intice you to insurrection:
if any idle headed libeller scatter papers amongst you, winne never
dying praise by detecting them.

(*A Student's Lamentation*, 1595)[1]

Famine is in thy cheeks,
Need and oppression starveth in thy eyes,
Contempt and beggary hangs upon thy back.
The world is not thy friend, nor the world's law.
The world affords no law to make thee rich.
Then be not poor, but break it . . .

(5.1.69–74)

"The aesthetic", as literary theory has taught us, is "contextually mobile".[2]
Construed, inescapably, within mutating fields of ideological sensitivity and
projection, textual 'meaning' lives in metamorphosis. Pressed into normative service, as Gary Taylor and Michael Bristol[3] have shown, by innumerable regimes of hierarchy and sensibility, Shakespeare's plays in particular
have become, in the words of Terry Eagleton, "products to be wrested if
possible from the grip of history and inserted instead into the matrix of
tradition."[4] The traditional constructions of the academy, poorly politicized
and frequently unhistorical, may easily miss or domesticate the political
risk and challenge decoded by the earliest audiences, cued by their cultural
moment to meanings *circumstantially* immanent. Conversely, social contexts centuries later may re-expose an old cutting edge of political suggestion, even polish it to a new and threatening sharpness. In the late 1980s,
for instance, it was reported in the British press that Israeli authorities had
prohibited possession of *Hamlet* by imprisoned Palestinians. In the crisis
years of the first *intifada*, this lofty Western classic of scholarly veneration,
this icon of civilising literary inwardness, had begun emitting intolerable
signals. To some readers it now heroized—once again—suicidal devotion
to extra-judicial assassination. For its brazenly seditious content, *Hamlet*
had to be proscribed.

In the case of *Romeo and Juliet,* the play's immediate political context has been obscured by a long tradition of appropriation of the play's meaning for an ethos of romantic 'transcendence'. Yet if aesthetic meaning turns out to be ineluctably conjunctural, then a work's founding meaning must be retrieved from vanished textual valences local to the circumscribed cultural conditions of initial production.[5] To re-embed this play in events and conditions in London between 1594–96—the escalating inter-class youth violence, the dearth of 1594–97, and the sensational London riots of 1595 which the combination precipitated—is to recuperate, I suggest, just such an originary and contingent salience, lost to posterity.

Recent work on the play has highlighted the importance of its violence. "With its feud, street fight, dueling, casualties, and deployment of combat imagery, *Romeo and Juliet* offers a panoramic view . . . of violence in Elizabethan England."[6] *Romeo* criticism to date, however, has addressed only *aristocratic* bloodshed: which was, I will argue, but one term of the *dialectical* violence of contemporary London and of the play. At the heart of a war-torn, over-taxed and now hunger-threatened nation, London in the mid-1590s was a congested, polarized and angry city, in which the crown and its officials had become hated, and the Lord Mayor made to fear for his life. This context of dearth and citizen violence, erupting in riot after riot, has never hitherto been noted in *Romeo* criticism; and examination of the play in this light reveals, I shall argue, a contextually implicit populist subtext of mordant political suggestion. As the crown and its agents, turning a blind eye to aristocratic mayhem, imposed upon the sometimes *technical* violence of famine-fearing lower-class Londoners punishments so severe that they triggered gigantic riots, *Romeo and Juliet* argued a counter-definition of the moral characters of elite and common citizenry. Shakespeare's humanitarian instincts, I shall argue, crafted within the romance narrative indictment of the irresponsibility of sated, self-indulgent wealth, and structurally juxtaposed the hunger, illiteracy and toil of the world of disprivilege. These relatively populist sympathies conferred on the drama—for an audience of London commoners at that particular historical juncture—many elements of a play of political protest.

* * *

The riots of June 1595 proved merely the sharpest flashpoint of violent tensions in class relations that had erupted sporadically in London from at least the 1580s, and which were notably exacerbated by food and price anxieties from 1594 through 1597. These general conditions thus existed as a resonant context of *Romeo,* at whatever point between 1594 and 1596 the play was written. A number of recent scholars have settled upon 1595–96 for *Romeo's* composition, a dating I find convincing, for I strongly suspect the June riots of 1595 and their political aftermath to have been a major stimulus to the play's creation.[7] "The London riots and rebellions of 1595 constituted the most dangerous and prolonged urban uprising in England between the accession of the Tudor dynasty and the beginning of the Long Parliament", notes Roger Manning. "There were at least 13 insurrections, riots and unlawful assemblies that year in a dozen parts of London and Southwark, of which 12 took place between 6 and 29 June."[8] Martial Law was imposed on July 4. ("For now, these hot days, is the mad blood stirring", shudders a fearful Benvolio, at 3.1.4.)[9]

Violent clashes in London that had "pitted apprentices against gentlemen . . . and against their servingmen"[10] can be traced back to at least June 1581, however, when apprentices fought the retainers of Sir Thomas Stanhope at Smithfield (towards which traditional sparring ground Gregory and Sampson appear bound at the play's beginning, as Edelman has noted.)[11] When the ringleader, accused of seeking to inflame one thousand apprentices "to make a rebellion against the gentlemen", was whipped for his offence, the apprentices rescued him from the cart on which he was being punished. Further large-scale brawls between gentlemen and apprentices are recorded for June 1584 on two successive days outside the Curtain theatre, and against Lincoln's Inn in 1590. The fragmentary nature of the source documents make it impossible to know, as Ian Archer suggests, the full extent of rioting before the 1590s.[12] However, the number of apprentices in London doubled between 1580 and 1600, reaching at least 30,000, and the number of domestic servants was equal or greater.[13] Further, the crisis-ridden condition of London's textile workers—many of whom inhabited 'the Maze', a pauper's "warren of tenements" which abutted the Southwark theatre district—led to serious, class-based rioting in May 1592, and the closing of the theatres.[14] Indeed many theatre closings, though discreetly ascribed by the Privy Council to plague prevention measures, were alarmed reactions to riot, as Barbara Freedman demonstrates. Taking the Privy Council's word at face value, literary critics and theatre historians from E.K. Chambers on have thus underestimated the true scale of contemporary popular disorder.[15] The riots of June 1595 began when, on the 6th, a silk-weaver, who had reviled to his face the government of Mayor Spencer—hated for his wealth and juridical severity—was arrested but then freed by a crowd of 200 or more persons.[16] As Richard Wilson sums up, "The modernist nostalgia for Elizabethan England as a model of some classless, pre-industrial *Gemeinschaft* cannot withstand the picture that is emerging of London's crystallizing class consciousness in the acute social and economic crisis of the 1590s."[17]

Crisis seems precisely the term. The harvests of 1594–97 were possibly the most catastrophic in English agrarian history. Further, these years "experienced the most sustained and severe inflation of prices in the sixteenth and seventeenth centuries and culminated in the lowest real wages in English history in 1597."[18] The impact of the failed harvests on a city whose population had doubled between 1580 and 1600, "more than doubled the price of wheat and carried that of barley, oats, peas and beans, the food of the poor, proportionately even higher. Probably for the first time in Tudor England large numbers of people in certain areas died of starvation."[19]

Famine seems eventually to have penetrated to the poorer pockets of London, for as Andrew Appleby records, 1597 saw an exceptional number of recorded burials across seven inner-city parishes.[20] But it was the *fear* of hunger, triggered by soaring prices, rather than its actualization, that typically provoked popular demonstration.[21] "It is difficult to exaggerate the extent to which people in the late sixteenth and early seventeenth century were conscious of the threat of dearth", write historians John Walter and Keith Wrightson. This was "the spectre which haunted early modern Europe, one of the principal factors contributing to the profound insecurity of the age."[22] Apprentices and serving men—populous in London theatre audiences, and given, we shall see, sympathetic prominence in *Romeo*—knew themselves to be in heightened danger: for, vulnerable to dismissal at any moment (as *As You Like It* illustrates), they were the first casualties when the prosperous sought economies. "The great dearth of victual which hath been continued these three years", wrote the city fathers to the Council, " . . . hath so impoverished the general estate of this whole city, that many persons, before known to be of good wealth [have been] enforced to dissolve their households", a "public calamity".[23]

In 1595 the Oxford preacher (and later Archbishop) George Abbot wrote that "The dearth which doth now raigne in many parts of this land . . . maketh the poore to pinch for hunger, and the children to cry in the street, not knowing where to have bread. And if the Lord do not stay his hand, the dearth may be yet much more".[24] Such fears seem to have set in however as early as November 1593, when Lord Cobham referred anxiously to "the present dearth of corn". By January 1594 the Aldermen of London had ordered a letter to Burghley requesting a ban on grain exports. Even before the first disastrous harvest failure, it was reported in London (in July 1594) that "the poorer sorte . . . are cheefely pinched with the dearthe"; and a committee to consider corn imports was established in the capital.[25] A ballad of 1594 clutched desperately at the miraculous, claiming that "a poor distressed widow and her seven small fatherless children lived by a burnt sixpenny loaf of bread and a little water above seven weeks in the Wild of Kent." As historian Peter Clark comments here, "begging burnt or mouldy bread from bakers, scavenging the yards of butchers and sifting the general wastage of fairs and markets undoubtedly produced many a semi-edible mouthful. According to one literary gentleman, fresh bread went further if one allowed it to go stale."[26] It had to. As Clark records of conditions, for example, in Kent, "the supply of grain reserved for the local poor was badly supervised and misused." The Mayor of Canterbury complained in 1597 that such was the grain shortage that "the poorest folk and a great part of the people being of small wealth are like to starve."[27]

M. J. Power develops the picture: a letter from the Lord Mayor to Burghley of September 1595 declared the city's wheat store to be already exhausted; in October he requested that any corn ships taken on the high seas be dispatched to London. November saw London commandeering food from other counties; and through 1594–95, various sites were sought in the city for the storage of any incoming grain.[28] The Stationer's Register listed on 5 November 1595 a work entitled *The poor man's Complaint*; and *Sundrye newe and artificiall Remedies against famyne . . . uppon the occasion of this present Dearthe* followed next August. For the harvest of 1596 was even more disastrous. "One year there hath been hunger", recorded a preacher that year; "the second there was a dearth; and the third there was great cleanness of teeth" (a caustic biblical phrase for starvation).[29] 'Dearth' was itself, of course, a euphemism for 'famine', aiming to disguise the state's own failure of distributive control.[30] These conditions would produce what Archer notes to have been the first food riots in London since the 1520s.[31]

The explosion came on June 12 1595, when in response to soaring food prices, a group of apprentices at Billingsgate compelled the sale of fish at the correct price, established by the Lord Mayor. The following day, in Southwark, another group of apprentices forced the sale of butter at 3d a pound rather than the 5d that the butter women were demanding. They also issued a proclamation (simply endorsing the law of England) that butter be brought for sale to the market, not sold in inns or private houses.[32] When officials attempted to make arrests, an indignant crowd sought to prevent the taking of prisoners. On the 15th, they went on to attack the Counter prison, and rescue prisoners being transported there. An inquest by the Lord Mayor established that there had in fact been at the 'butter riot' "nothing ells but a great concourse & presse of people for buying of butter & other victuals without any force or other disorder."[33] Notwithstanding this finding, the Privy Council, acting through the Court of Star Chamber, overrode the judgment of the mayor and enforced exemplary punishment— of apparently innocent men—so that on 27 June the 'butter rioters' were whipped, pilloried and imprisoned.

Such harsh punishment generated further popular outrage. Medieval canon law, we have seen, had been protective of the poor: it declared even the theft of food, in extreme necessity, to comprise not a crime but the exercise of a right. Whether or not commoners knew this, the Privy Council's action stood in shocking contrast to the traditional conditions prevailing in the countryside, where magistrates were normally lenient toward food rioters confining themselves to established ritual enforcement of sales at official prices. For the term 'riot' is a graphic misnomer here: these actions were something very different from our concept of riot today. Medieval implementation of the commonwealth ideal maintained the doctrines of a 'just price', and of fair market practices, to be observed by millers, bakers and others, and to be ensured by the authorities.[34] When in times of dearth magistrates proved lax in enforcing market regulation, 'food riots' developed which were in fact the orderly and semi-official initiatives of "disciplined crowds acting according to values which were shared to some extent by the elite in actions designed to remind the magistrates of their duties."[35] Since in the imposition of traditional prices the crowds merely exercised the office of the clerk of the market, we do better to term such activity (as does E. P. Thompson) "taxation populaire."[36] Grain 'rioters' in Canterbury in 1596, for instance, affronted by the spectacle of their local grain being carted away from their hungry district, "after taking the precaution of consulting an attorney's clerk as to the legality of their actions, took care 'not to meddle with the corn' and simply prevented the carriers from leaving the city."[37] We must "appreciate that riot was a negotiating strategy", insists Archer, designed to prod negligent officials—who might well be turning handsome personal profits from price escalation—into tightening up market regulations.[38] Where petitioning failed, 'riot' could usually "jolt the institutions of social regulation into effective operation."[39] (In this, the June '95 food riots were successful.) Moreover, such action was ritualized, to reassure the authorities that no political rebellion was intended. This was precisely the kind of assessment affirmed in Mayor Spencer's report.

Despite the clarity of such Tudor semiotics of class friction, however, and despite the element of traditional moral legitimacy to such corrective popular initiative, the crown, as we have seen, imposed flogging and imprisonment on the butter rioters. The consequence was a protest riot, in which a gathering of 1,800 people, assembling in Leadenhall and Cheapside, tore down pillories, attempted to break into the Counter and release prisoners, and finally proceeded to the lord mayor's home, where they erected a gallows outside his door and dared him to come out.[40]

Suggestively, the period produced even more riots of this type, protesting perceived injustice in sentencing, than it did 'food riots': fourteen of the former as against twelve of the latter between 1581–1602.[41] Anti-injustice riots might arise from a double-standard in punishment of violence, as when in 1591, following a skirmish between felt-makers and the Knight Marshall's men, a crown officer accused of manslaughter was released on bail, while a felt-maker was for the same crime hanged.[42] Or they might be sparked as protests against "the harshness and partiality of justice" frequently compelled upon the mayor and court of aldermen by the queen and privy council, whose intervention, for instance, included occasional order for the torture of prisoners under interrogation. In consequence, "Examinations of prisoners in the Marshalsea revealed that they talked freely of rebellion and killing the Queen."[43]

Friction between Londoners and crown officials thus burned with a white heat through June 1595, to culminate, one Sunday afternoon, in the astonishing Apprentice's Insurrection of June 29. A thousand people, including husbandmen, vagrants, 'apprentices' (a term used vaguely by contemporaries to denote youthful lower classes generally), discharged soldiers, silk-weavers, shoemakers and girdlers gathered at Tower Hill, intending to ransack gunmakers' shops. They were armed, according to the authorities, with pikes and bills, clubs, swords and daggers (Manning 210)—indeed much the same assortment of weapons as flourished in the opening brawl of *Romeo and Juliet*. The assembly and cohesiveness of so variegated a group, flourishing a banner defiantly, embodied a kind of elementary class-consciousness: one sustained, when the watch attempted to disperse them, by a former soldier sounding a trumpet to rally their forces, so that they were able to stone the watch back into Tower Street.[44] At this point the line had been crossed between riot and rebellion, whose "governing rules were quite different": the symbolism of carrying flag and trumpet were, as Buchanan Sharp notes, "acts associated since the late middle ages with the levying of war."[45] The scale of disorder, however, was scarcely such as to produce a "generalised social crisis in which all men of property feared for their lives."[46] Revolution was not in the offing. The Lieutenant of the Tower, for instance, actually hindered the efforts of the mayor's officers in making arrests, in order to score points in his long-running jurisdictional squabbles with the City. Nonetheless these actions now led the crown, deeply fearful of the alliance of apprentices and soldiery, to the exceptional step of hanging, drawing and quartering five apprentices in July, and imposing martial law.

Given the limited threat to authority even of the Tower riot; given the draconian order established by the rapidly hated Provost-Marshals, whom even constables soon came to disobey;[47] and given, too, the continuing fear of dearth in London: a sense of the many moral ambiguities of the entire month's events was presumably strong in the minds of most citizens. If the popular protest had grown out of hand, it had been innocuous enough initially, and had been propelled toward to rebellious violence by the harsh and anti-traditional responses of the Crown. Opinion in London, among the poor and 'the middling sort' at least, must have been passionate and divided. Further 'libels' were scattered about the city following the executions; and the government countered swiftly with a propaganda tract entitled *A Student's Lamentation*. Plainly fearful of continuing unrest, the *Lamentation* sought to justify the apprentices' execution, and to dissuade disaffected youths from further protest. It urged informers to report on anything seditious, and magistrates to punish with greater severity. Thus from early July 1595, London's lower classes were caught in a pincer movement of fear: squeezed between dearth-driven grievances—sustained, or even deepened, as the nightmare continued: 1596 brought both the worst harvest of the entire century—and a ferocious government crackdown, with two newly appointed Provost-Marshals (plus their twelve attendants)[48] seeking for informers, and hunting down offenders, whom it sought, in the words of the proclamation issued on July 4, "without delay to execute upon the gallows by order of martial law".[49] It is to precisely such conditions of fertile ambivalence and thrilling political charge that Shakespearean drama was frequently drawn. Indeed, to resituate *Romeo and Juliet* in this climate of explosive anxiety—to reread the play alongside contemporary government proclamations and its *Student's Lamentation*, juxtaposing these to *Romeo's* perspectives on urban violence, desperate hunger, and careless patrician feasting—is to perceive once more a political audacity characteristically Shakespearean.

The lower-class violence of 1595 had begun, as so often, with essentially *public* concerns: with peaceful attempts at popular market regulation as prices escalated, and subsequent mass protests against the ensuing harsh punishments and interrogation by torture. Aristocratic violence in London, however, was of a very different category, for this was characteristically a matter of endemic gang-feuding among the titled. As Lawrence Stone has written, "In London itself the fields about the city and even the main arterial roads were continual scenes of upper-class violence. Bloody brawls and even pitched battles occurred in Fleet Street and the Strand, and little protection could be offered by the authorities until hours or days after the affair was over". The behavior of the propertied classes, Stone notes, "was characterized by the ferocity, childishness and lack of self-control of the Homeric age"; while the language of "men of high social standing is often so intemperate as to be almost deranged".[50] Aristocratic retainers became little better than thugs, "armed bullies ready to serve their master's turn against his enemies, whether the poor and defenseless" or "a rival magnate", and were "ready to beat up or even occasionally to kill at a word from their master". The savagery of the so-called nobility acknowledged no rules. Sir Germaine Poole, for example, on getting his enemy Thomas Hutchinson to the ground, bit off "a good bit of his nose and carried it away in his pocket."[51] To these running brawls of the aristocracy Elizabeth turned a very blind eye. Indeed her occasional *protective* intervention in the trials of peers arraigned for killing in street-fights permitted great courtiers such as the Earl of Oxford and Sir Thomas Knyvett to commit in their feuding "murder after murder with complete impunity".[52]

In so permissive a climate, it is no surprise that the nobility raised the stakes in civil violence to a new level of deadliness, when, from the 1580s, they introduced use of the rapier. Previously, fighting had been conducted, as Edelman notes, with the heavy standard slashing sword, weighing at least three or four pounds, and a buckler (a small shield).[53] "These weapons", comments Stone, "allowed the maximum muscular effort and the most spectacular show of violence with the minimum threat to life or limb. Fighting with them was not much more dangerous than all-in wrestling" (Stone 118). The rapier, however, could run a man through the body as fast as lightning; and, combined with the code of honor (punctilio) establishing the rules of giving and the obligation to challenge even trivial slights, it introduced the duel to England, with the inevitable high death toll. Beyond limiting rapier length to "one yarde and halfe a quarter of the blade at the uttermost", however, Elizabeth, took no measures against swordfighting.[54] Dueling consequently increased during the 1590s.[55] England thus became, as a contemporary remarked, a country "wherein a poor man was hanged for stealing food for his necessities and a luxurious courtier . . . could be pardoned after killing the second or third man."[56]

* * *

Romeo and Juliet, I suggest, is permeated by the turbulence, class antagonism and passionately contested injustice of this juncture. In what follows, I shall be tracing what I believe to be some of the original political overtones in the play's presentation of class behavior. Though these overtones constitute significant dimensions of the drama, summoning powerful cultural reflexes to its allocations of sympathy or antipathy, I am not, of course, seeking to deny that the heart of the play's concern and of its lasting attraction is the romance of the young lovers. (Indeed I suspect that some of the conjunctural overtones of 'protest' here may have temporarily disappeared, along with the dearth, in 1598.) Nor do I suggest that Romeo emerges as an essentially negative figure. Shakespeare's genius for moral complication and abrupt reversals of sympathy or expectation nevertheless takes on political dimension, I suggest, in the characterization of Romeo, Capulet, Mercutio and the Prince. Moreover, though the narrative line activates topical popular angers and anxieties that at times may be relatively straightforward, its vision grows more complex through the very closeness with which the political is woven into the central ambiguities of the exquisite yet lawless romance. In the behavior, for instance, of Romeo, Shakespeare establishes resonant contemporary vignettes of both reckless rebel hero, and sneering, well-fed patrician. Even Juliet, prominently embedded in a language of revolt and plebeian unfreedom, figures herself occasionally in provocative metaphors of indefeasible wealth.

For even at the level of the main romantic action, the play pervasively elides the romantic with the political. Associating love with an imagery of violence, it plunges the feelings of its hero and heroine into amorous riot: "violent delights [that] have violent ends, / And in their triumph die like fire and powder, / Which as they kiss consume" (2.6.9–11).[57] Romeo twins Eros and riot: "O, brawling love, O loving hate / . . . Misshapen chaos of well-seeming forms" (1.1.169, 172). The essential narrative pits (and at points appears to endorse) passionate youthful insurgence against abusive authority: and remarkably, well-born Juliet is several times associated—like Katherine in the *Shrew*—not only with rebellion, but with the lower orders. Metaphors of specifically underclass suffering envelop her. She would have her lover safely *fettered* to her, "Like a poor prisoner in his twisted gyves" (2.1.224). Capulet threatens her that, should she refuse to go to Saint Peter's Church to marry Paris, he will "drag thee on a hurdle thither" (3.5.155)—a hurdle being the frame on which condemned traitors were dragged to their execution. He seeks to crush her resistance as a "disobedient wretch" by scanning, with secure contempt, the varied endings of the destitute, witnessable daily across dearth-racked London: "Hang! Beg!

Starve! Die in the streets!" (192; exclamation marks from Arden ed.).[58]
Joining her in death, Romeo describes their suicides as "a dateless bargain
to engrossing death" (5.3.115): engrossing meaning "To buy up wholesale
. . . for the purpose of 'regrating' or retailing at a monopoly price" (OED,
subst. 3).[59] Regrating was of course an illegal practice of the prosperous,
hated by the poor for escalating food prices: and one whose redress the
London council was urgently seeking in 1595 through the creation of new
committees.[60] Summing up her condition, Juliet, tyrannised instrument of
patriarchy, is explicit in self-alignment with embittered peonage:

> Bondage is hoarse, and may not speak aloud. (2.1.205)

It would seem that Shakespeare, the poet anguished that "gilded honour
shamefully misplaced" enforced an "art made tongue-tied by authority"
(Sonnet 66), could evince solidarity, as populist playwright, with the smouldering mutism of vassalage.

Romeo and Juliet's love, then, reckless in "the sin / Of disobedient opposition" (4.2.17–18), is defiant of authority, figuratively linked with violence,
and associated with outcast, criminal and plebeian status. Indeed, like the
political riots in the minds of their participants, it transgresses a prevailing
repression in the name of a higher principle. Like the impassioned popular
initiatives of moral redress which the authorities called riots, its course of
action offers, through a temporary and problematic disruption, the potential of a lasting harmony when all is clearly understood: and in this the
play shows it to be successful ("O brother Montague, give me thy hand",
5.3.295). It is thus tempting to speculate that Shakespeare, constrained by
censorship, has displaced the urgent ethical paradoxes of the riots—the
flagrant rebellion yet 'higher' justification—onto a parallel dynamic within
the framework of romance, wherein political morality could be subject to
debate and problematization on the wide public stage.

Less speculatively, the play is manifestly concerned to address street-
violence directly, hurling it repeatedly across center stage from the opening
cross-class mêlée to a pointedly blood-drenched finale. Just as Elizabeth had
notoriously authorized torture as a response to the riots, Shakespeare's Prince
Escalus confronts "Rebellious subjects, enemies to peace" with threatened
"pain of torture" (1.1.74, 79). In the heated contemporary context, however,
wherein such draconian monarchical measures had been directed exclusively
against *lower*-class violence, Shakespeare's treatment of violence and punishment assumes the aspect of a populist counter-indictment. For *Romeo and
Juliet*, we shall see, lays the blame for "mutiny" and civil bloodshed, even by
the lower classes, at the door of the urban elite, and contrasts a citizen activism of laudable responsibility, rebuking specifically the catastrophic effects of
a royal double-standard in punishment of bloody disorders.

To a remarkable degree, Shakespeare had taken over his primary characters and events from his manifest source, the 1562 translation from the

Italian by Arthur Brooke, and evidently knew Brooke's narrative well. Shakespeare, however, chose to centralize the master-class mayhem. He departs from Brooke by restructuring the entire story with symmetrical clarity through reiterated scenes of intra-elite fighting in public spaces. The opening, closing, and central scenes (with the Tybalt–Mercutio duel) each features patricians incorrigibly bent upon violence, and each involves the active intervention of regal authority itself, in the gathering of an entire community disturbed by "new mutiny", as "civil blood makes civil hands unclean" (Prologue, 3–4). Brooke's version had featured no opening brawl, giving merely an abstract statement of bloody feuding. Nor had Brooke conceived a belligerent Mercutio intent upon fighting Tybalt—an innovation producing two successive fights in mid-play. Shakespeare likewise transformed his source by inventing an anguishing finale of gentlemanly murder in the closing duel with Paris.

There is thus far more to the play's portrayal of violence than that generalized 'patriarchal' definition of 'masculinity' through violence of which critics have written.[61] In the contemporary contexts of *class*-generated violence, of officially allocated *class* culpability, and of differential *class* punishment, the play unsurprisingly dramatizes a class-differentiation in the character of violence. The very language of Prince Escalus' arraignment of violence underlines its pedigree: the "head, spring and true descent" of such "outrage" (5.3.217, 215) is to be traced, his terminology and the play suggest, to the upper orders. "By the stock and honour of my kin," explains Tybalt, in a couplet of obligingly pointed *hauteur*, "To strike him dead I hold it not a sin" (1.5.55–56).

The opening riot, with its "neighbour-stained steel" (1.1.75), foregrounds this proclivity to violence of the ruling class households of Capulet and Montague. Sampson and Gregory are no free-booting scrappers but enthusiastic agents of overlord will. Entering dressed in their master's livery, they subserve his traditional feud: "The quarrel is between our masters and us their men" (1.1.17). Sampson's excited brag—"I will show myself a tyrant" (1.1.18)—suggests a glamourized brutalism mediated from the ruling class model: cutting off heads bespeaks seigneurial verve. The opening jokes and Sampson's swaggering, with their display of lower-class snobbery—"We'll not carry coals." "No, for then we should be colliers" (1.1.1–2)—embodies the sparring superciliousness of retainers of the great, reiterated later in Peter's battle of wits with the musicians ("I will give you the minstrel." "Then I will give you the serving-creature" [4.5.138–39]), and presented elsewhere in the comic snideness of Malvolio and the murderous arrogance of Oswald. Capulet and Montague themselves leave no doubt as to the font of reckless belligerence, rushing onstage with eager calls for their weaponry. Shakespeare elsewhere confirms the double-standard to be commonplace, when in *Julius Caesar* Brutus directs that the conspirators should, "as subtle masters do, / Stir up their servants to an act of rage, / And after seem to chide em" (2.1.175–77).

Shakespeare maximizes the scale and disorder of the fracas, specifying a "washing blow" (55), stipulating an array of weaponry (swords and bucklers, long sword, rapier, clubs, bills and partisans), and bringing on a stream of further combatants as more retainers apparently arrive (107), along with citizens attempting to part them (66–67). Further, he appears to allocate the most formidable and most implacable violence not to the retainers but to their masters, in the graphic person of "the fiery Tybalt". "Peace? I hate the word, / As I do hell, all Montagues, and thee" (1.1.102, 63–64). Positioning Tybalt carefully at the centre of this mêlée, Shakespeare's treatment of him is notable in three respects. First, it was a conscious departure from Brooke to bring Tybalt onstage thus early in the action. Second, Shakespeare's specification that Gregory and Sampson were armed with sword and buckler will here find its point: for Tybalt, as an aristocrat or gentleman, bears a rapier (and probably dagger). The enforced contrast on stage, as the jocular and hesitant retainers with their largely token and demonstrative weaponry, old-fashioned and clumsy, are joined by the unappeasable patrician who closes upon Benvolio with lethal rapier, serves not just to escalate the violence but to highlight the greater threat to life posed by the city's most privileged youth. Third, Tybalt "swung about his head and cut the winds" (1.1.104). These blows, as Edelman and others have noted, identify Tybalt as fighting in the Spanish style, with its stylized cuts from the shoulder, elbow and wrist.[62] (Mercutio's later comments on Tybalt as fencing "as you sing prick-song", and fighting "by the book of arithmetic", 2.3.18, 3.1.97, confirm the identification.) Tybalt's erect back and skipping feet will have contrasted sharply with the Italian crouch of Benvolio, favoured by the English at this point. This identification of fighting styles will not have been lost on an audience accustomed to displays of fine swordplay traditionally staged at theatres, both as competitive fencing for prizes, or as part of a play's action. Though the significance of this specified contrast in fencing styles appears not to have been politicized by Edelman or others, we need only recall that in 1595 England was awash with rumours of an imminent and second Spanish armada (finally launched but shipwrecked in October 1596) to recognize that Tybalt's implacable onslaught, slashing from shoulder and elbow, would have triggered in audiences Hispanophobic revulsion; thus further demonizing that alien upper class violence of which he was the most virulent representative.[63]

Romeo himself is not exempted from this perspective. We are reminded of his class's propensity not only by his own language—"My man's as true as steel" (2.3.179)—and by Juliet's—"Romeo that did spit his body / Upon a rapier point" (4.3.55–56)—but by his action. The killing of Paris, a final outrage we saw innovated by Shakespeare, is particularly bloody, I suggest, as we may deduce from the triple references it evokes. ("What blood is this which stains / The stony entrance of this sepulchre?" asks the Friar. He later speaks of "masterless and gory swords / (That) lie discolour'd". The Watchman, entering shortly afterwards, notes "The ground is bloody".

(5.3.140–43,171)) The special bloodiness of this "foul murder" (5.3.197) may thus well have warranted use of the contemporary special effect of concealing a vinegar-soaked or blood-filled bladder under an actor's armpit, to burst and saturate him at the right moment as if skewered.[64] (Interestingly, it would seem that the compositor of Q2 regarded Romeo in such sanguinary terms. Misreading 5.3.198, "Here is a friar, and slaughter'd Romeo's man", he took Slaughter to be the name of Romeo's servant.)

Moreover, as Alan Dessen has noted, "the contrast between the two lovers of Juliet, one with flowers and sweet water, the other 'savage-wild' with mattock and crow of iron, could hardly be more striking". That contrast might have been further heightened if, as Dessen speculates, the 'tomb' into which Romeo forces his way was imaginary, rather than a verisimilar onstage structure (the evidence allows no certainty either way). "If Romeo uses verisimilar tools to pantomime an opening of an imagined tomb", then the action would acquire pronounced emblematic overtone, Dessen perceives. It could become a "highly disturbing" image, of violation and frenzy, of smashing one's way inside the jaws of death, "the savage-wild lover using a mattock and a crow of iron to rip open whatever separates him from his beloved." These may even have been the weapons used to kill Paris.[65]

The sustained and prominent rebuke of pedigreed mayhem structuring the play further includes the excoriation of punctilio as an unworkable code.[66] Ungoverned by the providential agency its proponents posited, its death-toll was catastrophic. As Alan Dessen elsewhere points out, Q1 makes it clear that even Benvolio dies: "the wiping out of the younger generation is complete."[67]

Finally, whereas Brooke had presented but a single pugnacious nobleman (Tybalt), and the rhetoric of Elizabethan authority was demonizing indolent apprentices and vagrants as the source of affrays, Shakespeare is at pains to reiterate an ominous scenery of idling *patrician* youths disposed to customary enlivenments of violence.[68] Establishing Mercutio as a second roving, insatiable belligerent (in Brooke he is merely a once-glimpsed, sedentary philanderer at home among "bashfull maydes"), and surrounding both Mercutio and Tybalt with a constant band of unnamed followers, Shakespeare presents Verona's "rebellious subjects, enemies to peace" (1.1.74) as the warring gangs of the aimless rich.[69]

The irony here in the 1595 context was particularly relishable. In response to the June riots Lord Burghley had issued an order urging that the city's masters—conceived, of course, as naturally peaceable—should restrain their apprentices: conceived, as usual, as the degenerate and natural source of public disorder.[70] (Officialdom's self-serving *idée fixe* of rebellion's demographics is exposed again some two years later in *2 Henry IV* as Westmoreland complains to the principled Archbishop of York that his rebellion came not "In his true native and most proper shape", "in base and abject routs, / Led on by bloody youth, guarded with rags, / And countenanced by boys and beggary": 4.1.37, 33–35.) The government's *Lamentation* likewise laid all blame for London's summer riots upon apprentices, abusing their 'liberty': "a headlong wilfulnes continued by custome of abused libertie, gave first fyre to this unadvised flame." It accordingly concluded with "A breefe Admonition to those idle persons living about London, whose sloth makes them apt for any sinne." "The roote of all evil is idleness, and idleness is your only exercise", it admonished.[71] The characterisation would apply handsomely, of course, to Tybalt, Mercutio and many of the red-blooded blue-bloods who are their sensation-seeking companions. *Romeo and Juliet*, grasped in its first performances, by the audiences for whom it was written, must thus have emerged, among other things, as an extended and graphic refutation of the government's conveniently one-sided and ideological myth of the genesis of contemporary violence: a retort of *vos quoque* to courtly persecution.

The double-standards of official punishment of violence, triggering anti-injustice riots in '95, are more than hinted in the play.[72] The most obvious instance is the sovereign's direct self-castigation for his disastrous Elizabeth-like lenience towards peer rioting. "I, for winking at your discords, too / Have lost a brace of kinsmen" (5.3.293–94). More subtly, the play closes in threat of underclass punishments to follow: "Some shall be pardoned, and some shall be punished" (5.3.307), concludes the Prince—although some sixty seconds earlier (or less) he had publically declared "All are punished" (5.3.294). The contradiction was unlikely to be lost on an audience inescapably aware of the recent food riots and their dramatic aftermath. The Friar, clearly terrified, and cringing in his speech, has been pardoned. However, Romeo's treacherous incrimination of the Apothecary whom he had bullied into breaking the law—a transaction Romeo had carefully recorded in an explanatory letter, and given Balthasar—suggests a grim fate ahead for that desperate victim of patrician hectoring should he prove identifiable. The threatful indeterminacy of the Prince's words which end the play, specifying retribution ahead, though not for whom, nor of what severity, must have recalled to the memories of many in the audience precisely that state of fearful anticipation of the authorities' reprisals against rioters, familiar from the summer. ("Well, Mercie hath taken Justice by the hand, and they that compassion cannot intreat, compulsion will inforce", threatened *A Student's Lamentation*.)[73] Brooke, by contrast, had cheerfully and approvingly related the execution of the apothecary: "Thapothecary, high is hanged by the throte, / And for the paynes he tooke with him, the hangman had his cote" (2993–94). Shakespeare's play, in sharp contrast to Brooke (and to Zeffirelli's influential film version, which comfortably excises the Prince's alarming resolution), thus closes on a note of punitive suspense: its post-crisis settlement juxtaposes freshly formed *beau monde* solidarity to overtones of authoritarian menace for members of the serving classes. The apothecary, the nurse, her 'man', and perhaps Romeo's 'man', who had fetched the 'cords' by which Romeo reascended to Juliet in "the secret night" (2.3.172), all lie under threat of angered royal retaliation.

Concluding contextualization of the play's violence in differential codes of class licence, we should note, finally, the role of Shakespeare's citizenry. Having cast the armigerous classes as the essential source of riot, and presented the disastrous lenity accorded their incorrigible violence in contrast to the menace of reprisals hanging over underclass heads, Shakespeare represents the citizenry as a kind of *anti*-mob: a collective body (the citizens are unnamed) whose spontaneous activism—like that of the crowd invading the palace at 3.2 of *2 Henry VI* to demand exile of murderous Suffolk— is prompt and responsible. Here again Shakespeare differs from Brooke, whose narrative pits the feuding families directly against the Prince's troops ("The townes men waxen strong, the prince doth send his force", 1039), and contains no concept of citizen intervention. To the contrary, in Brooke's account of the Tybalt-Romeo fray, townspeople simply choose sides with the warring families (983–84). Shakespeare however chooses to introduce concerned citizens making arrests: "Up, sir, go with me. / I charge thee in the Prince's name, obey" (3.1.134–35). His patrician brawlers are nervously aware that the citizens will do so: "Romeo, away, be gone. / The citizens are up" (3.1.127–28). Shakespeare introduces, too, a depth of class-anger felt by the citizens toward privileged hooligans and their lineage: "Strike! Beat them down! / Down with the Capulets! Down with the Montagues!" (1.1.66–67). Given the context of official reprisals against London's citizenry for their recent collective actions in spontaneous price regulation, it seems hard to resist the implication that Shakespeare through this aspect of the drama is crafting once again an implied and populist counter-definition of the role of the actors in the dusty mêlées of that desperate London summer. Royal proclamations in times of unrest typically ordered that "diligent inquiry shall be made of such as have been offenders in any the premises [*sic*], to the intent that due and condign punishment and correction may be to them ministered". Such a proclamation was nervously reissued in the first year of the dearth, 1594.[74] The drama's citizens seeking to arrest illegal brawlers and bring them to their Prince for justice are performing just the civic service demanded by the recent proclamation.

Annabel Patterson has persuasively argued that *A Midsummer Night's Dream*—penned within a twelvemonth of *Romeo*—seems to defend artisans and weavers against official suspicion of seditious turbulence in the wake of the Oxford Rising (1596), following their implication in numerous riots of the nineties.[75] In *Romeo and Juliet*, I suggest, Shakespeare performs for the metropolitan commons like service of revaluation in time of Martial Law. Having shown a society violent from the top down, its ruling classes fixated on feuding, its endemic brawls glamourizing brutality, its fashionable new weapon disastrously lethal, its sovereign injudiciously lax, Shakespeare interpolates a common citizenry whose concerted initiative— uncommended by their Prince—serves the good of the commonweal.

* * *

"Where shall we dine?" inquires Romeo of Benvolio, casually: in a year of ongoing disastrous harvests, and food riots in the capital. Some acts later he goads the starving apothecary from precisely the vantage of confident, well-fed privilege. "Art thou so bare and full of wretchedness, / And fears't to die?" he sneers. "Famine is in thy cheeks, / Need and oppression starveth in thy eyes, / Contempt and beggary hangs upon thy back" (1.1.166; 5.1.68–71). The play consistently places its gangs of disruptive idlers in contexts of abundant consumption, set against a backdrop of citizen dearth and toil. Governmental response to contemporary unrest, not unlike today's, entailed continuing demonisation of underclass youth and calls for increasing punitive harshness: "Lord roote them from this Citie and Suburbs, and put in the Magistrates heads to punish them with more and more severitie: for these and their companions are causes of all mutinies: and it is miraculous they have not long since wrought some great mischiefe."[76] The later 1590s indeed "saw an intensification of the use of the death penalty" by assize judges, "anxious to make examples."[77] *Romeo and Juliet*, by contrast, suggests the view from below. Its elements of political protest included not only the counter-indictment of aristocratic lawlessness we traced above, but a structural presentation of the *ground* of popular discontent, in extreme economic inequity and unsympathetic class relations.

To appreciate the force of the play's opposition of feasting and hunger, and to pre-empt charges from modern literary critics of imposing upon the play anachronistic political sympathies, we need to recall that the contemporary social teachings, both of church and state, enjoined a practicality of mutual Christian solicitude, insisting that wealth was possessed in public stewardship. Just as a "doctrine of economic ethics" sought to protect the poor against the possessing classes by criminalising food hoarding and price-gouging, so the paternalist ideal of the Commonwealth prescribed the charitable distributivist ethos of Christian tradition.[78] Though "a consideration which secular-minded twentieth century historians are apt to downplay", the Commonwealth ideal "was no empty rhetoric", explains Archer, since "it provided a set of values to which the disadvantaged could appeal, and because it shaped popular expectations of their rulers". The speeches of London's aldermen were "suffused in a commonwealth rhetoric"; London civic rituals, such as the Lord Mayor's processions, honored commonwealth ideals of mutual concern and service by placing freshly clothed paupers at the front of processions; and the clergy reminded the rich in general that their wealth obliged them to "an active duty to care for the poor, in giving alms . . . and in showing forbearance to poor debtors."[79] Queen Mary herself had maintained the monastic tradition of the *mandatum*, going down on her knees on Holy Thursday to symbolically wash, dry, and kiss the feet of selected poor folk, to "adore Christ in His poor", following which she would reclothe them, bestowing gifts of food, filled purses, and "aprons and towels which she and her ladies had worn."[80] "In dearth years in particular", observes Hindle, "governors played the commonwealth tune for all it was worth."[81]

Thus, in times of hunger, whilst the poor were commanded to patience, the rich were exhorted not only to acts of charity, but to moderation of their feasting. Lord Burghley, described by a contemporary as the "very Cato of the commonwealth", was acting within this centuries-old tradition when he issued through the Privy Council, in 1596, an order for the Restraint of Eating.[82] M. J. Power records that Burghley's letter of August 8th to the Lord Mayor and aldermen complained of "the custome of greater fare and excessive dyet" in London, and commanded the citizens "to use a more moderate and spare diet, to leave great feastinges and superfluous fare and to be contented with fewer dishes, converting the rest to the releif of the poore."[83] The Lord Mayor accordingly ordered citizens to forego two suppers per week, and to donate what was saved to the poor. A Privy Council order, exhorting "a better abstinence used than hath bin", was given out repeatedly that year, and reiterated the next year by both the Council and the Queen. The Archbishops of York and Canterbury likewise instructed the clergy to urge the rich once more to moderate their consumption, and increase their charity to the poor.[84]

These commonwealth teachings, then, exerting the force of hallowed moral tradition, became ever more urgent public standards at the forefront of popular consciousness as the continuing food and price crisis inevitably escalated class antagonisms. A ballad circulating in London in June 1596 (perhaps by Thomas Deloney) attacked magistrates for failing to implement relief measures, and parodied their Book of Orders.[85] A royal proclamation of November 1596 ('Enforcing orders against dearth') deplored and criminalized so-called 'badgers', secret purchasers of local grain for sale elsewhere at higher prices, and also commanded landowning revellers in London back to the shires, "there in charitable sort to keep hospitality".[86] The Elizabethan elite, as Archer (55) notes, were highly sensitive to "criticism for harsh treatment of the disadvantaged". London's mayor reported in September 1596 that four thousand twopenny loaves had been distributed to the poor since July: but this was "little more than a drop in the ocean, just enough to provide one day's ration in bread each week for one person in each of the households recorded as wanting relief at the beginning of the year."[87] An analysis of pauperism in 1597 gave as its principal causes continuing abuses by the wealthy: excessively luxurious expenditure, and excessive consumption of food, leading to rack-renting and sale of lands; gambling, usury, illegal inflation of corn prices; and unnecessary dismissals of servants and apprentices.[88] A libel circulating in 1595 put it more concisely: "For seven years space they [the rich] have fed on our flesh, on our wives and children . . . ; oh, who is the better for all the dearth? The rich."[89] A Somerset J.P. would write to Burghley in September 1596 complaining that the dearth was encouraging many "to all contempte of bothe of noble men and gentlemen, contynially bussynge into there eares that the ritche men have gotten all into their hands and will starve the poore."[90] It was rumoured in the autumn of 1597 that Mayor Spencer himself had kept back from the market the overseas grain he had purchased, to profit by rising prices.[91] The original audiences of *Romeo and Juliet*, wealthy and poor alike, must consequently have been very highly sensitized to portrayal of the class relations of wealth: in particular to the issues of extravagance in consumption, and of charity toward the hungry. If we are to recover the original political morality built into in *Romeo and Juliet*, we must imaginatively reenter this climate of heightened ethical assessment of wealth.

Capulet is a primary focus here. Shakespeare, we saw, conferred on Juliet's father intriguingly anti-populist overtones ("Hang! Beg! Starve! Die in the streets!"). As a rich and prominent member of the urban elite, he must have suggested to many in the audience a profile of the London rich in general. Since he is also extravagant and elite, authoritarian and self-absorbed, is it possible that in the figure of Capulet are suggested the lifestyle and limitations of London's leadership, the complacent and unpopular aldermen? In the alienated paternalism of the domestic father, is the *city* father analogized? Aldermen were "invariably the wealthiest members of city society" (Archer 51); and the traditional precepts on curbing lavish feasting, particularly when freshly urged by clergy and Council, were, as Power reflects, "doubtless unpopular with the aldermen" (Power 385), and presumably often ignored. The aldermen, moreover, were tending to neglect market regulation in the 1590s: "more ready to discipline marginal groups like fishwives and other hucksters than they were to restrain the wholesaling interests at which much popular anger was directed" (Archer 55). During the crisis years of 1594–97 the court of aldermen became actually *less* active than hitherto in fining bakers producing underweight wheaten loaves. They also failed to ensure city-wide poor relief, leaving this instead to parish officers. In their "complacency", the aldermen had to be "galvanized" by the parliament of 1597 to assume such a role (Power, 374–78). The aldermen had instead expended most of their energy during the crisis years in demonizing the underclasses as the source of disorder, to the point of introducing, in February 1596, street cages in which the disorderly were incarcerated [92]—a circumstance which again lends particular ideological irony to the presentation of those figures of urban nobility, Capulet and Montague, as themselves racing onstage inflaming their households in belligerent public disruption.[93]

Though foodstuff prices soar in London, Capulets and Montagues and their rank inhabit a virtual Land of Cockayne. "Sirrah", Capulet orders a serving man, "go hire me twenty cunning cooks" (4.2.3). His only worry, it seems, is for a suitably abundant and superior cuisine. Capulet's household is persistently identified with the tantalizing condition of food awaiting. "Madam", cries a servant to Lady Capulet, "The guests are come, supper served up, you called" (1.3.102–03). Capulet's two feasts, indeed, punctuate the action. At the first, where Romeo and Juliet meet, Capulet begs the disguised departing Montagues, with gloating false modesty, "Nay, gentle-men, prepare not to be gone. / We have a trifling foolish banquet towards" (1.5.118–19). This trifling banquet opens, appetizingly, with a stage direc-tion for servingmen to "come forth with napkins"; and it conspicuously involves reference to a 'court-cupboard' (1.5.5)—the most expensive house-hold item, used for public ostentation of goblets, ewers, silver plate, wine, fruit, etc.—which is possibly presented onstage, since we hear of the com-mand for its removal with the plate. Busy servingmen enter shouldering bas-kets of food. "Things for the cook, sir, but I know not what" explains one of them at 4.4.13. The household menials share surreptitiously the patrician plenty: "Save me a piece of marzipan" begs one to another (1.5.6). The second feast, to celebrate the Juliet-Paris wedding, causes Lady Capulet only one worry: "We shall be short in our provision. / 'Tis now near night" (4.2.38–39). The following morning, nonetheless, presents an imminent *embarras de richesse*.

Lady Cap.:   Hold, take these keys and fetch more spices, Nurse.
Nurse.:   They call for dates and quinces in the pastry . . .
Cap.:   Look to the baked meats, good Angelica.
             Spare not for cost. (4.4.1–2, 5–6)

The food predictably catches the attention of the musicians, mocked for their low income by Peter ("musicians have no gold for sounding"): "Hang him, jack! Come, we'll in here, tarry for the mourners, and stay dinner" (4.5.160,165–66).

The Capulet household however enjoys no monopoly of the theme of well-fed revels. Romeo's insouciant "Where shall we dine?" is echoed by Mercutio's "Romeo, will you come to your father's? We'll to dinner thither" (1.1.166; 2.3.126). Their jestings run to sharp sauce for a sweet goose, and disparage the meagreness of hare pie (2.3.65–71, 118–25). Jarringly unap-preciative of his privilege, Romeo expresses his lovesickness for Rosaline by declaring himself

    Shut up in prison, kept without my food,
    Whipp'd and tormented. (1.2.53–54)

By coincidence or otherwise, these are the same four conditions that befell the butter rioters: hunger, imprisonment, whipping, and "torments" (the pillory). Indeed it is at just this moment, as if a corrective class perspec-tive were called for, that Romeo is interrupted by an illiterate member of the lower orders: "God gi' good e'en. I pray, sir, can you read?" (1.2.56). (Literacy, we recall from the rebellion in 2 *Henry VI*, could be perceived by the underclasses as a working marker of resented class privilege.) "Ay, mine own fortune in my misery" responds Romeo, unbudged from self-pity. Such contrasts haunt the play; and it is hard to avoid the view that they will have helped in that intermittent targeting of Romeo for audience derision or antipathy which is effected by a thematic 'effeminating' of Romeo remarked by many critics.[94] ("Like a mishaved and sullen wench, / Thou pouts", the Friar comments, at 3.3.143–44).

Romeo, perhaps infuriatingly, is associated with banquets. "I have been feasting with mine enemy", he relates to Friar Laurence (2.2.49). The Friar compares Romeo's love for Rosaline to a dish he seasoned, but threw away without tasting (2.2.71–72). Later he links romantic intemperance to epicurean excess: "The sweetest honey / Is loathsome in his own deliciousness, / And in the taste confounds the appetite" (2.5.11–13). Romeo, indeed, will describe the Capulet tomb as a "detestable maw", "gorged with the dearest morsel of the earth"(5.3.35–36,45–46). Breaking into its "jaws", he declares "I'll cram thee with more food." Juliet's body, he feels, makes the vault "a feasting presence" (5.3.48, 86). In the light of such imagery, Juliet seems to function as a further, if sublime, appetite of the self-indulging Romeo: "dearest morsel" of a leading scion of the banqueting class.

From *2 Henry VI*, with its spurning of commoners petitioning against illegal enclosure (1.3.24–26), to the pathos in *The Tempest* of the torture-threatened Caliban protesting to Prospero that he had taught him the fertile places of the isle (1.2.340–41), Shakespeare trained a humanitarian eye on access to food as a foundational shibboleth of social justice. Following *Romeo and Juliet*, working men in *I Henry IV* would refer casually to the death of 'Robin Ostler': "Poor fellow never joyed since the price of oats rose; it was the death of him", 2.1.10–12. The thematic will be centralized again with the next major food riots, *Coriolanus* responding to the Midlands Risings of 1607–08 ("What authority surfeits on would relieve us", 1.1.13).[95] In *Romeo and Juliet*, as emblematic climax to its dearth-amidst-surfeit complex, comes the youthful diner's direct encounter with cadaverous desperation. In the apothecary, famine is graphic, both as corporal emaciation and broken-spirited surrender. The contrast with Brooke's treatment of this incident is again instructive. Both narratives explain the apothecary's motivation in breaking the law to be the bite of poverty. "For nedy lacke is lyke the poore to compell / To sell that which the cities law forbiddeth him to sell" notes Brooke laconically (2573–74). Brooke's Romeo, however, does not indulge in pauper-bullying, but simply asks outright for poison. His Romeo has no recourse to taunting, for Brooke presents the apothecary as eager to break the law, immediately "inflamed" by the sight of "glittring gold." "The wretch by covetise [*not*, we note, by reluctant desperation] is wonne" (2576, 2581) glosses the censorious and self-contradictory Brooke. His apothecary becomes a somewhat sinister figure, prompt to sell poison, who whispers conspiratorially in Romeo's ear (2584). He appears to believe the "poyson stronge" is for murder, since Romeo gives no hint of suicide as the intention. By contrast, Shakespeare's apothecary had been asked for a dram that would kill "the life-weary taker" (5.1.62). Further, Shakespeare's apothecary initially resists the illegal request; and even as he caves in before

Romeo's persuasions, he registers his moral disapproval of the transaction: "My poverty but not my will consents" (5.1.75).

If Shakespeare's apothecary thus becomes a figure for whom any audience, especially famine-fearing commoners in 1595–96, may feel sympathy, Shakespeare's Romeo becomes far more problematic. Defined now in terms of haughty class-superiority even as he seeks the means of final self-sacrifice to Love, Romeo—whose loudness of voice surprises the apothecary (57)—commands his lowly instrument with peremptory authority:

> Come hither, man. I see that thou art poor. (5.1.58)

The Shakespearean 'targeting' effect becomes clear here, as Romeo, volleying rebuke and supercilious command, instantiates once more the figure of the brusquely domineering lord whom we noted opening *Shrew* and other plays. "Art thou so bare and full of wretchedness, / And fear'st to die? Famine is in thy cheeks, / Need and oppression starveth in thy eyes, / Contempt and beggary hangs upon thy back" (5.1.68–71). Like the hierarchically insentient Duke Theseus ("To you your father should be as a god", 1.1.47), who opens *A Midsummer Night's Dream* by revelling in his own ardour for Hippolyta while condemning Hermia's love and coolly sentencing her "To death or to a vow of single life" (121), Romeo, "over-full of self affairs" (*Dream* 1.1.113), is culpably blind to the suffering humanity of a social inferior.[96] Twenty lines of preceding meditation (5.1.37–57) on the apothecary's penury—"Sharp misery had worn him to the bones" (41)—have evoked in Romeo, as his soliloquy plainly informs the audience, not compassion, but merely a sense of the man's fitness as a tool in shady dealings, an assessment driven by open contempt. "Beggar" (56), "beggarly account" (45), and "caitiff wretch" (52) convey the tone of indiscriminating class-condescension: a blanket derogation resembling the Elizabethan authorities' classification of a range of lower-class ranks and occupations with the vague and disparaging term 'apprentice'.[97] Romeo's callous instrumentation here may even carry echoes of those contemporary libels circulating in London which accused aldermen and magistrates of turning the commons' hunger to personal interest, through forming *pactes de famine*.[98] Certainly, the conclusion of their business touches one more time the nerve of contemporary anxiety: "Farewell, buy food, and get thyself in flesh" bids a sardonic Romeo (84).

Nothing in the drama, however, had prepared us for the breathtaking radicalism of Romeo's well-chosen line of persuasion.

> The world is not thy friend, nor the world's law.
> The world affords no law to make thee rich.
> Then be not poor, but break it, and take this. (5.1.72–75)

In simple monosyllables, with patronizing plainness, Romeo spells out, as though to a child, the brutal catechism of class-consciousness. Perhaps nowhere else in the Shakespearean canon is there a more candid instance of ideological subversion. The very essence of the spirit behind the London riots, and behind dozens of others across England in the two closing decades of the sixteenth century, seems here summed up: the nation's laws are inimical to the interests of the poor, and quietism only leaves the poor clamped in their hopeless condition. The case seems the more compelling coming from one for whom the Prince himself recently "hath [b] rush'd aside the law", as Friar Lawrence twice points out: "The law that threatened death becomes thy friend, / And turns it to exile" (3.3.26 and 138–39). Having digested this recognition that his class privilege extends to juridical functioning itself, Romeo turns it witheringly upon the apothecary. The demystification of law as repressive social control is, moreover, diagrammed here to incite immediate lawbreaking. In the political context of the riots and their aftermath, it is remarkable that Shakespeare dared to do this; and even more remarkable that he got away with it.

Perhaps one factor in his success here was the strategic impact of the gloss that Shakespeare cunningly allocated Romeo as soon as the apothecary had capitulated:

> There is thy gold—worse poison to mens' souls,
> Doing more murder in this loathsome world,
> Than these poor compounds that thou mayst not sell.
> I sell thee poison; thou hast sold me none. (5.1.80–84)

These sentiments would prove immediately reassuring to authority and its censors, striking an absolving, almost homiletic tone of Christian piety. Indeed, in disparaging wealth as injurious to the possessor, the self-serving rhetoric further articulated, paradoxically, an article of dominant ideology, thus closing the scene on the safe note of class orthodoxy. For the dispraise of riches and privilege as a burden unappreciated by the vulgar, was an article of faith among the jewelled classes: a favoured courtly trope of the sixteenth century enunciated in Castiglione, and reiterated in Elyot's *Book of the Governor*.[99] Sir John Cheke, castigating the hatred of gentlemen demonstrated by Kett's rebels, likewise asks in *The Hurt of Sedition* (1549) "Whi should ye thus hate them, for their riches or for their rule? . . . If ye felte the paine that is joined with governaunce, as ye se and like the honoure, ye woulde not hurte otheirs to rule them, but rather take great paine to be ruled of them."[100] In Thomas Lodge's *Rosalynde, or Euphues Golden Legacie* (1590), from which Shakespeare borrowed the plot of *As You Like It*, Lodge frequently muses thus: "Ah *Rosalynd* what cares wait upon a crown, what griefes are incident to dignitie? What sorrowes haunt royal Pallaces? The greatest seas have the sorest storms, the highest birth subject to the most bale, and of al trees the Cedars soonest shake with the winde: small Currents are ever calme, lowe valleys not scorcht in any lightnings, nor base men tyed to anye balefull prejudice. Fortune flies, & if she touch povertie, it is with her heele."[101] Sidney elaborated in *Astrophil and Stella* on the sleeplessness often denied the rose-garlanded chambers of the privileged, for sleep was "The poore mans wealth, the prisoners release".[102] Demystifying the motif, Shakespeare presents this perverse transfiguration of opulent privilege into bemoaned oppression at many points: in Henry V's self-pitying dismissiveness of "the intertissued robe of gold and pearl" and "thrice-gorgeous ceremony", for instance, which disallows him (he claims, fresh from encountering commoners insomniac with military terror) the contented sleep of the peasant (4.1.244, 248). Likewise his father complains that "in the perfumed chambers of the great, / Under the canopies of costly state" the sleep is elusive that blesses "smoky cribs" (2 *Henry IV* 3.1.12–13, 9). Henry VI laments lack of a shepherd's contentment "far beyond a prince's delicates, / His viands sparkling in a golden cup" etc. (3 *Henry VI* 2.5.51–52). Richard II will prove prompt, he feels—for about a minute—to exchange riches for simplicity: "I'll give my jewels for a set of beads, / My gorgeous palace for a hermitage, / My gay apparel for an almsman's gown" etc. (3.3.146–54). Richard III, feigning reluctance to accept "the golden yoke of sovereignty"—the throne, for which he had murdered so many—coyly protests "Will you enforce me to a world of cares?" (*Richard III*, 3.7.145, 213). Elizabeth herself was to remark to Parliament in 1601 that "To be a king and wear a crown is more glorious to them that see it, than it is pleasant to them that bear it."[103] Wealthy young Romeo's words thus vary a gilded topos, structural to power—the myth of the happier poor, spared the anguishes of affluence—and provide his dangerous earlier perspective with a kind of ideological alibi: the law may deny the poor opportunity for enrichment, but they are fortunate to be so unencumbered.

A second 'alibi', of course, was Brooke. Geoffrey Bullough, introducing Brooke's *Romeus and Juliet* long ago in the first volume of his *Narrative and Dramatic Sources of Shakespeare*, accurately termed it "a leaden work", and remarked that "The surprising thing is that Shakespeare preserved so much of his source in vitalizing its dead stuff."[104] Shakespeare's unusually close dependence on his source may thus have been, I suggest, a conscious tactic, securing himself an easy line of defence of a content only now rendered dangerously 'political' by current events.[105] For although Shakespeare made a number of significant modifications of Brooke to suit his own purposes, the playwright had shrewdly found a tale in which reckless upper-class violence, a self-inculpating, lenient prince, and poverty-driven crime (the apothecary) all lay innocuously to hand in a thirty-three year old narrative poem on long-ago in wicked Italy.

* * *

The opposition of feasting and hunger that Shakespeare has woven through his play is but one element in its sustained populist sensitization to social inequity. The exotic high fashions that the wealthy can parade are not only mocked by Mercutio but exhibited by Romeo, who apparently sports a 'slop', the wide, loose breeches of the French style ("There's a French salutation to your French slop", snorts Mercutio, at 2.3.39–40.) Further, Jean MacIntyre has noted that "the play may well have strained the wardrobe resources" of the company, given its requirements for costuming forty-one speaking parts, many of which require 'best apparel': the guests and gentlewomen at Capulet's first feast, for instance, "an occasion for which Elizabethan decorum would expect fine clothes", as well as Romeo and Juliet, still wearing their 'best robes' in the balcony scene. Such costuming demands, I suggest, would have furthered the class-polarization emphatic in the play; for as MacIntyre interestingly observes (without politicizing the perception), "By parsimony with some characters' costumes, Shakespeare may have been compensating (or overcompensating) for the lavishness of apparel at the Capulet feast late in Act one."[106]

Privileged idleness allows Romeo a perverse (and highly fashionable) nocturnalism, wandering abroad before dawn, then locking himself up during daylight to "make himself an artificial night" (1.1.133), so that he loses his sense of time (1.1.153–54), just as Capulet and Paris can spend all night together in celebrating the betrothal to Juliet.[107] ("Get you to bed. Faith, you'll be sick tomorrow / For this night's watching" the Nurse scolds Capulet (4.4.7–8). Their wealth is repeatedly displayed in an effortless tipping and procuring ('tantalization effects' of the kind we shall discuss in *As You Like It*): Romeo dispenses coins to the Nurse for bringing Juliet's message, to Balthasar in the churchyard, and of course to the apothecary for his poison; Juliet sends a ring to her "true knight", twice displayed (3.2.142; 3.3.162). Capulet dispatches first a servant for "twenty cunning cooks", then the Nurse for baked meats ("Spare not for cost", 4.2.2; 4.4.6). At the play's conclusion, the bereaved parents pledge themselves to commissioning statues of the lovers, to be raised, astoundingly, "in pure gold" (5.3.298). The contemporary context is again suggestive. In 1595, the hated Lord Mayor of London, Sir John Spencer, against whom death-threats were made, whose home was threatened with arson, and outside whose door the rioters had erected a gallows, was bitterly nicknamed, for his great wealth, simply 'Rich' Spencer.[108]

In sustained contrast to the conspicuous wealth and tantalizing feasting, is the insistently scripted presence of toiling underclasses. In another notable departure from Brooke, the drama counterpoints gangs of idle patrician youths to knots of busy servants, who bustle in repeatedly to service their superiors' demands. Act one scene three closes with a frantic servingman who emerges from hall and pantry to announce supper served, "everything in extremity", his own need to dash away and wait at table, and the plea that Lady Capulet "follow straight". Capulet's feast (act one scene five) opens with the entry of at least three servants. "Where's Potpan, that he helps not take away?" (1.5.1) establishes immediately the tone of strain, whilst, as Romeo's exuberant masquers "march about", the servants hurry on with napkins, prepare the table, bundle away joint-stools and cupboard, turn the tables up (a complex operation, as an Arden note suggests, requiring removal of pegs, lifting of table tops, and stacking of these with their trestles against a wall), and supply more light. Stage directions for a later scene (act four scene two) again specify opening with "two or three servingmen", now taking orders for guests and cooks. At 4.4.13 "three or four servingmen" enter, "with spits and logs and baskets", to be peremptorily ordered by Capulet "Make haste, make haste!" and "Sirrah, fetch drier logs!" The major characters each have their personal servant: while Juliet has the Nurse, the Nurse herself has her "man" (2.4.19), just as Romeo has his "man" (2.3.4.169, 179) to bring cords for his ascent to Juliet. Mercutio, who bristles into hostile punning when Tybalt refers to Romeo as "my man" (3.1.51–54), will demand "Where is my page? Go, villain. Fetch a surgeon" (3.1.90), just as Tybalt orders an underling "Fetch me my rapier, boy" (1.5.52). The Nurse, her bones (she claims) aching, sums up the point of so much intrusive stagecraft:

I am the drudge, and toil in your delight. (2.4.74)

The contrast of indolent privilege and toiling subaltern is thus not mere empiric 'reflection' of a class-stratified social formation, but a representation calculated, in a time of heightened and bloody class friction, to appeal to populist resentments. Romeo, we have already seen, is perhaps the principal figure of such political targeting, his self-pitying patrician self-absorption several times juxtaposed directly to underclass disadvantage or misery in such a way as to highlight his enviable social privilege. The puncturing of his pampered Petrarchanism through contrast with the illiterate serving man, we have noted already; and the play's contrast of literacy and illiteracy appears systematic.[109] We have seen, too, his hectoring and subsequent betrayal of the apothecary "worn to the bones" by "sharp misery" (5.1.41), as well as the carefree masquing of Romeo and his companion *bon vivants* about the stage as a set of busied servants lay out their feast. One final example may serve to illustrate how much of the play's original meaning has been lost through the combination of a traditional scholarly exegesis paying little attention to the plays *qua* plays, and the depoliticised interpretation of the play as essentially honoring a 'transcendent' love.

In Romeo's first sight of Juliet (1.5) we have some of the most celebrated lyric lines in the English language. "O, she doth teach the torches to burn bright" gasps a Romeo forever transfigured (41). The original feeling generated here, however, appears to have been rather more complex and problematic than the uplift of the exquisite. The stage on which Romeo speaks is crowded with many figures, the primary contrast of worker and reveller having been established from the outset by those four or more servingmen whose activity sets them off from the guests, and whose speaking parts compel our observation of them. Capulet keeps them harried by a volley of disparaging commands (lines 25–26). Ordered by Capulet to produce more light ("More light, you knaves") at line 25, they are apparently unsuccessful, being commanded again at lines 84 and 122 ("More light! More light!" and "More torches here!"). It is in this context that Romeo speaks—to the servant, the script suggests—his celebrated exclamations.

Romeo: What lady's that . . . ?
Servant: I know not, sir.
Romeo: O, *she* doth teach the torches to burn bright!" (1.5.41; emphasis added)

In the midst of such stage activity, Romeo's words as directed to a servant failing to produce better light acquire overtones of rebuke or disparagement. Reflex contempt, we have seen, is habitual to this master class ("Where is my page? Go, villain"; "More light, you knaves"; "Art thou so bare and full of wretchedness / And fear'st to die?"etc [3.1.90; 1.5.27; 5.1.68–69]). Romeo's continuing language of epiphany—Juliet becomes "a rich jewel", and "Beauty too rich for use" (43, 44)—resonates likewise with the elite values of confident opulence and work-free leisure. Juliet's raptures at her wedding had been similarly provocative. "They are but beggars that can count their worth", she cried, in what is easily construed as a sneer. "But my true love is grown to such excess / I cannot sum up sum of half my wealth" (2.5.32–35). The self-delighting sybaritics of their transports would not be missed by a popular audience, with its vocal component of maids and servingmen, porters and mechanics, apprentices, journeymen and labourers. In the midst of sublime ecstasy, Romeo and Juliet are simultaneously in the midst of the frictions of class. In the starvation years of the mid-nineties, how could they not be?

The players and their playwright know just where, in this graphic contrast of lifestyles and dignities, they are themselves sited. If, in the "two-hours' *traffic* of our stage", anything should "miss", apologises the Prologue, "our *toil* shall strive to mend" [italics mine]. The unusual term 'traffic' (rare, notes the OED, before 1600), normally signified trade or commerce; and allied to the Nurse's emphatic word ("toil"), the players thereby mark—perhaps announce—discrete awareness of their own class-position. ("It is probably not an overstatement" declares Gurr of patrician perspective upon common players, "to say that to the aristocracy they were at best befriended parasites.")[110] Shakespeare, despite the coat-of-arms obtained for his father, never secured the right to put 'Gent' after his name on the title pages of his works.[111] Technically classified as retainers, labouring in an intensely precarious new profession, and often poorly paid, it is no surprise that Elizabethan dramatists and licensed players could be sympathetic at a time of crisis to the perspectives and grievances of the subordinate classes. The fortunes of the two groups in fact were frequently linked: following the 1595 riots, the Lord Mayor urged the Privy Council in September to suppress the theatres, as having helped "infect" "the late stirr & mutinous attempt of those few apprentices."[112] Such circumstances lent economic incentive to the theatre to become, in diplomatic degree, spokesman and defender of a commons demonized by authority.

* * *

In light of the historical class-tensions and populist sentiments traced above, further moments of the play may now perhaps recover lost political valences. When, for instance, the discovery of Juliet's 'corpse' by her heartbroken parents is suddenly 'capped' by a series of jests between Peter, the Nurse and the musicians, the brusque eruption of comedy would seem not a lapse of taste or abrupt comic relief, but the supply of a form of audience 'retaliation' against the banquet-happy and authoritarian Capulets. By involving the audience in a burst of merriment that actively contradicts the Capulets' suffering, the sharp juxtaposition constitutes another 'populist' refusal of sympathy for the grief of the elite that we have seen structuring the presentation of Romeo. Indeed the pointedly visible *onstage* contrast between the doomed bustle of the Capulet household and Juliet's 'deathbed'—it is apparently unremoved and in plain view from 4.3 throughout the feasting anticipations opening 4.4—may likewise have afforded the audience (knowing what Capulet does not) a kind of conspiratorial gratification, as they anticipated an imminent counterstrike against the domineering will of the sybaritic master of the house.

At one final point in the play, thinly veiled political language takes on a new bite. Elizabethan audiences, heir to medieval allegoric traditions of construing art and nature, were highly alert to symbolic overtones in popular drama—political overtones in particular. Drama, after all, showed "the very age and body of the time his form and pressure", Hamlet noted; and as Leah Marcus has remarked, Renaissance plays were enjoyed most for their spicy topicalities.[113] Censorship only heightened the will to cunning decipherments. "The institutionally unspeakable makes itself heard inferentially, in the space between what is written or acted and what the audience, knowing what they know, might expect to read or see", observes Annabel Patterson.[114] Kett's Rebellion, according to Holinshed, had been sparked by a play.[115]

It is consequently not perverse but proper to note suggestively political dimensions to the language of this drama. Gregory's line in the opening minutes of the play, for example, "the quarrel is between our masters and us their men" (1.1.17)—given in response to Sampson's threats against Montague's "men" and "maids", and at once dismissed by Sampson ("'Tis all one")—would seem to push the meaning of a line artfully ambiguated by Shakespeare in the direction of signifying "the quarrel is that of the masters against us their servants", rather than "the quarrel is between two masters, and involves their respective servants". If spoken as admonition, with a clear break after the word "us", the line is at once disambiguated: "the quarrel is between our masters and us, their men". Witty and sceptical Gregory, who has been puncturing steadily the vainglorious bragging of Sampson, thus establishes a note of contemporary political resonance from the play's opening minutes, with the exasperated retort to a fellow serving man to get his priorities straight and remember which class he belongs to. Shakespeare's ingenious capability for producing such sentences, charged with a political ambiguity whose preferred meaning can be selected and projected in delivery, was, I suggest, another of his tactics for outflanking Elizabethan censorship. (We might compare the perspective on kingship, as admiration or exposé, in Horatio's response when Hamlet reveals that he has sent Rosencrantz and Gildenstern to their deaths, and probably to Hell, yet feels no pity: "Why, what a *king* is this" [5.2.63; emphasis mine].)

The disagreement between Gregory and Sampson proves highly topical. Its suggestion that the kind of class-solidarity manifested in the Apprentices' Riot was emergent, unsettled and contingent, is born out by *A Student's Lamentation*, which remarked just such divisions among apprentices, claiming the riot to have failed precisely because many apprentices had thought their primary duty to be to their masters, and reported to them the imminent mass gathering.[116]

In Gregory's words here, appealing for underclass solidarity—"The quarrel is between our masters and us their men"—surfaced just that note of inflammatory appeal that the thoroughly alarmed government was seeking to root out. "If any trecherous insinuater goe about to intice you to insurrection: if any idle headed libeller scatter papers amongst you, winne never dying praise by detecting them", urged the *Lamentation*.[117] It is Romeo, conversely, who acts in unproblematic class allegiance. Fingering the impoverished Mantuan apothecary in the note he gives to Balthasar for delivery to his father (5.3.274, 287–88), he fulfils the role of government informer praised by the *Lamentation*. First seducing the apothecary in the language of a treacherous insinuater ("The world affords no law to make thee rich. / Then be not poor, but break it"), then promptly betraying him, Romeo emerges a virtual *agent provocateur*. "O true apothecary" Romeo exclaims at point of death (5.3.119): testifying to a one-way class fidelity. His treachery appears to have been lost upon modern literary criticism; but that it would not have been lost on contemporaries is clear from a recent proclamation, 'Protecting Informers', of 1594. So hated were government informers—termed 'promoters' in contemporary argot—that they found themselves "beaten and very evil treated" by "light and evil-disposed persons . . . in great routs and companies."[118] To meditate, therefore, the response of contemporary audiences to discovering Romeo's meticulous betrayal of a starving commoner, revealed indeed during the menacing inquisition of a wrathful Prince interrogating "the parties of suspicion" (5.3.221), might prove useful schooling for those asserting Shakespeare's patrician affiliation or transcendence of the political.

* * *

There will be readers who view the kind of interpretation of Shakespeare set forth here as hopelessly tendentious. Shakespeare, they may affirm (as has Alvin Kernan in a notable work), was a thoroughly conservative play-wright.[119] Traditional criticism often assumes Shakespeare's concerns to be largely apolitical, construing Romeo as an essentially romantic hero: the play dwells upon love, not politics. In brief response I would argue that Shakespeare's presentation of Romeo and Juliet's love did not conceal its mediating class conditions; that the existence of a noble-souled Romeo does not banish his evil twin; and that Shakespeare the problematizer reveled in precisely such complication, thematic, moral and political. The love between Romeo and Juliet certainly possesses rare sensitivity and sanctity, brilliantly counterpointed as it is by Mercutio's obscenities, Capulet's brutish imprecations, and the Nurse's roistering prurience. Yet their love is deeply shadowed—as traditionalist criticism has long acknowledged—by the obtrusive Roman Catholic imagery that articulates its inception ("shrine", "pilgrim", "palmer" and "saint" at 1.5.91–103), by the 'feminization' of Romeo which it effects, and by the Renaissance horror of suicide which terminated it. Why, then, should we rule out the *political* as a further dimension of such sustained artistic ambiguation, enveloping both Romeo and his class? At the very climax, after all, of Romeo's apotheosis, as he eternalizes his passion and presses into "death's dateless night", we are propelled by his penultimate sentence into memory of others' physical pains—those of the victims of poverty: "O true apothecary", he cries, "Thy drugs are quick!" (5.3.119–120).

The overtones of political protest for which I have been arguing in this play projected in their cultural moment, moreover, an interestingly ambiguous relation towards authority. For the most part these perspectives were not 'radical' in the modern political understanding of that word, but 'medieval populist'; and as such they embodied the paradox of a loyal disaffection or licensed indictment. For the play's demystifying presentation of the city's ruling classes could claim to be a dutiful echo of higher authority, its barbs activating the ancient civil ideal of Commonweal paternalism shared by monarch, church and Privy Council. Much in *Romeo and Juliet*'s sceptical portrayal of the urban rich would have been shared by the nation's rulers, for 1594–97 saw considerable friction between city leaders and the crown.[120] The Privy Council, and later Parliament, were much irritated by what they saw as the failings of mayor and aldermen during the twinned crises of price inflation and public disorder. Indeed, notes Archer, "a common explanation for outbreaks of disorder in London was the 'want of government' in masters over their servants":[121] a perspective surely evoked in *Romeo*'s opening scene of boisterous servingmen anticipating loyal household violence. Capitalizing on the tension between ruling class blocs, Shakespeare could critique the lower authority from the protective shelter of the higher. It was a pattern, after all, often repeated in the period, as the court protected the public theatres against the wrath of City Fathers who would close them.

Yet this is not to deny that Shakespearean political critique was, in the terms of his own culture, marked by radicalism. As a number of critics have pointed out, merely to 'problematize' dominant ideology, to suggest alternative perspectives upon official Tudor historiography or the distribution of wealth, was to occupy, dangerously, an 'oppositional' position.[122] To place alongside *Romeo and Juliet's* presentation of class the keystone tenet of dominant ideology, articulated in Cranmer's words to the Western rebels in 1549—"The greatest multitude [is] for the most part always wicked", for "A gentleman will ever show himself a gentleman and a villein a villein"—is at once to perceive, I suggest, the founding heterodoxy of Shakespeare's political sympathies (and that of many contemporary dramatists).[123] Gregory's arresting cry, during the angry days of the London Riots, that "the quarrel is between our masters and us", not to mention Romeo's catechism to the apothecary on the class-interest of the law, suggest it to be more reasonable to place consideration of Shakespeare's plays in the context of a ferment of angry dissidence, of an intellectually exciting interrogation of traditional wealth and class, than to assign to them a putatively consensual dominant ideology. Bishop Bancroft was worrying, rightly, in the mid-1590s over "what John Cleveland was to call 'that levelling lewd text' . . . which dated from the late fourteenth century and was never forgotten":[124]

> When Adam delved and Eve span
> Who was then the gentleman?

It was, one might guess, on the tip of Gregory's tongue.

8   *As You Like It*
Political Topicality

> This great dearth of victuals causeth men to keep as little houses
> and as small hospitality as they possibly may, and to put away their
> servants. Whither, I pray you, but a-begging, or else (which these
> gentle bloods and stout stomachs will sooner set their minds unto)
> a-stealing?
>
> (More, *Utopia*, Robinson trans., p.31)

In his opening oration to the 1597–98 parliament, Lord Keeper Egerton
praised Her Majesty—formidably in attendance—for so great a care in
preserving her kingdom to the benefit of her subjects "that the simplest
among them could not but see, and the wisest but admire, their happiness
therein; the whole Realm enjoying peace in all security."[1] Yet this was to
prove, in J. E. Neale's words, a parliament "into which rushed concern
for the economic disorders of the day", lamenting problems in the rural
world of catastrophic magnitude: enclosures, dispossession, depopulation,
vagabondage and hunger. On the first day of business, November 5th 1597,
Francis Bacon condemned, probably by governmental direction, "Lords
that have enclosed great grounds and pulled down even whole towns and
converted them to sheep pastures". All shame for such proceedings had
now disappeared, he said, "and therefore there is almost no conscience in
destroying the savour of our life—I mean bread."[2] Bacon's motion sought
to replace privately lucrative pastures by publically beneficial agriculture,
reconverting to cultivation all fields taken out of longstanding tillage since
the queen's accession. Supporting the bill, one speaker noted bitterly that
"There groweth cleanness of teeth through scarcity of bread."[3] "The eyes
of the poor are upon this Parliament", he warned. "This place is an epitome
of the whole Realm . . . We sit now in judgement over ourselves." Echoing
More's *Utopia*, he deplored a state very different from the happy kingdom
of Egerton's official rhetoric—a "brutish land, where sheep shall devour
men"; and he blamed "gentlemen", who "will become . . . grinders of the
poor, whereby, if not the heart of Cain, they yet strive to bring the punishment of Cain upon their younger and weaker brethren, to make them
vagabonds and runagates upon the earth."[4]

As You Like It, staged less than two years later, likewise takes itself as
"an epitome of the whole Realm", piercing, like Jaques "through / The body
of country, city, court" (2.1 58–59), and it likewise focuses "vagabonds

and runagates upon the earth." Literary criticism has not always taken the play's measure here, sunnily asserting, for instance, as recently as 2005, that from the moment it escapes the world of Duke Frederick, "all the rest of the play is one long celebration of benign comic freedom".[5] Anne Barton likewise finds it impeturbably harmonious, with "a stillness at the centre which no turn of the plot, apparently, can disturb".[6] Even the well informed Edward Berry concludes that Shakespeare's Arden "seems to have only one definitive attribute: an exclusion of contemporary reality."[7] Yet *As You Like It*, with its cast of malnourished cottager, bankrupt gentleman, starving vagrants, scathing malcontent, and assorted political refugees, takes pains to foreground anti-Arcadian perspectives, evoke political ills, and countervaluate harsh contemporary attitudes. Sparkling as the play often is, its tonal range and nuances, as well as its targets of hilarious political mockery, have yet to be fully identified.

"PRETTY COUNTRY FOLKS" (5.3.22)

As You Like It's remarkably spirited politics of resistance are plain as a wayside oak when we resituate the drama in three political contexts that overarched English life in 1599–1600; indeed their sturdy, broad-boughed visibility may explain why this drama, despite much near-Falstaffian hilarity, went unpublished before the first Folio, in 1623. The first two contexts, rural distress and the government book burning of early June, will be addressed in this chapter; Chapter 9 will sketch the populist ire mounting against the church in the late Elizabethan culture wars.

The engulfing misery of rural England was highly topical: a problem addressed both by royal proclamations in 1598 and 1600, and by the 1598 parliament. Historians have well mapped this terrain, and recent literary studies are now absorbing its significance.[8]

In the late sixteenth century aristocratic attitudes to greenwood and flock were sharply contradictory. On the one hand, these were idealized, in the pastoral tradition so fashionable at court, as the playworld of passionate lovers and idling herdsman flortists; but to the eyes of the authorities concerned with realpolitik, sylvan underclasses were anathema. For it was to wastes and forests that the poor, the evicted and the unemployed drifted, since there, by a law of 1550, they could build cottages and claim grazing rights.[9] A tradition of independence flourished in such areas, permissive of far more mobility and freedom than the regulated arable regions. The wealthy accordingly favoured disafforestation to destroy the resorts of masterless men. Indeed to the propertied classes, as Camporesi demonstrates, pauperism often suggested "a tide of human insects that would rise until finally submerging them."[10] "The poor increase like fleas and lice, and these vermin will eat us up unless we enclose", declared one seventeenth century pamphlet.[11] Shakespeare's play, however, contradicts patrician perspective in both its aspects: demystifying its fake golden world as a realm of injustice and desperate poverty, the drama conversely rehumanizes its economic victims, the demonized woodland vagabonds.

The idyllicism of the lilting pastoral songs, we will see, is thus ironized by stage incident; a strategic erosion of mythic surface which recalls Shakespeare's technique in *Henry V*, where propagandist courtly voice (the Chorus) is likewise sabotaged by the disclosures of staged action.

By 1599, Arden had ceased to be dense forest. Already by the early sixteenth century a mix of woodland and pasture, the encroachments of mining, local population growth (rising nearly forty per cent from 1570–1600), and further conversions to arable and pasture, were thinning Arden's remaining woodland. These woods, moreover, far from offering green haunts of popular freedom, were increasingly controlled by local landowners, who, thanks to illegal enclosures, owned by 1550 over ninety per cent of the woodland.[12] The ensuing social destabilization, combined with the rocketing prices of the 1590s, inflicted "increasing polarisation within local society and the creation of a landless proletariat."[13] Trees retreated before desperate squatters' cottages and a commons overstocked with animals. Always regions of exceptional poverty, disorder and class conflict, forests came packed with political disaffection: even more so in decline. "It is surely no coincidence" writes David Underdown, "that between 1590 and 1620 the Henley in Arden court leet regularly presented people for engaging in violent affrays, in numbers out of all proportion to the population."[14] "The forest", notes Buchanan Sharp, "supplied important supplements to income: pasturage for a few cattle, pannage for swine, game to be poached, and wood which could be used for building materials and fuel." Deforestation could consequently trigger riots. Even as *As You Like It* was likely still playing to London crowds, Rockingham Forest exploded, in 1603, as "the base sort" attempted to prevent felling of trees and removal of deer.[15] During the 1580s and 1590s, "the Forest of Arden was one of the most disaffected agrarian regions in the Midlands, intermittent commissions of enquiry ordered by the Crown providing neither solution nor more than temporary alleviation."[16] Since even well-to-do farmers suffered economically from the enclosure of former forest areas, "propertied opinion" could prove ambivalent, even sympathetic to rioters, local authorities taking only "half-hearted measures", with "foot-dragging and excuses" to restore order.[17] Home in Stratford, Shakespeare would have been inescapably aware that around one quarter of the township, in the year he penned *As You Like It*, had been reduced by failed harvests, fire and enclosures, to poverty.[18] The year before Shakespeare wrote this play, Sir Fulke Greville "without warrant illegally denuded large tracts of their trees" in Arden.[19]

Vagrancy was an allied problem—more for the desperately trekking unemployed themselves, than for the Tudor state which endlessly vilified them and hysterically exaggerated their numbers—as wandering, dispossessed folk, criminalized *per se* by legislation, sought forest and commons wastes where they might elude the further catastrophes of bloody lashings, ear-boring, branding, incarceration in bridewells, impressment, summary execution under martial law, or even the penal slavery twice legislated by parliaments.[20] "No-one could guess, by reading this Act [of 1597], that there was any lack of employment in England as the century drew to its close."[21] In the mid-1590s, "Whipping posts appeared all over London, and payments in accounts show that they were regularly used in ensuing years."[22] The parliament of 1597 decreed that itinerant paupers as young as seven years old should be punished as vagrants; and in February 1598, London's Court of Bridewell Hospital was flogging 25 to 50 vagrants *every* day. An alarmed contemporary in the early seventeenth century estimated the English vagabond horde at eighty thousand—a figure corroborated by some historians today.[23] The parliamentarians of 1597 even decreed that the wandering destitute should be dispatched to the galleys. No evidence has been found, however, that suggests this barbarism was enforced.[24]

Yet "It is difficult", writes J. A. Sharpe, "to draw any real distinction between the vagrant and the unstable poor of the parish, the migrant workers, servants or poor labourers who had no real stake in the community, and who were terribly vulnerable to the economic crises of the period."[25] Woodland sanctuaries, as we have seen, were however disappearing, as the wealthy waged campaigns of expulsion, and as the great trees were hacked into timber. "Rosy prospects for large profits encouraged men for whom the greenwood was just so much minstrelsy nonsense to move in with the axe ... So just at the time when Robin Hood's Sherwood was appearing in children's literature, stage drama, and poetic ballads, the greenwood idyll was disappearing into house beams, dye vats, ship timbers, and iron forges."[26]

For the destitute who stayed put in their parishes, the traditional relief of 'hospitality' was disappearing, the monasteries having been abolished, and the doors now increasingly locked on the hall tables of the great as they absconded to London pleasures. By statute of 1563 compulsory wage-labour was imposed for life, without choice of employment, upon all indigents over the age of twelve. Parliament legislated the death penalty upon any who three times fled. (Fortunately, "Tudor magistrates were not as savage as parliament.")[27] Unremitting hard labour was, of course, for the moral and spiritual benefit of the poor. As Sir Edwin Sandys expressed it, petitioning (successfully) the Privy Council for permission for the Virginia Company to kidnap the children of vagrants for deportation to the colonies, "under severe Masters they may be brought to goodness."[28] Worse, in a century of galloping inflation Justices of the Peace fixed the wages of forced labour below subsistence level (reasoning that several family members would be employed), thus making savings unthinkable, the education of one's children impossible, and very survival problematic. Associating to improve wages was criminalised, as was any private act of kindness by which an employer might raise wages above the specified level.[29] By 1600, between a quarter and a third of the rural population was thus trapped, with no hope, in the new agrarian proletariat.[30] Remarkably, "Those entirely dependent on wage-labour were so badly off in the sixteenth and seventeenth centuries that 'neither contemporary nor modern economists can explain how they lived.'"[31]

This condition of permanent landless bondage was profoundly resented as 'slavery'.[32] ("What reverence he did throw away on slaves" Richard II sneers languidly of Bullingbrooke's courtship of the lower orders [1.4.26], in superbly chosen deictic insult.) The new social meanness towards those committing the sin of poverty was becoming commonplace. For the poor man, "the bitterest thing he suffers is his neighbours", John Earle would write. "All men put onto him a kind of churlisher fashion."[33] Suggestively, actors too could be placed in these denigrative categories, as a species either of vagrant (as in the 1572 'Act for the Punishment of Vagabonds' wherein "Common Players in Enterludes" might be liable for punishment as "roges Vacaboundes and Sturdy Beggars" unless duly licensed by dignitaries),[34] or of wage-labourer, stigmatised with the insulting term 'hireling'. "Gosson denounced stage players as 'hirelings', and in 1615 one of the worst things that could be said against an actor was that 'his wages and dependence prove him to be a servant of the people'".[35]

In these conditions, *As You Like It* sets up anticipations of idyllic country retreat—

> They say he is already in the Forest of Arden, and a many merry men with him; and there they live like the old Robin Hood of England. They say many young gentlemen flock to him every day, and fleet the time carelessly, as they did in the golden world (1.1.114–19)

—only to undermine them, despite much song and celebration, by incursions of cold realism. Just as Shakespeare exposes the court's *urbs in rure* through the Touchstone-Corin dialogue ("Those that are good manners at the court are as ridiculous in the country as the behaviour of the country is most mockable at the court"; 3.2.40–42), and renders Petrarchan figurines (Sylvius and Phoebe) stylised against more realist portrayals of love, so he demystifies Arcadian projections of country life through inductions of contemporary actuality.

The shepherd, Corin, recalls the venerable literary stereotype of the innocently assiduous *vetus colonus*: "Sir, I am a true labourer. I earn that I eat, get that I wear; owe no man hate, envy no man's happiness; glad of other men's good, content with my harm; and the greatest of my pride is to see my ewes graze and my lambs suck" (3.2.64–67; compare Amien's standard pastoral song on the retired man's life, "Seeking the food he eats / And pleased with what he gets", 2.5.34–35). Yet Corin is a propertyless hireling, abandoned by a master "of churlish disposition" to impotent hunger. "At our sheepcote now / By reason of his absence there is nothing / That you will feed on" (2.4.75, 79–81). At risk of starvation and vagrancy through no fault of his own, Corin presents the pathos of pauperized wage-labour, facing displacement. In Shakespeare's source, Thomas Lodge's *Rosalynde*, the runaway heroines had by contrast "made merrie" in the house of Coridon the shepherd upon "countrey fare", and counted "no content [compared] to the blisse of a Countrey cottage."[36] Shakespeare's introduction of a shepherd unable to offer hospitality is unprecedented (as Renato Poggioli noted) in all pastoral literature.[37] Tudor poor law initiatives, despite proliferation and complexity, attained very limited success in relieving either malnutrition (especially in bad harvest years), or "that general impoverishment of the labouring poor suggested by our sources for the half-century after 1580."[38] "The slender resources available for poor relief meant that the bulk of what was available went to the aged, impotent, and very young", rather than to people of labouring age and capacity—ever assumed to be mere idlers.[39] Rosalind and Celia, even on the run from despotic power, can effortlessly buy Corin up, "his cot, his flocks, and bounds of feed" (2.4.78): an instance of wealth's casual appropriation of helpless rural humanity that, though sympathetically motivated, reminds us of the desperate extremes of rural poverty in contemporary England, so deeply contradictive of both the commonwealth ideal officially regulating the Elizabethan economy, and of that peaceful peasant well-being envied by the propertied in their pastoral verse and by so many of Shakespeare's kings. ("Care cannot harbour in our cottages", warbles Lodge's Coridon, "nor doo our homely couches know broken slumbers: as we exceede not in diet, so we have inough to satisfie.")[40]

Shakespeare's treatment of rural refugees and the dispossessed is likewise a politically charged departure from both political and literary norms. That outlaws holed up in the forest seek "sermons in stones, and good in everything" (2.1.17), proving morally superior to the court, which (again very topically) banishes and seizes at whim,[41] has some basis in the conventions of pastoral romance and in *Rosalynde*. Yet Lodge's greenwood is studiedly a courtly paint-job: in its elaborately Euphuistic rhetoric, its frolicking swains and nobly Latinizing heroes, the entire confection is a bravura gentlemanly fantasy into which no reality intrudes. For Elizabethan gentlemanly reality consisted in a near-pathological hatred of the roaming and propertyless as 'vagabonds', whether in forests or on the roads. In literature, best-selling works claimed to profile their true nature as 'cony-catchers and bawdy baskets': professional criminals opting freely for a life of pleasurable wandering over decent Christian labour, their fleshly sores and emaciation mere self-inflicted tactics to fleece gullible citizenry.[42] Thomas Harman's *Caveat for Common Cursitors*, an early classic of the emergent genre of rogue literature, claims to survey at first hand a worthless and predatory 'fraternity' organized into criminal specializations (rufflers, priggers, palliards, Abraham men), armed with a horrifying repertoire of stratagems, and protected by an arcane language of its own. Harman, who delights in recounting anecdotes of his harassment and even torture of vagrants, appears to have invented the term 'rogue', from the Latin 'rogare', to ask: thus eliding a plea for bread with criminal status. Thereby popularized, the term became, as Linda Woodbridge has noted, "elevated to the status of a legally defined technical term in a statute" in the 1572 Poor Law act.[43]

Reprinted in 1573 and 1592, Harman's writings on the "scelerous secrets" of the "rowsey, ragged rabblement of rakehells" spawned many imitators, most notably in the pamphlets and plays of Robert Greene and Thomas Dekker multiplying through the 1590s and the early Jacobean period.[44] The copiousness of the literature became such that some modern literary historians, such as Arthur F. Kinney, have been deceived into accrediting this farrago with sociological verity. The myth has been exploded, however, by analysts like Camporesi and Woodbridge.[45] The latter sensibly notes, for instance, that the use of a secret language alleged of rogues ('Pedlar's French') would have been "a dead giveaway" of tricksters and wrongdoing, and appears rather to be one of Harman's own self-projections, "madly minting strange new words".[46] Further, the familiarly scurrilous realm, with its frequently self-contradictory admiration of criminal ingenuity, has been plausibly classified by Woodbridge, following a hint in Greenblatt, as a subspecies of jest book, in vogue among Humanists and general public alike through the sixteenth century.[47] Yet it is also perceptibly the world of emergent City Comedy, projected onto field and footpath. Peddling vagrant Volpones to a readership of Politic Would-Bes, Harman and his ilk market a demonizing displacement of precisely those ruthless pecuniary energies, entrepreneurial, specializing, insouciantly transgressive of medieval class propriety, that typified the appetency of the rising bourgeoisie in the early capitalist city.[48] Welcomed by the propertied classes, and helping drive the penal legislation of branding and ear-boring, of bloody floggings across country to houses of correction, rogue literature functioned as projection, as well as furnishing a legitimate discourse.[49] "Rarely has any culture fashioned so wily and powerful an enemy out of such degraded and pathetic materials", comments William Carroll.[50] Conveniently repealing the medieval sanctity of poverty and mendicancy, and displacing the passionate tradition of Christian distributivism urged by the Commonwealthmen, the rogues' gallery of cheerily cunning parasites ideologically anaesthetized guilt over re-enserfing victims of enclosure, depopulation and ill-chance in the ghastly new proletariat.[51]

What must also, I think, have consolidated late Tudor 'terror of the tramp' were propertied nightmares of underclass revolt, following Germany's Peasants' War of 1525, Anabaptist egalitarianism at Munster (1533–35), and at home, the rebellions of 1549. The literature of the rogue as tramp gained its large popularity in decades following Kett, with Awdeley's *Fraternitie of Vacabondes* (1561) and Harman's *Caveat* (1566; reprinted 1573 and 1592).[52] Further, "the new surge of cony-catching pamphlets in the 1590s . . . followed the demobilization of the militias" raised in the war with Spain and Ireland, for veteran soldiers were stereotyped as dangerous rogues.[53] In England this literature was much harsher, judges Pugliatti, than its comedic, Italian models.[54]

Medieval attitudes, schooled by the Church Fathers, had favoured unconditional almsgiving to the indigent. ("Extende manum tuam, ne sit contracta. Non sumus vitae examinatores", urged John Chrysostom.)[55] "In the early Middle Ages . . . It was the Church's mission to help the poor, and a third or a fourth part of Church income was to be allocated to them on a regular basis."[56] The general principle was trenchantly affirmed by Tertullian: "Deus semper pauperes justicavit, divites praedamnat".[57] To revile the poor, warned Ambrose, was to commit murder.[58] Yet by the sixteenth and seventeenth centuries, medievalism's sorrowing mendicant had been stigmatised into early modernity's disorderly vagabond: "sine re, sine spe, sine fide, sine sede," in the words of one disgusted magistrate.[59] As Pugliatti's fine research has shown, statutes converting destitute humanity into a cheap supply of forced labour—a necessity of developing capitalism—began, in France and England, in the fourteenth and fifteenth centuries: "provisions for the poor and the repressive and compulsive measures which accompanied them were a matter of economic policy long before becoming a matter of Protestant ethics." Systematized poor relief measures, which "bear striking similarities" were springing up across Europe in the 1520s.[60] When, belatedly, England came to companion its anti–vagrancy laws with relief mechanisms, "the English statutes were probably the most aggressive and virulent."[61]

Robert Crowley had pithily expressed the older attitude to poverty in 1550, "Yet cesse not to gyve to all, / Withoute anye regard; / Thoughe the beggers be wicked, / Thou shalte have thy rewarde."[62] His fellow Commonwealthman, Bishop Ridley, had urged William Cecil in 1552 to take over Bridewell palace for the relief and retraining of the destitute: "I must be a suitor to you in our good Master Christ's cause; I beseech you to be good to him. The matter is, Sir, alass! he hath lain too long abroad (as you do know) without lodging in the streets of London, both hungry, naked and cold."[63] Likewise, the Elizabethan 'Homilie of Almes deeds' taught that "He that receiveth the poore and needy, and helpeth them in their affliction and distresse, doeth thereby receive and honour Christ their Master".[64] Yet these very homilies were deep in Tudor denial: "povertie followeth idlenes . . . For a great part of the beggary that is among the poore, can bee imputed to nothing so muche, as to ydlenes, and to the negligence of parentes" (*Homily against Idleness*, 1563).[65] Influential Puritans like William Perkins—whose teachings on the vagrancy issue were published in just the period of *As You Like It*, appearing between 1597 and 1601—were now arguing that it was spiritually sinful to give alms to vagrants, since this encouraged parasitism.[66] And by the mid-seventeenth century, Puritanism had hardened its heart further: "ordinarily it is a duty rather to die than to take another man's goods against his will", admonished Richard Baxter.[67]

"In many parish records", the historian Joyce Youings noted, vagrants were called 'wanderers' (283); and the proclamation against vagabonds of

September 1598 twice refers to "idle people and vagabonds" as "wandering".[68] We should accordingly note, I think, what editors have missed, that Shakespeare has semantically linked his knot of delightful forest outlaws to the reviled condition of vagabondage. Informing Oliver and the audience near the play's beginning that Duke Senior has been banished and his supporters expropriated, Charles jokes of the usurper that "therefore he gives them good leave to wander" (1.1.90). (It was wandering without the good leave of a magistrate, as recorded in a licence, that established the criminal offence of vagrancy.) Though promptly glossed by the wrestler Charles in the machismo terms of Robin Hood fantasy (100–103), the hinted counter-definition of vagrancy's origins in social injustice, not avidity for crime, is soon developed, with the bite of harsh realism, in Orlando's response to his own sudden dispossession.

> What, wouldst thou have me go and beg my food,
> Or with a base and boisterous sword enforce
> A thieving living on the common road?
> This must I do, or know not what to do (2.3.32–35)

Bestowing a moment of sympathetic understanding on the plight of those turned highwaymen, these lines belong to the play's clear intention (among others) of humane counter-valuation of the condition of vagrancy: a project in sympathy furthered by the fact that, despite his immediate disavowal ("Yet this I will not do, do how I can"), Orlando's despairing cry defines what he *does* do, commanding the men he encounters to share, at point of sword, their food with him.

Such incidents were commonplace in Elizabethan England, and would prove an abiding problem. A letter to Lord Burghley speaks in1596 of rebellious men who "stick not to say boldly 'they must not starve, they will not starve'", and who protest "that the rich men have got all into their hands, and will starve the poor."[69] The parliament of 1597–98 had considered no less than fifteen bills to remedy poverty and vagrancy, in what Bacon called "a feast of charity"[70] But so incorrigible proved gentry self-interest that parliament diluted the bill to suppress enclosures; and to the anger of the queen herself, it actually rejected such anti-poverty bills as that to enforce the provision of hospitality (thus failing to heed, as the bill's sponsor put it, "the lamentable cry of the poor, who are like to perish"), as well as rejecting a bill criminalising those practices of forestalling and regrating ("odious to the commonwealth") that inflated food prices.[71] For the impoverished of England, consequently, little was to change, as a Digger pamphlet (1650) would show.

> We have spent all we have, our trading is decayed, our wives and children cry for bread, our lives are a burden to us, divers of us having five, six, seven, eight, nine in family, and we cannot get bread for them by

our labour. Rich men's hearts are hardened, they will not give us if we beg at their doors; if we steal, the law will end our lives. Divers of the poor are starved to death already, and it were better for us that are living to die by the sword than by the famine."[72]

When Shakespeare's Duke Senior, menaced at sword point, freely grants to the armed vagrant Orlando his fill at the banquet—"Sit down, and feed, and welcome to our table" (2.7.104)—his calm and remarkable mercy works as humanitarian rebuke to the Puritanism of Perkins and the hardened heart of Elizabethan officialdom, adamant in parliament and proclamation. Cued by Orlando's pleading speech ("If ever you have looked on better days . . . / If ever sat at good man's feast"), the Duke's reply

> True it is that we have seen better days
> And have been knolled with holy bell to church
> And sat at good men's feasts and wiped our eyes
> Of drops that sacred pity hath engendered

movingly summons an older tradition, aligning Christian duty with hospitality, whose stage effect of large and beautiful compassion traduces the meanness of Elizabethan ruling discourse. This is, in effect, indiscriminate almsgiving of the kind urged by the Church Fathers, at odds with the unwearying Tudor discrimination between the deserving and undeserving poor. The poignant speech by Jaques on the seven ages of man which immediately ensues, and the re-entry of Orlando with the aged Adam in his arms—"his youthful hose, well saved, a world too wide" (159), in his helplessness close to "second childishness and mere oblivion" (164)—infuse the graphic, transforming pathos of a common humanity into the perception of vagrants, the reviled terrorists of official discourse. The move is typical of the values of As You Like It, precipitating traditional popular perspectives against what we shall see to be the new authoritarianism.[73] Orlando had a parallel in the Elizabethan gentleman, Thomas Stanley, once an Inns of Court gentleman, obliged for a time to turn highway robber. Stanley would write in a pamphlet to King James that "The Poore may be whipped to death, and branded for Rogues, and so become Felons by the Law, and the next time hanged for vagrancie . . . before any private man will set them to work."[74]

There was considerable sympathy among common folk for 'spirited crime', evident both in the ballads of the period, and in reluctance to invoke the law's full penalties against vagrants even when they stole. "In the latter half of the sixteenth century there must have been few peasants who could be confident that eviction and vagrancy might not be their ultimate fate."[75] One troubled Justice of the Peace had complained to Burghley in 1596 that "the simple countryman and woman . . . are of opinion that they would not procure a man's death for all the goods in the world."[76] Harman's Caveat was repeatedly vexed that beggars did receive alms and compassion from the public; and Beier records instances of constables indicted for ideological negligence in the punishing or pursuing of vagrants ("the weather was very hot"). As Linda Woodbridge notes, such traditionalist sentiments were fighting a reaguard action internationally.[77] More's Hythlodaeus, deploring the avarice and heartless policies of the aristocracy which produced begging in the first place, had recognised almost approvingly that stealing was preferable to begging for "gentle bloods and stout stomachs"; and Andy Wood demonstrates the preference to 'die like men' rather than starve to have been "a cliché of rebellious plebeian masculinity."[78]

Shakespeare's plays are haunted by concern for the victims of dispossession. Mindful of "unaccommodated man" long before the dark climactic explosions of *King Lear*, Shakespeare's sensibility here would require an entire volume for thorough documentation. Among many examples we might note the following. *2 Henry VI* (1.3) presents commoners petitioning against enclosures and protesting that house and land have been taken from them, only to meet with abuse from the queen and Suffolk. *The Merchant of Venice* has Shylock skewer the Venetians with the home truth of their double-think in protesting his dehumanization of Antonio, since they take slaves, whom "like your asses and your dogs and mules, / You use in abject and in slavish parts" (4.1.90–91). In the same play, Portia is sensitively aware that the very instant of her marriage to Bassanio deprives her of her "fair mansion", her servants, and even of the mastery of herself (3.2.166–171). Dispossession by impressment is glimpsed in *Henry IV*, with terrified men bribing Falstaff into allowing them return to all they love, just as in *Henry V* Williams laments soldiers dying overseas "crying . . . upon their wives left poor behind them, some upon the debts they owe, some upon their children rawly left" (4.1.132–34). Similarly Bullingbrooke, though publically loquacious in *sententiae* of exile consolation, privately rejected all such attempted comforts (*Richard II*, 1.3.256 ff). Mark Anthony installed in power is prompt "to cut off some charge in legacies" in Caesar's will (*Julius Caesar*, 4.1.9), whilst Malcolm in *Macbeth* threatens that as king he would "cut off the nobles for their lands, / Desire his jewels, and this other's house" (4.3.80–81). *Macbeth*'s murderers are "reckless what [they] do to spite the world" because a thane has, in Macbeth's words, "bowed you to the grave / And beggared yours forever" (3.1.111–12, 91–92). Central to *The Tempest* is Prospero and Caliban's hate-spitting exchange over the latter's dispossession: "This island's mine, by Sycorax my mother, / Which thou tak'st from me" (1.2.334–35). Poor Tom's cryptic refrain in *Lear*, "Through the sharp hawthorn blows the cold wind" and "Still through the hawthorn blows the cold wind" (Conflated Text 3.4.47, 91) may derive, I think, from the fact that hawthorn was the Tudors' quick-set hedge of choice for establishing new enclosures, "meant to afford an impenetrable barrier to man and beast."[79] Closing Shakespeare's career in fantasies of restitution, *Cymbeline*, *Pericles* and *The Winter's Tale* take the startling and improbable beauty of their finales from forced and terrible separations magically repaired. Forcibly thrust from household and security, the transformative miseries of Orlando and Adam are thus deeply intrinsic to the Shakespearean imagination, to an outlook permanently impacted by the trauma of loss. The Shakespearean anagnorisis of absolute need, starkest in Orlando and *Lear*, is probably one consequence, I suspect, of Shakespeare's childhood experience of a father spiralling down from civic preeminence into outcast debt and prosecution. Wandering without master, lacking work and wielding a sword, Orlando is in Elizabethan legal terms a "sturdy beggar"—capable of work yet without it—and in precisely the category of vagabondage against which Elizabeth had just issued a proclamation in 1598: for Orlando is a man "wandering in the common highways", who possessed "forbidden weapons", and who attempted armed robbery. Establishing Martial Law for the summary lynching of such disorderly vagrant persons, the proclamation could not but have been in the minds of audiences in 1599–1600. Indeed the crown issued another in January 1600, renewing the command to all officers to suppress and punish "rogues and vagabonds wandering up and down this realm idly and insolently".[80] Yet if Her Majesty was, as the 1598 proclamation (perhaps uneasily) explained, "compelled to look with the eye of severity into these growing outrages" (p. 197), Shakespeare presents a vagrant himself the victim of outrage; and one who, despite drawn sword, can plead convincingly that he goes "like a doe . . . to find [his] fawn / And give [it] food", by introducing "an old poor man . . . oppressed with two weak evils, age and hunger", who has "many a weary step / Limped in pure love" (2.7.127–31).

The ensuing song, commanded by the Duke whilst the starved fall upon nourishment—

> Blow, blow thou winter wind
> Thou art not so unkind
> As man's ingratitude

—may even hint at another topical grievance to which the 1598 proclamation alludes: the presence of multitudes of discharged or deserting soldiers among England's penniless wanderers.[81] The proclamation gestured angrily at vagrants "colouring their wandering by the name of soldiers lately come from the wars"; but the reality was the discharge of many servicemen with little or no pay, in many cases unable to work through injuries incurred in the defence of their country: precisely the grievance we saw hotly discussed in *2 Henry VI* , and later hinted in the death of Jack Cade. The dramatist's apparent sympathy for fugitive ex-soldiers was shared by commoners: for as Breight records, in the face of government-directed pursuit, often "country people harbored the men and helped them escape."[82] Shakespeare presented the condition again, almost simultaneously with *As You Like It*, in the case of Pistol (*Henry*

V), whose crucial defence of a bridge against the French made him, in Fluellen's admiring words, "as valiant a man as Mark Anthony" (3.6.11), yet who ended up friendless, wifeless, unrewarded, and cudgelled by the very officer who so fulsomely had praised him. "*Fico* for thy friendship!" exclaimed Pistol (3.6.51): whom the drama's close found gloomily resolving "To England will I steal, and there I'll steal" (*Henry V* 5.1.78).

> Freeze, freeze, thou bitter sky,
> Thou dost not bite so nigh
> As benefits forgot.
> Though thou the waters warp,
> Thy sting is not so sharp
> As friend remembered not. (*As You Like It* 2.7.184–89)

Shakespeare, then, has transformed a pastoral archetype (Corin) into a sixteenth century starving cottager, and enveloped Lodge's coterie of exquisitely idyllic gentry in touches of realism that evoke the ugly desperation of contemporary wanderers: victims whose demonization he thereby exorcises through humane counter-definition.[83] Seeing suffering individual lives where officials saw vice, Shakespeare stages in his vagrant-at-the-banquet scene of 2.7 a *lyric* compassion, a traditionalist perspective of humane concern and respect ("Good old man, / Thou art right welcome . . .", 2.7.200–01).

Further induction of contemporary rural realism into the forest idyll comes with the motif of heartless invasion by the privileged. Introduced in the extensive descriptive passage on the dying deer, its agony moralised by Jaques, the theme unfolds suggestive imagery of "native burghers of this desert city", "gored" in "their own confines" (2.1.23–25). The process, Jaques comments, is a 'usurping' worse than Duke Frederick's (2.1.27–28), a tyrannical visitation on lives abused "In their assigned and native dwelling place" (63). Crying out as it does for allegoric attentions in its length, stilted diction, and anomalous descriptive precisions, we shall revisit the passage hereafter; but it is evident at once that its import goes beyond the established topos of anti-hunting sentiment, as it "most invectively . . . pierceth through / The body of the country, city, court" (2 1.58–59). The pathos of destructive intrusion by the powerful into a quiet traditional green world was of course the fate we saw befalling Arden and other sixteenth century forests, as the wealthy felled and enclosed, or bought up poor cottages to gain grazing rights for their own livestock: an invasiveness ideologically fortified as scouring away those fleas and lice, masterless men. Such sylvan purging is just what Duke Frederick attempts, we learn at the drama's close: for hearing of men resorting to the forest every day to swell the ranks of opposition, he resolves armed extermination of the threat. When, having "Addressed a mighty power, which were on foot, / In his own conduct, purposely to take / His brother here, and put him to the sword" (5.4.145–47), and having come to "the skirts of this wild wood" (148), he suddenly recants, we feel wondrous relief.

Yet despoliation of woodland innocence by Touchstone is successful. Supervening upon simplicity with casual destructiveness, sporting, in aristocratic tradition, with underclass woman as sexual toy (3.3.62), he employs bamboozling false promise to Audrey (a marriage engineered for subsequent self-extrication) and threats of violence to uproot a sincere rustic courtship ("I will kill thee a hundred and fifty ways", 5.1.51–52). Pitched though the proceedings are into clowning mode and bumpkin obtuseness, Touchstone's sexual predation completes the play's picture of callous dispossession: its gloating expropriation of sexual capital sustained throughout by strident expressions of class contempt for "country copulatives" (5.4.53). "A poor virgin, sir, an ill-favoured thing, sir, but mine own" mocks Touchstone (5.4.55–56), but the point, precisely, is that she never will be: fated to be "forsworn" "as blood breaks" (5.4.54–55), when supercilious courtly hilarity, retired from its playworld, abandons rustic casualties like "winter to foul weather" (5.4.125). Should Audrey become pregnant, in the police-state climate enforcing the new Poor Laws in the 1590s, Touchstone will be liable to financial support of his child for up to fourteen years—but only if she can demonstrate to magistrates evidence of her marital status. Strategically dispossessed of this by Touchstone, she will face flogging, with possible incarceration, as a poor woman convicted of bastardy. For Touchstone, "the good of our returnèd fortune" (5.4.163); for Audrey, like hundreds of other single mothers in poverty, "hard labour and due correction".[84]

"SINCE THE LITTLE WIT THAT FOOLS HAVE WAS SILENCED . . ." (1.2.83): THE BOOK BURNING OF 1599

When *As You Like It* opened in 1599, it followed upon a blaze of state destructiveness. By Star Chamber decree of 1586, John Whitgift, as Archbishop of Canterbury, shared with the Bishop of London the power to licence all publications in England; and by command of Whitgift, officials on June 4 1599 entered the book mart area of London by St. Paul's, seized as many as possible of what were termed "unseemly satires and epigrams", and roasted them on a great public bonfire in the Stationers' Yard.[85] As the executioner stoked the flames, Kit Marlowe's translation of Ovid's *Amores* blackened and disintegrated, all that could be found by Nashe crisped and glowed, Marston curled over and Middleton vapourised, Guilpin charred and Hall went up in smoke, Cutwode and John Davies crumbled in sparks. When it was over, Elizabethan satire blew about the streets in ashes.

The severity of the action was shocking: these works had passed the censor, yet "previously issued licenses were not honoured; books were burned on suspicions alone."[86] Shakespeare must have been particularly stung: both Nashe and Marlowe had been among his professional associates. Marlowe had been a rival, a source of inspiration, a fellow star of the London theatrical world. Nashe (almost certainly) was one of Shakespeare's collaborators in the composition of *1 Henry VI*, and had enjoyed, like Shakespeare, the patronage of both Ferdinand Stanley, Lord Strange, and later, the Earl of Southampton. Worst of all, this fiery annihilation of popular reading owed not, as many modern critics have thought, to moral disapproval of these works' erotic elements, but rather, as Cyndia Clegg has argued, to Archbishop Whitgift's personal intervention in the political climate, to protect from satiric shafts his friend the Earl of Essex, vulnerable while campaigning in Ireland. As Clegg notes, this was in fact the second of three occasions when the Archbishop used his powers of censorship to protect crisis-ridden Essex.[87] Armouring whom Shakespeare would pierce, the Church was improperly burning licensed works to protect the nation's super-militarist Protestant hero, the great earl who was becoming, as *Richard II* and *Hamlet* testify, Shakespeare's *bête noire*. Little wonder that Shakespearean reference to Essex became, this year, fully explicit, in the Chorus' effectively damning parallel in *Henry V* of its pseudo-populist, war-seeking king with the "general of our gracious empress" (5.0.30).[88]

With *As You Like It*, Shakespeare hit back. With truly remarkable audacity, Shakespeare countered castration of printed satire with a roistering apotheosis of satire on the stage. Replete with belly-laughs, clowning and cross-dressing, with its songs, wrestling and flaunted sexuality, *As You Like It* swaggers a pot-belly of carnival, a festival from which Falstaff would have stolen relished quips. Its protests, predictably, include some six references to Marlowe and his work, including direct quotation from the "dead shepherd" at 3.5.82.[89] And Nashe receives perhaps even more attention in the play, as very possibly the subject of the curious allegoric particulars of the wounded deer passage.[90]

The play's defence of satire is textually plain, and has often been noted. Critically neglected, however, has been that public incineration of satires, whose effect was to place the drama's championing of satiric prerogative, value and insuppressibility at the very edge of sedition. It is true that the popular theatres were traditionally licensed, of course, to express *some* degree of anti-authoritarianism; and Whitgift was censor of printed works, not staged. Moreover, this play was not *ad hominem* in its satire—a consideration not insignificant, I suspect, for Whitgift, whose views on the genre were probably coloured by a Marprelate tract's accusation that he had enjoyed sodomitic relations with the Master of Peterhouse.[91] Nonetheless, *As You Like It* was never printed in Shakespeare's lifetime; and we have no record of it staged at court.[92]

The play opens indeed with a tyrannical court, whose arbitrary actions propel into exile not one satirist but two (Jaques and Touchstone).[93] Banishing ruthlessly by paranoid reflex, its commandments, under questioning, prove devoid of rationale: "Let it suffice that I trust thee not", Duke

Frederick lamely tells Rosalind when she pleads to know "the knowledge of [her] fault" (1.3.49, 40). Significantly, this Duke issues orders for "search and inquisition" (2.2.20): and the needless cramming of the words "seize" and "seizure" into the same line at one point (3.1.10) may have activated memories of the books so recently subject to search and seizure. Crucially motivating the despotism is fear of popular forces: Rosalind is banished because "the people praise her"; "Her very silence, and her patience / Speak to the people, and they pity her" (1.2.247; 1.3.72–73). Orlando likewise is plotted against by his brother because he is "so much in the heart of the world, and especially of my own people . . . that I am altogether much misprised" (1.1.143–44).

As You Like It deplores at regular intervals the silencing of "fools" and satirists. "The more pity that fools may not speak wisely what wise men do foolishly" observes Touchstone. "By my troth", answers Celia, "thou sayest true; for since the little wit that fools have was silenced, the little foolery that wise men have makes a great show" (1.2.72–76). Jaques defends satire for some forty lines in act two (2.7.42–87), and even Duke Senior initially appreciates critical expression: disparaging the "peril" of "the envious court" he counterpraises "counsellors / That feelingly persuade me what I am" (2.1.4, 10–11). Relish of high-impact language turns motif: as the girls bid Touchstone "unmuzzle your wisdom", Celia invites Rosalind "come lame me with reasons", and Touchstone, noting escape from violence through turn of nuanced phrase, praises "much virtue in 'if'" (1.2.58; 1.3.5; 5.4.92). Banishing Rosalind, Duke Frederick tells her to leave soon lest "In the greatness of my word, you die" (1.3.83). Celia slyly observes that—like satires and plays, of course—being "news-crammed", she will be "the more marketable" (1.2.79–80).

Yet satiric defiance of authority is ultimately embodied in Rosalind: not only as insuppressible wit ("you shall ne'er take her without her answer unless you take her without a tongue", she boasts to Orlando, 4.1.148–49), but as the transgressively independent woman, flaunting sensuous insubordination through to the very epilogue. Tireless in jokes about cuckoldry, ignoring her father and deceiving her husband-to-be, Rosalind is a masterless *woman* among masterless men. Touchstone's triumphal crow, "By my troth, we that have good wits have much to answer for. We shall be flouting; we cannot hold" (5.1.10–12) sums up the jubilation of satire risen from the ashes.[94]

The very centrality of satire as theme in this play supports the suggestion, as I have argued elsewhere, that the curious passage on the sobbing deer in 2.1 may well evoke the June book burning. Insisting on the wounded animal as a 'fool' or jester ("poor dappled fool", 22, "hairy fool", 40), the excursus laments invasion of its urban setting ("native burghers of this desert city", 23, "fat and greasy citizens", 55) by "usurpers" (61), who wreak destruction in another's sphere ("their own confines", 23, "assigned and native", 63). "A language of class-opposition is, indeed, pronounced here:

we have "burgher" against "tyrant" (22 and 61), and then "leathern coat" against "velvet" (37, 50)."[95]

We have discussed the play so far in terms of the plight of the destitute, and the celebration of satiric perspective: and there might seem some incongruity between these concerns. What logic, if any, connects the play's partnering of carnival roistering with sympathy for the poor, its elision of compassionately transvalued vagabondage with a festival of wit? There is in fact a profound historical congruence to these values: and, in Jaques' suggestive phrase, "The why is plain as way to parish church" (2.7.52). If we would reconstruct the drama's broad agenda, we need, literally, to travel back along this way to the parish church: to explore the world of ridiculed Sir Oliver Martext, and the emerging functions of the national church in the late 1590s. It is to this, the drama's third contemporary context, that now we turn.

9 "Betrayed To Every Modern Censure"
As You Like It and Vestry Values

Many parishes had a 'church house'—a community centre or club at which church ales and other parochial functions were held . . . As such activities declined, it might become the place where the poor were set on work . . . There is an ironical symbolism in this end of 'merrie England', of the village community: the community centre becomes the house of correction.

Christopher Hill, *Society and Puritanism
in Pre-Revolutionary England*, 366

The most ubiquitous and therefore perhaps the most significant politics in early modern England were the politics of the parish, and especially those of the poor rate.

Steve Hindle, *The State and Social Change*, 237

Thou thyself hast been a libertine,
As sensual as the brutish sting itself,
And all th'embossed sores and headed evils
That thou with licence of free foot hast caught
Wouldst thou disgorge into the general world.

As You Like It, 2.7.65–69

Dost thou think because thou art virtuous there shall be no more cakes and ale?

Twelfth Night 2.3.103–04

Arrived in Arden and praising the freedom attained when "exempt from public haunt", Duke Senior moves in a single speech from lauding liberation from "the envious court" to extolling the liberty of finding "sermons in stones" (2.1.15, 4, 17). The movement of thought hints a double escape, from a regime of constraint entwining courtly authority with *ecclesiatical*. That coupled oppression I shall argue to lie at the heart of the drama.

For there is a missing link in literary criticism's connection between *As You Like It* and that 'freedom' of medieval carnival values which the play is often noted to celebrate. There is more to this transmission than a broad matter of folk festivity as generally bequeathed to London's new professional theatres (Barber), or of the state continuing to license a temporary, politically tranquillising revolt by anarchic bodily values (the Bakhtin school), let alone of an undiscriminating conflation of carnival and popular culture with riots and crime (Wilson).[1] Though there is some truth in all these models, the connection between *As You Like It* and carnival values must also be grasped at the level of social and political topicality. The drama is a response, I suggest, to the intensifying, nation-wide conflict over cultural regulation of the English parish, a conflict whose escalation paradoxically produced in the Parliament of 1597–98 both angry complaints and a consolidating statute. At the heart of the friction was the aggressively authoritarian alliance of divisive parish oligarchies with the state church: a union, legislatively empowered, whose culturally repressive dynamic was the campaign to exalt local hegemonies by extirpating folk revels. Blessed by the crown, the censorious campaign grew notably harsher through the 1590s, to the point of detonating explosions of protest against Church courts in the last parliament of the sixteenth century.

"TO SEE NO PASTIME, I" (5.4.184)

Certain features of this pattern were not new. Central government's alliance with local officers had been longstanding in Tudor England. Lacking a national salaried bureaucracy, the dependency of the state on local self-government through rotating, parish-elected officers was such that one historian has described local English politics as an unacknowledged "Saxon republicanism".[2] And crackdowns on the poor were routine in periods of economic distress (for example the 1550s), suppressing alehouse keeping, promiscuity and traditional parish revels. May Day rites were under especial suspicion following the Evil May Day riots of 1517: "By the later sixteenth century May Eve was regularly accompanied by orders for a doubling of the city [i.e. London] watch".[3] Moreover, Reformation zeal had stigmatised calendar festivals as pagan and was phasing out community drama as papist. "We increase the wrath of God more on holy days than on others", Luther had warned, and in England by Order of 1536 these were abrogated, as the occasion, as Hill notes, of idleness, riot and superfluity— and the decay of crafts.[4] Ales and feastings, sexual licence and folk recreation, were associated with Catholicism.[5]

Yet by the end of the century, a new level of censoriousness had developed, assisted by an extraordinarily tight embrace between central authority and local elites.[6] Officers in town and village were flooded with new directives (for road maintenance, provision of militia weapons, regulation and relief of the poor), and to administer this 'increase in governance' they were more highly empowered by the late Elizabethan state. "Having to a very large extent functioned outside the state system," observes Steve Hindle, "the parish now changed its character, becoming to an unprecedented extent a local expression of state authority."[7] Simultaneously, parish self-representation had disengaged itself from a broad-based local franchise to establish the self-perpetuating rule of elite 'select vestries'. As Christopher Hill long ago noted, "From the mid-sixteenth century we find groups of richer parishioners formally agreeing to exclude 'the rest of the common people', although not the leading families of the parish, who would be consulted on important matters even if not members of the vestry . . . Select vestries from about 1590 onwards aspired to have their authority confirmed by a faculty from the bishop. They appealed to the bishops' dislike of democracy, against the 'great confusion' which would result 'if the whole parish should be electors' . . . and 'excite the ruder sort to extreme liberty.'"[8] When Elizabethan vestries "met in parish churches they did so in the presence of the royal arms, the 'dragon and the dog' having replaced Christ as *a*, if not *the*, central symbol in parochial political culture."[9] This late sixteenth century secession of the prosperous notables of town and village from the wider local community generated a new, penal severity of class-control: an almost adversarial, policing relation to social inferiors, aggressively seeking to enforce, as a 'reformation of manners', substantially 'Puritan' values of industrious abstinence and righteous sobriety.[10]

Yet the militant culture of discipline with its inculpatory assault of plebeian pleasure was not confined to Puritanism, occurring often "in the absence of puritan influence". Its impetus seems rather to have derived, in the words of an authoritative recent study by Steve Hindle, from "the extraordinary arrogance and anxiety of the authorities", local and central, as they confronted the immiserising 1590s, with its war-exhaustion, dearth and pauperization: it was "orchestrated by a regime whose concern with order, and with the maintenance of its own authority, had reached almost paranoid levels."[11] Thus central government suspiciously invigilated justices of the peace and parish officers, through the new and intensive usage from the mid-1590s of circuit charges and articles of inquiry, just as local authorities nervously policed the behaviour of their own underclass.[12]

In the minds of the parish elites governing early modern England there thus emerged a distinctively post-medieval structure of feeling, whose ingrained Victorian familiarity perhaps disguises its emergence in the sixteenth century: the 'bourgeois' attachment of snobbery not to wealth or to birth but to a staid and readily reproving civic respectability. These vestry values, as we shall call them, imposed on community by the bureaucratic regimentation of reforming oligarchies, established a monied authoritarian primness, a new snobbery of sanctimonious suppressiveness, that rejoiced in scapegoating the poor and prohibiting their folk celebrations. The old feastings and merry-makings had comprised "shared recreational activity", expressing "communitarian sentiments"[13] and fostering "a strong sense of neighbourly identity":[14] one in which the poor had their rightful place. But now, in the name of public order, anything scandalising the godly was to be extinguished. Like the religious agenda which Weber characterised as "this-worldly asceticism" (*innerweltliche Askese*), the tightening of social control in the Black Nineties dictated hostility to festal pastime.[15]

The result was a clash of cultures, fought out in village and parish across late Elizabethan England, in bitter local wars over civic control and the *mores* of Christian neighbourhood, that escalated through the 1590s and would reach its fiercest point in the first decade of the seventeenth century.[16] "Swearing, tippling, sexual irregularities, 'night walking', absence from church, feasting and merry-making, and general idleness: these were the common targets of reformers everywhere."[17] Maypoles were sawn down, pregnant brides whipped, and drunkards hauled from ale-houses. In parliament, "The rhetoric of the late Elizabethan Commons' debates on drunkenness was both hysterical and class-specific."[18] "The sheer *range* of personal conduct which was now subject to regulation seems particularly novel", observes Hindle. Further, "the fines, penances and evictions which had been generally imposed in the fifteenth and early sixteenth centuries were now increasingly supplemented, or replaced, by scolds' bridles, ducking-stools, stocks, whipping posts and bridewells."[19] Clergy fulminated that after Sabbath revels of bear-baiting, dancing and drunkenness, "men could not keep their servants from lying out of their houses the same Sabbath day at night."[20] The curate of Winsley in Wiltshire, infuriated by midsummer feasting, thundered in 1602 "that all women and maids that were singers and dancers were whores, and as many as did look upon them no better than they." As Peter Burke observes, "It did not escape the godly that the maypole is a phallic symbol."[21] Indeed, "The phallic maypole", noted Hill, "was for the rural lower class almost a symbol of independence of their betters": so that opposition to the strict rule of city fathers might express itself in the erection of maypoles and playing of May games (e.g. Lincoln 1584–85). At Shrewsbury in 1588 prohibition of the maypole saw protestors jailed.[22]

A gentleman at Poyningham in Somerset in 1606, aspiring "to get the love and affection of the common people", was prosecuted for his strategy of promoting a church ale with bull-baiting, and personally joining in the morris dance.[23] We might compare Shakespeare's Henry V bidding for solidarity from his soldiers in his St Crispin's Day speech before Agincourt, by projecting a tipsy calendar wherein each man "yearly on the vigil feast[s] his neighbours", with "flowing cups" (4.3.45, 55): a calculatingly populist transgression of vestry values, companioning a scorn of "gentlemen in England now abed" who will "hold their manhoods cheap" for missing Agincourt (64, 66). Indeed, the great playwright must have chafed over the irony that at Stratford-on-Avon the "Puritan-leaning" authorities prevented the performance of drama in his home town: by 1602 fines were to be imposed on anyone who permitted playing.[24] In popular reaction, a September fair there, as late as 1619, saw rioting when local officers tried to take down the town maypole. Several "prominent townsmen" who had been Shakespeare's friends became involved and championed the old ways, so that the maypole, along with morris dancing and a Robin Hood play, survived until at least 1622.[25]

Late Elizabethan class conflict thus pitched 'emergent ideology' against 'residual' through rival ideals of community.[26] An "ethics of solidarity" was challenged by "one of civility."[27] Feudalism's superstructure had promoted, in David Underdown's words, "the traditional concept of the harmonious, vertically integrated society", whose bonds of paternalism and good neighbourliness were expressed in "familiar religious and communal rituals": a scheme rebuffed by the vestrymen's emergent ideology, with its accent upon "the moral and cultural distinctions which marked them off from their poorer, less disciplined neighbours.[28] Archer writes similarly of the new oligarchic values being imposed in London: "the expression of the social bond [as] a much more hierarchically articulated one than the older practices of commensality among neighbours", the emergent model emphasising "the extraction of deference in return for patronage, in particular through the exercise of poor relief."[29]

We should not, of course, sentimentalize the traditionalist parish. As Hill warns us, a propos of the old church ales, "It had long been a class-divided group", its church providing, for instance, "two categories of communion wine—claret for the vulgar, muscatel for the gentry."[30] Nor, as Archer cautions, should we "exaggerate the divorce which . . . opened up between popular and elite cultures": bear-baiting and public theatre "united spectators from a broad cross-section of society." Yet even these two activities, he concedes, were "much more anonymous forms of recreation than the parochially based activities of the pre-Reformation period."[31] The 1590s, observes Peter Clark, "unstopped a cascade of internal community vendettas . . . the new machinery of the poor law allowed parish busy-bodies to victimise any poorer villager whose face they happened to dislike."[32] In Underdown's summative words, "Whether initiated by county JPs or borough corporations, by village notables or reforming ministers, the campaign against popular festivals was almost invariably divisive. In that campaign Puritans naturally took a leading part. Puritan insistence on the distinction between the elect and the reprobate made the ideal of all-inclusive parish harmony unrealizable . . . Examples of urban conflict can be culled from every part of England."[33] The new divisiveness, judges Hindle, was more than merely cultural: "the most ubiquitous and therefore perhaps the most significant politics in early modern England were the politics of the parish, and especially those of the poor rate."[34]

The new schism helps explain the non-emergence, which we noted in Chapter 3, of any serious rebellions against Elizabeth in the last decades of the century, since what historians call 'the middling sort' found their staunchest ally, in local hegemonic struggle, in the state and its church. Conversely, when, from the second decade of the seventeenth century the crown would begin to antagonise 'Puritan' oligarchies through a reversed policy of support for folk revels (beginning with Robert Dover's revival of Cotswold Games, and eventually eliciting James' 1618 Declaration of Sports[35]), and when Laud thereafter came to intervene in the rule of select vestries in matters of social justice,[36] the standing opposition of the two "socio-cultural constellations" formed that "division in the body politic which erupted in civil war in 1642."[37] The politics of revelry, which in *As You Like It* were anti-establishment, would be reappropriated for monarchism in Robert Herrick's *Hesperides*.[38]

Critical to *As You Like It*, and hitherto unrecognised in studies of our play, I believe, is the absolute centrality of the state church to the prosecutorial climate of the new repressiveness. "The ecclesiastical unit of the parish had been completely fused with the administrative hierarchy of the civil State."[39] In the campaign against folk merriment, the church now expanded the range of activities it punished, and received parliamentary support for its censures through "unprecedented statutory backing".[40] Indeed, a rhetoric developing from the 1580s into early Stuart culture insisted upon a partnership in chastisement between magistracy and ministry, between "the sword of justice and the word of God".[41] It is against just this state-abetted church of penality, with its sword-and-word regime, that Shakespeare's exiled Duke appears to be reacting, relaxing in that freedom from "public haunt" which, evading perilous state power, finds "Sermons in stones and good in everything" (2.1.4, 15–17).

Traditionally, the church had itself been the site of community recreations—and in places still struggled to be. "In 1602 players were given 1s. not to perform in the church at Syston, Leicestershire. In 1612 at Woburn the curate baited a bear in church."[42] But by the late sixteenth century, "Alehouse culture and common village life were worlds apart from the parson's study . . . Improving standards of clerical education and the beginnings of recovery in the economic fortunes of the clerical estate did little to ease social difficulties."[43] The killjoy campaign of the late sixteenth century accordingly began with the church's own institutions. First, Church ales—festivals of wassailing (or pledging one's neighbours) used to raise money to pay the parish clerk and support the parish poor—were becoming replaced by the direct, fun-free cash demands of parish rating. In Somerset, Wiltshire, Worcester, Berkshire, Devon, and other cloth-counties, we find church ales prohibited from the 1590s on grounds of order: a suppression fomenting bitter county county disputes, and even fistfights in church.[44] Zachary Some, at Sandon in Essex, 1592, reviled his parson as "a prattling fool, for preaching against drunkenness", and hurled hassocks at the sexton.[45]

Second, crucial to the ferocious bite of the new parish elites—as to the salve of *As You Like It*—was their escalating empowerment as Churchwardens. The Churchwarden, as Eric Carlson records, had thirteenth-century origins, but his duties were standardized under the Tudors as the upkeep of church property and valuables.[46] It was important that he be man of some prosperity, as he would have personally to outlay expenses in advance; and from the 1580s on, his social status rose further, as more gentry, moved by a "desire to enforce their own social attitudes", held the office.[47] Elected in church after evensong, the Churchwarden was powerful as the crucial arbiter of fluctuating social status in the parish: for nearly everywhere it was he who allocated seating positions in the church, pinpointing the hierarchic location of each member of the congregation. Those who paid the highest church rates ranked supreme; but with local fortunes rising and falling, accusations of bias and favouritism grew commonplace.[48] Parish snobbery's Master of Ceremony, all too often deference was his exaction and abasement his métier.

For, charged with checking church attendance, the Churchwarden's duties extended to breaking into alehouses to haul off roisterers to church, and presenting moral offenders to the ecclesiastical courts. It thus lay substantially with him to report and prosecute the culture of revelry—men and women caught dancing, drinking, fornicating, even harbouring pregnant women.[49] Subject to periodic review, Churchwardens failing to present such reprobate cases might themselves be prosecuted.[50]

It was upon the government's further elevation of these formidable ecclesiastic powers of underclass suppression and chastisement that the counter-cultural riposte of *As You Like It* was written: for by statute of the 1597–98 parliament, "Churchwardens of every Parishe" were made also Overseers of the Poor.[51] It was now their additional role, throughout the realm, to assess their fellows for the poor rate, and to place paupers and their children from six years old in work. Positioned to classify the poor as deserving or undeserving, the Churchwarden as Overseer, in concert with "fower substancial Howsholders" as fellow Overseers, enjoyed discretionary powers to supplement—or not—the income of the workers paid too little to survive: a brutally substantial number.[52] For, as Paul Slack's masterly study noted, records in counties such as Essex in 1598–99, for instance, show that twenty per cent of those *in work* were "not able to maintain themselves and their charge by their labour".[53] The most recent book-length study of poor law relief, Steve Hindle's *On the Parish*, reveals that Elizabethan statutes conferred no entitlement upon even the poorest: of the twenty per cent or so of the early modern population officially recognised as destitute ('paupers'), only about five per cent finally received cash disbursements (becoming 'collectioners'). The remainder, though aged, infirm or ill, were to be found work, or encouraged to attempt survival through solicitation of family and neighbours, or to subsist in an 'economy of makeshifts', being granted rights of pasturage, gleaning and fuel gathering. Parish officers, Hindle insists, "negotiated" relief with the paupers—making eligibility depend upon criteria of social respectability such as sobriety, deference and church attendance.[54] These officials—self-appointing vestrymen "recruited almost exclusively from the upper stratum of village society"[55]—now came to use poor relief as a means of social control. "Vestries are found removing disorderly pensioners from their almshouses or temporarily depriving them of poor relief in hope of 'amendment' of their behaviour."[56]

Furthermore, the same parliament now granted powers of summary justice to constables: permitted, now, to flog the vagrant poor, or to imprison them in stocks for up to three days, without recourse to a Justice.[57] Consequently the "urban oligarchs and village notables who dominated local government" possessed "the authority to police their inferiors almost at will."[58] John Downame, for instance, deplored the unchristian way that the prosperous would "browbeat the poor with proud, sour, and severe looks"; and he enjoined "kind and loving language" to them, "contrary whereunto is the practice of those who join with their alms proud expostulations, harsh words, and upbraiding speeches."[59] The handbook for Overseers (1601) itself deplored the potential of these new "governors of the poor" to "looke like a lyon and domineer like a devil over the poor", exercising "no felicite but in taunting, reviling and abusing the poor". It prescribed nonetheless "a countenance mixt with some austeritie", for mildness encouraged idleness.[60] Central government had handed "power of summary justice to officials in every parish in the land, which they eagerly took up. Who would judge that to be an insignificant extension of state authority?"[61] Wielding a power which might prove that of life or death, the vestrymen were positioned, like modern *mafiosi*, to make to any pauper an offer he couldn't refuse.

It was in the church porch, often after divine service or attended with ringing of church bells, that dole was distributed to the very few of the destitute permitted to become collectioners. It was to the church porch that the desperate came, sometimes whole families, to pass the night out of the rain, and to advertise their plight to the community. ("The why is plain as way to parish church" is a phrase of the scornful Jaques, arguing for a roving liberty, 2.7.52.) And it was in that church porch, surely ironising for many that symbol of ecclesiastic beneficence, that the unsuccoured were sometimes found dead, from starvation and exposure.[62]

Where non-paupers were concerned, the campaign against plebeian revelry utilised yet another church institution: the church courts. Over two hundred and fifty of these existed in Shakespeare's day, and to these 'bawdy courts' men and women might be taken not only for failure to attend church regularly or pay the poor rate but for drunkenness, swearing, ribaldry, whoring, 'wickedness of life' or defending allegedly 'popish' ways. Disciplinary cases in ecclesiastical courts worked not by jury, but usually by compurgation: they could indict, that is, simply on the basis of sworn testimony by locals to the *general belief* that the offender had committed the sin alleged. Thus to anyone with a grudge to pay off or a threat to fulfil, the courts presented a field day for revenge and scandal. "Mean persons", it was complained in parliament in 1598, had to appear "for small causes" whilst there was "a toleration of offences in great persons". Further, "In 1600–01 a man acquitted of the charge of lying with a neighbour's wife, still had to pay costs of £1 3s. 4d. on pain of excommunication."[63] Defendants, that is, found themselves obliged to pay court fees even if found innocent: so that many of the poorer sort were unable to appear to plead their case.[64] The church, conversely, was turning a handsome profit from what was increasingly viewed as a scam. "You keep your apparitors to go pricking up and down the country . . . that they should cite for your own gains" complained one victim in 1591.[65] "An extensive literature of denigration [emerged] in which the church courts were characterised as oppressive, unjust, corrupt and inefficient."[66] The church felt impelled to defend itself, commissioning Richard Cosin—whose government defence of the execution of William Hacket we discussed in chapter three—to publish the propagandist *Apologie of and for Sundrie Proceedings by Jurisdiction Ecclesiastical* in 1591. Hatred intensified as ecclesiastical courts arbitrarily raised their fines, sometimes exponentially: it was complained in 1597 that in some places they had shot up from one shilling to twenty.[67]

Public anger was such that even parliament expressed outrage. "There were attacks on church courts in the Parliaments of 1586 and 1589. In 1593 the outcry against them was so great that the Queen promised that Whitgift would inquire into the state of all the church courts in his province."[68] By the 1598 parliament, finally, it seemed that the dam was finally about to burst. The archbishop now "observed that the 'multitude of complaints' in the last Parliament had endangered the very existence of church courts"; and in alarm he sent circular letters of thundering denunciation to his bishops, deploring "the infinite number of apparitors and petty summoners hanging upon every court; two or three of them at once most commonly seizing upon the subject for every trifling offence, to make work to their courts." He also issued a table of revised fees and charges: "But this did not stop fees being raised."[69] The parliament of 1598 actually proposed "a roving commission on ecclesiastical abuses", but was prevented by royal intervention, since this allegedly would encroach upon crown prerogative as Supreme Head of the Church.[70] The next parliament (1601) introduced a bill (apparently put to sleep again by authority, Neale records) for "the putting down and abolishing of certain idle courts, kept every three weeks by archdeacons and their officials and commissaries and registrars."[71]

A final cause of smouldering anti-ecclesiastical resentment was church intrusion into matters of marriage. This went beyond both vestry tendencies to try to prevent pauper marriages,[72] and ecclesiastical hostility to large and raucous wedding processions. As Hill records, the church was campaigning nationally to invalidate 'informal' weddings, "ignoring the many variant marriage customs",[73] and insisting upon clerical solemnisation: for which, of course, it demanded a substantial sum. "Contemporaries had little doubt that the main interest of the clergy was in the fees payable". From the vestrymen's vantage point, the resultant parish registers were useful to facilitate proper descent of family property, and to forestall false claims to poor relief by verifiably allocating each to their parish. "The introduction of parish registers was an essential part of [the] campaign to make a formal church ceremony the only legal form of marriage."[74] But for centuries, church weddings had co-existed with marriage by simple hand-clasp in front of witnesses; the Lollards, like seventeenth century radicals, had championed such free self-marriage. Popular resentment of enforced church marriage was widespread. "We finde not in the Scriptures the gyv-ing and joyning in matrimonie to be an action of the church", protested John Greenwood, in *A Collection of Certaine Sclaunderous Articles Given Out by the Bisshops* in 1590.[75] Literary expression of such bitterness could mark Robin Hood ballads, insisting that Robin had married Maid Marian informally, without church fee.[76] Puritans, Huguenots and English Catho-lics likewise resented enforced Anglican wedding, as requiring communion and the 1559 Prayer Book.[77] Whitgift's alarmed 1601 circular to his bishops, denouncing church court abuses in the wake of parliamentary criticism, likewise deplored public scandals over marriage licenses.[78] Convocation was compelled to enact canons regulating the issue of marriage licenses in 1597, and again in 1604. "The law prescribed that clandestine marriages, though irregular, were valid and binding . . . But offenders were subject to punishment", in church courts, where they were excommunicated.[79]

When *As You Like It* was written (1599), the church had thus become the fat and active spider at the center of a web of repressive and disciplinary institutions.[80] Abetting through select vestries the interests of a disenfran-chising, newly domineering parish elite; sermonizing upon an industrious and killjoy godliness; suppressing church ales; prosecuting merrymakers and calendar festivity through church courts; functioning through Church-wardens to arbitrate parish status and regiment the desperate poor, few of whom gained succour in the church porch; coercing all regions and all social classes into the costliness of church weddings; incinerating, at the command of the Archbishop of Canterbury, licensed satirical books: the Church of England by 1599 had clamped into place and was contentiously policing a counter-traditionalist order of disciplinary vestry values—a kind of usurping cultural totalitarianism, wherein many commoners feared that they might, in Rosalind's phrase, "betray themselves to every modern cen-sure" (4.1.6). "The humour of the time is grown to be too eager against all ecclesiastical jurisdiction", complained Bishop Bancroft in 1605.[81]

"HOT AND REBELLIOUS LIQUORS IN MY BLOOD" (2.3.50): *AS YOU LIKE IT*

In that closed off, licensed other world of the Globe playhouse, its appeti-tive hubbub placed amongst brothels and close to a bear baiting house, its pleasures sequestered by the bought privacy of forty-two foot high walls,[82] wherein alcohol was on sale and whores swaggered their allure, there was, we have noted, no raising of a curtain or dimming of lights to subdue the boisterous audience mood as Elizabethan plays began. It is into the midst, therefore, of exuberant carnival forces that the haughty young gentleman walks who opens *As You Like It*; and this impeccably dressed figure, "point-device in [his] accoutrements, as loving [himself] than seeming the lover of any other" (3.2.346–47), commences with a torrent of class snobbery. He is, he insists, through to his exit near the end of the first scene, a "gentle-man of birth" (1.1.8). He seeks "Gentleman-like qualities", and "exercises as may become a gentleman" (59, 61). He invokes his "gentle condition of blood" (38), and his quarrel with his brother is that he "mines my gentility with my education". He aspires, he says, to "good education"—hardly an exciting prospect in the carnival world, as *Love's Labour's Lost* under-lines—and he laments being "marred" with "idleness" (28–29). Since the rebuke of 'idleness' was a staple invective of anti-theatrical discourse, the term sets him further at odds with audience values, and the high-minded disgust may have been received as auditorium insult. (Contrast the celebra-tion of idleness elsewhere in the drama: Charles on the banished Duke's men who, like Robin Hood's men "fleet the time carelessly as they did in the golden world", 1.1.102; and Amiens' song praising pastoral *otium* "Under the greenwood tree", 2.5.1–8.) For Orlando is correspondingly abusive of the lower classes. "You have trained me like a peasant", Orlando complains to his elder brother. He must "feed with hinds." "Shall I keep your hogs" he protests (31), as the climax to his lofty scorn.

Most tellingly of all, Orlando is shrill with self-pity because he is not rich enough. He has, he blurts before an audience packed with servants, maids, labourers, apprentices, tradesmen and ex-soldiers, "but poor a thousand crowns" (2). He insists again on the sum as minuscule at line 62 ("the poor allotery my father left me"). Though no critic seems to have remarked on it, a thousand crowns (£250) was in fact the approximate equivalent of £125,000, or around $200,000 in today's currency.[83] The groundlings must have wept for him. In that period, when Orlando pronounced £250 inadequate to his gentility, an unskilled labourer earned £7 per year, a schoolteacher only £20 per annum, and Shakespeare may have paid only £60 for the second largest house in Stratford. In law, theft of a mere two shillings (and a crown was five) was in principle a capital crime. A con-temporary playwright of good standing would receive only £5 for a new drama. To be considered a true gentleman, one needed to spend at least £60 per year: and at this rate, Orlando was set up for over four years without having to breakfast before noon.

Orlando, it seems clear, and through him, gentlemanly self-pity, are being set up by Shakespeare for carnival targeting. Meanwhile, a few feet away, silent as always in canny Shakespearean tradition yet surely responsive to this flow of insult, is one of the "hinds" with whom Orlando feels insulted to eat. "Call you that breeding for a gentleman of my birth, that differs not from the stalling of an ox?" asks Orlando (7–9): but Adam says not a word in agreement. "Yonder comes my master, your brother" (22) is his only, apparently belated reply after twenty-five lines of gentlemanly class contempt. Like Alexander Court following *Henry V's* critical debate before Agincourt, like Jessica, "Lorenzo's infidel", silent at the close of *Merchant of Venice* as Christians celebrate her father's anticipated death in unmoderated racist terms, like the ultra-chaste nun Isabella at the finale of *Measure for Measure*, frozen into silence by the Duke's casual announcement that he will marry her, this charged silence, as Adam listens to Orlando's tirade, constitutes that very typical Shakespearean device, the overdetermined framing commentary. His body language, receiving the hammer blows of derision, are a gift in graphic, wordless judgement, a study in pain or retaliatory resentment beyond the censor's ken. Played at court for studied impassivity or wise acquiescence, in the carnival amphitheatre his eloquent corporal potential includes sardonic disgust or parodic fastidiousness reflecting groundling bristling or whistling. (After all, though later he will pledge his savings and his servitude to an outcast Orlando, at this early point Orlando is still a relatively intact member of the master class, and Adam's own master has yet to cast out of doors Adam's "unregarded age" (2.3.43) with "Get you with him, you old dog", 1.1.69). Shakespeare's audience would thus be watchful of old Adam, I suggest, expectant of reciprocated class hostilities, keyed by familiarity with Shakespearean framing actions to find wry solidarity with their underclass holiday perspective.

Yet they are not, I would speculate, granted this satisfaction. In a kind of miniature action of carnival frustration, whose logic we will only later find unfolded, Adam the hind will not return the class contempt, remaining so sympathetically in ideological complicity with overclass scorn that Orlando confidently includes him in a trick on Oliver: "Go apart, Adam, and thou wilt hear how he will shake me up" (1.1.23–24).

It turns out to be the elder brother who channels at Orlando the latent carnival targeting, initiating a deixis that renders Orlando the butt of audience mockery through very much of the drama. When Oliver crosses the encircled Globe stage, he asks Orlando in startled tone—as well he might—"Now sir, what make *you here?*" (italics mine). "Nothing", replies Orlando snobbishly, for he is "not taught to make anything", but is being "marred", "with idleness." As Orlando rails, Oliver responds with horror—and a presumable glance at the thousands of people watching—"Know you where you are, sir?" When Orlando replies in deictic naivety, "O sir, very well: here in your orchard", he must have been met by audience laughter. Yet Oliver persists, with a gesture perhaps at the groundlings, "Know you before whom, sir?" "Ay, better than him I am before knows me" counters Orlando, in catastrophically haughty deictic ignorance. In a piece of brilliantly scripted stage ambiguity, then, Orlando's ideological posture, defined through his loud class superciliousness, is being punished as misfit through a pattern of audience interaction. Where other characters acknowledge or tease the

Globe community, Orlando is apparently unaware of the spectators' (presumably often vocal) existence. He inhabits the drama as a deictic outsider. In a pastoral play, he complains from the outset against being kept "rustically" (6); and, disapproving of the forest as "desert", he will hang tongues on every tree "That *civil* sayings show" (3.2.113, 116, emphasis mine). In contrast to the Duke's description of the happily sequestered life "exempt from public haunt", Orlando defines himself contrariously as "inland bred" (2.7.96): a phrase evoking, perhaps, the realm across the water from the Globe, beyond the Liberty. He belongs to officialdom's realm, willing subject of gentlemanly authority.

Orlando, then, is sequestered from us, marooned inside the fiction amidst a lapping sea of spectators. In Shakespeare's theatrical targeting of Orlando, the kind of deictic lobotomy that excises his auditorium consciousness renders his vision not strictly sightless but site-less. To Latinize the condition, we might say that Orlando is hic-gnorant, or ille-terate. This politically strategic privation, a recurrent device of Shakespeare, we might christen *claustration* (from the Latin 'claudere, claustrum', to enclose, or bar up), Orlando being only one of many *claustrati* in the plays who have been sealed off by an invisible dramaturgic wall from audience awareness. (We saw Eleanor and York make sport of other characters through this device in *2 Henry VI*.)

Yet this stagecraft-punished overweening gentility is but one aspect of a crucially ambiguous and ideologically destabilized Orlando, in whom thwarted pretension to class superiority becomes paradoxically articulated through a discourse that smacks of underclass rebellion. Orlando insists that he is treated like an animal—precisely as were the poor. "Hounds were better fed than servants, and they were sometimes better housed", records historian Keith Thomas. He cites a Stuart commentator who noted masters to care so much more for their dogs than their servants, that "you may see in some men's houses fair and fat dogs to run up and down and men pale and wan to walk feebly."[84] In More's *Utopia*, Hythlodaeus similarly judges that the poor, who live "by so great and continual toil as drawing and bearing beasts be scant able to sustain", nonetheless "get so hard and poor a living, and live so wretched and miserable a life, that the state and condition of the laboring beasts may seem much better and wealthier".[85] One of the leaders of the 1596 Oxford Rising held that "servants were so held in and kept like dogs that they would be ready to cut their masters' throats".[86] Accordingly, Orlando is on familiar ground for many in the audience when he complains that his condition at the hands of Oliver "differs not from the stalling of an ox" (9): a perspective that goes some way to explaining Adam's apparent sympathy, as a servant who anticipates how poorly he will be treated "When service should in my old limbs lie lame, / And unregarded age in corners thrown" (2.3.42–43). Orlando persists with "His animals on his dunghills are as much bound to him as I" (12–13), and wonders whether he will have to share husks with the hogs (31). His bitter claim that "his horses are bred better" (9) is a standard plaint of class resentment: found in Jack Cade (*2 Henry VI*) who, arraigning Lord Saye, declares "thou oughts't not to let thy horse wear a cloak when honester men than thou go in their hose and doublets" (4.7.42–43).

Orlando's conclusion is likewise politically charged. His spirit, he claims, "begins to mutiny against this servitude. I will no longer endure it" (1.1.19–20). He will rebel against what sarcastically he terms "the courtesy of nations"—an angry indictment of social convention that anticipates the explicitly subversive intentions of another wronged younger brother, Edmund in *King Lear*, who cheerleads groundling mutiny against "the curiosity of nations" (Conflated Text 1.2.4). ("Why brand they us / With base? With baseness? Bastardy? Base? Base?"1.2.9–10.)[87] True to his word, Orlando erupts into violence, when insulted (or perhaps struck) by his elder brother. With a deftly immediate success, which must have won a gust of admiration from the crowd, he pinions Oliver into pain and concession. "Wert thou not my brother, I would not take this hand from thy throat until this other had pulled out thy tongue for saying so" (50–52). Yet even here, the offence is to have been termed low born (villain / villein, 47).

In the context of the populist theatre, then, its carnivalesque orientation still close to the surface in the play's opening minutes, Orlando will be received as an arrestingly contrary figure. Alienating in his shrill class contempt, offensive in his whining genteel insistence on the insulting insufficiency of the wealth bequeathed him, comically hapless in his claustration, he yet echoes the language of underclass resentment, and embodies the exciting spirit of active resistance—a cocktail of ideological contrarieties at times promising a Molotov cocktail. This Elizabethan Angry Young Man also possesses street-smart combat skills of the kind that might prove very handy in London's back-streets, as he will demonstrate a second time against Charles the wrestler; yet the charismatic masculine potency, we will see, is cross-grained by sermonizing self-obsession, and he will prove for nearly the length of the drama the dupe and doting puppy of overmastering Rosalind. Punished by duping, targeted by comical deictic unknowingness, and mocked in the allocation of execrable verse, his sneering hubris is humbled: and the ideologically conflicted Orlando of the play's opening, already destabilized by his ambiguous class position, becomes incorporable into the playhouse's community of revellers.

For Orlando resembles many in Shakespeare's carefully appraised audience, victims of the severest form of primogeniture practised in Europe, who are thus appropriable by a politically disaffected and sceptical theatre. Primogeniture, objected more learned Elizabethans, lacked biblical authority, and as Christopher Hill shows, the plight of the younger brother, so frequently showcased in Shakespeare, would be taken up by Levellers, Quakers, Diggers and other radicals in the Republic.[88] Louis Montrose has aptly noted that, since "Shakespeare's audience must have included a high proportion of gentleborn younger sons" acquiring law at the Inns of Court, as well as large numbers of apprentices and servants, then "Youths, younger sons, and all Elizabethan playgoers who felt that Fortune's benefits had been "mightily misplaced" could identify with Shakespeare's Orlando."[89] Yet Montrose misses the strident negatives in Orlando's early characterization, like almost all critics (the play's latest editor, for instance, pronounces Orlando "a thoroughly likeable and good-natured young man", and thinks his opening speech on "but poor a thousand crowns", to "establish immediate sympathy for young Orlando").[90] Conversely, the rare voice of percipient repulsion, trumpeted in Bernard Shaw, discerns only the "safely stupid and totally unobservant young man."[91] But to miss either the supercilious misfit, stuffy fall-guy to carnival values, or the stirring martial mutineer, is to miss the crucial political redirection of Orlando's development from intense ambiguity towards the telos of *As You Like It*: the play's triumphant incorporation of deflated genteel resistance, the ludic rout of vestry values.[92]

Initially, however, the preponderantly outsider status is reprised in the scene where Orlando and Adam resolve to flee on Adam's savings (2.3.39–77). Announcing to Orlando his brother's murderous intentions, the hitherto near-silent Adam breaks out into fourteen lines of a curiously exclamatory homage to Orlando. Commencing, tellingly, in reiteration of Oliver's opening and deictically fraught question, "Why, what make you *here?*" (2.3.4, italics mine), Adam continues "Why are you virtuous?" and eventually concludes "Know you not, master, to some kind of men / Their graces serve them but as enemies? / No more do yours. Your virtues, gentle master, / Are sanctified and holy traitors to you." The strong possibility of deixis here, Adam indicating the groundling sea early antagonised by Orlando's hubristic self-pity, looks clinched by Adam's concluding lines:

> O, *what a world is this*, when what is comely
> Envenoms him that bears it! (emphasis added) (2.3.14–15)

"This" is an habitual deictic pointer; and the Globe theatre as "the world"—its motto was *totus mundus agit histrionem*, The entire world moves the actor—would, many critics assert, become a self-referential commonplace.[93] It is frequently taken so where Jaques' "All the world's a stage", 2.7.138, is concerned. It has not been recognised in this passage, however, even though Adam's melodramatic staccato "This is no place! This house is but a butchery! / Abhor it! Fear it! Do not enter it!" (28–29) would be consonant with the earlier audience estrangement, and produce hilarious carnival targeting.[94] (Frankie Howard's fixated, classic face of scandalised Puritanical horror in *Up Pompeii*, itself derived from vaudeville tradition, comes irresistibly to mind). These deictic histrionics are precisely consonant, too, with what follows: for Adam and Orlando now launch into an enthusiastic Puritan sermon traducing carnival joys.

Traditionally construed, ahistorically, in terms of noble old man and compassionate youth (Burnett sees only wisdom from a "trusty manservant", and even Shapiro merely "an emblem of devotion between old and young"), the values of this scene in 1599 were wholly different in tone.[95] First, Adam lauds his own "thrifty" lifestyle (40) that made possible his savings. Thrift was of course a cardinal virtue of Puritanism and of vestry values, and by definition antagonistic to the priorities of the pleasure-seeking, theatregoing crowd. (Jaques' speech on the seven ages of man indeed fires the riposte, when Adam is carried in, in the "youthful hose well saved, a world too wide / For his shrunk shank", 2.7.159–60.) Next, the sermonizing tone becomes explicit, with "He that doth the ravens feed, / Yea providently caters for the sparrow, / Be comfort to my age" (44–45). If the Almighty however will provide for Adam in age, what need the lifetime of thrift? The contradiction swells the surreal unease of the moment, as Adam discloses himself to be startlingly wealthy, the possessor of five hundred crowns (£125: or over $100,000 by today's measure), yet begs Orlando to maintain him in servility ("Let me be your servant. / Though I look old, yet I am strong and lusty", 47–48). The moment must surely have been close to incomprehensible to many of the humbler spectators, whether servants, apprentices or labourers, as the very reverse of their own attitudes and aspirations: particularly in an age when apprentices, as historians tell us, "were exposed to an almost limitless sadism from their masters."[96] Adam's gesture looks less like Christian generosity than bizarre preference for abasement over personal freedom. The London underclasses who flocked to liberatory wish-fulfilment in *Tamburlaine* would have found Adam's will-to-servitude a hard sell. Indeed, it will be populist Iago, exuberantly bonding with the groundlings (for the first two acts) through beer-swilling, drinking songs, direct address, lewd jokes, patriotic compliment, and the engineering of exciting sword fights, who utters the perspective of the rowdy, carnivalesque playhouse upon the ideal of indefeasible servility. And it will sound almost like a reminiscence of old Adam.

> You shall mark
> Many a duteous and knee-crooking knave,
> That, doting on his own obsequious bondage,
> Wears out his time much like his master's ass
> For naught but provender, and when he's old, cashiered.
> Whip me such honest knaves. (*Othello*, 1.1.44–49)

So large a sum of money as Adam possesses required, moreover, an enviably fat and bulging super-purse. (One authority estimates that it would have to have weighed close to one and a half kilograms, "more than a bag of sugar".)[97] As Adam holds out to Orlando that clinking, mesmerising bag—"Here is the gold. / All this I give you" (46–47)—the groundlings, so close to this numinous object, must momentarily have suspended their collective breath. This, I would argue, is a tantalization effect. Its recurrence marks a favourite Shakespearean device: the hurled rings and proffered coins of *Twelfth Night*; the bag of gold tendered for a seance by Dame Eleanor in *2 Henry VI* ("Here, Hume, take this reward: make merry, man", 1.2.85); the coins that Romeo has ever to hand for sweetening persuasion, as he placates the nurse, and later drives away Balthasar (2.3.164; 5.3.41); the sudden tips with which a Prince procures the silence of Bardolph and the page in *2 Henry IV* 2.2.139, just as he will use a glove, filled onstage with crowns, to try to bribe the soldier Williams from hostility in *Henry V* 4.8.52; the two purses thrust by vindictive great men in *Richard III* upon messengers of other men's disasters (Hastings at 3.2.102, King Richard at 4.4.514 in Folio); the gold with which Cleopatra comically over-rewards the messenger for disparaging dispraises Octavia's looks ("There's gold for thee: / Thou must not take my former sharpness ill", *Anthony and Cleopatra*, 3.3.33–34). The obtrusively displayed wealth of buying actions functioned, in their immediate material reality, clunky, tinkling, glittering, to inflame envy: the aroused anguish establishing alienating distance from such insouciantly privileged characters.[98] In *As You Like It* both Adam and Rosalind dispense redemptive gold: but in Rosalind's case, as she relieves Corin's necessity (2.4), the script suggests no mouth-watering purse displayed.

Climaxing the estrangement, Adam now plunges, deictically or otherwise, into pointedly antagonising homiletics.

> In my youth I never did apply
> Hot and rebellious liquors in my blood,
> Nor did not with unbashful forehead woo
> The means of weakness and debility. (49–52)

Delivered to a pit of cheery youthful swillers, located in a red-light district, and in the midst of a comedy, the chances of success for such sentiments look unpropitious. Just Say No was a message that, here, did not exactly sing. These godly imperatives of meek teetotalism and retiring chastity summed up, of course, the coercive regime of the new vestry values, inflicted on the socially inferior, the poor, and where possible, the young. Adam, neocon, is specifically assailing youth culture ("In *my youth*, *I* never did . . ."; emphasis added), whose heartland lay in the riotous freedoms of Liberties such as Southwark, and the pleasures of the playhouse. In 1600, perhaps half of England was under twenty years old, as was much of the theatregoing public.[99] The number of apprentices in London had doubled between 1580–1600, rising to some 30,000—two to three times the normal proportion—and the number of servants became possibly even greater.[100] To the authorities, we saw with *Romeo and Juliet*, such figures posed an alarming threat, particularly as London apprentices developed their own, rowdy subculture. In the Bridewell of 1602, ninety-seven per cent of the imprisoned were under twenty-one.[101] "At any sign of general disaffection, the city's first precaution was always to order a curfew for apprentices and servants, and to close the alehouses where they would loiter with intent."[102]

As Roger Manning records, even though "these discontented younger sons of the gentry added an articulate and politically sophisticated leaven to the London crowd", "[t]o contemporaries, gentlemen apprentices were associated with riotous living".[103] Disparagement of drinking, linked with festal suppression and crackdown on alehouses, could "subsume, focus and articulate", notes historian Keith Wrightson, "conflict between godly and ungodly, governor and mastered, master and servant, employer and employee, rate-payer and actual or potential charge upon the poor rates."[104] Indeed Adam's charge that sexual and alcoholic licence "woos . . . weakness and debility" echoes the refrain of local elites and parish officers (noted by Wrightson) that feasting and alehouses ruined a man, thereby raising the local poor rate.[105] Pitched into Elizabethan culture wars, then, thrifty Adam, censorious gerontocrat, far from comprising the elevated exemplar for which Shakespearean criticism has always sentimentally mistaken him, would have commanded at a public theatre much the same reception that a TV evangelist might expect from an inset cameo sermon in *The Rocky Horror Picture Show*.

In Lodge's *Rosalynde*, Adam had assisted Orlando ('Rosader'), who had broken open the family wine-vaults, in serving up a drunken feast, to celebrate Orlando's wrestling victory. Later, Rosader being tied up in the hall by his carousing elder brother and friends, Adam releases him, suggesting that the pair of them can "make havocke among them", "with a couple of good pollaxes" (which indeed they do). When both starve in the forest, Adam suggests "I will presently cut my veynes, &, master, with the warme bloude relieve your fainting spirits". United with the banished king's men, Adam proves ever merrily ready with "a peece of red Deere and a bottle of wine". This swashbuckling servitor ends up appointed by the restored king to the position of Captain of the King's Guard.[106] Though both loyal Adams decently wish repair of family integrity, the contrast between Lodge's mettlesome halberdier and Shakespeare's anaemic, clerical teetotaler could hardly be more telling.

Further suggestive for the concerns of this drama was the fact, noted by historians, that since in this, the golden age of flogging, many apprentices ran away, and servants were often laid off at short notice, youth culture tended to overlap with the vagrant population.[107] (The "extraordinarily high drop-out rate among London apprentices" saw nearly three-fifths failing to complete their terms.)[108] *As You Like It* surely maps just this confluence, its political stance thus both compassionate and commercially astute. Indeed an almost precisely contemporary tract (first edition 1603) articulates just this conjunction, the fate dreaded by Adam "When service should in [his] old limbs lie lame" (2.3.41):

> It is the custom of most men nowadays (so wretchedly covetous are they grown) that they toil their servants while they can labour, and consume their strength and spend them out: and when age cometh,

and the bones are full of ache and pain, they turn them out of doors, poor and helpless into the wide world to shift for themselves as they can; and they must either beg or steal or starve, for any relief they shall receive from their masters . . . and thus it cometh to pass that many become thieves and vagrant beggars through their master's niggardliness that would not do his duty in bestowing some proportionable and competent relief upon them.[109]

Yet as out-of-touch, gentlemanly Orlando responds to Adam's words, he completely misses the injustice of his own class, so accurately foreseen by Adam, projecting instead the denigrative authoritarianism visited by the well-born on servant and vagrant alike:

O good old man, how well in thee appears
The constant service of the antique world,
When service sweat for duty, not for meed!
Thou art not for the fashion of these times,
Where none will sweat but for promotion,
And having that do choke their service up
Even with the having. (57–63)

Presented, in Adam's crowns, with an immediate instance of astounding subaltern loyalty and magnanimity, Orlando perversely attacks underclass shiftlessness. The true note of ideology ("pleasurable, intuitive, self-ratifying", "In the sphere of ideology, concrete particular and universal truth glide ceaselessly in and out of each other, by-passing the mediation of rational analysis")[110] is sustained as his tirade sketches an almost demented extreme of patrician deserving. Indifferent to the harshness of sixteenth century treatment of elderly workers (though More, in *Utopia*, 1516, had lamented just such behaviour)[111] Orlando lauds labouring dutifully, apparently forever, with no thought of wages (devoted or "constant service", that will "sweat for duty, not for meed").

Furthermore, the unctuous anti-materialist sermon contradicts his own aching self-pity on inheriting "but poor a thousand crowns" (1.1.2). The complacent self-contradiction forms another instance of that repulsively blind, self-pitying plaint of the well-born, tellingly juxtaposed to the desperate plight of commoners, that we saw articulated and targeted in Henry VI and Romeo, and that recurs in Henry V—all of them "superfluous and lust-dieted men" in the words of *King Lear*, who "will not see / Because [they] do not feel" (4.1.67–69).[112] Finally, Orlando's reproach of material self-interest in the lower orders establishes—in a principle pervasive in Shakespeare, and narratologically structural to *Henry V*—the sly spectacle of dominant ideology's fervent theory dealt demolition by staged actuality: had servants indeed been heedless of pay, Orlando would not have had those crowns to aid him.

If Adam's rectitude of abstinence was dear to the heart of every Church-warden, Orlando's ideology of underclass fecklessness came straight from the tightened lips of Overseers of the Poor. Adam and Orlando embrace in a tender duet of vestry values: unconquerable servility in a joyless work ethic kneels to hierarchism's calm deserving of feeless underling duty. The self-congratulatory duo of the dour Puritan work ethic unite proudly against the scandal of the lower classes: vice-ridden ("unbashful forehead[s]"), ignobly concerned about their wages ("sweat . . . for meed"), and disrespectful to their betters (swilling "hot and rebellious liquors"). They are oligarchy's newly-weds, melting into a marriage made in the very heaven of early capitalist accumulation.

Then Orlando swiftly pockets the chunky bag of coins proffered by Adam.

The moment, rich in satiric potentiality, suggests, at the very least, the double standard of those who deplored lower class cries in their parish for financial help whilst making hefty sums themselves. It may even have hinted at the widespread contemporary suspicion of embezzlement by vestry officers. The 1597 parliament, for instance, legislated temporary imprisonment for Overseers and churchwardens failing to tender "a true Accompte" of their income and spending;[113] and the 1601 parliament, meditating a bill compelling churchwardens to resume levying shilling recusancy fines against the very poor, feared lest churchwardens compile a secret list, and "take fourpence for themselves and dispense with the rest."[114] Indeed, in the very parish in which this play was being performed (the Globe was located in St. Saviours, Southwark), an intense resentment gathering against restriction of the traditionally universal parish franchise was being buoyed by accusations that the vestrymen were spending the monies gathered for poor relief upon "private feasting". An appeal to parliament would eventually be launched in 1607, and a 1608 ruling restored traditional voting rights.[115] Generally, however, "Before Laud the Church seems to have had no 'social justice' policy which would challenge the rule of local oligarchies"; and consequently "embezzlement by town and parish oligarchies of funds intended for poor relief proceeded apace in the century between the Reformation and Revolution."[116]

"I BLUSH, AND HIDE MY SWORD" (ORLANDO, 2.7.118)

Given Adam and Orlando's embrace of the anti-populist discourse of hand-wringing self-righteousness, kin to the Overseers' "felicite but in taunting, reviling and abusing the poor", and given Orlando's double standard on cash, it is no wonder that Orlando's incorporation into the drama's community of revellers is *purgatorial*, proceeding both by personal suffering and stage humiliation. In 2.5 the Duke's forest lords deck a table with food, but the Duke is absent and his men leave to find him. Stage directions, and common sense probability, suggest the loaded table did not leave with them: and indeed that laying of the table, enforced by the script, was needless to the scene. A feast set for a Duke thus remains onstage (I would bet center stage) throughout the following scene, in which a starving Orlando and collapsing Adam totter at the brink of death. Critics have noted with puzzlement the near-certain presence of the table in 2.6, but failed to recognize the deducible political effects.[117] First, the spectacle of a laden board juxtaposed to terminal starvation must have formed a graphic, visually dominant tableau of contemporary social injustice. And it is probably no accident that when, in the ensuing scene, Orlando returns to steal food, Jaques and the Duke, laughing amid plenty, are debating the propriety of satire, and bourgeois transgressions of courtly dress codes (2.7.42–87). Aristocracy and bourgeoisie are thus locked cheerfully in ethical contention, while the Third Estate, desperate and indigent, roam famished as complete outsiders to the political conversation. Second, as Adam collapses from hunger and Orlando begs him not to die, promising desperately to find food—somewhere, somehow— the Duke's stacked table sits just feet away: and Orlando never sees it. That complex stage moment serves not only to emblematize Elizabethan inequity but to make Orlando look something of an idiot. Our gentleman protagonist, alienatingly censorious and moralistic, is metaphorically and literally unseeing, missing what exists literally almost under his nose. Orlando the unseeing is perpetuated at the deictic level, too: his language is conspicuous once more for comical auditorium misprision: "If this uncouth forest yield anything savage, I will either be food for it or bring it food for thee . . . thou shalt not die for lack of a dinner if there live anything in this desert" (2.6.4–6, 13–14). Invisible on the page but stark on the stage, such performance dimensions disclose a mordant populist politics, often pointed through hilarity.

When in 2.7 Orlando discovers the Duke's company and demands food at sword point, he becomes the deictic fall-guy once again. "Speak you so gently? Pardon me, I pray you. / I thought that all things had been savage here" (2.7.105–06). The moment can be played for a thrilling turn of high adventure, or can be keyed into another instance of Orlando Claustratus, audience-insulting and impercipient; especially as he then launches into what sounds like unconscious audience address, conceiving the community of the Forest / Globe as godless idlers—just the view, of course, that Perkins and Puritanism held of vagabonds.[118]

> whate'er you are
> That in *this desert inaccessible,*
> Under the shade of melancholy boughs,
> *Lose and neglect the creeping hours of time,*

If ever you have looked on better days,
If ever been where bells have *knolled to church* . . . (2.7.108–13;
   italics mine)

That the Globe was situated very close to St. Mary Overbury, so that her
knolling bells must have been regularly audible in the roofless theatre,
introduced yet another ironising instance of auditorium cluelessness on
the young gentleman's part. Further, the machismo credentials of tough-
guy Orlando, destroyer of the Duke's wrestler, now bursting in with sword
brandished, are successfully mocked by languid Jaques:

Orl.:   Forbear, and eat no more!
Jaques: Why, I have eaten none yet.
Orl.:   Nor shalt not till necessity be served.
Jaques: Of what kind should this cock come of? . . .
Orl.:   But forbear, I say.
            He dies that touches any of this fruit
            Till I and my affairs are answered.
Jaques: An you will not be answered with reason, I must die. (2.7.88–91,
            97–100)

   Yet with Orlando humiliated, the scene then modulates into an intense
poignancy. In a deeply Shakespearean dramaturgical pattern of gratifying vengeance pressured rapidly into compassion—the principles we saw
governing presentation of Dame Eleanor, Queen Margaret and Surrey in
2 Henry VI—the play grants the audience delicious 'punishment' of these
misfit sneerers, then under the power of a crafted intensity of pathos,
relents to forgive and include them. Just as impoverished, sword-wielding
Orlando suffers comical humiliation by Jaques' aristocratic contempt, so
Puritanical Adam, vaunting his toughening by abstinence from sex and
booze—"Though I look old, yet I am strong and lusty" (2.3.48)—has been
reduced to whimpering for death: "O I die for food. Here lie I down and
measure out my grave" (2.6.1–2). Act 2 scene 7 then progresses to a moving hospitality, as "an old poor man"(128)—all bravado drained and no
crowns in sight—now wordless, broken, slumped helpless on Adam's shoulder, becomes cared for, fed, and respected ("Good old man, / Thou art right
welcome . . . Support him by the arm", 200–02). The tonality is heightened
by the delicate, paradoxically stately lyric poetry of Orlando's imploration,
echoed by the Duke ("If ever you have looked on better days / . . . If ever sat
at any good man's feast"; "True is it that we have seen better days, / And
sat at good men's feasts, and wiped our eyes / Of drops that sacred pity hath
engendered", etc.). It is then poetically deepened by the climax of Jaques'
Seven Ages of Man speech ("second childishness and mere oblivion"), to
which the pair reappear, and is further overlaid by the power of song,

supplied by Amiens. The fashioning of touching moral beauty effectively 'forgives' Adam, redefining him in terms of simple human need.

Status-anxiety, it seems, had lain behind the Calvinistic sentiments of Adam and Orlando, the former forfeiting standing through "unregarded age" (2.3.43), and the latter through the tensions between gentlemanly and younger brother status. Such anxiety links them with the violently persecutory Antonio of *Merchant*, racked by homosexual guilt ("I am a tainted wether of the flock", 4.1.113), with the confrontationalist testing of boundaries by Richard II, destabilized by child-king contradictions between personal vulnerability and divine right rhetoric, and with Prince Hal the usurper's son, trickster voyeur of the commons' mind. Orlando, however, differs suggestively from these men. Purged, he moves beyond the fires of self-obsession, discovering humility and pity. In a striking prefiguration of *King Lear*, where Lear, Gloucester and Edgar each plummet from comfortable privilege into the humbling strokes of eye-opening poverty, Adam and Orlando, pitched into the desperate paths of "bare distress" (2.7.95) have found that sermonizing snobbery cannot survive the experience of unaccommodated man. Exposed themselves to feel what wretches feel (*Lear*, 3.4.35), discovering in the acid of their own bellies a society heedless that "distribution should undo excess, / And each man have enough" (*Lear*, 4.1.70–71), they follow, respectively, the terminal options of either broken-spirited death ("O, I die for food", 2.6.1) or of robbery with violence. Unaccommodated Orlando, stumbled upon the banqueting Duke, now redefines in desperate hunger what it means to be a gentleman. It is no longer a matter of scorning servants as "hinds", disparaging their concern for adequate wages, or pining for "such exercises as may become a gentleman" (1.1.61). "If you", he begs the Duke, have

> ever sat at any good man's feast,
> If ever from your eyelids wiped a tear,
> And know what 'tis to pity, and be pitied,
> Let *gentleness* my strong enforcement be. (2.7.114–17; emphasis added)

The personal experience of starvation and outcast status have dissolved, it seems, the brusque class haughtiness. ("O how bitter a thing it is to look into happiness through another man's eyes", 5.2.38–39.) Following this scene, Puritanical Adam disappears from sight, and Orlando ceases to be a disapproving, anti-carnival figure, becoming puppet instead in Rosalind's playful subversions.[119] Invited hereafter by Jaques to "rail" satirically against the world, Orlando's answer is remarkable.

> I will chide no breather in the world but myself,
> against whom I know most faults. (3.2.256–57)

He continues to be something of a gull, however, twisted around Rosalind's transvestite finger, his poetry mocked (in sharp contrast to Lodge's original), and his somewhat wan residual personality easily upstaged by perfervidly passionate Silvius. Pitifully duped until the very denouement, it is Orlando, when Duke Senior seems close to rumbling Rosalind's identity, who reiterates her preposterous lies in a burst of heartfelt naivety:

> But, good my lord, this boy is forest-born,
> And hath been tutored in the rudiments
> Of many desperate studies by his uncle,
> Whom he reports to be a great magician
> Obscured in the circle of this forest (5.4.30–34).

"HOLY-DAY FOOLERY" (CELIA, 1.3.11)

If the fortunes, then, of Adam and Orlando present vestry values fusilladed by carnival targeting, and a subsequent movement into chastening, diminishing forgiveness as suffering dissolves their pusillanimous righteousness, the values of Rosalind and Celia are substantially those of *As You Like It* itself. It was overwhelmingly the women who were As They Liked It, bouncing into the Globe's enclave of exuberant misrule as the bearers of carnival values. Quipping transgressors of patriarchy, their crime of cross-dressing carried severe Elizabethan penalities, and struck at the very foundation of political rule. Yet their primacy is not only the matter, widely observed, of Rosalind receiving more lines than any other Shakespearean female, and proving the only woman in Shakespeare to speak an Epilogue. Where Orlando had sneered at underclass concern about wages, the women are prompt to rescue from poverty. "Buy thou the cottage, pasture, and the flock, / And thou shall have to pay for it of us" Rosalind immediately promises Corin. "And we will mend thy wages" adds Celia (2.4.87–89). Little noted by literary critics today, such sympathy must have stolen the breath away from poorer audience members, for wage complaints from the propertyless were currently pouring in to justices of the peace. Cottagers wholly dependent on wages, often in the western forests, were petitioning magistrates for relief, Buchanan Sharp records; and in 1595, for instance, come bitter complaints of wage-cutting.[120]

Rosalind and Celia in fact establish a frequent solidarity with working people and their world in turns of language somewhat improbable for court-bred ladies. "How full of briars is this working day world!" sighs Rosalind (1.3.9–10); and will later joyously exclaim, in the mood of the audience, "I am now in holiday humour" (4.1.59). Commending Touchstone, Celia invokes the bricklayer—"That was laid on with a trowel!" (1.2.87)—before moving on to taverns: "The oath of a lover", she jokes, "is no stronger than the word of a tapster. They are both the confirmer of false reckonings" (3.4.27–29). Rosalind, too, is apparently experienced in the world of the bibulous plebeian: "Good wine needs no bush" she observes in the epilogue (3). The key to such idiom lay perhaps in her plea to Duke Frederick:

> Good my liege, mistake me not so much
> To think my poverty is treacherous. (1.3.58–59)

Chastising supercilious Phebe as tyrannical to the helpless—"you insult, exult, and all at once, / Over the wretched" (3.5.37–38)—she climaxes the rebuke in roundly demotic terms: "Sell when you can. You are not for all markets" (3.5.60).[121]

Market forces and wretchedness turn out, in fact, to be surprisingly definitional of Phebe and Silvius. Shakespeare resets these ostensibly Italian-ate figurines into an English foreground imposing sharp political outlines, much as he had wreathed the romance of Romeo and Juliet, we saw, in terms figuring power-relations on the hungry London streets. In Silvius, submissive love-starvation evokes the pathos of pauperism. Desperate in his "poverty of grace" for the merest scraps of attention from Phebe, he will "think it a most plenteous crop / To glean the broken ears after the man / That the main harvest reaps"(3.5.101–04)—one of the slender perks, as we have noted, potentially awarded to the 'deserving' destitute by Overseers of the Poor. But gleaning, though no critic has noted this, was currently a shibboleth. The parliament of 1597–98 sought to criminalise this tra-ditional use-right of the indigent, in a propertied reconceptualisation of the action as theft by idlers, not an entitlement of the needy. The Queen refused assent to so stony a bill; yet so obdurate proved oligarchic illiber-ality that the legislation was resubmitted, and it passed in the parliament of 1601.[122] From 1601 come accounts of gleaners now being stocked, and from 1603, of being assaulted by farmers or their hirelings.[123] "Wherever sorrow is, relief would be" (87), urges the agonizedly dependent Silvius: but the pitiless Phebe, while defensively claiming to be "neighbourly" (91)—a key term of the traditional charitable ideal—rebrands his importuning, like an implacable 1590s parliamentarian, as "covetousness" (92). The comfortable domineering of Silvius by "proud disdainful" Phebe (3.4.43) thus silhouettes a familiar spirit of demeaning denial currently practised by the gentry and unsympathetic farmers. Phebe will further press Silvius to labour for her, like an indigent compelled by Poor Law into employ-ment irrespective of its wages and conditions. "I'll employ thee, too. / But do not look for further recompense / Than thine own gladness that thou art employed" (3.5.97–99). Reprising the startlingly imperious notion of employee relations that we saw hymned by pre-hunger Orlando ("con-stant service . . . / When service sweat for duty, not for meed", 2.3.58–59), Phebe in her contemptuous instrumentation again projects familiar ves-try values; and broken-spirited Silvius is pathetically eager for even this:

"Loose now and then / A scatter'd smile, and that I'll live upon" (104–05). Rosalind's castigation of delusive superiority exulting over the wretched is in political terms highly suggestive: as is, perhaps, the irritating (and Adam-like) spectacle of invincible servility in her pauper. In a small-scale parallel to Orlando's trajectory, Phebe will be punished for her contumely when she succumbs herself to humiliating dependency, *qua* romantic need. Both cases theatrically grant that curative reversal of fortune for insentient power which will be craved by Gloucester in *Lear*: "Let the superfluous and lust-dieted man, / That slaves your ordinance, that will not see / Because he does not feel, feel your power quickly" (4.2.67–69).

Wage-mending Rosalind and Celia are thus sharply populist in contrast, and it is they who supply much of the delighting spirits of carnival (or "holy-day foolery" as Celia calls it, 1.3.11): so it is no surprise that it is to them that bonding deixis is most allocated. When in act one Le Beau announces a wrestling match imminent and Touchstone suggests this scarcely "sport for ladies" (1.2.114), Rosalind calls out, in terms very strange if her only audience is Celia, "But is there any else longs to see this broken music in his sides? Is there yet another dotes on rib-breaking?" (116–17). Clearly deictic, the cheerleading appeal (and presumable enthusiastic response) heighten the carnival bonding that Rosalind's exuberant transgressiveness will sustain right through to the epilogue. It is deeply familiar role, since it draws on medieval traditions, much noted by critics, of May Queens presiding over holiday games, of Maid Marions in Robin Hood festivities, and of electing "a king and queen to preside at a banquet 'for laughter's sake.'"[124] Privileged in her deixis and insuppressible in her wit, Rosalind is a *reine pour rire* come to the professional theatre.

When consequently Duke Frederick banishes Rosalind as a traitor, threatening death if she be found within twenty miles of the court, giving no reason why ("Let it suffice thee that I trust thee not", 1.3.49), and remaining unmoved by an appeal that must have resonated strongly with the commons audience—not to think that her "poverty is treacherous" (59)—his subsequent warning to Celia that "Her very silence, and her patience / Speak to the people, and they pity her" (72–73) must have carried deictic actualism.

Celia shares occasionally in the deixis. Arrived in Arden, she slyly opines, with approving audience survey, "I like this place, / And willingly could waste my time in it" (2.4.89–90). Chiming with the drama's numerous pastoral endorsements of fleeting the time carelessly as in the golden world, the merry response contrasts again with Orlando's [initially] disapproving line on forest dwellers who "Lose and neglect the creeping hours of time" (2.7.111).

The word 'forest' in fact occurs no less than twenty-three times in this play, though never more than three in any other.[125] Yet as these deictic instances cumulatively suggest, a master motif of this drama is that the 'forest'—so lovingly scrutinised by generations of critics for its environmental details, so lauded for its clarifying, therapeutic effects as a sanctuary in great creating nature—this forest is in fact no more sylvan than mustard and pancakes. "The circle of this forest" (5.4.34) denotes the theatre itself.

BAPTISING IMPUNITY

Christopher Hill noted that "London was for the sixteenth century vagabond what the greenwood had been for the medieval outlaw—an anonymous refuge."[126] Our play confirms the shrewdness of this insight, since on a primary level its forest—safely sequestered from the world of courtly authority, a place of idleness, free speech and pleasure, often egalitarian in tone, and abounding, we are told, in horned creatures (cuckolds)—proves manifestly to signify the Globe and its creatures. "Now my co-mates and brothers in exile", the Duke exultantly introduces the theme, "Are not these woods / More free from peril than the envious court? / Here feel we not the penalty of Adam" (2.1.1, 3–5). The deixis here not only establishes camaraderie with the co-mates and brothers in the Bankside playhouse, but perhaps functions also as fleeting commentary on preceding action. Stirring memory of the Adam whom we have recently seen spurned by his master ("Is 'old dog' my reward? Most true, I have lost my teeth in your service", 1.1.70–71), the ducal deixis congratulates his co-mates on escaping the world of ingrate hierarchism. Further, since 'Duke Senior' is almost certainly and recognisably the same actor who, seconds earlier, had been Duke Frederick tyrannically banishing poor Rosalind ("Her very silence, and her patience / Speak to the people, and they pity her", 1.3.72–73), he is able to 'recall' the hostilities of the audience to that action—an outcry from those very co-mates whom now he commends. For to the *"churlish chiding* [my emphasis] of the winter's wind"—and wind, breath or odour are habitual markers, we have seen, of audience reference—he now responds, he says, with a smile. "This is no flattery. These are counsellors / That feelingly persuade me what I am" (2.1.7, 10–11).[127] Doubling and deixis thus lace the passage with enriched comedy and intensified bonding, the Duke enjoying a festal, teasing relation with his encircling hearers. (Like the "churlish" wind, the allegedly valuable 'toad', "ugly and venomous", 13–14 , may reference plebeian members of the audience, in lost Elizabethan slang. The word was common as invective, as in insults of Richard III, 1.2.147; 1.3.244; 4.4.81; and Richard II likewise refers to toads in a major passage of pleading deixis, 3.2.15). The giddy quick-change in attitude established by the ducal doubling may also set up in overtone that tutelary mistrust of great lords wooing commoners which we saw plotted by stagecraft in *2 Henry VI*: a suspiciousness vindicated a little later, for Duke Senior will turn abruptly upon merry-making Jaques, and with him, upon the primary sympathies of the drama, by reproving satire (2.7.62–69), and denouncing "licence of free foot" (2.7.68).

Deictic elision of forest with playhouse abounds in the play, its success facilitated by the absence of any stage props to instal a separate world.[128] "Well, this is the forest of Ardenne", says Rosalind, gazing around, mischievous and appraising. "Ay, now I am in Ardenne; the more fool I" mocks Touchstone (2.4.11–12). When Rosalind and Touchstone debate Orlando's execrable verse, Touchstone resolves, with sweeping democratic gesture, "Let the forest judge" (3.2.111). "Here we have no temple but the wood", he later jokes, "no assembly but horn-beasts" (3.3.40–41). The dislike of pre-conversion Orlando for the "uncouth forest", his thinking "that all things had been savage here", his reassurance to Adam that he will find food "if there live anything in this desert"(2.6.4; 2.7.106; 2.6.13–14) perpetuate in contrast his outsider status, the comic targeting of his snobbery and impercipience. Audrey, by contrast, hopes "it is no dishonest desire, to desire to become a woman of the world" (5.3.3–4). The most manifest instance of this deixis has been universally remarked and savoured:

Duke: Thou seest we are not all alone unhappy.
          This wide and universal theatre
          Presents more woeful pageants than the scene
          Wherein we play in.
Jaques: All the world's a stage . . . (2.7.135–38)

The Duke's opening praise of "this our life, exempt from public haunt" clarifies the purpose of this running deixis. Jokes about "the circle of this forest" (5.4.34), reversing pastoral's customary *urbs in rure* for *rus in urbe*, serve not only to raise laughter, define character and promote a commercially shrewd audience–actor bonding. They define or christen the theatre and its constituency. For the Globe has recently opened: many critics think this probably Shakespeare's second, or even first, play written for the new theatre.[129] And the Globe has been carefully located across the water from the regulated city of London, in a traditional 'Liberty' where the city authorities lack jurisdiction. (Rosalind's "Now go we in content, / To liberty, and not to banishment", 1.3.131–32, possibly winks at this in pun.) As Gary Taylor notes, "In the Renaissance theatre you could not escape the sense of communal response, of a common sensing. The physical crowding of three thousand people into a small arena—many of them standing on the undemarcated floor of the pit, the rest huddled together in galleries stacked precipitously one on top of another—ensured that they all remained conscious of one another . . . The audience was as visible and present to itself as the actors onstage."[130] What is introduced, I suggest, by *As You Like It*'s identification of Bankside's new theatre with merry greenwood refuge is the bestowal upon that spectator self-presence of a camaraderie of transgression. The forest identification baptises impunity, sparking the encircled Globe community of players and spectators alike into collective self-celebration as holiday outlaws, relishing a realm of counter-cultural freedom and flourishing satire. Laying on (with a trowel) the carnival roistering suppressed by the vestrymen, its gregarious hilarities restore that lost experience of neighbourliness and community, rebuilding, like medieval festivity in Bakhtin's words, "a second world and a second life outside officialdom".[131]In this festal wooden O bathed in broad daylight, the consciousness of co-celebration with neighbours, of engulfing public comradeship, would have been an immediately visual and sensory affair quite lost in modern theatres.[132] As anyone can testify who has seen a play in London's reconstructed Globe, the playhouse's scale is such that, despite an audience in the thousands, the changing facial expressions of spectators on even the far side of the auditorium are clearly perceptible.

To this end, *As You Like It* staged at the Globe restored the full range of traditional pleasures enjoyed at carnival time. The Bankside location, replete with bear-baiting pit nearby, and the sale of ales in the theatre, re-established in itself a climate of festivity and licence: to which the play added a wrestling match, dancing, minstrelsy, songs on idleness and calendary sexual licentiousness ("Between the acres of the rye . . . / These pretty country folks would lie, / In spring-time" (5.3.20, 22–23), satiric jesting at upper-class culture (e.g. Touchstone on the ritual of the quarrel, 5.4.50–92), a satiric flouting (of the Reverend Martext), what is possibly a folk-mime at 4.2 with mummer-style dressing in antlers; and centrally, of course, the erotic irregularities of a forward maiden, cross-dressing, the pleasures of courting, and a mock wedding.[133] This, surely, explains the extended hilarities of courtship between capering Rosalind and muted Orlando that so dominate the play. It is not, as so often solemnly declared, a matter of pursuing moral reform in the introspective peace of timeless woodlands, of Shakespeare's concern that Rosalind 'educate' her mate in the nature of true love[134]—her talk is often desperately improvised and delirious prattle—but rather of the dramatist giving delicious scope to the traditional carnival opportunity, anathematised by reformers, for flirtation and sexual conquest. Rosalind herself, notably screening her identity from her father, links her romance with carnival licence: "Come, woo me, woo me, for I am now in a holiday humour, and like enough to consent" (4.1.59–60).

The strategically communitarian merrymaking of *As You Like It*, the calculated affront to official values through galvanising Bankside audiences with the gift of carnival *redivivus*,[135] took its cue from the heightened perils of the Chamberlain's Men in 1599. Only a few dozen yards away, Henslowe's celebrated Rose Theatre (opened in 1587) was enjoying continuing success with its staple of traditional 'citizen' plays, their values patriotic and martial, whilst Boys companies, just started up at Paul's and the Blackfriars, were finding great success with their 'railing' satire and indoor theatre. Further, the Lord Chamberlain's men appear recently to have lost (or expelled) their hugely successful clown, Will Kempe, whose "departure left the company hazardously poised for a new beginning in conditions of unprecedented competition."[136] Shakespeare himself, as a future 'sharer' in the new theatre, had invested deeply from his own funds in the approximately £700 construction of the Globe, whose furnishing of a merely thatched roof (unlike the tiled finish of the neighbouring Rose and the Swan) suggests insufficient funds: "the Globe was a distinctly cut-price job."[137]

To the intense new struggle between professional theatres Shakespeare brought, however, his own public following—as this play's very title suggests. For by 1598, publications of his dramas (beginning with a quarto of *Love's Labour's Lost*, followed by a quarto of *Richard III* and two of *Richard II*) were advertising his name on their title pages. As an actor that year he may actually have headed the cast-list of Ben Jonson's *Every Man in His Humour*.[138] *Palladis Tamia, Wit's Treasury* (an inventory of quotations and maxims published in 1598 by the amateur enthusiast and Cambridge graduate Francis Meres, listing England's finest plays) saluted the supremacy of Shakespearean drama. Comparable with both the comedies of Plautus and tragedies of Seneca, it was "among the English . . . the most excellent in both kinds for the stage." Shakespeare's company was therefore not, I suggest, agonizedly facing "a choice, between going the Henslowe way and catering for an increasingly narrow and old fashioned citizen taste or competing with the boys and their new fashions."[139] Undismayed by the new competition, Shakespeare's new dramas at the Globe (*Henry V, As You Like It, Julius Caesar, Hamlet*) maintained their traditional orientation, proclaimed with the title *As You Like It*. Shunning both the simplistic heroics of the citizen plays, and the acerbic railing against social types (lawyers, merchants and gallants) of the kind the Boys exemplified—a social rather than political genre, comprising merely "a weapon of social class allegiance"[140]—Shakespearean drama courted instead, as this book has tried to make clear, a constituency of popular political disaffection. That dissidence was both topical and fundamental, both scathingly anti-authoritarian and generously humane, and it comprised in its sceptical compassion a kind of underdog populism rather than that nationalist populism of the northern theatres which was a form of underclass conservatism. Around six months after the Globe's opening, the Rose Theatre acknowledged defeat and fled Bankside, relocating to the north of the city as The Fortune.

A final instance of the play's telos of subversive auditorium bonding lies in its treatment of poaching, generally overlooked. Although by common law wild animals were part of nature's providence (*ferae naturae*) and thus free to all, England's Game Laws had from the fourteenth century sought restriction of hunting to gentry and nobility: a condition bitterly resented by the commons, subject to such ferocious medieval penalties as eye-gouging and castration when caught hunting. Since huntsman and steed became the proud, privileged image of resented aristocratic rule, poaching evolved on one level into a cultural language of insubordination or retribution. Political revolts, for instance, were accompanied by popular attacks on deer parks in 1549, 1569, and 1641; and mass poachings were sometimes organised as a form of popular justice in retaliation against lords perceived to have offended the community through enclosures or failure to provide hospitality.[141] (There is very possibly truth to the legend of Shakespeare poaching at Charlecote, suggests Roger Manning, since for Tudor youth, poaching was almost an anti-authoritarian rite-of-passage.)[142]

When Duke Senior and his men hunt deer in *As You Like It* they are of course poaching, as the deposed Duke no longer owns the forest; and poaching an enemy's deer was a standard expression of contumely among feuding nobility, as in the deer-wars between the Earl of Pembroke and Sir Maurice Berkeley running from 1591 to Berkeley's death in 1601.[143] The Duke's trespass, as I have argued elsewhere, is aggrandised in the drama into a shared revelling of players and audience. "In the culture wars of the late sixteenth century, poaching culture and theatre culture disreputably overlap."[144] Two factors lent special intensity to the scene of sly poaching celebration.

First, poaching in 1598–1600 was a matter of hot topicality. *A Treatise of the Laws of the Forest,* published in 1598 by Lincoln's Inn lawyer Sir John Manwood who clearly felt the Elizabethan age to be soft on poaching, lovingly set out the full panoply of terrifying medieval penalties for the crime. The following year saw a crackdown on black market venison by the Attorney-General, who brought prosecutions for deer poaching to no less a court than Star Chamber. It was in these 1599 Star Chamber prosecutions, notes historian Roger Manning, that Attorney-General Coke indeed introduced into the English language the compound word "deer-stealer". The Privy-Council subsequently (re)ordered the lord mayor of London, in 1599, and again in 1600, to prevent sale of poached game in its taverns—one of these taverns, to common knowledge, being in Southwark, the nearby St. George's.[145] As a poacher in 1600 could earn as much in one night as an artisan in a month, and as poaching was sometimes the last defence against family starvation, the authorities' campaign was resented and resisted.

Second, particularly alarming to the Tudor ruling class, was that "poaching bands transgressed hierarchy, promoting insurrectionary bravado and even 'Levelling' associations. For poaching gangs placed a genteel leader at the head of armed commoners; and their expeditions, moreover, were customarily organized and afterwards celebrated in the rowdy, subversive milieu of alehouses."[146] It is just such an instance of jubilantly defiant, cross-class bonding that *As You Like It* supplies, I have argued, when in 4.2 Jaques and other outlaw lords celebrate their illegal deer-slaying. In traditional ritual, notes Manning, as the kill was being eviscerated, "the hunters who had horns blew the *mort,* while others hallooed and the hounds were encouraged to bay. This must have been an emotionally satisfying release, which also served to reinforce communal bonds and, on a smaller scale, to elicit a sense of fraternity. Depending on the formality of the occasion, the hunters would march in procession homewards."[147] As Jaques and his fellows march and halloo about the stage ("Then sing him home", 4.2.12), the scene, I suggest, appears to recreate that elating process: the "sense of fraternity" which "served to reinforce communal bonds" is precisely what is being produced between actors and spectators.[148] Given, then, that deer poaching was coded insubordination, and given too the contemporary official backlash against underclass poaching, its savoury yield discreetly available in local taverns to which audience members might afterwards mirthfully repair, "Act four scene two in an early Globe performance becomes an exultant ritual of demotic political transgression,"[149] a communal raspberry blown at the 'inland men' in civic authority across the water. Suggestively, the very terms in which Coke was busy prosecuting poaching bands in 1599—"verie dissolute, riotous and unruly persons, common nightwalkers and stealers", who offend against "industrious subjects", "confederatinge themselves with dyvers others of their companyons and adherents . . . whereof great multitudes doe swarm"—participate, we might note, in the established discourse for vilifying theatre audiences.[150]

"WIND AWAY, / BE GONE, I SAY, / I WILL NOT TO WEDDING WITH THEE" (3.3.86–88)

"It was not until the late sixteenth century that a church wedding was required everywhere", historians recount. Catholic and Protestant churches alike were then campaigning to emphasise the religious character of weddings.[151] Yet for Shakespeare's society some ambiguity remained, since "England had quaintly retained medieval canon law on contract marriage despite its abolition in Europe by the Council of Trent."[152] We discussed above the unpopularity of what was perceived as avarice-driven ecclesiastical destruction of that centuries-old liberty of common law marriage expressed in the simple expedient of the 'handfast'. Such violation of the plebeian tradition of free self-marriage filled yet deeper the dark reservoir of popular resentment of the church, its angry waves stirred further by the class double standard: for the upper classes could, effectively, bribe the church to dispense with formalities such as the banns or the prohibition of marrying in Lent. ("And all this for money, and such a sum of money as the poor man cannot reach unto.")[153] The parliament of 1598 introduced a bill against the scandal of "covetous use of dispensations" (anomalous and costly marriage licenses and dispensations), only to have it quashed by Elizabeth as encroaching on her prerogative as Supreme Head of the Church.[154]

In this context, Shakespeare introduces a character and scene nowhere in his source: the clergyman Sir Oliver Martext, indignant over impropriety in a proposed wedding ceremony. His name, as editor Hattaway remarks, "suggests an illiterate 'hedge-priest' who could not expound upon scriptures";[155] and his inarticulate haplessness in the face of disrespect from both Touchstone and Jaques may bring to mind Rosalind's earlier jest on "a priest that lacks Latin" who "sleeps easily because he cannot study"

(3.2.292–94). His presence is doubly gratuitous. Not only is he absent from the source, but he is unnecessary to Touchstone's ploy: the Clown's desire for a 'deniable' marriage would better be served by a swift rhetorical moment of unwitnessed troth-plighting. Since he involves a clergyman at all, this must reflect Shakespeare's desire to introduce one: a figure he promptly subjects to ridicule, and through whom he presents for jest ecclesiastical solemnization. "This fellow will but join you together as they join wainscoat; then one of you will prove a shrunk panel and, like green timber, warp, warp" (3.3.71–73). Through Touchstone's stratagem ("he is not like to marry me well, and not being well married, it will be a good excuse for me hereafter to leave my wife", 75–77) gloat the contemporary politics of anti-clerical backlash: the congenial retort to clerical officiousness of inept officiation.

For good measure, to laughter at clerical incompetence Shakespeare adds outright satiric flouting. Touchstone's leave-taking of Martext is song-and-dance mockery.

> Farewell good master Oliver. Not—
>
> O sweet Oliver,
> O brave Oliver,
> Leave me not behind thee
>
> But—
> Wind away,
> Begone, I say,
> I will not to wedding with thee.

Capering about the solemn minister (or even jigging: Kemp's favourite satiric mode), pillorying propriety with the confrontational exuberance of revels, the clown comically redirects the rejection motif, in what was a popular song, from the implied lover towards the reddening vicar himself.[156] The witless sniffing of Martext's response confirms him the easy fall-guy to carnival values—"'Tis no matter. Ne'er a fantastical knave of them all shall flout me out of my calling" (89–90). "Ne'er a . . . knave of them all" suggestively implies a climate of contemporary derision. "My calling", of course, carried Puritan overtones. ("The experience of mockery confirmed anxious ministers in their own sense of righteousness . . . [and] helped bond the puritan godly as a moral elite", notes historian David Cressy.)[157] "Fantastical" is a word which Shakespeare associates with carnival;[158] so that we have in microcosm here the drama's foundational project of flouting the new authoritarianism of vestrymen and clerisy.[159]

The perspective is hinted again in the mock-wedding of 4.1, where Rosalind elbows the clergyman's role aside. "I might ask you for your commission", she laughs at Celia, playing the minister, "but"—and she runs on as though such matters were footling—"I do take thee, Orlando, for my husband." And she at once underlines that overturning of proper ceremony: "There's a girl goes before the priest" (4.1.117–19). Inconspicuous in Rosalind's breathless key, the potential anti-clericalism of this passing instant would count for little (though it could easily be played up in performance by a shove aside or turned back) were it not that it reprises the derogation of Martext, and that this perspective culminates in Hymen.

We shall deal more fully with the Hymen scene in the following chapter, but we should note here that 'Hymen' effectively usurps the role of church minister. Climaxing the play's joys, the multi-marriages are notably conducted without banns, with no church, and with no clergyman. (In Lodge, the weddings had been very properly conducted, in Church before a priest, who "solemnely solemnised" their marriages [253].) The Duke's command "First, *in this forest* let us do those ends / That here were well begun, and well begot" (5.4.159–60; emphasis added) certainly makes overt the eschewal of the new due process. Such avoidance is the more remarkable as foregoing in favour of woodland nuptials the newly regained possibilities of marriage in palatial pomp and splendour. With its mockery of Martext, its girl going before the priest, and its conspicuously rural marriage, it seems clear that affectionate endorsement of extra-ecclesiastical wedding is one more plank in the oppositional populism of *As You Like It*.

Companion to the position is the scattering of casually anti-clerical moments through the play. Rosalind is consistent here. To her earlier jest on priests without Latin, and the rebuff of "There's a girl goes before the priest" (4.1.118), we should add the terms of her rebuke to Celia's long recitation of Orlando's risibly giftless effusions: "What tedious homily of love have you wearied your parishioners withal, and never cried 'Have patience, good people!'" (3.2.143–45). Her promise to love Orlando "Fridays and Saturdays and all" (4.1.99) volleys carnivalesque libido against Sabbatarian fasting. Predictably, contrast emerges with the early Orlando. He expects sympathy, he tells the Duke, "If ever [you have] been where bells have knoll'd to church" (2.7.113). This sounded a note, however, to which the 'integrated' Orlando never recurred.

The true, indeed adversarial, contrast is with Jaques. Seeking an image for a self-evident condition, he comes up with "The why is plain as way to parish church" (2.7.52). And it is most notably Jaques who insists upon church marriage: "Get you to church, and have a good priest that can tell you what marriage is" (3.3.70–71). Michael Hattaway's (undeveloped) suggestion that Jaques's language, "filled with revulsion against 'the foul body of the infected world' (2.7.60), seems to derive from the pulpit of a fundamentalist preacher" possesses, I think, some cogency—at certain points.[160] For it is Jaques who incongruously echoes the bible ("I'll rail against all the first born of Egypt", 2.5.54–55), and who also displays competitive piety in disdaining the Duke: "I think of as many matters as he, but I give heaven thanks, and make no boast of them", he boasts (2.5.29–30).

It is Jaques who will abandon his fellows for the sake of religious discussion with a "convertite" (5.4.173), and who pointedly forsakes their joyous songs and dancing at the finale with a Puritan sneer—"To see no pastime, I" (5.4.184). Shakespeare indeed underlines Jaques' final stance through the familiar technique of (brief) carnival frustration. The marital couples being joyously united, the Duke announces "rustic revelry", and actually utters the command "Play, music" (167). It is at this moment, as perhaps the dancers begin to line up, as musicians take up instruments or even launch into an opening bar or two, that Jaques halts festivity in its tracks. One can imagine him holding up a cold, obstructing hand: "Sir, by your patience . . .", he begins. "Compact of jars", as the Duke had rightly called him (2.7.5), he announces his departure ("If I heard you rightly . . .", 169) and exits pronouncing sour disdain of "dancing measures" (5.4.182).

Yet Jaques had earlier proven a bearer of carnival pleasure. His deadpan scorn to Amiens and the musicians in 2.5 ("I do not desire you to please me, I do desire you to sing", 2.5.14) is frequently hilarious, just as his defence of satire aligns him with Touchstone and our heroines. His extended exculpation of satire—"Who can come in and say that I mean *her* / When such a one as *she*, such is *her neighbour*?" (2.7.77–78; emphasis added)—is of course a rollicking tour de force of deixis: the longest indeed in the play. As the former libertine strolls the platea or stage-rim, studying the spectators and delightedly picking out his victims—

> There then! How then! What then! Let me see wherein
> My tongue hath wronged *him*. If it do *him* right
> Then he hath wronged himself . . . (2.7.83–85; emphasis and
>   exclamation marks added)

—we have the reverse of Orlando's claustration. A feast of audience bonding ensues, whose choice teasing effectively cancels out its ostensible disapproval of sumptuary violations, and virtually celebrates the transgression of suddenly spotlit auditors, presumably writhing, laughing, interacting by gesture or voice. This delighting, boisterous collusion would heighten the outsider status of Orlando, suddenly entering an auditorium which he declares to be a "desert inaccessible" (109).

This melancholy moralist, then, though he "most invectively pierceth through / The body of the country, city, court" (2.1.58–59), and invites Orlando to sit and "rail against our mistress the world, and all our misery" (3.2.254–55), has nonetheless a celebrative side. On the one hand, he is relentlessly analytic in his pessimistic intelligence, "full of matter" (2.1.68), travelling widely ("Monsieur Traveller", 4.1.29), his large intellectual appetite restlessly in quest, ever scrutinising and moralizing spectacles into a thousand similes (2.1.45). Though he loves fine reasoning ("have a good priest that can tell you what marriage is", 3.3.70–71) and enjoys giving it ("Go thou with me, and let me counsel thee", 3.3.78), his is too paradoxical and ingenious a mind for a fundamentalist preacher ("you do more usurp / Than doth your brother that hath banished you", 2.1.27–28). Yet though he brags "my often rumination wraps me in a most humourous [peculiar, fantastic] sadness" (4.1.17–18), it is Jaques who commands Amiens "Come, more, another stanza" (2.5.15), and he who even sets afoot the stomping procession with the slain deer at 4.2 ("Let's present him to the Duke like a Roman conqueror . . . Have you no song, forester, for this purpose"?, 3–6).

Psychologically, the key to Jaques would seem to be that he is a manic depressive, a sufferer, in more recent terminology, from bipolar disorder. The "melancholy Jaques" who, beholding the dying deer by a brook, "augment[s] it with his tears" (2.2.41, 43), recounts that on seeing Touchstone in the forest, "my lungs began to crow like chanticleer" (2.7.30).

And I did laugh sans intermission,
An hour by his dial. (2.7.32–33)

The acuity of Shakespeare's pyschiatric diagnosis here is once more confirmed, I suggest, by modern research codified in the DSM.[161] "Major depressive episodes" are confirmed not only by Jaques' heavily self-advertised melancholy, which the Duke, aware of its actual intermittency, perceptively terms "sullen fits" (2.1.68). It appears also in his observed tearfulness (DSM-4, p. 326 symptom 1), and in his "diminished interest or pleasure in all, or almost all, activities most of the day" (symptom 2). Jaques has no interest in hunting, in fellowship, or in 'disputation' with the Duke ("I have been all this day to avoid him", 2.5.28), but instead begs Amiens for more of his sad music ("I can suck melancholy out of a song as a weasel sucks eggs. More, I prithee, more", 2.5.11–12). His sleep problems ("insomnia or hypersomnia nearly every day", symptom 4) are suggested as he exits 2.5, apparently in the middle of the day: "I'll go sleep if I can; if I cannot, I'll rail . . ." (2.5.53–54). "Manic episodes", by contrast, appear in Jaques' "abnormally and persistently elevated, expansive" mood in 2.7, as he enters euphorically, having laughed for an hour, demands to be invested in motley ("They may change their dress, makeup, or personal appearance to a . . . dramatically flamboyant style that is out of character for them", DSM-4, p.330), and finally proceeds to the uproarious deictic teasing of members of the audience (exhibiting "indiscriminate enthusiasm for interpersonal . . . interactions", the person "may spontaneously start extensive conversations with strangers in public places", DSM-4, p. 328). Sufferers of the disorder may also "travel impulsively to other cities, losing contact with relatives and caretakers", and their mood disturbance may generally "cause marked impairment" in "usual social activities or relationships with others" (DSM-4, pp. 330, 332): all of which strongly recall Jaques' behaviour at the play's close. Intense irritability ("I pray you mar no more trees with writing love-songs in their barks", 3.2.237–28; "I do not like her name", 3.2.243) is a symptom common to both manic and depressive episodes: the "railing" to which Jaques twice refers includes both the exuberantly satiric shafting of the audience and the scowling session to which Jaques invites Orlando.[162]

Much of this sounds like Ben Jonson, emerging rival of Shakespeare, currently engaging Shakespeare (and other dramatists) in a public war over modes of comedy (Jonson's Aristophanic comical satire disdaining Shakespeare's Plautine festive comedy).[163] Many critics have indeed seen Jaques as an embodiment of Jonson and his genre's values (though to the best of my knowledge no-one has yet diagnosed him as a clinically accurate portrayal of bipolar disorder), and have construed Jonson as given a 'purge' by Shakespeare in this play: 'jakes' was Elizabethan slang for a privy. Like Jaques, Jonson possessed a restless, judgmental intelligence proud of its authoritarian moral analyses, plus a high-spirited extraversion, gay and elated in satiric proceeding, as his plays reveal. Like Jaques, too, was his competitive defensiveness ("I think of as many matters as he", 2.5.29) and the intellectualist scorn of vulgarity that would seek to diminish Shakespeare for his "little Latin and less Greek". The contrariety of Jaques, initiating revelry over the deerkill at 4.2 only to shun "pastimes" in act five, would emerge in the polar movement of Jonsonian drama from the bursting energy and euphoric laughter of the early plays to the black pessimism of *Sejanus*.

The truth seems to be that, like notoriously domineering Jonson, Jaques will not participate where he does not command. His final denial of the joyous common bond proceeds from a personal need for predominance, an egoistic aversion to eclipse through festal group-immersion ("There is sure another flood toward, and these couples are coming to the ark. Here comes a pair of very strange beasts, which in all tongues are called fools", 5.4.35–37). His instant reversion in 2.7 from jubilant audience-baiting to rancid dismissiveness of rapier-brandishing Orlando, entering to usurp his auditorium primacy—"Of what kind should this cock come of?", 2.7.90—exhibits just this jealous ascendancy. "Inflated self-esteem"(DSM-4, p.328) and "excessive involvement in pleasurable activities that have a high potential for painful consequences" (DSM-4 p.332) are manic features less clear in Jaques than Jonson. The latter was twice imprisoned for outspokenly satiric plays (*The Isle of Dogs* and *Eastward Ho!*), and summoned before the Privy Council on charges of treason for *Sejanus*.

More speculatively, and perhaps more suggestively, roistering, brawling Ben Jonson was a fresh convert to Roman Catholicism when Shakespeare put Jaques, the church-minded ex-libertine, upon the public stage.

Shakespeare's repudiation of Jonsonian values in Jaques, then, rejects not only the new form of invective comical satire, combatively vaunted by Jonson in *Every Man Out of his Humour* (1599) which appears to have mocked Shakespeare in the figure of Sogliardo.[164] The ecclesiophobe telos of *As You Like It* engineers a dramaturgic 'turn' against Jaques as a figure aligned with ecclesiastical authority and vestry values. Initially seductive in his sardonic wit, and elevated to his zenith of magnetism in charismatic goading of spectators for their 'bravery' of dress (2.7.80), Jaques is thereafter subjected by Shakespeare to a gradual phasing out of stage appeal. It would seem that the turning point, significantly, was precisely that scene, pivotal for Orlando and Jaques alike, wherein Jaques' scintillation yielded abruptly in a display of supercilious chill to starving vagrants approaching the banquet. Thereafter Jaques actually loses battles of wits: first with Orlando, where he is deeply uncharacteristic in slowness of wit—"[a fool] is drowned in the brook. Look but in, and you shall see him." "There I shall see mine own figure." "Which I take to be either a fool, or a cypher" (3.2.262–65)—and next with Rosalind, debating melancholy, where he exits in complete discomfiture, without even a farewell salvo after Rosalind's "[they] will scarce think you have swam in a gondola" (4.1.1–34). In between the two defeats he enters to hector Touchstone on the necessity of church marriage (3.3). Yet Touchstone retains easy comic predominance here by flouting Martext as Jaques stands silent (and horrified?) by. Though Jaques makes something of a comeback at 4.2 by instigating the huntsman revel, his vitality and presence have been trounced and subordinated by both Rosalind and Orlando; and he is finally outshone by Touchstone in the dazzling comedics of the seventh cause of the quarrel. This technique of reducing a charismatically comic figure during the second half of a drama, substantially through allocation of disappointingly few or poor jests, such that critique and rejection of the character's values can be implemented effectively, we have dubbed carnival repudiation. As with Richard III, Falstaff *et al.*, the turn against Jaques as a formerly irresistible lord of misrule is established by that dampening out of formerly bright wit which accompanies graphic exposure of his inhumanity. "To see no pastime, I", he sneers, exiting for the convertite. He had been notably anti-demotic all along, mocking "beggarly thanks" (2.5.23), deploring "fat and greasy citizens" (2.1.55), offering no syllable of goodwill to starving Orlando and Adam, and being alarmed by Touchstone's rustic nuptial only insofar as he was "a man of . . . breeding" (3.3.69–70). In the finale of his coldly chosen, self-regarding alignment with religious contumely against common festivity, Jaques, like Ben Jonson and his railing satire, is in the last analysis on the side of pulpit and vestry values against neighbourliness and the jig.

10 *As You Like It,* Part Three
Dysresolution, Sexual Politics
and the Public Sphere

On his appointment as Director of the National Theatre in 2002, Nicholas
Hytner published a meditation on the endings in Shakespearean comedy.
Though tempted, perceptively, "by the idea that, in Shakespeare, there is
always a secret play behind the official play", he nonetheless argued Shakespeare to have allowed his psychological and social realism, his "addiction
to the truth", to be undermined by "respect for the rules of the genres
in which he worked" to the point where his endings "land [him] in real
trouble." Surveying comedic closure in *Twelfth Night* (Shakespeare has the
drama "shoot itself in the foot by marrying Viola to Orsino"), *Measure for
Measure* (conclusions "throb like raw wounds on the body of the play"),
as well as *The Winter's Tale* and *As You Like It,* he concluded "You can
sense the playwright's unease with the ending demanded by the genre." It
reminds him, he says, of "low-rent *opera buffa*". Yet he abruptly rebukes
his own verdict of Shakespearean insincerity, on opining peremptorily "the
truth is that when Shakespeare seems unplayable, it is almost always our
fault."[1] Professional literary critics, however, have often shared the unease.
Even the astute Louis Montrose, for instance, reads Shakespeare in *As You
Like It* as attempting to "resolve conflict" (that of the younger brother specifically, and more generally of Elizabethans lacking full identity through
not being male heads of household), and succeeding only "by the conjurer's
art".[2] Occasional voices have been raised in protest: "In essence, Montrose
sees the comic form as a vehicle for articulating, only to erase, the contradictions of a particular social formation. I would simply argue that a text
such as *As You Like It* is more subversive of formulations of reconciliation
than Montrose's reading allows", counters Jean E. Howard.[3] Yet it remains
to examine the particulars and deduce the model of what alternative goal
Shakespeare might be pursuing. It is therefore to this project that I now
turn, positing that the unease of *As You Like It*'s finale is calculatingly
designed, its anti-realism pointed, and its telos that subversive effect of
flaunted political disavowal one might christen the *dysresolution.*

Shakespeare emphasises for his audience the sheer improbability of
an eager octet of imminent spouses, through Jaques' mockery that there
must be "another flood toward, and these couples are coming to the ark"

(5.4.35–36). Shakespeare further imposes on the closing settlement three major elements of incongruous miraculism: two astounding conversions, and the purportedly supernatural figure of Hymen.

First comes the instantaneous transformation of evil elder brother Oliver into the loving benefactor to his arch-enemy, Orlando, bequeathing him his "father's house and all the revenue that was old Sir Rowland's." Oliver will, he claims, having conveniently fallen for Celia, "here live and die a shepherd" (5.2.9–11): a proposition intrinsically ludicrous for a gentleman, and rendered further preposterous by the play's ample demystification of rustic condition. (Nor indeed has Celia made any vow of *stabilitas loci*. Do we really believe she will remain in the country when her beloved Rosalind returns to court?). Like Jaques, Oliver pointedly underlines the unlikeliness of affairs: "Neither call the giddiness of it into question, the poverty of her, the small acquaintance, my sudden wooing, nor her sudden consenting" (5.2.5–7). There had been some plausible motivation to the passion of Lodge's Celia: the elder brother had fought to save her from assaulting forest brigands. Shakespeare, however, departed here from his source, then added extravagantly to Lodge's lion, which had threatened sleeping Oliver, "a green and gilded snake" that apparently wreathed itself "about his neck"—without waking him—and, "nimble in threats, approached / The opening of his mouth" (4.3.107–09).

The play's very language shifts here into the register of the fantastic. The abruptly stylised, heavily fictional effect is heightened by contrast not with one, but with two immediately preceding forms of realism. First had been the sophisticated realism of the metropolitan theatre-goers, raised to consciousness by the auditorium in-joke when Oliver asks how to locate Rosalind "in the purlieus of this forest". Given the literary fictiveness of this forest, constantly cued to deictic actualism, it follows that when Celia instructs Oliver, tongue-in-cheek, to look for "The rank of osiers by the murmuring stream / Left on your right hand brings you to the place" (4.3.78–79), the audience must have savoured her resourceful improvisation of airiest pastoral vacuity. Realism of another order lay in the play's customary discursive naturalism, exemplified minutes earlier in Rosalind's derision of Phebe: "She has a leathern hand, / A freestone-coloured hand. I verily did think / That her old gloves were on; but 'twas her hands" (4.3.24–26). Then suddenly emerges the tone of hoary fable.

> Under an old oak, whose boughs were mossed with age
> And high top bald with dry antiquity,
> A wretched, ragged man, o'ergrown with hair,
> Lay sleeping on his back. (4.3.103–06)

This discrepant tonality introducing the Oliver miracle simultaneously announces and undercuts the formula of romance narrative.[4] The remoteness of literary artifice is sustained by Oliver's melodramatic recounting

("Lo what befell!", 101), his interspersing of Latinate diction ("dry antiquity", "indented glides"), and his elevated aphorisms ("For 'tis / The royal disposition of that beast / To prey on nothing that doth seem as dead", 104, 111, 116–17; "But kindness, nobler ever than revenge, / And nature, stronger than his just occasion, / Made him give battle to the lioness", 127–29). To these is added a somewhat wooden rhetorical loftiness ("betwixt us two / Tears our recountments had most kindly bathed", 138–39). The answering vernacular, jesting yet polyvalent in Rosalind's discomfiture—"I pray you, tell your brother how well I counterfeited. Heigh-ho!"(166–67)—confirms the episode as a kind of stilted foreign overlay upon realism.

Having rendered Oliver's conversion more fantastical than had his source, Shakespeare presses the abrupt elimination of Duke Frederick into the realm of the discreditably incredible. The usurper in Lodge (King Torismond) had been slain in battle; in Shakespeare, however, having assembled and led his army to the forest, he "meeting with an old religious man, / After some question with him was converted / Both from his enterprise and from the world" (5.4.149–51). Aware of the absurdity here, even the messenger feels obliged to close his account with

> This to be true,
> I do engage my life. (154–55)

Keen hearers may have caught in "an old religious man" the echo of Rosalind's whopping fib, to an Orlando suspicious of her "accent", that she had been taught in the forest by "an old religious uncle", who had forsworn being "an inland man" (3.2.313–14). Patently a desperate fiction in its first instance, its reprise would swell the undertones of amused scepticism.

Third and heaviest element, however, in the conclusory "incongruous miraculism" is the figure of Hymen. "It is left to the producer to decide whether the masque shall be plainly a charade got up by Rosalind, or whether it is pure magic" noted Agnes Latham.[5] But a third possibility is more likely, I suggest. Hymen descends neither from Rosalind's brain nor the realm of supernature, but condenses the customary terminal spirit of romance genre. Hymen is the *deus ex machina* as built to creak.

Assessment of Hymen must be more speculative even than most of our dramaturgical arguments are constrained to be, in the absence not only of detailed stage directions and eye-witness accounts but of convincingly definitional dialogue. ("Still music" is apparently provided at [or following] Hymen's entry with Rosalind and Celia: but how long does it last?) Nonetheless, what look like some telling features emerge on close scrutiny of the script. Hymen's first verses are suspiciously amenable to subversive interpretation.

There is, as editor Hattaway notes, "no indication that [Hymen's] lines were originally sung, although they have been put to music".[6] I strongly suspect them to have been spoken on the common stage (though perhaps not at court).

Then is there mirth in heaven
When earthly things made even
Atone together.
Good Duke receive thy daughter;
Hymen from heaven brought her,
Yea, brought her hither,
That thou mightst join her hand with his
Whose heart within his bosom is. (97–104).

The first clue here is that the last line is sheer doggerel—and doggerel effort-lessly avoidable, since "his" could have rhymed promisingly, for instance, with "bliss", "kiss", etc. The rhyming of "daughter" with "brought her" likewise suggests humour, as the usual function of feminine end-rhymes on couplets. Next, "Hymen from heaven brought her" is palpably, indeed hilariously untrue. This is a whopper, and gratuitously so (reminiscent of Shakespearean association of religion with duplicity elsewhere, as in Edgar's lies to his father at Dover Cliff). The following line—"Yea, brought her hither"—thus sounds like a retort to audience murmurs or laughter of denial. Further, the verb to "atone", given suggestive prominence by abbre-viation in the third line, sounds oddly disapproving of human affairs in the context of marital joys, even comically inappropriate. For although the word could mean simply to bring into concord, it was used (as the OED documents) in Tyndale, the Geneva Bible, and other English translations to signify the reconciliation of God with sinners, and thus is heavy with impli-cations of mortal wrongdoing. (Other Shakespearean usages confirm this: in *Merry Wives*, for instance, Parson Evans volunteers to reconcile Shallow and Falstaff saying "I am of the church, and will be glad to do my benevo-lence to make atonements and compromises between you", 1.1.27–28. The rebel Archbishop in *2 Henry IV* speaks of seeking to "make our atone-ment" with the King, 4.1.219.) There is a definite hint of the dourly clerical here then, perhaps even of Puritan temperament.

When Rosalind then speaks to Orlando, her father and Phebe, Hymen interrupts with what sounds like peremptory displeasure. "Peace, ho! I bar confusion, / 'Tis I that must make conclusion / Of these most strange events" (114–17). Hymen, it seems, feels undermined in due officiation. Here again, it seems, "there's a girl goes before the priest"; and Hymen is determined not to be flouted out of his / her calling. Continuing, with banal decorum, "Here's eight that must take hands / To join in Hymen's bands", Hymen adds "If truth holds true contents"—a line that sounds perilously like doggerel once again.[7]

As the above implies, Hymen, far from being a truly Classical personage, would appear to evoke a contemporary clergyman—"wedlock hymn', at line 126, makes this clearer still—and Shakespeare would seem to be eliciting targeting responses. In line with the play's preceding treatment of clergy-men and clerical wedding, unpopular clerical officiation is simultaneously bypassed in the Hymen figure, and satisfyingly snubbed even in the substitution. Hymen is then sidelined by the arrival of Jaques de Boys, and tacitly rebuked by Jaques (who had likewise, of course, insulted 'Martext' for incompetence) in his own ritual-sounding bestowal of blessings, which contradict Hymen in the case of Touchstone and Audrey ("thy loving voyage / Is but for two months victualled", 180–81).

What would render the process emphatically parodic would be the playing of Hymen by 'Adam': conspicuously vanished from the playful band after 2.7. If the same actor doubled as Adam, Sir Oliver Martext, and Hymen—which the onstage groupings permit[8]—both persuasive thematic consistency, and climactic stage hilarity, would be generated. All three roles, as we have seen, are associated with grave and disapproving vestry values of Puritan overtone, and all three figures are mocked. Between Hymen's doggerel verse and Martext's learning-challenged ineptitude derided by Jaques ("have a good priest that can tell you what marriage is. This fellow will but join you together as they join wainscot"), there seems also comic consonance. With a Hymen who was visibly Adam *redivivus*, the tall claim that he came down from heaven ("Yea, hither brought her"), would acquire enhanced comedic logic, as part of his invincibly superior self-regard. The whole conclusory scene as hilarious demystification of mysterious providentialism would also be the plainer.

"FEED YOURSELVES WITH QUESTIONING, / THAT REASON WONDER MAY DIMINISH" (5.4.127–28)

We should ask finally the *purpose* of erecting the play's concluding triumphal gateway from the conspicuously aerial masonry of a triple anti-realism. Hytner's thesis of a Shakespeare servile to dictates of genre—a conclusion shared by eminent critics such as Anne Barton[9]—seems as implausible as Duke Frederick's conversion: for Shakespeare exposes generic form's inadequacy to reality not only in his caricature of Polonius's epistemologically challenged flailings ("comedy, history, pastoral, pastoral-comical, historical-pastoral, tragical- historical, tragical-comical-historical-pastoral", *Hamlet* 2.2.379–81), but in his own widely remarked, lifelong dramaturgic practice of mingling and problematising genres.[10] Alternatively, the view that Shakespeare's goal is the celebration of wonder, as benevolent supernatural agency discloses itself upliftingly in the redemption of human affairs, is an argument radically untenable in the light of what seems to be in Shakespeare an essentially secular, even anti-religious vision. Why, for example, would a devout Shakespeare produce so many tragedies, becoming prolific in a genre whose burden is the anti-providential demonstration of earthly injustice and whose foundational premise is the absence of afterlife? (Tragic effect is lost if we assume Romeo and Juliet risen hand-in-hand to heaven. The Nurse's "Ah sir, ah sir, death's the end of all!" is tragedy's enabling, terrible conviction.)[11] Destitute of answers to prayer, of divinely conferred protection of the innocent, demystifying the divine right of kings and portraying the natural man acting in the natural world, Shakespearean drama seems rather the product of that widespread "disintegration of providentialist belief" for which Dollimore argues so cogently.[12] It is a perspective of disillusion entirely consonant, after all, with a Shakespeare packed off at sixteen years old to Hoghton Tower as subseminarian and disciple of Campion, only to experience the panicked break-up of the Catholic centre, the news of Campion's arrest, torture and execution, and the failure of the Jesuit mission in England. Again, if Shakespeare seeks in *As You Like It* to affirm religious wonder, why does he not enunciate closing developments in specifically supernaturalist terms, Christian or mystic? He labours, quite to the contrary, both to make the miraculism look implausible, and to deprive it of legitimative Christian language and reference. And his treatment of Hymen, we have seen, reduces allegedly supernatural apparatus to parodics.   Shakespeare's purpose in furnishing a stylised, flamboyantly improbable pseudo-resolution to the hopeless entanglements and endemic injustice inflicted by hereditary aristocratic governance, in a social formation most legibly his own, is surely political. As a corny or parodic providentialism, a deliverance rendered fake through maximised improbability and continuance of clashing linguistic registers, this is a *dys*-resolution: a self-exposing cover-up of the natural outcome of class rule. "Feed yourselves with questioning, / That reason wonder may diminish" (5.4.127–28). The salvationary miraculism patently disavowed, its operation simultaneously mystifying and demystifying, what emerges is the persisting and terminal delegitimation of the political system. (What would it take to restore justice to our kingdom? Only a concatenation of miracles could achieve it.)

For there is more at stake than pastiching the endings of traditional romance narrative, which regularly concluded, as had Sidney's *Arcadia*, that "all had fallen out by the highest providence."[13] The official governance of Elizabethan society by the approximately three per cent of the population born as nobility and gentry, this elite's expropriation of food and leisure from the labour of the common people, the derivation of a lifetime's power, pomp and privilege from "the brief and aching lives of the permanently cheated",[14] all rested upon patrician claim to the manifest operation of divine will. Celestial superintendence ordained, sustained and delivered its chosen rulers. When, consequently, Shakespeare precipitates that class into folly, vicious action and catastrophe (conventionally enough), but adds strong topical overtones and constructs a risible, self-disowning deliverance fiction, the effect of that non-stick remystification is to render unreal the legitimative metaphysics itself. To discredit aristocratic romance salvation is to expose and corrode its underpinning ideology, rendering untenable that entire style of ideological thought. When beleaguered Stuart kingship soon after sought reaffirmation of just that metaphysical register, elaborated through masque, this was possible only through flight from popular disaffection and the abrasive climate of the common stage. Masque could only exist as an exquisite refugee, sequestered from naturalism in the precincts of the court.

In the autumn of 1599, as *As You Like It* was probably joining the repertoire, the Chamberlain's Men played Jonson's *Every Man Out of His Humour.* This stinging satire on contemporary humours closed, somewhat startlingly, with the seeming appearance of Queen Elizabeth, whose bedazzling majesty flung the character Macilente (Envy) overwhelmed to the floor, and induced his instantaneous moral reform. The crowd, however, made its dislike of this notion so very plain that Jonson was obliged to change the ending. That conclusion, Jonson later confessed, "many seem'd not to relish . . . and therefore 'twas since alter'd."[15] Modern critics have accounted for this as the high-toned disapproval by a devoutly monarchist audience of a mere actor impersonating Elizabeth. ("The theater was considered to have overstepped its bounds").[16] More probable, I suggest, was that Jonson's reverential miraculism foundered upon the conditioned political scepticism of Globe audiences. Crowds who had that season devoured *Henry V* and *Julius Caesar* found in Jonson's resolution, in effect, a dysresolution: and one without the winking self-deprecation of the Shakespearean model.

Shakespearean abolition of fairytale providentialism through a dysresolution returns us to the world of the Histories and Tragedies: realist studies of agony, disaster, and prevailing injustice. Shakespeare's technique of dissolving metaphysical ideology in an acidic potion of intense scepticism is itself, I suggest, transgeneric. In *Macbeth*, for instance, the lengthy dialogue at 4.3 between Malcolm and Macduff effectively criminalises the track record of kingship, as Malcolm predicts his own reign would bring royal rape, murder, theft, "confineless harms" (56), yet Macduff urges him not to worry about this since such things are customary ("But fear not . . . the time you may so hoodwink . . . do not fear", 70, 73, 88). When, in this climate of harsh realist exposé, an English doctor enters to sing the magical powers of English kingship—possessed of gifts of prophecy, healing the dying merely by touch, "Hanging a golden stamp about their necks, / Put on with holy prayers" (154–55)—the misfit propaganda, smothered by preceding cynicism of thought and action, systematically denied the oxygen of magical thinking, perishes in incredulity or even laughter.[17]

Closing almost abruptly with an unpersuasive wonder, breathtaking, touching, and preposterous, subtextually urging the real-world insolubility of problems imposed by aristocratic misgovernance, the dysresolution is deployed in a host of Shakespearean endings: among them the closures of *The Comedy of Errors, Much Ado, Twelfth Night, Measure for Measure,* and *The Winter's Tale.* And the dysresolution brings always to the party a companion feature pointing up the unquiet subtext of a dark realism not truly escaped: a character whose suffering, contempt, or reindicated untrustworthiness maims the closing unworldly innocence. In *As You Like It,* that person is not only sneering, departing Jaques: it is the stranger come upon the scene, the other Jaques, "the second son of old Sir Rowland" (5.4.141).

Critics have been perplexed by the gratuitous recurrence of the name 'Jaques', but to the best of my knowledge have yet to ponder the *social effects* of this wholly unnecessary arrival of a second son unmentioned since the play's fifth line ("My brother Jaques he keeps at school, and report speaks goldenly of his profit", 1.1.4–5). Since an anonymous messenger announcing Duke Frederick's conversion would have adequately served that purpose, Shakespeare clearly intends more by the intrusion of Oliver's younger brother. Suggestively, though the Duke cries joyously "Thou offerer'st fairly to thy brothers' wedding" (156), no welcome whatever is given their brother by either Oliver or Orlando. (In *Rosalynde*, he was met with friendly greetings by both brothers and led to dinner.) And a moment's reflection, once we are freed from the illusion that Shakespeare inevitably intends concluding higher harmony, suggests why this is so.

In *Rosalynde*, the reappearance of the middle brother appears due to the romance convention of wondrous familial reunion. He is joyously assimilated into the group, and his tone of alarm owes to his message of imminent invasion ("from daintie cates rise to sharpe weapons", 255). Following the battle, in the concluding settlement of fortunes he is elevated to the post of Principal Secretary by the restored monarch. In Shakespeare, though the bearer not of alarum but the news of fabulous restoration, young Jaques remains a strangely tense and joyless figure, no syllable of rejoicing uttered. His speech closes in anxiety ("This to be true, / I do engage my life", 154–55), and he is left unrewarded.

Two implications seem suggested here. The first lies here in the physical appearance of Jaques de Boys. Since he has arrived in an army, then penetrated "this wild wood" (148), he is at least wearing and probably holding a sword, and may look unkempt or dirty. Both his sudden entry, and his opening line, devoid of courteous address—"Let me have an audience for a word or two" (140)—seem abrupt, incongruously intrusive, dramatically transforming the tone after Hymen's hymn and Phebe's loving pledge to Silvius. Have we not encountered such a figure before, supervening, martial and disconcerting, upon communal hilarity? The probability is strong that we are being reminded of the earlier Orlando, sword in hand, and the worse for wear, surprising the ducal banquet. Since the Orlando of the present moment will be well attired for his wedding day, having been instructed by Rosalind "put you in your best array" (5.2.63), a deeply suggestive tableau will result, as a younger son, visibly the outsider, surveys his prosperous sibling's happy inheritance. (Costuming could easily make the visual echo unmistakable.) In this pregnantly silent figuration, Jaques de Boys turns out to be appropriately named after all, beneficiary of the role of 'Jaques' in Act Six as another melancholy malcontent. As unpropertied Jaques de Boys gazes on wordlessly ("How bitter a thing it is to look into happiness through another man's eyes!", 5.2.38–39), the narrative of the younger brother nightmare ends, with sceptical realism, back at square one.

A second implication may be that for Jaques de Boys, the spectre looms of unjust dispossession, since the family lands, forsworn by Oliver, should have passed to himself, as next in succession, and not to the youngest brother. The script indeed hints that the problematic settlement of fortune may indeed be indicated to him, in Jaques's farewell to the brothers: "You to a love that your true faith doth merit; / You to your land, and love, and great allies" (177–78). Though modern editions interpolate the addressees here to be first Orlando and next Oliver, the order may in fact be the reverse if Jaques knows, as possibly he may, of Oliver's romantic forswearing of his estates for Celia. Jaques de Boys would thus be astonished to see Orlando apparently inheriting the family "land and great allies".

To the modern world, the shattering financial implications of the intruding second son are lost: we are long rid of the curse of primogeniture. But for Elizabethans, exposed in vast numbers to the younger brother predicament, and for whom "'Younger son' meant an angry young man, bearing more than his share of injustice and resentment",[18] the announcement "I am the second son of old Sir Rowland" would be an arresting lead clause in a thoroughly financial language. Is Jaques de Boys visibly aghast, if he learns the nature of the new family order? Will he join the tight-knit band of revellers, or stand outside, awkward and excluded? He is clearly ruled out from Duke Senior's concluding promise of rewards: "every of this happy number / *That have endured shrewd days and nights with us* / Shall share the good of our returned fortune" (161–63, emphasis added). No Principal Secretaryship there.

The closing moments thus impose a crux: that Shakespearean device we might call the shibboleth of terminal gesture. Like the stage directing of lonely Jessica at the close of *Merchant*, as her husband greets joyously the prospect of her defeated father's death; like the response of ultra-chaste Isabella in *Measure*, when the Duke casually announces his intention to marry her; like the group reaction closing *Twelfth Night* when Malvolio exits screeching "I'll be revenged on the whole pack of you" (5.1.365): we have the construction of a last-minute crux, giving potential, even probable rise to a dominating bodily commentary, undisclosed within the script, which powerfully defines end-tones. Outflanking censorship by triggering on the stage dimensions invisible on the page, such carefully constructed and recurrent Shakespearean shibboleth helped also solve the problem of politically polar theatrical venues, by motivating on the common stage a prominent gestural subversion of supernal harmony or aristocratic 'justice' which could be omitted in court performance, where body language would safely articulate politically appropriate rapture. In such 'stagecraft secrets', Shakespeare the common player tutors Shakespeare the playwright in sophistication of the medium.

"IT IS NOT THE FASHION TO SEE THE
LADY THE EPILOGUE" (EPILOGUE 1–2)

It is commonly observed of the later middle ages and early modern period that popular resistance to perceived injustice or exceptionally repressive conditions conceived as their remedy not the construction of some enlightened novel alternative, but return to a lost ancestral paradigm. Against baronial oppression were claimed an egalitarian state of nature, or the freedoms of Saxon England throttled by the Norman Yoke. Extortionate ecclesiastical opulence was denounced against the primitive church of the apostles. Indicting early capitalist individualism was the true Christian commonwealth. To counter the bad new things, one sought the good old ways. Progress is thus backward-looking; oppositionality deeply conditioned by notional conservatism. Such political ideality (to steal Auden's memorable binarism) is Arcadian, not Utopian.[19]

It is to this paradox of progressive conservatism that *As You Like It* clearly belongs in fundamental ways. Its major features comprise, we have seen, a virtual inventory of medieval carnival delights, and it opposes to the new authoritarianism the spirit of popular liberties centuries old. Yet Shakespeare's sceptical genius is not, I would argue, in thrall to dreams of happier forefathers. Just as his Histories, we saw, build consonances of contemporary calamity and medieval horror, so *As You Like It* refrains from urging ascent to the past. The drama's ending makes the point forcefully, not only in the dysresolution's political anti-fideism—the sabotage of faith in providentially aided aristocratic governance—but in the play's sexual politics, figured in an unresubjugated Rosalind.

Audience approval of her entrepreneurial way with nuptials had been secured in part by the Martext episode (3.3), which had pointedly raised the Church of England's resented ceremonial demands. Marry properly in church, insisted Jaques; "Truly she must be given, or the marriage is not lawful", dogmatized Martext (57). Rosalind was thus the more likeable in her breathtaking bridal independence. Not only does she engineer a priest-free woodland wedding, in the popular tradition of *sponsalia per verba de praesenti*, thus suggesting satisfying snub to resented ecclesiastical *diktat*; and not only does she pointedly give *herself* away, doubly violating patriarchal authority, ducal and paternal. In a fine dialectical reversal, she inverts patriarchal authority at its foundation by in effect choosing her father, rather than yielding in traditional passivity to her own bestowal:

> (To Duke) To you *I give myself*, for I am yours.
> (To Orlando) To you *I give myself*, for I am yours. (105–06;
>   emphases added)

Critics have seen in this ending quite literally a closure, the repressive conservatism of a patriarchal telos, which slams down on female freedom like a heavy-lidded box. Peter Erickson, for instance, writes of Rosalind's marriage as crowning "the conservative countermovement by which, as the play returns to the normal world, she will be reduced to the traditional woman who is subservient to men."[20] But this is to aggrandize, in each of the sentences quoted above, the concluding clause, conventionally devotional, at the expense of the middle one: vehement in anti-patriarchal self-determinism. Such criticism has simply missed, in "I give", the performative semantic of marital ritual. Erickson (25) for instance reads "To you I give myself" merely as Rosalind's submissiveness to a new and necessary passivity in "the role of male possession"; but this overlooks the transgressive meaning, "*I myself* give myself": a sensational violation of ritual male "giving", made the clearer by contrast with Reverend Martext's patriarchal indignation: "Truly she must be given" (3.3.57). (Such usurpation would make the funnier Martext-in-Hymen's affronted sense of loss of face: "Peace ho! . . . 'Tis I must make conclusion . . ."). In Lodge's original, fatherhood had likewise presided over smooth transference of patriarchal possession: "Rosader [Orlando], take her, she is thine, and let this day sollemnise . . . thy nuptialls" (253). Shakespeare's heroine, breathtakingly, is self-betrothing, self-affiliating, freely self-positioning within familial bonds. The female subject in such an economy of belonging can be no mere commodity, circulated at will among males.

Rosalind, then, is created by Shakespeare to be charismatic in prerogative transgression. Reinforcing the emphasis and extending the prerogative is the whole tenor of the courting scenes between Rosalind and Orlando: which, though jocular and hyperbolical, have effectively established new and emancipatory terms of marriage, abolishing the sexual double standard. "Maids are May when they are maids, but the sky changes when they are wives", warns Rosalind. "I will be more jealous of thee than a Barbary cock-pigeon over his hen, more clamorous than a parrot against rain . . ." "You shall never take [your wife] without her answer, unless you take her without her tongue" (4.1.125–28, 147–49).[21] Rethinking of marital relations was just what was happening in many regions in England, historians record, where women were gaining a greater sense of independence from the expansion of the market economy (in dairy regions women were responsible for both producing and marketing butter and cheese), and from Puritan teachings on spousal partnership in marriage. "The popularity of advice manuals and conduct books in this period suggests that people were having to work out a new relationship between spouses, one that could no longer be taken for granted."[22] The profile must surely have appealed to the citizen wives who were "regular playgoers" throughout the period, and to the ladies who "were in numbers at the Globe from 1599 to 1614."[23]

Radically self-bestowing, leaving her menfolk gasping in astonishment ("If there be truth in sight, you are my daughter!", 5.4.107), and textually undiminished by any closing action of masculine resubordination, Rosalind revels on through the very close of the play, a woman married but unmastered in the very epilogue, where, though effectively now a married woman, she nonetheless flirts with the audience ("My way is to conjure you").[24] "It is not the fashion to see the lady the epilogue" Rosalind admits to them; then fires back the riposte: "But it is no more unhandsome than to see the lord the prologue"(Epilogue 2–3). Teasingly strolling the stage rim to the final seconds, surveying the upturned faces with impudent caprice for beards that pleased her and complexions that "liked" her, and close enough, she says, to "perceive . . . your simpering": maintaining power in her own white hands even after the script is done, by compelling tantalised focus upon her actions—"when I make my curtsy, bid me farewell" (and how long will she deign, deliciously, to keep them, waiting and simpering?)—Rosalind in her unrebuked mocking-mastering epitomises female independence triumphant.[25]

Critics have sometimes defused such conclusions by repositioning Rosalind in the tradition of carnival, whose inversions of gender and domineering Maid Marion may paradoxically have functioned to support hierarchic and patriarchal normativity, as both accommodative ritual catharsis, and as reinforcement through parodied reversal.[26] But we must avoid the falsifying conflation of medieval ritual with Elizabethan drama: institutions crucially distinct in provenance, duration, location, means, financial yield, audience expectations, and authorial ambitions. When carnival exuberance and *reines pour rire* are relocated to Elizabethan professional theatres, the medieval quietist functions may be problematised, even annulled, by the new representational framework. For the epistemological paradigm of the new theatres—the *theatrum mundi* of Montrose's cogent exposition—is characterised not only by imports of clown and fool, cross-dressing and festive misrule, but by constitutive induction of realism, by topical allusiveness, psychological profiling, individualist self-determinism: in short, a version of reality substantial, analytic, and thus tutelary, as carnival-time frolics could rarely be. Thus upon charming, challenging Rosalind, at work on amatory critique in *As You Like It* with its rich social mimesis, is conferred an intrinsic propositional realism, an exemplary appeal to paradigm shift in gender relations, generically denied to the grotesqueries of plainly transvestite Maid Marion.

Indeed Rosalind's autonomy is the more marked and startling, I suggest, in the context of another ludic convention, the Tudor popular wedding dance—surely to the forefront in contemporary spectators' minds at this point in the action—in which newly made brides had customarily to submit to every male who sought them as his dance partner. "There is such a lifting up and discovering of the damsel's clothes and of other women's apparel that a man might think all these dancers . . . were sworn to the devil's dance. Then must the poor bride keep foot with all dancers, and refuse none, how scabbed, foul, drunken, rude and shameless so ever he be."[27] We can never know, of course, precisely what has ensued in the "rustic revelry" (166) just instigated by Duke Senior on Jaques' final departure;

but power-relations in the epilogue are writ large. Though both the wedding dance context and the drama's imminent termination require her surrender to others' will ("What a case I am in then", 6), Rosalind at this very point—like Cressida captive in the Greek camp, power-jesting her way out of sexual harassment—resists ritual submission, through supremacy by teasing. ("I am sure as many as have good beards, or good faces, or sweet breaths, will for my kind offer, when I make curtsy bid me farewell".) The contrast powerfully demonstrates, as does so much else with Rosalind, that Shakespeare's political sensibility is not simply oppositional-conservative, but actually 'progressive', in the modern sense, instilling novel reflexes of delighted admiration for female empowerment and independence. The novelty is of a piece with Shakespeare's sympathy for self-determining Juliet, and what Gurr calls "Juliet's rebellion."

> Shakespeare's presentation of marriage was relatively 'new', in that his plays uphold the power of love over parental authority. Juliet's rebellion . . . was an act of disloyalty which few London citizens were ready to applaud. Shakespeare's heroines were an alarming novelty. When Beatrice challenged the convention of women undergoing arranged marriages, and the young lovers in *A Midsummer Night's Dream* rebelled against the harsh Athenian laws they were voicing kinship with Juliet.[28]

Indeed the emerging prerogative of filial autonomy in marital choice—a consequence of Protestant emphasis upon marriage for spiritual companionship—was in the later 1590s facing patriarchal backlash in the courts and parliament. Thomas Thynne and Maria Audley, the teenage children of prominent and rival West country families, had married secretly in 1594 to the mutual horror of the parents, and the Thynnes were continuing their struggles in court, even as *As You Like It* was being performed, to have the marriage declared invalid. Their argument was that the wedding had been conducted without due process: no banns, priest, or in-church ceremony.[29] Members of the 1598 Parliament, too, had become distressed by a recent rash of eloping heiresses. "A staid trio of gentlemen" sponsored a bill to prohibit church sale of licenses to forego reading of banns, thus effectively closing a loophole that permitted youthful marriages to be hidden from fathers.[30] A daughter's rebellious marriage was conceived normally as a disgrace for the father. Just months before the play opened, the dashing and bankrupt William, Lord Compton had eloped (in April 1599) with the only daughter of the unpopular and immensely wealthy former Lord Mayor of London, Sir John Spencer, and married her, despite a paternal detestation of Compton so bitter that Spencer had beaten and hidden his daughter: for which the lord had managed to have him briefly imprisoned. These events were the talk of London in 1599, of which Shakespeare could not have been ignorant (particularly as Spencer was living in a vast, eye-catching mansion in St. Helen's, Bishopsgate: Shakespeare's own parish from probably 1596–99). The humiliation of 'rich' Spencer'—the very Mayor threatened in 1595 by angry crowds protesting miscarriage of justice, and thus part, as we saw, of the political context of *Romeo and Juliet*—occasioned delight to the citizenry.[31]

Little concerned for fathers ("what talk we of fathers, when there is such a man as Orlando?" 3.4.33–34), Rosalind had at the eleventh hour, of course, enjoyed her father's approbation of her choice of spouse. She had, however, presented him with what was all but a *fait accompli*, wrapped in magical improbability ("I have since I was three year old conversed with a magician", 5.2.53–54; "Dost thou believe, Orlando, that the boy / Can do all this that he hath promised?", 5.4.1–2), and the whole emphasis of the play is upon a daughter independently instigating both courtship and nuptials. *As You Like It* thus positioned itself to celebrate female and filial autonomy at a precise historical point when patriarchal reassertiveness was seeking juridical and statutory constraint of self-bestowing daughters. Such emancipatory sexual politics may have been in part local, since Southwark, among other institutionalised anomalies, seems to have provided elopement oppportunity.[32] Though these politics were in part nostalgic (spiced with connotations of old literary romance, and sustaining free marital choice in the *per verba de praesenti* tradition), they were also pioneering—unsanctioned, that is, by idealizing conservative retrospect—in their pleasuring redefinition of female domestic prerogative, celebrating latitude for female speech and energy within matrimony itself.

"THEN SHALL WE BE NEWS-CRAMMED"(1.2.79): THE GLOBE AND THE FLEDGLING PUBLIC SPHERE

In *The Structural Transformation of the Public Sphere*, Jurgen Habermas recognised the development at the close of the seventeenth century of a 'bourgeois public sphere': a network of clubs, coffee houses and periodicals fostering a culture of informed, rational interchange of thought and social critique, effectively independent of the traditional authority of church and crown.[33] Habermas' dating of the sphere has been much contested, however, since his account entirely overlooks England's mid-century Republic, its political revolution and astonishing effloresence of cultural and political perspectives. "For a time, the sphere was far wider than merely 'bourgeois.'"[34] Habermas also fails to reckon, as David Norbrook has pointed out, with the *Jacobean* emergence of literary clubs meeting in taverns around St Paul's in London. "These clubs brought together figures with Parliamentary, legal and courtly connections across a broad range of political sympathies."[35] Indeed, London life was evolving through the sixteenth century an institutionalised discursive plurality which contributed to that sphere's emergence. "Young men about town gathered outside and inside St Paul's

Cathedral, where all three forces Foxe had singled out as great vehicles of the reforming spirit—preachers, players and printers—were offering their wares."[36] Habermas's model remains, however, "heuristically valuable", Norbrook notes, because it "encourages us to locate pressures towards a wider political community, contesting top-down models in which monarch and court set the ideological agenda."[37]

In England a fledgling 'public sphere' can arguably be traced early in the century to the Humanist anti-aristocratic discourse of the More circle (*Utopia, Of Gentleness and Nobility, The Spider and the Fly*), and to the sermons and publications of the Commonwealthmen. Fierce campaigns of ideological control, however, waged subsequently by Henry VIII, Protector Northumberland, then by Mary and Elizabeth in the wake of massive popular unrest, polar religious changes, and large-scale revolts such as Kett's Rebellion (1549) and the Northern Rising (1569), drove underground the spirit of bold public critique. The drying up of Crowley's political polemic after his spirited *The Way to Wealth* and *Philargyrie* (1550–51) is representative. Proliferating treason laws, repeated impositions of Martial Law and the creation of Provost Marshals, the development in the 1590s of not one but two, competing espionage systems (run by Burghley and Essex respectively), Machiavellian fabrication of pseudo-plots against the crown, the crackdown following the Martin Marprelate tracts, the springing of surprise house-to-house searches across the country producing detailed intelligence documents, the increasing use of juridical torture, and initiatives such as Burghley's (in the royal proclamation of October 1591) establishing nation-wide, domestic "inquisition of all manner of persons" (which we examined in relation to *2 Henry VI*), all combined to manufacture a punitive 'national security state', and thus to discourage revival of arenas for public articulation of political challenge to crown and peer.

Yet the construction in London of permanent professional theatres from the 1580s on effected a major intervention in public life. Its authors and players in large degree independent of the patronage system of the court and nobility, theatre was an institution endowed, we have seen, with a highly ambiguous relation to political discourse.[38] Since, to the authorities the theatres were to function as a political safety-valve, ideally contained by censorship, plays were licensed in limited expression of disaffected perspective. Shakespeare's were regularly enriched, as we have seen, by topical allusiveness.

Ros.:   Then shall we be news-crammed.
Celia: All the better: we shall be more marketable. (1.2.79–80)

Much Elizabethan drama was, of course, celebrative of national militarism, monarchy, and traditional hierarchy. And even at its most independent, the new professional drama, unlike the discourse of the fully developed public sphere, was still *counter*hegemonic, its oppositionality substantially subtextual since delimited by state censorship. Further, in its ecumenical interplay of rhetoric and high learning with folk cultural elements, it offered a polyphony that would be pointedly excluded from the rationalist and scientific discourse of the bourgeois public sphere.[39] Yet insofar as it comprised the voluntary mass participation of citizens in a civil discourse, a discourse often deeply public and topical in character, and insofar as its audiences formed a heterogenous, cross-class bloc, committed to intensive playgoing (commercial theatre in the period 1574–1642 saw "on average . . . as many as a million visits to the playhouse a year"),[40] Elizabethan theatre in general, and, I would argue, Shakespeare's plays in particular, mark the charismatic resuscitation and expansion of a nascent public sphere.[41]

As You Like It, we have suggested, is as a defining masterwork of countercultural perspectives. The play champions satire in the wake of the 1599 book-burning, sympathises with underclass distress, saturates its audience in the forbidden delights of traditional festal pastimes, repudiates the authoritarian meanness of vestry values, celebrates poaching, mocks the church and rejects its self-serving dismissal of extra-ecclesiastical weddings, instills heady pleasure in transgressive expansion of female prerogative, and deictically identifies, as its master movement, the freedom-giving, anti-hierarchic forest with the Globe theatre itself. In all these ways—not to mention, as other critics have shown, in its playful demystification of such aristocratic poetic conventions as Petrarchan pedestalisation of women, and the superiority of pastoral life—this drama critiques and combats the ideologies, genres and prohibitions of both official and aristocratic culture. In the new stronghold of the Globe Theatre, where the Lord Chamberlain's Men possess finally a home of their own, the play announces the continuity of the company's perspective ('As You Like It'), celebrates the impunity enjoyed in the liberty of Bankside, and, to sure commercial advantage, consolidates its constituency through the particularly potent spell of deictic revel. For the script's many invocations of the playhouse community ("Let the forest judge") regenerate what the vestrymen have expelled from London: carnival's generation of a jubilation in mass fellowship, a "strong sense of neighbourly identity".[42] In *As You Like It*, Shakespeare infuses elated camaraderie into the counterhegemonic spirit of the struggling public sphere.

11 Conclusion

> It must not be forgotten, however, that just as the landowning classes
> were obliged to serve their economic purposes by contriving a depres-
> sion of the social and legal status of the peasantry whom they con-
> trolled, so the peasants in fighting against economic oppression were
> also fighting for wider human rights. They strove not merely for a
> reduction of rent but for human dignity.
>
> (Rodney Hilton, *Class Conflict and the
> Crisis of Feudalism*, revised ed., 65)

> The rabble should have first unroofed the city
> Ere so prevailed with me! It will in time
> Win in power and throw forth greater themes
> For insurrection's arguing.
>
> (*Coriolanus*, 1.1.207–10)

The Black Nineties, we saw, unfolded for the masses as one of the harsh-
est decades in English history. In that extraordinary world, of a harrowing
underclass misery so desperate it could view Spanish armadas as emancipatory, of a turbulent religio-political inheritance vitalising multiple lineages of oppositional thought, and of a social order fissiparous at both
elite and parochial levels, we found in Shakespeare an habitué of critical
perspectives on power, steadily publicising its discrediting abusiveness, and
emerging at many points as a risk-taking radical. Himself the product of an
economically destabilised family and township, and writing for the arena
theatres in the transgressive Liberties, Shakespeare was persistent, we saw,
in the exposure of a society comprehensively obtuse and repressive in its
hierarchic ideologies of class and gender.

Resituating dramas in their individual political moments, we discovered
Shakespeare articulating public angers through what we dubbed the art
of toxic parallel. *2 Henry VI* paraded the festering grievances of military
disasters, unpaid troops, and territorial losses; of hyper-taxation, forced
loans, and ruinous alliance with a French monarch. Lord Burghley, we
saw there, was indicted, *qua* Gloucester, for peculation and torture. The
contemporary plight of deserting common soldiery we saw glanced at in
both *As You Like It* and the sudden poignancy enveloping the terminal
Jack Cade. Through the Cade rebellion were broadcast such longstanding underclass angers as the aristocratic treatment of animals better than

servitors, and the institution of neck verses, which left only working men executed. Plebeian hunger in the midst of insouciant patrician banqueting we found structural to *Romeo and Juliet*, composed during the starvation years and traumatising food riots. The late Tudor requirement of in-church weddings—expensive violations of ancient popular prerogative—was countered in *As You Like It* by a concluding nuptial simultaneously clergyman-free and satiric of clerical officiation. The harshness of primogenture was explicit in the same play, whose abrupt introduction of the younger Jaques de Boys at the play's very close, in a kind of *déja vu* refiguration of the earlier Orlando, emphasised that the younger son problem remained glaringly unresolved, whatever the luck of Orlando himself.

Close contextualisations further revealed that, in what looks to have been a settled stratagem of discursive rejoinder in a budding counter-public sphere, Shakespeare countered official doctrines of demonisation by flipping them back against the establishment. The allegedly constitutive intemperance and violent irrationality castigated in women by patriarchy is diagrammed, in *Shrew*, as permissible injuriousness in a head of household; and the drama's anguishing finale generalises to the entire political order the prerogative of character-crippling personal repression. In the wake of London's 1595 riots, that responsibility for street violence attributed by government tract and crown proclamations to underclass youth is volleyed back against the feuding upper class and troublemaking heads of household in *Romeo and Juliet*: wherein anonymous townspeople do their repeated, uncommended best to maintain the peace gored by bloodletting superiors. The spectre of nation-wide anarchy, inveterately blamed by government homiletics on rebel commoners, is exposed in *2 Henry VI* as the calculated product of dementedly ambitious noblemen, responding to criminally incompetent monarchy. Government seizure of satires elicited the same year as *As You Like It* the sustained defence and practice of that genre, just as the criminalising of vagrancy by legislation in the most recent parliament and by recent proclamations stimulated that drama to humane counter-valuation of homeless wandering. The vestry values exercised by freshly empowered Churchwardens and divisive local oligarchies to domineer the poor and suppress folk revels was countered with *As You Like It*'s anticlerical jibes, and its entire muster-roll of roistering festal recreations. The very title *As You Like It*, we suggested, advertised continuity of Shakespeare's sceptical fare, and celebrated, through that drama's deictic conflation of Arden Forest with the Globe theatre, the flourishing of greenwood freedoms across the water in the new home of the Lord Chamberlain's Men.

Finally, beyond the topical playwright who pressed hot-button issues and penned discursive rejoinders, the historicist dimension to our analyses uncovered a Shakespeare of systemic challenge to the foundational hierarchic principle. Interlinking despotic brutalities of patriarchy and class, *Shrew*, *Romeo* and *As You Like It* all associated female victimisation with the sufferings of the poor. Conversely, these plays applauded female insurgence:

piteously devotional in Juliet, charismatic in unresubjugated Rosalind, and vexatiously thwarted in carnivalesque Catherine. In *Henry VI* the crown itself forfeited the axiomatic loyalty propagandised by the Tudors. The picture of irresolvable claimant problematics in *Henry VI Parts Two* and *Three*, disturbingly contemporaneous as the end approached for the Tudor dynasty, de-absolutised simple fealty to hereditary succession, much as Catholic propaganda was seeking to do. Sworn crown allegiance was suggested a revocable sin by Salisbury's principled argument in *2 Henry VI*: a play which—astoundingly, in the teeth of Burghley's national surveillance proclamation of October 1591—foregrounded both resistance theory, and the subversively charged trope of 'commonwealth' rights. *2 Henry VI*, we saw, whilst repudiating Jack Cade as a genuine representative of the commons, lent conditional endorsement to armed popular revolt; and it supplied, in the spectacle of patriotic pirates executing Suffolk on behalf of the nation, the experience of a populist class vengeance through a Martial Law from below. Indeed the egalitarian pirates of *2 Henry VI* demonstrated that Shakespeare, "ever receptive to oppositional thought and experience— the proletarian radicalism of Cade's followers, the regicidal indictments in *Hamlet* and *Macbeth*, the resistance theory behind *King Lear*, the outlaw greenwoods of *As You Like It*—has here tapped another source, the early stirrings of the maritime radical tradition."

Having established through a close-hewn historicism the frequently subversive thrust of Shakespeare's plays at the thematic level, we re-identified such values at the level of form, in excavating the politics of the stagecraft. The original meanings of Shakespearean drama, we argued, can best be recovered by thinking through their valences as scripts, fashioned to generate meaning through interaction in the carnivalesque auditorium: a space wherein late Tudor audiences, conditioned by the binaristic thinking of rich against poor, came easily to collective self-identification as 'the trewe comons' or 'the poorality'. The court censor, engaging these plays through private and silent reading, missed the festal dialogic which activated 'constructed performance latencies' enhancing and transforming meaning in the amphitheatres.

Prominent here was actor-author Shakespeare's pressuring audacity in sleight of deixis, buttonholing surrounding spectators in a collusion of jest, teasing insults, appeals for solidarity, or even menacing hostility: a process of outreach we found habitually signalled in imagery of wave and sea, breath or wind, stench or vapour, ground or lowness. Central, too, was Shakespeare's apparently unique repertoire of manipulative carnival dynamics, deployed throughout his career, and perfected as early as *The Taming of the Shrew*. Carnival targeting exploited the anti-authoritarian orientation of the arena theatres, relatively unsubdued in a play's opening minutes, by exhibiting authority figures, often of the highest level, for audience hostility. Men of power alienate the vacationing throng through such various autocratic behaviours as the frigid threatening of innocence, the immediate firing of a tirade of commands, or an arrogant insulting of the underclasses and their pleasures. Tantalization effects may further such estrangement, as dense description of sybaritic luxuries, or an effortless bestowal of rings and jewels, coins or bulging purses, underline a lifestyle of privilege and an insouciant liquidity of riches so hypnotically proximate, yet so agonizingly beyond reach, for the close-packed underclass masses in the beggaring 1590s. Conversely, through carnival bonding, comedic masters delight the community of revelry with a reign of misrule that travels far beyond quips and clowning to exposé and violation of the quotidian hierarchic order. "As men of some consequence transgressing against figures of still higher authority, the wide field of their antics can both unmask and exemplify heartless typicalities sustaining the social and political order—the ideologies of the class system, the ruthless mechanisms of court realpolitik, the baseless propaganda of patriarchy." But against these demystifying bearers of carnival Shakespeare engineers always a gradual turn, and dissolves the admixture of comedic delight with rising moral disquiet through final repellence by moments of unmitigated cruelty. Carnival repudiation's final exposé of the reveller's ugly brutalism sunders us in some measure from his values and perspective: a potential suspension or problematisation of the subversive critique enunciated in Iago and Edmund, Falstaff or Thersites, that may seem to question the ethical tenability of seditious thought, and to which we shall return. In *The Taming of the Shrew*, however, repudiation of the whimsically despotic Petruccio is heightened through the additional technique of carnival frustration. Stoking joyous expectations of sensational climax, Shakespeare turns the victorious reimposition of patriarchal authority into the sickening extermination of a craved and beloved vitality. Such manipulation by exasperation resembles Shakespeare's device of carnival suppression, widely recurrent when authority-figures, in a kind of dramaturgic insertion of vestry values, confiscate from the recreative community the pleasures of roistering, of instrumental music, and even of madrigal.

As You Like It, we saw, worked not only through the ubiquitous dynamics of carnival bonding and targeting, but pursued its countering of the new cultural authoritarianism through such further stagecraft techniques as deixis, doubling, and the dysresolution. We followed the targeting of Orlando as an antipopulist gentleman, rendered an outsider to the Globe's metaphoric forest by the same technique of deictic 'claustration', or contrastive sightlessness of the audience, by which populist York had winkingly mocked the auditorium-blind Warwick and Salisbury in *2 Henry VI* with assurance that they were reliably beyond anyone's hearing. We observed the characteristic Shakespearean clemency with which Orlando, initially humiliated by both vagrancy and auditorium solecisms, becomes integrated into the festal community after loss of class arrogance. Buoyantly contrastive was the deictic bonding with the populist young women, who cheerlead enthusiasm for playhouse pastimes, prove spontaneously compassionate to the indigent, and out-joust the ethically supercilious, clerically respectful, and suggestively Jonsonian Jaques. The overwhelming probability that puritanical old Adam doubled both as Reverend Martext and Hymen underscored once more the play's anti-clerical animus, as bumbling Hymen, spouting doggerel verse, finds for a final time his authority jostled and pronouncements gainsaid. The finale, we found, was in fact a dysresolution, its flamboyantly self-exposing implausibilities functioning as terminal delegitimation of dominant ideology on its supernaturalist plane, and returning us to the providentially denuded world of the Histories and Tragedy.

2 Henry VI revealed a playwright precociously brilliant in crafting a clandestine politics of performance. In their powerfully recurrent outreach into the auditorium, highly varied deictic modalities induced a kind of simulated playhouse activism: inflaming, soliciting, satirising along populist lines, and exciting to a kind of theatrical plebiscite the phenomenon of mass political arousal that was anathema to the authorities. For Eleanor's mime of heaving up the crown from the groundling pit figured just that spellbinding latency which was the nightmare of the Tudors and the structural heart of this drama, the king-making powers of the commons. These powers were refused, however, by a Gloucester ambiguously audience-sighted yet mainly remaining in principled remoteness from the unquiet spectators. The contrast was thus with York, firebrand demagogue of the surrounding commons, and the play on one level comprises York's electoral campaign for the throne. Opening with his candid bid for followers, outraged like him by the national catastrophes inflicted by incompetent monarchy, it closed in act five with his appeal for insurrectionary support as King Henry attempted his arrest: a call to arms which, by that point, fell on disapproving ears. The primary rhythm driving this drama was an audience goading by figures of supreme power—Dame Eleanor threatening "headless necks" to "base" men, Queen Margaret cursing the hostile "sea" and "waves", Suffolk screeching class abuse—which then granted spectators delicious retaliation, only to melt that political revenge into pity or irresolution in the spectacle of extreme suffering (Eleanor's public shaming and exile, Margaret's loss of her lover, Suffolk's murder). Cade's revolt likewise laid on a rapture of reprisals, as carnival broke out in the congeniality of the gamehouse, releasing a dizzying disinhibition of political expression, and a wisecracking world-turned-upside-down where violence was mere playworld romping. Yet the revolt turned shaming, as a restored realism rendered Saye's execution sadistic, and a climate of blind London slaughter suddenly ensued. Surprise pathos enveloped the rebel Jack Cade, however, as it had encompassed the Duke of Suffolk: a sympathy attained through more virtuoso stagecraft. Iden and his complacent enunciation of private property rights were targeted through deictic blunder, wherein his loud, repeated claims of owning the locality unwittingly established jarring overtones of expropriation of the local commons in occupation of the playing space. Iden's murder of Cade unfolded as a sickening replay of the contest between Thump and his master: the scene, now leeched of comedy and clemency, became redolent instead of sadistic gentlemanly injustice as a single, starved, and little man was repeatedly stabbed by a well-fed one who towered above him, and was backed by five henchmen.

In summary, then, we can respond to the not uncommon claim that Shakespeare turned radical in his middle age, with *King Lear* or *Coriolanus*, by demonstrating that William Shakespeare, on both thematic level and dramaturgic, proved a radical political thinker from the outset. Not only does he appear to have shared precisely the set of political heresies that historian Andy Wood has recently uncovered in underclass 'memories' of Kett's rebellion in the 1580s and 1590s: "that the gentry could not be trusted; that organised resistance could be both feasible and effective; and that it was possible for labouring people to advance political claims".[1] With the lampooning of Jack Cade's followers for dissolving at the mere name of charismatic kingship, and through the "derision medicinable"of courtly demystification, Shakespeare goes further, to burn away that trusting reverence of kingship which had delimited traditional rebellion's counter-politics of monarcho-populism.[2]

Yet our *tour d'horizon* of Shakespeare the subversive does not take in the entire dramatic landscape. The relentless protest playwright emerges also, and structurally, as a pessimist.

First, the dynamic of carnival repudiation, integral to the closure of so many plays, may prove in fact an anti-dynamic, severely problematising endorsement of the carnival protagonist's sceptical perspectives. Strikingly, there seems to be nowhere in Shakespearean drama a figure of articulate political scepticism who remains trustworthy and humane. Second, the typically Shakespearean rhythm of *2 Henry VI* manipulated playgoers from subjection to goading into retaliative gratification, only to find the payback foundering into pathos or horror, into revisionary, compassionate assessment of a fellow human become an underdog. The aim here may simply have been indictment of political reprisals at the individual level— suggesting, in today's terms, a Shakespeare who would favour only a post-rebellion Truth and Justice Commission—but ambiguously, that surprise rehabilitation of political adversaries through their suffering humanity may have effected suspicion of insurgency *per se*: a kind of conservatism of compassion. Third, this drama further establishes the sterile dialectic of a negation of the negation, as York and Cade crusade against a nation-wrecking kingship, only to preside in turn over criminality equal or worse. Fourth, there is paradoxically rebuff to political hope in even Shakespeare's generous and insistently repeated moral vision of our human commonality, as a universal condition which overrides and falsifies all hierarchic orderings of class, race, religion and gender. On the one hand, this is a warm-hearted, counter-demonising, and profoundly subversive vision: "I live with bread, like you; feel want, / Taste grief, need friends. Subjected thus, / How can you say to me I am a king?" (*Richard II*, 3.2.171–73); "Hath not a Jew eyes?" (*Merchant of Venice*, 3.1.49 ff.); "What art thou, thou idol ceremony? . . . Art thou aught else but place, degree and form / Creating awe and fear in other men?" (*Henry V*, 4.1.222, 227–29). On the other hand, the insistence carries with it the apparent, unsparing correlative of our universal political shortcomings, such that suffering plebeians as well as the feasting privileged would seem untenable vehicles of reform. ("Use every man after his desert, and who should scape whipping?" [*Hamlet*, 2.2.508–10].)

A bleak assessment of humanity was currently pervasive. As Jim Sharpe has noted, a "general mood of pessimism . . . formed an important strand in the late-Elizabethan mentality." Many English Protestants believed themselves living in the 'Last Days', an Augustinian sense of human depravity colouring their thinking. "This abstract notion of the corruptibility of human beings interacted in the elite consciousness with the concrete realities of vagrancy, grain riots and the rising levels of crime . . . A faltering war effort restricted the opportunities for optimism still further."[3] Yet Shakespeare's plays themselves demonstrate a steady empiricism behind such unhopefulness. That the ideological consciousness of the lower orders was a volatile mix, commoners thus proving agonisingly gullible, was dramatised in the lightning *volte face* of the Cade rebels, surrendering disaffection at the merest touch of such alternative discourses as patriotism and the sharing of warrior-heroism with kings and great men: precisely the sentiments to which Henry V will confidently appeal in his St Crispin's day speech. The problem of leaderless dissension in the late Tudor period was presented in the melding of Cade into Hacket. That impasse in turn arose partly from the nation-wide phenomenon of oligarchic self-dissociation from wider local community in a puritanical anti-populism: the 'vestry values' combatted by *As You Like It*. That the oppositional ideology of the urban underclasses was still a vulnerably non-consensual affair we observed in the exasperated retort of one retainer (Gregory) to another (Samson)—"the quarrel is between our masters and us, their men"—who, in his infatuation with lordly swashbuckling, seemed incapable of grasping the point.[4] In the conditions of late sixteenth century England, then, Shakespeare's paradoxical outlook (as it may seem to moderns), his sustained but pessimistic demystification, perhaps constituted objective realism: it was not until the 1620s and beyond that the preconditions for substantial political change—cross-class alliance in political opposition—began to emerge. Historical unpropitiousness limited Shakespearean dissidence to a resourceless delegitimation of power.

Shakespeare's horizon of aspiration thus lacked the confident amplitude predicating modern radicalism. Whatever Francis Bacon's dreams of an emancipatory revolution in the scientific sphere, the transformation of human potential through foundational restructuring of political and economic system, the passion of today's political radicalism, would have seemed absurdly unrealistic in the 1590s to the most ardently egalitarian:

although a "golden uncontrolled enfranchisment" (*Richard II*, 1.3.90) via a new constitution would be explicitly meditated, and as an imminent possibility, for his daughters' generation, at the Putney Debates of 1647. Yet if Shakespeare embodied the paradoxical limits of an Elizabethan radicalism—foundationally subversive yet not revolutionary, delimited by lack of agency to an almost impotent exposé—he did not permit his political pessimism to erase his *saeva indignatio*, or to justify retreat into prosperous indifferentism. Compassionate anguish on his scale allows no such luxury. (We must have hope, suggested Brecht, on behalf of those who have no hope.) Despite both the limited compass of resistance available to him, and the literally eviscerating penalties of dungeon and executioner's bonfire awaiting those found transgressing power at its fundamental level, Shakespeare remained, very remarkably, what today we term an activist. Refusing both political passivity, and a mere play of ambiguation, radical Shakespeare continued to work through his playwrighting for a more humane society, in four evident ways.

First, Shakespeare's endings, no matter how pessimistic, do not relegitimate the deconsecrated political order. Shakespeare's vision continues one of *smouldering* subjection, closes with *unreconciled* demystification. In the plays we have examined, no elevating harmonic bonds us finally with court and kingship, repositioning us in confident submission to hierarchy. No religious or political insight restores allegiance to a system stripped bare to a self-serving hierarchy, of often murderous human callousness, spun out of control. *Romeo* ends with Capulet and Monatague still locked in competition, as they seek to outbid each other in the lavishness of their proposed funerary commemorations; and the closing speech from the Prince evoked, we saw, a climate of reprisal for scapegoated underlings. *The Taming of the Shrew* terminates in callous crowing over victorious psychic disintegration of a patriarchal captive. *As You Like It* foregrounds once more the younger brother tragedy inflicted by primogeniture. *2 Henry VI* ends amid national destabilization and slaughter, just as *Part Three* ends without solution to that perennial aporia of monarchic government, succession crisis. The History plays demonstrate, indeed, that accommodation to the Tudor establishment and its dogmata was impossible within Shakespeare's thinking, since sovereign power was characterised—in a vision kindred to Original Sin—not by that wily impersonal insuperability imputed it by Foucault and Greenblatt (any "oppositional practice that failed to deliver the New Jerusalem on schedule must have been controlled all along from a secret office in Babylon", comments Jim Holstun),[5] but by the age-old hold, over the court as over commoners, of personal self-obsession, perilous duplicity, and often gross manipulability: attributes that rendered state power perennially untrustworthy, often incompetent, and prone to lurching, like Elizabeth, from crisis to crisis.

Second, Shakespeare committed his hopes for human betterment, as we have seen, to the project of popular education, effected through the tutelary drama of the public playhouse. Exposing the impostures of power, he sought to refashion the moral sensibilities of the commons: thus occupying a zone of engagement delimited yet vital, in a logic not unfamiliar to radicalism today in the impasse of resistance to global capital.[6] Breaking their normative incorporation in a range of political ideologies, Shakespeare sought to render his audiences, "through the art of known and feeling sorrows . . . pregnant to good pity" (*King Lear*, 4.6.217–18). Pessimism over institutional reform thus partly displaced the political agenda into the project of fostering complex critical thinking; repeated infliction of emotional sensitisation to human suffering helped counter habits of demonisation.[7] Shakespeare's plays could thus forge alterity of values, if not of political formation. The appeal to audience percipience here implies some residual confidence in the potential judgement of the masses, and thus in popular possibilities, at odds with any wholesale political defeatism.[8]

Deployment of eloquence for persuasion of the multitude was a precept, of course, of Tudor humanism. Rhetoric was conceived, however, as an elite class weapon: the oratory of the privileged would contain the tumults of the populace. Rhetorical training was accordingly to be withheld from commoners, for in the minds of noblemen and gentry, Peltonen observes, "There was nothing more dangerous than the power of eloquence being wielded by or even for the common people."[9] Shakespeare, conversely, appropriated rhetorical brilliance to educate his audiences *against* manipulation by official political rhetorics. Preconditional to any reform of power was disseminating deconsecration of the existing political order. In a memorably brisk formulation of Franco Moretti, "Having deconsecrated the king, tragedy made it possible to decapitate him."[10]

Third, Shakespeare's complex dramatisation of underclass rebellion, far from simple defeatism, contained encouraging elements. Not all the sufferings of the body politic were immedicable. *2 Henry VI* demonstrated (as would *Coriolanus*) the feasibility of attaining limited political goals, in this case the expulsion from court of a hated magnate of disastrous national influence. And the play's direct presentation of a universal pardon granted to rebels—a spectacle produced only by breaking with the Chronicles— hardly suggests that traumatised deterrence was the bard's goal.

Finally, Shakespeare's resolute interventionism in contemporary political process is most daringly visible in his crusade, as well we might term it, against the Earl of Essex, and against nearly everything that England's most popular man was fighting for. The epitome of aristocratic privilege and power, militaristic, compulsively confrontational, scornful both of commoners and common law, Essex was equally threatening to eirenic and humanitarian values in his passion for Protestant supremacy abroad, escalation of war with Spain, and at home the implicit continuation of a governance of frequent resort to Martial Law and hyper-taxation. Shakespeare responded with a counter-campaign of determined exposé, puncturing Essex as posturing, embryonic tyrant first as York in *2 Henry VI*, and then later as Machiavellian Bullingbrooke in *Richard II*. Whatever the private cost thereby incurred to Shakespeare's relations with Essex's friend Southampton, Shakespeare would continue this operation through the *Henry IV* plays, and then bolt Essex fast onto his depiction of ruthlessly fraudulent Henry V through an explicit comparison established by the Chorus. At the height of the Essex crisis mounting through the later 1590s, and just months before the February 1601 coup which sought to enthrone King Robert I, Shakespeare would finally pen another script of sensationally subversive stagecraft effects taking aim at the pseudo-demotic Earl: the tale of that populist yet treacherous swordsman-courtier, the charismatic but half-demented Hamlet. But this larger narrative of principled Shakespearean activism must be relocated, for reasons of space, to a successor volume.[11]

Formed amid immensities of human suffering, witness to haughty ideologies maiming human life, provoked by successive crises to foundational political critique, the greatest literary genius of the Elizabethan age emerged, from the outset, as a radical playwright.

Notes

NOTES TO CHAPTER 1

1. Steve Hindle, *The State and Social Change in Early Modern England, 1550–1640* (Basingstoke: Palgrave 2002), 233.
2. Roger Manning, *Village Revolts: Social Protest and Popular Disturbances in England, 1509–1640* (Oxford: Clarendon, 1988), 202.
3. Orazio Busino, cit. *Harrison's Description of England in Shakspere's Youth, Being the Second and Third Books of his Description of Britaine and England*, ed. F.J. Furnivall (London: 1878), Part 2, Book 3, 53. I take this quotation from the excellent article by Barbara Freedman, 'Elizabethan protest, plague, and plays: rereading the "documents of social control"' in *English Literary Renaissance* 26 (1996) Spring, 17–45.
4. John Dover Wilson, *The Essential Shakespeare: A Biographical Adventure* (Cambridge: Cambridge University, 1932), 6.
5. On the transformation of the bust, see Brian Vickers (whose work draws on that of Richard Kennedy), letter to *The Times Literary Supplement*, June 30, 2006, and also Vickers' *TLS* article of August 18, 2006, 16–17. It seems that at some point after William Shakespeare was buried beneath the chancel floor, his admirers may simply have added the plaque of Latin and English verse commemorating William to the base of the nearby family monument, with its bust of John, rather than commissioning a new monument.
6. Quotation from *King Lear* 3.4.35.
7. 'Historicizing Shakespeare's *Richard II*: current events and the sabotage of Essex' in *Early Modern Literary Studies* 11.2 (September 2005), 1.1–47.
8. Manning, *Village Revolts*, 183.
9. David Underdown, 'The taming of the scold: the enforcement of patriarchal authority in early modern England' in *Order and Disorder in Early Modern England* ed. A. Fletcher and J. Stevenson (Cambridge: Cambridge University Press, 1985), 116.
10. Curtis C. Breight's outstanding work, *Surveillance, Militarism and Drama in the Elizabethan Era* (New York: St. Martin's, 1996), discusses the Armada aftermath on 40–42,176–80.
11. Susan Frye, 'The Myth of Elizabeth at Tilbury' in *Sixteenth Century Journal* 23.1 [1992], 114.
12. Felipe Fernandez-Armesto, *The Spanish Armada: the Experience of War in 1588* (Oxford: Oxford University Press, 1988), 271–73.
13. William Leahy, *Elizabethan Triumphal Processions* (London: Ashgate, 2005), 127.

14. Fernandez-Armesto, *Spanish Armada*, 220, 223.
15. *State Papers Relating to the Defeat of the Spanish Armada*, ed. J. K. Laughton, 2 vols: (London: 1894–95), vol. 2., 138–39, 95, 159–60; cit. Fernandez-Armesto, *Spanish Armada*, 224, 71, 66.
16. P. L. Hughes and J. F. Larkin, eds., *Tudor Royal Proclamations* (New Haven: 1969), no. 735.
17. A. L. Beier, *Masterless Men: the Vagrancy Problem in England 1560–1640* (London: 1985), 153.
18. Cit. Beier, *Masterless Men*, 153.
19. Hughes and Larkin, *Tudor Royal Proclamations*, nos. 735 and 740.
20. Breight, *Surveillance*, 86.
21. Ian Archer, *The Pursuit of Stability: Social Relations in Elizabethan London* (Cambridge, 1991), 9.
22. Fernandez-Armesto, *Spanish Armada*, 89–90.
23. Christopher Hill, *Liberty Against the Law: Some Seventeenth Century Controversies* (London: Penguin, 1996), 164; *The Century of Revolution* (Wokingham, Berkshire: Van Nostrand Reinhold, 1980), 21.
24. Manning, *Village Revolts*, 161.
25. Park Honan, *Shakespeare: A Life* (Oxford: Oxford University Press, 1998), 241; James Shapiro, *A Year in the Life of Shakespeare: 1599* (New York: Harper Collins, 2005), 238.
26. Cited by Christopher Hill, 'The Many-Headed Monster' in *Change and Continuity in 17th Century England* (1974; rpt. New Haven and London: 1991), 187.
27. Fernandez-Armesto, *Spanish Armada*, 44, 47. Compare Breight, *Surveillance*, 42.
28. Peter Clark, *English Provincial Society from the Reformation to the Revolution: Religion, Politics and Society in Kent 1500–1640* (Hassocks, Sussex: Harvester, 1977), 249.
29. Cit. Clark, *English Provincial Society*, 454 n.2.
30. Manning, *Village Revolts*, 224. Manning's important study concludes riots to have been essentially "sub-political" (3): a view I find untenable in the light of subsequent studies by Andy Wood, Keith Wrightson and others discussed hereafter, as well as much of his own evidence.
31. Jim Sharpe, 'Social strain and social dislocation, 1585–1603' in *The Reign of Elizabeth I: Court and Culture in the Last Decade*, ed. John Guy (Cambridge: Cambridge University Press: 1995), 199. The soldier is quoted 199–200.
32. Keith Wrightson, *English Society 1580–1680*, 2nd ed. (New Brunswick: Rutgers University Press, 2003), 148.
33. Ibid., 149.
34. Though James Holstun is in my view shrewdly accurate that the 1590s was a "post-revolutionary era", strongly impacted by the defeat of Kett's Rebellion in 1549, and that "late-Tudor turbulence was far from mid-Tudor crisis" ('"Damned Commotion": riot and rebellion in Shakespeare's histories' in *A Companion to Shakespeare's Works, Volume 2, The Histories*, ed. Richard Dutton and Jean E. Howard [Oxford: Blackwell, 2003], 197–98), this was the *objective* situation as we know it in hindsight. If radical success enjoyed poor prospects in the mid-1590s, due to the absence of cross-class insurrectionary bonds, many contemporaries nonetheless feared "impending breakdown of the social order" (Underdown, 'Taming', 116) ; and radical thought and impulse were kept on the boil by almost unendurable conditions.
35. Christopher Hill, *Reformation to Industrial Revolution, 1530–1780* (Harmondsworth: Penguin, 1969); Andrew Appleby, 'Diet in sixteenth century England: sources, problems, possibilities' in Charles Webster, *Health,*

Medicine and Mortality in the Sixteenth Century (Cambridge: Cambridge University Press, 1979), 108–12.

36. Archer, *Pursuit*, 10.
37. Hindle, *State and Social Change*, 40.
38. Hill, *Century of Revolution*, 19.
39. Archer, *Pursuit*, 10,13.
40. Manning, *Village Revolts*, 187.
41. Archer, *Pursuit*, 13.
42. Hill, *Century of Revolution*, 19.
43. Between 1540 and 1550, food and woollen cloth prices virtually doubled, and many rents rose by over 50 per cent. Neal Wood, *Foundations of Political Economy: Some Early Tudor Views on State and Society* (Berkeley, 1994), 222.
44. R.H. Tawney and Eileen Power, *Tudor Historical Documents* (1924; rpt. London: Longmans, 1953), 2.233–34; compare 243.
45. See Archer's discussion in *Pursuit*, 9–14 and 35; quotation from 13.
46. Tawney and Power, *Tudor Economic Documents*, 2.240.
47. C. S. L. Davies, 'Popular Disorder' in *The European Crisis of the 1590s* ed. Peter Clark (London: Allen and Unwin, 1985), 244.
48. *Historical Manuscripts Commission, Salisbury,* XIII, 168–9; cit. Andy Wood, 'Fear, Hatred and the Hidden Injuries of Class in Early Modern England' in *Journal of Social History*, Spring 2006, 815. Here the mid-century plebeian conviction that the gentry sought to starve the commons to death (Wood, *1549 Rebellions*, 169–72) is reappearing—if it ever entirely vanished.
49. Cit. J. Sharpe, 'Social strain', 200.
50. Wood, 'Fear, Hatred', 813.
51. Cit. Wood, *1549 Rebellions*, 203, and discussed 202–07.
52. Lawrence Stone, *The Causes of the English Revolution, 1529–1642* (London: Routledge and Kegan Paul, 1972), 56–117.
53. Lawrence Stone, *The Crisis of the Aristocracy, 1558–1641* (Oxford: Oxford University Press, 1967) 303–31.
54. Stone, *Causes*, 85–88.
55. Perry Anderson, *Lineages of the Absolutist State* (London: Verso, 1979), p.129; Stone, *Causes*, 79–83.
56. Lawrence Stone, 'Review' in *English Historical Review*, 77 (1962) 328.
57. Stone, *Causes*, 95–97, 113–14.
58. Ibid., 79, 116.
59. Hill, *Liberty Against the Law*, 325. The law was in fact a complex and ambiguous terrain, sometime open to usage (especially customary law) by the poor against their governors: see J.A. Sharpe, 'The people and the law' in *Popular Culture in Seventeenth Century England* , ed. B. Reay (London: Croom Helm, 1985), 244–70. Nonetheless, English rebels indicted the legal system for its inability to restrain gentry predation: see Wood, *1549 Rebellions*, 103.
60. Archer, *Pursuit*, 237.
61. John Howes, cit. in Tawney and Power, *Tudor Economic Documents*, 3. 441–42; cit. William C. Carroll, *Fat King, Lean Beggar: Representations of Poverty in the Age of Shakespeare* (Ithaca: Cornell University, 1996), 30.
62. From the burial list of St Botolph's without Aldgate, 1593–98; cit. Beier, *Masterless Men*, 46.
63. Robert Crowley, *An Infomacion and Peticion* (1548) in *Select Works of Robert Crowley*, ed. J.M Cowper (London: Early English Texts Society,1872), 159–60.

64. Robert Crowley, *The Opening of the Wordes of the Prophet Joell* (written in the 1540s), sigs. F5r-v; cit. David Norbrook, *Poetry and Politics in the English Renaissance* (London: Routledge and Kegan Paul, 1984), 53.

65. *Policies to reduce this realme of England unto a prosperous wealth*, in Tawney and Power, *Tudor Economic Documents*, 3.336. On frequent underclass protestation of willingness to rise and fight against oppression, see Andy Wood, 'Poore Men woll speke one daye: Plebeian Languages of Deference and Defiance in England c. 1520–1640' in Tim Harris, ed., *The Politics of the Excluded, c.1500–1850* (New York: Palgrave, 2001), 67–98; and Whitney R. Jones, *The Tudor Commonwealth 1529–1559* (London: Athlone, 1970), 51–55.

66. Andy Wood, 'Poore men woll speke", 81.

67. John Ponet, *A Shorte Treatise of Politike Power* (1556) in *John Ponet: Advocate of Limited Monarchy* ed. Winthrop Hudson (Chicago University Press, 1942), 61.

68. Brents Stirling, 'Shakespeare's mob scenes: a reinterpretation' in *The Huntingdon Library Quarterly*, 3 (May 1945), 213–40.

69. Andy Wood, *Riot, Rebellion and Popular Politics in Early Modern England* (Basingstoke: Palgrave, 2002), 32–38.

70. "Much as the magistracy might resent and resist government policy on particular issues . . . there was no disagreement on the basic question of the need to advance and preserve good order among its inferiors." Wrightson, *English Society*, 162.

71. Elliot Rose, *Cases of Conscience: Alternatives Open to Recusants and Puritans Under Elizabeth I and James I* (Cambridge: Cambridge University Press, 1975), p.1. Peter Lake, 'Religious identities in Shakespeare's England' in *A Companion to Shakespeare* ed. David Scott Kastan (Oxford: Blackwell, 1999), 59–67.

72. Beier, *Masterless Men*, 16; Peter Clark, *The English Alehouse: A Social History* 1200–1830 (London: Longman, 1983), 129.

73. Derek Hirst, *Authority and Conflict 1603–1658* (Harvard University Press, 1986), 15.

74. See Louis Montrose, 'The place of a brother in *As You Like It*: Social Process and Comic Form' in *Materialist Shakespeare* ed. Ivo Kamps (London: Verso, 1995), 39–70.

75. The Essex revolt could easily have succeeded had Essex gone ahead with his plan to take Whitehall Palace with his elite swordsmen, since the queen, on the night planned for the *coup*, was poorly defended. See Mervyn James, *Society, Politics and Culture: Studies in Early Modern England* (Cambridge: Cambridge University Press, 1986), 446, 448.

76. Hill, *Century of Revolution*, 21; Manning, *Village Revolts*, 329.

77. Youings, *Sixteenth Century England*, 219; see also chapter 8 above.

78. Quoted in *Tudor Rebellions*, by Anthony Fletcher and Diarmaid MacCulloch, 4th ed. (London: Longman, 1997), 10.

79. Andy Wood, *The 1549 Rebellions and the Making of Early Modern England* (Cambridge: Cambridge University Press: 2007), xiii. These historians include Keith Wrightson, Steve Hindle, Andy Wood, Ethan Shagan, Tim Harris, Mark Goldie, David Rollinson, John Cooper, R. B. Goheen, and I. M. W. Harvey: for bibliographic discussion, see the Introduction to Harris, *Politics of the Excluded*; the Introduction to Andy Wood's *Riot, Rebellion*; and the Preface to Andy Wood, *The 1549 Rebellions*.

80. Wood, *1549 Rebellions*, 104.

81. Harris, *Politics of the Excluded*, 6.

82. Ethan Shagan, *Popular Politics and the English Reformation* (Cambridge: Cambridge University Press: 2003); Andy Wood, *1549 Rebellions*.
83. Markku Peltonen, 'Political rhetoric and citizenship in *Coriolanus*' in *Shakespeare and Early Modern Political Thought* ed. D. Armitage, C. Condren and A. Fitzmaurice (Cambridge: Cambridge University Press: 2009), 237–38.
84. Hindle, *State and Social Change*, 24.
85. Mark Goldie, 'The unacknowledged republic: officeholding in early modern England' in Harris, *Politics of the Excluded*, 153–94.
86. Archer, *Pursuit*, 64.
87. Goldie, 'Unacknowledged Republic' in Harris, *Politics of the Excluded*, 153. "Order and authority did not merely 'trickle down' but 'welled up' within society itself", concludes Hindle: *State and Social Change*, 132. Patrick Collinson likewise discusses "quasi-republican modes of political reflection and action" under Elizabeth, suggesting that "citizens were concealed within subjects" and terming contemporary England "a monarchical republic": *Elizabethan Essays* (London: Hambledon, 1994), 18–19, 31–58.
88. Phrase from Hindle, *State and Social Change*, 233.
89. On circuit charges and articles of inquiry, see Hindle, *State and Social Change*, 4–8.
90. "At every level, from council chamber to quarter sessions bench, from magistrate's parlour to parish vestry meeting, the enforcement of social policy had to be negotiated . . . [It] stood or fell by the achievement of parish officers." Hindle, *State and Social Change*, 175.
91. *The Rape of Lucrece* in the Arden edition of *The Poems*, ed. F. T. Prince (London: Methuen, 1960), lines 615–16, 607–09.
92. Thomas More, *Utopia*, translated by Ralph Robinson, 1551 (rpt. New York: Barnes and Noble, 2005), 143.
93. Markku Peltonen, *Classical Humanism and Republicanism in English Political Thought 1570–1640* (Cambridge University Press, 1995), 11, 35–39, 64, 71, 79–80, 110, 112; F. Heal and C. Holmes, *The Gentry in England and Wales 1500–1700* (Stanford University Press, 1994), 30–33.
94. More, *Utopia*, trans. Robinson, 23.
95. Erasmus, *Adagia* 3.7.1, ed. W. Barker (Toronto: U. Toronto Press, 2001), 284–85.
96. Thomas More, *Quis optimus reipublicae status* in *The Penguin Book of Renaissance Verse 1509–1659*, selected by David Norbrook (London: Allen Lane Penguin, 1992), 82.
97. Juan Luis Vives, *Concerning the Relief of the Poor*, trans. Margaret Sherwood (New York: New York School of Philanthropy, 1917), 6: quoted in Linda Woodbridge, *Vagrancy, Homelessness and English Renaissance Literature* (Urbana and Chicago: University of Illinois Press, 2001), 169.
98. John Rastell, *Gentleness and Nobility* in *Three Rastell Plays*, ed. Richard Axton (Cambridge, 1979), ll.1154–62.
99. Jones, *Tudor Commonwealth*, 24.
100. Wood, *1549 Rebellions*, 31–32.
101. *Henry Brinklow's complaynt of Roderyk Mors*, ed. J. Meadows Cowper (Early English Text Society, extra series 22, London: 1874), 33; cit. Wood, *1549 Rebellions*, 32.
102. *Brinklow's complaynt*, 12, 73 ; cit. Wood, *1549 Rebellions*, 34.
103. Shagan, *Popular Politics*, 280.
104. Norbrook, *Poetry and Politics*, 51.
105. Neal Wood, *Foundations*, 171–72.
106. Crowley, *Infomacion and Peticion*, ll.378–82.

107. *Shakespeare and Early Modern Political Thought*, 9–10. Skinner himself knows better: *Foundations of Modern Political Thought* (Cambridge University Press, 1978), vol.1, 215, 224–28.
108. Crowley, *Infomacion and Peticion*, ll.302–308.
109. Hugh Latimer, *Sermons of Hugh Latimer, sometime Bishop of Worcester, Martyr, 1555* ed. G. E. Corrie (Cambridge: 1844), 100; cit. Wood, *1549 Rebellions*, 34.
110. Wood, *1549 Rebellions*, 30–40, esp. 40.
111. Shagan, *Popular Politics*, 273–286, quotation from 275.
112. R. H Tawney, *Religion and the Rise of Capitalism* (1922; rpt. Harmondsworth: Penguin, 1980), 147.
113. Bernard Gilpin, *A godly sermon preached at the court at Greenwich . . . 1552* (1581), 45–46; cit. Wood, *1549 Rebellions*, 35.
114. James Holstun, 'The spider, the fly, and the commonwealth: John Heywood and agrarian class struggle' in *English Literary History* 71.1 (Spring 2004), 53–88.
115. John Chrysostom, *De Lazaro Concio*, 2.4; cit. Charles Avila, *Ownership: Early Christian Teaching* (Maryknoll, NY: Orbis, 1983), 83. See also Michel Mollat, *The Poor in the Middle Ages*, trans. Arthur Goldhammer (New Haven: Yale, 1986), 20–23.
116. Debora Shuger, 'Subversive fathers and suffering subjects: Shakespeare and Christianity' in *Religion, Literature and Politics in Post-Reformation England*, ed. Donna Hamilton and Richard Strier (Cambridge: Cambridge University Press: 1996), 62 n.7. Even Shuger's pioneering essay, however, does not take the full measure of the Fathers' position, revealed in Avila's neglected study.
117. Basil the Great, *Homilia in illud Lucae, 'Destruam'*, 7; cit. Avila, *Ownership*, 133.
118. Ambrose of Milan, *De Nabuthe Jezraelita*, 1; cit. Avila, *Ownership*, 135.
119. Avila, *Ownership*, 132.
120. Ambrose, *Expositio Evangelii secundum Lucam*, 7; cit. Avila, *Ownership*, 139.
121. A. O. Lovejoy, 'The communism of St. Ambrose' in *Essays in the History of Ideas* (Baltimore: Johns Hopkins, 1948), 301–02. See Ambrose, *De Nabuthe Jezraelita*, 7.35, 8.40.
122. Ambrose, *De Nabuthe Jezraelita*, 13.56; cit. Lovejoy, 'Communism of St. Ambrose', 300.
123. Basil the Great, *Homilia in illud Lucae, 'Destruam'*, 7; cit. Avila, *Ownership*, 135.
124. Brian Tierney, *Medieval Poor Law: A Sketch of Canonical Theory and its Application in England* (Berkeley: 1959), 34, 117; cit. Shuger, 'Subversive fathers', 53.
125. John Milton will re-urge the Christian distributivist logic through the Lady in *Comus*, declaring that natural bounty should relieve "every just man that now pines with want" by dispensing her blessings, currently amassed by the few into "lewdly pampered luxury", with "unsuperfluous even proportion" (ll.768–74).
126. Neal Wood, *Foundations*, 28.
127. Cit. Neal Wood, *Foundations*, 82–84.
128. *Dialogue between Pole and Lupset* ed. T. F Mayer (London: Royal Historical Society, 1989), 86–87, 124–31; see Wood, *Foundations of Political Economy*, 148–49.
129. Neal Wood, *Foundations*, 5.
130. Ibid., 37.

131. Andy Wood, *Riot, Rebellion*, 5–23; David Underdown, *A Freeborn People: Politics and the Nation in Seventeenth Century England* (Oxford: Oxford University, 1996), 7–9; Harris, *Politics of the Excluded*, 1–3; William H. Te Brake, A *Plague of Insurrection: Popular Politics and Peasant Revolt in Flanders, 1323–1328* (Philadelphia: University of Pennsylvania,1993), 5–8; Wayne Te Brake, *Shaping History: Ordinary People in European Politics 1500–1700* (Berkeley: University of California,1998), 2–21.

132. James C. Scott, *Weapons of the Weak: Everyday Forms of Peasant Resistance* (New Haven: Yale University,1985), xv, 319; *Domination and the Arts of Resistance* (New Haven: Yale University,1990), xii. I gratefully acknowledge Annabel Patterson for introducing Scott to Shakespeare scholars in *Shakespeare and the Popular Voice* (Oxford: Basil Blackwell, 1989).

133. E. P. Thompson, *Customs in Common* (1991), 66; cit. Hindle, *State and Social Change*, 200.

134. Underdown, *Freeborn People*, 106–30; quotation 107.

135. Christopher Hill, *Puritanism and Revolution* (Harmondsworth: Penguin, 1986), 58–125; quotation from 65. See also Hill, *Liberty Against the Law*, 83–90.

136. Hill, *Puritanism and Revolution*, 76.

137. Wood, *The 1549 Rebellions*, 7–8, 154–60; Sharpe, 'The people and the law', 244–70.

138. On the historical associations of this proverb see Christopher Hill, *The English Bible and the Seventeenth Century Revolution* (London: Penguin, 1994), 202–03; also Hill, *Milton and the English Revolution* (London: Faber, 1977), 71–72; Rodney Hilton, *Bond Men Made Free: Medieval Peasant Movements and the English Rising of 1381* (London: Routledge, 2003), 211–212; and A.B. Friedman, '"When Adam delved . . .": contexts of an historic proverb' in Larry Benson, ed., *The Learned and the Lewd: Studies in Chaucer and Medieval Literature* (Cambridge, Mass: Harvard, 1974), 213–30.

139. Lovejoy, 'Communism of St. Ambrose', 307.

140. Peter Brown, *The World of Late Antiquity* (New York: Norton, 1989), 66–68.

141. See Norman Cohn, *The Pursuit of the Millennium*, (St Albans: Paladin, 1970), esp. chapters 10–13 and Conclusion. We "probably shall never know fully", concludes Christopher Hill, "how much continuity of underground radical use of the Bible there was from Lollards through Foxe's martyrs down to the apparently sudden appearance of Biblical radicalism in the 1640s": Hill, *English Bible*, 197.

142. Jean Froissart, *Chroniques*, ed. Luce and Raynaud, 11 vols., (Paris: 1869–99), vol.10, 95; cit. Cohn, *Pursuit of Millennium*, 199.

143. Rastell, *Gentleness and Nobility*, lines 606, 611–12.

144. Richard Woods, *Norfolkes Furies, or A View of Ketts Campe* (1615), B1v–B2r; cited by Patterson, *Popular Voice*, 42. Andy Wood discusses the question of the authenticity of the ventriloquised voices of Kett's rebellion in *1549 Rebellions*, 91–108.

145. Hill, *English Bible*, 202.

146. Hilton, *Bond Men*, 211–12, 221–32, quote from 229; Hill, *World Turned Upside Down*, 166; 115–23. See also Hilton, *Class Conflict and the Crisis of Feudalism*, 143–53.

147. See Wood, *1549 Rebellions*, 4; 150; 151–64; quotations from 163–64.

148. On monarcho-populism see Holstun, 'The spider, the fly', 53–88; and Wood, *1549 Rebellions*, 7–9, 154–64.

149. Harry Levin, *The Myth of the Golden Age in the Renaissance* (Oxford University Press, 1969); Raymond Williams, *The Country and the City* (Oxford: Oxford University Press, 1973), 13–19, 42.

150. Woodbridge, *Vagrancy*, 118.
151. Crowley, *Select Works*, 142–43.
152. Article 38 of The Thirty-Nine Articles, in *The English Creede* (London, 1587), 86.
153. *Mother Hubbard's Tale*, lines 132–53, 368–74.
154. See Hill, 'The many-headed monster' in *Change and Continuity*, pp.183–85; Stephen Greenblatt, 'Murdering peasants: status, genre and the representation of rebellion' in *Representing the English Renaissance* (Berkeley: University of California, 1988), 1–29.
155. Charles Hobday, 'Clouted Shoon and Leather Aprons: Shakespeare and the Egalitarian Tradition' in *Renaissance and Modern Studies* vol. 23 (1979), 64.
156. Peter Milward, S.J., *Shakespeare's Religious Background* (Chicago, 1973); also *The Catholicism of Shakespeare's Plays* (Southampton, 1997). Richard Wilson's more objective points were set out in 'Shakespeare and the Jesuits', *TLS* December 19 1997, 11–13 ; see also his less persuasive argument for Shakespeare as a *politique* in *Secret Shakespeare* (Manchester, 2004). Shakespeare's Jesuit connection has been questioned by, among others, Peter Davidson and Thomas McCoog, SJ, in *The Times Literary Supplement*, March 16 2007.
157. Antonia Fraser, *Faith and Treason: the Story of the Gunpowder Plot* (New York: Anchor, 1997), 114; Collinson, *Elizabethan Essays*, 247.
158. Breight, *Surveillance*, chapters 4–6.
159. Michael Questier, 'Elizabeth and the Catholics' in *Catholics and the 'Protestant Nation'* ed. Ethan Shagan (Manchester University Press, 2005), 81. Quotation of Cardinal Allen, 70.
160. Fernandez-Armesto, *Spanish Armada*, 44.
161. John Carey, *John Donne, Life, Mind, and Art* (London: Faber, 1981), 16.
162. Diarmaid MacCulloch, *The Reformation* (London: Viking, 2003), 381.
163. Substantial study of these parallels is in Breight, *Surveillance*.
164. Fitter, 'Historicizing Shakespeare's *Richard II*'.
165. Medina Sidonia cit. Fernandez-Armesto, *Spanish Armada*, 39.
166. Thomas Cotton was arrested on arrival at Dover in 1580, and executed at Tyburn in May 1582. His brother at Stratford would seem to have been the linkman in Campion's postulated recruitment of Shakespeare for Hoghton Tower in the winter of 1580.
167. Ponet, *Shorte Treatise*, 109.
168. Donald R. Kelley, 'Ideas of resistance before Elizabeth' in *The Historical Renaissance* ed. R. Strier and H. Dubrow (Chicago: University of Chicago,1988), pp.48–76; see also Skinner, *Foundations*, vol.2, 189–358. Resistance theory by no means wilted away with Elizabeth's accession to power, insists Collinson, *Elizabethan Essays*, 43–48.
169. *Rape of Lucrece*, ll.1692–93.
170. Richard Strier, 'Faithful Servants: Shakespeare's Praise of Disobedience' in *The Historical Renaissance* ed. Dubrow and Strier, 119–20.
171. Linda Anderson, *A Place In the Story: Servants and Service in Shakespeare's Plays* (Newark: University of Delaware, 2005), 202–18. Anderson does not politicise this fact, despite its tell-tale occurrence in *Lucrece*: "servitors to the unjust, / [should] cross him with their opposite persuasion " (285–86).
172. Andrew Hadfield, *Shakespeare and Republicanism* (Cambridge: Cambridge University Press: corrected ed., 2008), 187.
173. Skinner, *Foundations of Modern Political Thought*; J. G. A. Pocock, *The Machiavellian Moment* (Princeton: Princeton University Press, 1975).
174. Anderson, *Lineages of the Absolutist State*, 420–28.

175. Norbrook, *Poetry and Politics in the English Renaissance*; also *Writing the English Republic* (Cambridge University Press, 1999). See also David Weil Baker, *Divulging Utopia: Radical Humanism in Sixteenth Century England* (Amherst: University of Massachusetts, 1999).

176. Patrick Collinson, 'De Republica Anglorum' and 'The monarchical republic of Queen Elizabeth I' in *Elizabethan Essays* (London: Hambledon, 1994), quotations from 19.

177. Collinson, *Elizabethan Essays*, 47.

178. V. Conti, 'The mechanization of virtue' in *Republicanism: A Shared European Heritage* ed. Martin van Gelderen and Quentin Skinner (Cambridge: Cambridge University Press, 2002), vol. 2, 73–83 .

179. Norbrook, *Poetry and Politics*, revised ed., 87.

180. Hadfield, *Shakespeare and Republicanism*, 40.

181. Starkey, *Dialogue between Pole and Lupset*, 121–22.

182. Oliver Arnold, *The Third Citizen: Shakespeare's Theatre and the Early Modern House of Commons* (Baltimore: Johns Hopkins, 2007), 54–56, 64–65; quotation of Coke from 15.

183. Hadfield, *Shakespeare and Republicanism*, 51–53.

184. Ibid., 17, 7.

185. Ibid., 25, 22, 41.

186. Philip Sidney, *The Countess of Pembroke's Arcadia (The Old Arcadia)*, ed. Jean Robertson (Oxford: Oxford University Press, 1973), 320; cit. Norbrook, *Poetry and Politics*, 85.

187. Norbrook, *Poetry and Politics*, revised ed., 93–94.

188. Hadfield, *Shakespeare and Republicanism*, 57, 13. Hadfield's sunny appraisal of Elizabethan Shakespeare as confidently republican misses, I feel, the bleak intensity of Shakespearean scepticism, in both its scale of demystification, and its pessimism regarding reforming political agency.

189. Andrew Hadfield, *Shakespeare and Renaissance Politics* (London: Thomson, 2004), 127, 134.

190. The Attorney-General fired such paramount distinction at William Hacket in his prosecution in 1591, as we shall see in chapter three: "Yf a nobleman rebell, his meaninge ys onlie to usurpe the Crowne, not impayringe the governmente; but ther can be no means to these peasants to accomplishe ther purpose, excepte by the absolute extirpation of all governmente, magistracy, nobility and gentrye." *The Manuscripts of Lord Kenyon*, Historical Manuscripts Commission, 14th Report, Appendix, Part IV, 609.

191. See Tobin Siebers, *Cold War Criticism and the Politics of Class* (Oxford: Oxford University Press, 1993); Ian Tyrrel, *The Absent Marx: Class Analysis and Liberal History in Twentieth Century America* (New York: Greenwood, 1986).

192. See Lawrence Stone, 'The revolution over the revolution' in *The New York Review of Books* 11 June 1992, 47–52; James Holstun, *Ehud's Dagger: Class Struggle in the English Revolution* (London: Verso, 2000), pp.42–45; Perry Anderson, 'Civil war, global distemper' in *Spectrum: from Right to Left in the World of Ideas* (London: Verso, 2005), 232–276.

193. See James Holstun, 'Ranting at the New Historicism' in *English Literary Renaissance* vol. 19, number 2 (1989); David Norbrook, 'Life and Death of Renaissance Man' in *Raritan*, vol.8 issue 4, Spring 1989.

194. Wood, *Citizens to Lords*, 9.

195. Holstun, *Ehud's Dagger*, 328.

196. *Skinner, Foundations of Modern Political Thought*; Pocock, *Machiavellian Moment*. A notable follower is Peltonen, *Classical Humanism*. Their limited purview is reproduced in the disastrously cramped and insubstantial

cartography of Armitage, Condren and Fitzmaurice in *Shakespeare and Early Modern Political Thought*; and it confines the focus of Martin Dzelzainis, 'Shakespeare and political thought', and of David Harris Sacks, 'Political Culture', both in *A Companion to Shakespeare*, ed. David Scott Kastan (Oxford: Blackwell, 1999). For the reduction of the battlefield of political thought to a disembodied textualism of the privileged classes, characterising the Skinner / Pocock Cambridge School of the history of political theory, see Ellen Meiksins Wood, *Citizens to Lords: A Social History of Western Political Thought from Antiquity to the Middle Ages* (London: Verso, 2008), 7–12; Perry Anderson, *English Questions* (London: Verso, 1992), 290–93.

197. On Brinklow's *Complaynt*, see Neal Wood, *Foundation of Political Economy*, 156; for *A ruful complaynt* see Andy Wood, *1549 Rebellions*, 34–35. "Historians, themselves the product of a literary culture, relying so much on written or printed evidence, are always likely to underestimate verbal transmission of ideas", notes Christopher Hill. "Men did not need to read books to become acquainted with heresy: indeed censored books were the last place in which they would expect to find it." *Milton and the English Revolution* (London: Faber, 1979), 76–77.

198. John Guy, *Tudor England* (Oxford University Press, 1988), pp.208–11; Fletcher and MacCulloch, *Tudor Rebellions*, ch.6 and Document 12.

199. Peltonen refutes Tacitean displacement of the Ciceronian, but remains within their parameters: "The unearthing of the classical humanist vocabulary in Jacobean England elucidates not only the development of the theory of citizenship in England but also, and more particularly, the full range of political thinking of the period."(*Classical Humanism and Republicanism*, 16). Why pass over the terms 'Levellers' and 'Diggers', with their perspectives, emergent in 1608?

200. Armitage, Condren and Fitzmaurice in *Shakespeare and Early Modern Political Thought* 8–9, quotation from 13.

201. On riot as treason, see Manning, *Village Riots*, 206–07, 228, 311–12.

202. Hindle, *State and Social Change*, 67.

203. The fear of a 'middling-sort' official expressed in a wardmote petition of 1597 in London's Tower ward: Corporation of London Record Office, Samuel Barton's Book, folio 46; cit. Archer, *Pursuit*, 9.

204. For example Psalm 12.5; Proverbs 21.13; James 5.1, 4; 2.5–6; Luke 6.24–25. On kingship, see Isaiah 1.23; Samuel 8.10–18.

205. "Israel's politics have been mined for the support of the divine right of kings, revolution against unjust authority, covenanted commonwealths, liberal democracy, nationalism, capitalism, and socialism" observes Norman Gottwald, *The Politics of Ancient Israel* (Louisville, KY: Westminster John Knox, 2001), 250. "Used as rag-bag of quotations", concludes Christopher Hill, "the Bible ultimately contributed to pragmatism, lack of theory, the rise of empiricism": *The English Bible*, 188.

206. Aristotle, *The Politics*, 1301b26–1302a2; quotation from Penguin translation by T.A. Sinclair and T. J. Saunders (Harmondsworth: 1981), 299.

207. Cicero, *De Republica*, I.XXXI, trans. C. W. Keyes (Cambridge, MA: Harvard University Press, 1959).

208. Hadfield, *Shakespeare and Republicanism*, 103–29; quotation 63.

209. Thomas Hobbes, *Leviathan* 2.21; 2.29, ed. C.B. Macpherson (Harmondsworth: Penguin, 1968), 268, 369; cit. Norbrook, *Writing the English Republic*, 34–35.

210. Wood, *Citizens to Lords*, 236.

211. G.E.M. de Ste. Croix argues that Christ's teachings on distributivism, emphatic in Mark, are vitiated by comprise as early as the Gospel of Matthew,

and become further diluted by the Fathers: *The Class Struggle in the Ancient Greek World* (Ithaca: Cornell, 1981), 425–441.

212. Bronislaw Geremek, *Poverty: A History*, trans. A. Kolakowska (Oxford: Blackwell, 1994), 25–28.

213. Cohn, *Pursuit of the Millennium*, 201–02.

214. Shuger, 'Subversive fathers', 52.

215. A breaker of illegal gentry enclosures at Frome, Somerset during the Western risings of 1549; cit. Wood, *1549 Rebellions*, 48.

216. Hugh Latimer, *Sermons*, 134; cit. Wood, *1549 Rebellions*, 108.

217. Katherine, *The Taming of the Shrew*, 4.3.77–78.

218. "The rhetoric of justice, peace and welfare—whether it found expression in royal proclamation and parliamentary statute or in popular petition and seditious libel—therefore presupposed cultural norms which were by their very nature vulnerable to rival interpretation . . . remaining in a continuous dialogue of challenge and reaffirmation in which the vocabulary was one of resistance as well as of obedience." Hindle, *State and Social Change*, 237.

219. James Holstun, 'Damned commotion', 195. Shakespeare's "rational sympathy with the dead", Holstun argues, "extends . . . to the gibbets of London, the starving streets and fields of England, and the slaughterhouse of Robert Kett's Norwich." 'Damned Commotion', 215.

220. Archer, *Pursuit*, 259. On Renaissance vilification of the masses compare C.A. Patrides, 'The beast with many heads: Renaissance views of the multitude' in *Shakespeare Quarterly* 16, no. 2 (1965), 241–46.

221. "The objective basis of the co-existence, for a long historical epoch, of feudalism and capitalism within transitional social formations was their common definition as systems of private property . . . There was always the possibility of a scale of mutually advantageous transaction—up to 'organic' compromise—between the nobility and bourgeoisie as social classes." Perry Anderson, 'The notion of bourgeois revolution' in *English Questions* (London: Verso, 1992), 111.

222. Christopher Hill, 'The many-headed monster' in *Change and Continuity*; 182.

223. Archer, *Pursuit*, 260.

224. Jan Kott, *Shakespeare our Contemporary*, trans. B. Taborski (1965; rev. 1967); Patterson, *Shakespeare and the Popular Voice*; Jonathan Dollimore, *Radical Tragedy: Religion, Ideology and Power in the Drama of Shakespeare and his Contemporaries* (Sussex: Harvester, 1984); Breight, *Surveillance*.

225. A.P. Rossiter, *Angel With Horns: Fifteen Essays on Shakespeare* (1961; rpt. London, 1989), 62.

226. The publisher and dramatist Henry Chettle noted "Nor doth silver-tongued Melicert / Drop from his honeyed Muse one sable tear / To mourn her death": Ian Wilson, *Shakespeare: the Evidence* (New York: St. Martin's Griffin, 1993), 295. Andrew Hadfield remarks that "Shakespeare stood out as one of the few prominent writers who neglected to celebrate the accession of James with a poem": *Shakespeare and Renaissance Politics*, 113.

NOTES TO CHAPTER 2

1. Ann Pasternak Slater, *Shakespeare the Director* (Brighton: Harvester, 1982), 31, 33.

2. Ibid., 15.

3. Tiffany Stern, *Rehearsal from Shakespeare to Sheridan* (Oxford: Oxford University Press, 2000), 65.

4. Court productions would take much preparation, but "The fee for taking a play to court was £10, comparable for the income they would get from a good day in their common playhouse." Andrew Gurr, *The Shakespearean Stage* (3rd ed., Cambridge: Cambridge University Press, 1992), 24. "There is no evidence", notes Lois Montrose, that any Shakespeare play was originally written with court or aristocratic household in mind, as opposed to being later performed and perhaps adapted for it. *The Purpose of Playing* (Chicago: Chicago University, 1996), 177.

5. Gurr, *Shakespearean Stage*, 212–13.

6. M. H. Wikander, *Princes to Act: Royal Audience and Royal Performance 1578–1792* (Baltimore: Johns Hopkins, 1993), 6.

7. Cit. C. D Bowen, *Francis Bacon* (1963), 141.

8. Leah Marcus, *Puzzling Shakespeare: Local Reading and its Discontents* (Berkeley and Los Angeles: University of California, 1988), 29.

9. C. L. Barber, *Shakespeare's Festive Comedy* (Princeton: Princeton University, 1972), 7. Among many related titles, see *Shakespeare and Carnival: After Bakhtin*, ed. Ronald Knowles (New York: St. Martin's, 1998); and *Carnival and Theater: Plebeian Culture and the Structure of Authority in Renaissance England* by Michael Bristol (New York: Methuen, 1985).

10. Barber, *Shakespeare's Festive Comedy*, 7; Montrose, *Purpose of Playing*, 19.

11. C. R. Baskerville, *The Elizabethan Jig and Related Song Drama* (Chicago: Chicago University, 1929), 47, 62.

12. Robert Weimann, *Shakespeare and the Popular Tradition in the Theater* (Baltimore: Johns Hopkins,1978), 24.

13. See Natalie Zemon Davis, 'The reasons of misrule' and 'The rites of violence' in *Society and Culture in Early Modern France* (Stanford: Stanford University Press, 1975), 152–87; also her 'Women on top: symbolic sexual subversion and political disorder in early modern Europe' in *The Reversible World: Symbolic Inversion in Art and Society*, ed. Barbara Babcock (Ithaca: Cornell University Press, 1978), 147–90. Likewise Emmanuel Le Roy Ladurie, *Carnival in Romans*, trans. Mary Feeney (New York: George Braziller, 1979); Wood, *1549 Rebellions* 164–66 on the spirit of play and festivity in Tudor rebellion.

14. Steven Mullaney, *The Place of the Stage* (Ann Arbor: University of Michigan, 1995), 43.

15. Joseph Lenz, 'Base trade: theater as prostitution' in *English Literary History* 60.4 (1993), 837.

16. Gary Taylor, *Reinventing Shakespeare: A Cultural History from the Restoration to the Present* (Oxford: Oxford University Press, 1989), 390. Compare the interchangeability of whoring and playgoing in John Davies' epigram, 'In Fuscum', cit. Gurr, *Shakespearean Stage*, 7.

17. Charles Edelman, *Brawl Ridiculous: Swordfighting in Shakespeare's Plays* (Manchester: Manchester University,1992), 5–7.

18. Alfred Harbage, *Shakespeare's Audiences* (1941; rpt. New York: Columbia University, 1964), 68.

19. Richard Wilson, *Will Power: Essays on Shakespearean Authority* (Detroit: Wayne State University,1993), 34.

20. Stern, *Rehearsal*, 119.

21. Gurr, *Shakespearean Stage*, 119.

22. *Thomas Platter's Travels in England*, 1599 , trans. Clare Williams (London: 1959), 171.

23. Harbage, *Shakespeare's Audience*, 80.

24. Mullaney, *Place of the Stage*, 31.

25. Montrose, *Purpose of Playing*, 34.

26. *Homily Against Disobedience and Wilful Rebellion* (1570) in *Certain Sermons or Homilies: A Critical Edition*, ed. Ronald B. Bond (Toronto: University of Toronto, 1987), 213.

27. Matthew Parker, *Correspondence* (London: Parker Society, 1853) p.61; cit. Christopher Hill, 'The Many-Headed Monster' in *Change and Continuity in Seventeenth Century England*, 2nd ed. (New Haven: Yale University Press, 1991), 189.

28. Robert Cecil, *Proceedings in the Parliaments of Elizabeth*, ed. T. E Hartley, (London: Leicester University Press, 1995), 3.398.

29. Andrew Gurr, *Playgoing in Shakespeare's London* (Cambridge: Cambridge University Press, 1987), 153.

30. Stern, *Rehearsal from Shakespeare to Sheridan*, 114. On "the elective power of the audience" in Shakespeare see Arnold, *Third Citizen*, 161–66: a process he engagingly dubs "the politics of halitosis" (161).

31. Thomas Dekker, *The Gull's Hornbook* (1609); cit. Harbage, *Shakespeare's Audience*, 13.

32. Jean E. Howard, *The Stage and Social Struggle* (London: Routledge, 1994), 31.

33. Taylor, *Reinventing Shakespeare*, 325.

34. John Northbrooke, *A Treatise wherein Dicing, Dauncing, Vaine Playes . . . are reproved* (1577); cit. Chambers, *Elizabethan Stage*, 4.198. It should also be noted, however, that some two-thirds or so of London's population were not playgoers. And the period's best-selling books were not plays, but sermons, by authors like the Puritan William Perkins.

35. Montrose, *Purpose of Playing*, 209–10. Montrose expands here on the germinal perceptions of Weimann in *Shakespeare and the Popular Tradition*, 169–77.

36. Edmund Dudley, *The tree of commonwealth: a treatise* (1509), ed. D. M Brodie (Cambridge: Cambridge University Press, 1948), 45.

37. On the requirement of silence in women, servants and the poor, see Wood, *1549 Rebellions*, 108–22; quotation from 113.

38. Harbage thought the vast majority of the groundlings to be artisans, their families and apprentices (*Shakespeare's Audience*, 60), but an account of affairs at the Curtain in 1613 indicates that the yard there was for working men and the unemployed (discussed in Gurr, *Playgoing*, 71). Gurr, in 1997 ('The Shakespearean Stage' in *The Norton Shakespeare*, 3284) suggested the majority of the audiences were artisans and apprentices, along with law students, who would have preferred the galleries (a silent contrast with his earlier speculation that citizens and apprentices were the probable majority (*Playgoing*, 64–65). Ann Jenalie Cook's speculation that the amphitheatres played to the privileged few (*The Privileged Playgoers of Shakespeare's London* [Princeton,1981]) has been demolished by Martin Butler, *Theatre and Crisis 1632–42* (Cambridge, 1984), Appendix 2, as well as refuted by Gurr, *Playgoing*, 3–4, 49–79.

39. Gurr, *Playgoing*, 38–39, 45.

40. Gurr, 'The Shakespearean Stage' in *The Norton Shakespeare*, 3287, and *Playgoing*, 22, 16.

41. *Romeo and Juliet*, 2.4.69–70; *Richard III*, 3.5.8–10; see Gurr, *Shakespearean Stage*, 98–103.

42. John Middleton, *The Roaring Girl*, 1.2.29–32. Middleton, of course, was an assistant of Shakespeare in the Jacobean period.

43. Gurr, *Shakespearean Stage*, 138–39.

44. It is true that for groundlings scanning the stage at an angle, the lowest galleries at the sides of the stage would be in the line of vision. For all groundlings,

however, the galleried majority would have been out of sight. Moreover, the distance between the stage front and the rear galleries at the Fortune (which appears to have resembled the Globe), was substantial, comprising some 27 feet: Gurr, *Shakespearean Stage*, 138.

45. The alteration is usually construed in depoliticised terms, as simply "improved design", e.g. Gurr, *Shakespearean Stage*, 146.

46. A satire from Dekker suggests perhaps the active auditorial custodianship of the commoners, in relating that audiences annoyed by the behaviour of wealthy gallants onstage would vocally assault them, with what he terms "the mewes and hisses of the opposed rascality". (*The Gull's Hornbook*, ch. 6, cit. Gurr, *Shakespearean Stage*, 228.)

47. Grace Ioppolo, *Dramatists and Their Manuscripts in the Age of Shakespeare, Jonson and Heywood* (New York: Routledge, 2006), 65; Gurr, *Shakespearean Stage*, 33.

48. Margot Heinemann, 'Shakespearean contradictions and social change' in *Science and Society* 41 (1977), 11.

49. Montrose, 'Place of a Brother', 50.

50. Gurr, *Playgoing*, 52.

51. Manning, *Village Revolts*, 53.

52. Wood, 'Fear, hatred', 812.

53. Wood, 'Poore men woll speke', 83.

54. "Theatrical experience is . . . generally far more permissive than our socially regulated experience of everyday life. It is especially conducive to the representation and entertainment of fantasies that are usually relegated to the background of our consciousness outside the theater. As a result, it is particularly geared to satisfy a playgoer's longing for a release from normative constraints." Thomas Cartelli, *Marlowe, Shakespeare, and the Economy of Theatrical Experience* (Philadelphia: University of Pennsylvania, 1991), 10.

55. Ibid., 55–56.

56. Ibid., 121, 31.

57. Letter by city authorities of 1574, cit. Gurr, *Shakespearean Stage*, 8. "Stage plays" wrote hostile city fathers to the Privy Council in 1595, "are so set forth that they move wholly to imitation and not to the avoiding of those vices which they represent, which we verily think to be the chief cause . . . of the late stir and mutinous attempt of those few apprentices and other servants, who we doubt not drew their infection from these and like places." Chambers, *Elizabethan Stage*, 4.318.

58. Harbage, *Shakespeare's Audiences*, 11.

59. Howard, *Stage and Social Struggle*, 73, 83.

NOTES TO CHAPTER 3

1. Giovanni Nenna, *Nennio: or a treatise of nobility*, trans. William James, 1595, folio 80r; cit. Peltonen, *Classical Humanism*, 112.

2. Richard Cosin, *Conspiracie for Pretended Reformation*, September 1592, 72.

3. Geoffrey Bullough believed it to date from late 1591 (*Narrative and Dramatic Sources of Shakespeare*, London: Routledge and Kegan Paul, 1960, vol. 3, 89); and, though the exact date of the play, and its place in the compositional sequence of the *Henry VI* trilogy, remain unproven, most modern scholars, following Stanley Wells and Gary Taylor in the *Oxford Shakespeare* (1988) and Michael Hattaway in the Cambridge edition (1991), likewise date the drama between 1591–92. Henslowe's 'Harey the vj, ne' is dated March 3 1592; Nashe's

reference to Talbot (of *Part One*) dates from August 1592; and Green's "Tiger's heart" allusion to *Part Three* dates from September 1592. See Hattaway, *The Second Part of Henry VI* (Cambridge University Press, 1991), 60–68.

4. "Mr. Sollicitor" compared Hacket's rising with the rebellions of "Cade, Taylor [i.e.Wat Tyler], and them of Norfolke" [i.e. Kett's Rebellion of 1549]. 'Memorandum of the arraignment, at Newgate, of William Hacket, of Northamptonshire, for high treason', in *The Manuscripts of Lord Kenyon*, Historical Manuscripts Commission, 14th Report, Appendix, Part IV, 609.

5. Henry Arthington's contritional pamphlet, *Seduction of Arthington by Hacket*, was also published in 1592; Throckmorton's *Defence of Job Throckmorton*, detailing his blameless association with the conspirators, came out in 1594, and was replied to by Matthew Sutcliffe's *Answere unto a certain caluminous letter published by M. Job Throckmorton* in 1595; and Thomas Cartwright's account of his guiltlessly peripheral association with the conspirators appeared in his *Briefe apologie* of 1596, to be contested by Sutcliffes' *Examination of M. Thomas Cartwight's late apologie* of the same year. Richard Bancroft spent the last forty of his 180 pages in *Daungerous Positions and Proceedings . . . under Pretense of Reformation* in 1593 dramatizing the sedition of the Hacket affair. For these and fuller references, see Curtis C. Breight, 'Duelling ceremonies: the strange case of William Hacket, Elizabethan Messiah,' in *Journal of Medieval and Renaissance Studies* vol. 19, 1 (1989), 35–67; and John Booty, 'Tumult in Cheapside: the Hacket conspiracy' in *Historical Magazine of the Protestant Episcopal Church* [Austin, Texas], 42 (1973), 293–317.

6. Richard Verstegan, *A declaration of the true causes of the great troubles, presupposed to be intended against the realm of England* (1592), 39–42; Robert Parsons, *Elizabethae Angliae Reginae haeresis Calvinianam propugnatis* (1592), 39–40; Robert Southwell, *An humble supplication to her Maiestie*, ed. R.C. Bald (1953), 26–27, 41.

7. *The Works of Lord Bacon* (London: William Ball, 1837),1.383; *The Works of Thomas Nashe*, ed. R.B. McKerrow (Oxford: Basil Blackwell, 1958), vols. 1.295 and 3.99.

8. Keith Thomas, *Religion and the Decline of Magic* (1971; rep. Harmondsworth, Peregrine: 1978), 159. Compare likewise Samuel Rowland's verse history of the rise and fall of Munster, *Hell's Broke Loose* (1605), which numbered Hacket with Jack Straw and Wat Tyler among Anabaptist 'Commonwealth men'.

9. Richard Helgerson, *Forms of Nationhood: the Elizabethan Writing of England* (Chicago: University of Chicago, 1992), 214, 240, 235.

10. Walter Cohen, *Drama of a Nation: Public Theater in Renaissance England and Spain* (Ithaca: Cornell University Press, 1985), 227–28.

11. David Bevington, *Tudor Drama and Politics* (Cambridge, MA: Harvard University Press, 1968), 239, 241.

12. Phyllis Rackin, *Stages of History: Shakespeare's English Chronicles* (Ithaca: Cornell University Press, 1990), 219.

13. Carroll, *Fat King*, 155–56. Carroll even compares Shakespeare's presentation of the beggar Simpcox with the stony hearted perspective of much rogue literature: "the pleasure taken in the exposure is exactly like Harman's in the story of the Dommerar": *Fat King*, 153.

14. Wilson, *Will Power*, 27, 29, 30.

15. Hill, *Change and Continuity*, 185; *Liberty Against the Law*, 258.

16. Thomas Cartelli, 'Jack Cade in the Garden' in *Enclosure Acts: Sexuality, Property, and Culture in Early Modern England* ed. Richard Burt and John Michael Archer (Ithaca: Cornell University Press, 1994), 61.

17. Patterson, *Popular Voice*, 48.
18. Stephen Longstaffe, '"A Short Report and Not Otherwise": Jack Cade in *2 Henry VI*' in *Shakespeare and Carnival: After Bakhtin* ed. Ronald Knowles (New York: St. Martin's Press, 1998), 13–35, quotation from 26.
19. Ellen C. Caldwell, 'Jack Cade and Shakespeare's *Henry VI Part Two*' in *Studies in Philology* 92.1 (1995), 18–79; misprisions of the carnivalesque 52–54.
20. Jean Howard, introduction to 'The First Part of the Contention' in *The Norton Shakespeare*, ed. cit., 210.
21. Paolo Pugliatti, '"More than history can pattern": the Jack Cade rebellion in Shakespeare's *2 Henry VI*' in *Journal of Medieval and Renaissance Studies* 22.3 (Fall 1992), 456, 458, 477.
22. Victor Kiernan, *Shakespeare Poet and Citizen* (London: Verso, 1993), 36–37. Shakespeare, "like any other sensible person, disliked the thought of anarchic disorder. It is about the *causes* of disorder that he must have differed from many others." "He may fairly be called a 'progressive' . . . [though] only with due caution" (11–12).
23. For the most recent and authoritative account of the historical revolt, see I.M.W. Harvey, *Jack Cade's Rebellion of 1450* (Oxford: Clarendon Press, 1991).
24. Edward Hall, *Chronicle: Union of the Two Noble and Illustre Famelies of Lancastre and Yorke* (1542, 1548, rpt. 1809), 221.
25. Raphael Holinshed, *Chronicles of England, Scotland, and Ireland* (2nd ed., 1587, rpt. 1808), vol. 3.218.
26. Holinshed, *Chronicles* (this vol. rpt. 1807), vol. 2.739.
27. Stirling, in 'Shakespeare's Mob Scenes', enumerates many examples, 228–39. The quotation is from *Caesar's Dialogue* (1601), 52, cit. Stirling 232.
28. Cit. Fletcher and MacCulloch, *Tudor Rebellions*, 5. See Hill's classic essay on the politics of fearful patrician contempt of the people, 'The Many–Headed Monster', 181–204.
29. Hall, *Chronicle*, 219–20.
30. Phrase from Patterson, *Popular Voice*, 36.
31. Patterson, *Popular Voice,* 38. On this tradition, see Patterson, ibid, 32–51; Charles Hobday, 'Clouted Shoon', 63–78; Hill, *Puritanism and Revolution*, 58–61; *Change and Continuity*, 183–85; *The English Bible*, 202–03; Cohn, *Pursuit of the Millennium*, 187–330; William Te Brake, *A Plague of Insurrection.*
32. James Holstun, 'Damned Commotion', 194–219.
33. See Andy Wood, *1549 Rebellions*, chapter 6.
34. Patterson, *Popular Voice*, 42.
35. Indeed, the quotation itself proves slippery on inspection, and may contradict construal as mere reveling in anarchy. As the reply to news that the Staffords and their army "are all in order, and march toward us," the basic meaning of Cade's words here may be merely that the rebels *achieve* a certain order (military cohesion, solidarity), in the approaching act of resistance that puts them outside state law. Compare "even your hurly / Cannot proceed but by obedience" in Shakespeare's addition to *Sir Thomas More*, Addition 2 D, ll.123–24 (*Norton* 2017–18).
36. Francois Laroque, *Shakespeare's Festive World: Elizabethan Seasonal Entertainment and the Professional Stage* (Cambridge: Cambridge University Press: 1991), 251.
37. Public Record Office SP12/263/86 (I); SP1/120, fols 100r–4v; cit. Andy Wood, '"Poore men woll speke', 84–85.

38. Wood, ibid., 87. Wood echoes here the arguments of James C. Scott, on the exhilarating "saturnalia of power" that results from "public declaration of the hidden transcript" (i.e. underclass oppositional ideology). See *Domination and the Arts of Resistance*, 202–227.

39. Dollimore, *Radical Tragedy*, 60–61.

40. Stern, *Rehearsal*, 99.

41. Cosin, *Conspiracie*, 55.

42. Breight, 'Duelling ceremonies', 49. I base my own account here upon those of Cosin, *Conspiracie*; Booty, 'Tumult in Cheapside'; and Richard Bauckham, *Tudor Apocalypse* (Appleford, Oxfordshire, Sutton Courtenay Press: 1979).

43. Breight, 'Duelling ceremonies', 52.

44. Cosin, *Conspiracie*, 56.

45. Ibid., 56–7.

46. Ibid., 58.

47. Ibid., 59.

48. For slightly contradictory accounts of these various writings, see Cosin, 32, 38–42; Booty, 307–08; Kenyon MSS, 608–09.

49. Cosin, 32.

50. Kenyon MSS, 609.

51. Ibid., 609.

52. Cosin, 38–41.

53. Cosin, 56.

54. Also tortured in Bridewell, with its rack and manacles and whipping room with walls painted black, were Thomas Kyd (1593), who therein denounced Christopher Marlowe for sedition, and Bartholomew Steere, organiser of the Oxford Rising (1596). See Carroll, *Fat King*, 118–20.

55. Cosin, 61–62, 64–69.

56. *Acts of the Privy Council*, New Series, ed. J. R. Dasent, vol. 21 (1906), 325–26; cit., Booty, 'Tumult', 313.

57. Cosin, *Conspiracie*, 71–72.

58. On the Lambeth circle's exploitation of the Hacket rising to discredit Cartwright and other eminent Puritans, see Bauckham, *Tudor Apocalypse*, 191–207; Alexandra Walsham, 'Frantic Hacket: Prophecy, Sorcery, and the Elizabethan Puritan Movement' in *History Journal* 41.1 (1998), 26–66, esp.32–38; Patrick Collinson, *The Elizabethan Puritan Movement* (Berkeley and Los Angeles, University of California Press:1967), 424–25. For the 1590s and early Jacobean campaign by the authorities to associate popular rebellion with Anabaptist levelling, see Stirling, 'Shakespeare's Mob Scenes', 213–40.

59. Bacon, 1.383.

60. I follow the Folio, and the Arden and New Cambridge editions, in calling the character Bevis, rather than 'Second Rebel' as in the Norton.

61. Cosin, 6, 46, 58.

62. Ibid., 57–58. This incident of humiliating recognition is perhaps apocryphal, particularly since a related motif occurs in Hall concerning the historical Cade, who put to death in London "divers persons . . . of his olde acquayntance, lest they should blase & declare his base byrthe": *Chronicle*, 4.7. Cosin, present at Newgate when the Solicitor-General compared Hacket with Cade, would presumably have been familiar with the Cade of the Chronicles.

63. Thomas Nashe, *Works*, 1.295.

64. *Calendar of State Papers, 1591–94*, 75–76.

65. Kenyon MSS., 608.

66. On the politics of prosecutorial withholding of the 'dementia' classification, see Walsham, 'Frantic Hacket', 48–65.

67. 'Besom' (brush) is from the Geneva Bible's version of Isaiah. The Geneva Bible, cheaply available from 1576, and the most popular version in England until the King James version appeared in 1611, is the one Shakespeare normally echoes, and probably possessed, although he sometimes shows familiarity with the Bishops' Bible, the official version read in church. Though the Douay-Rheims Old Testament also chooses 'besom', it did not appear until 1609–10. See Naseeb Shaheen's *Biblical References in Shakespeare's History Plays* (Newark: U Delaware P, 1989), 17–20, 23, 42–61: which, however, does not note this allusion. The Genevan provenance of the edition echoed is distinctly appropriate to Cade the Puritan.

68. Michael G. Baylor, editor and translator, *The Radical Reformation* (Cambridge University Press: 1991), xii.

69. Excerpt from Nicholas Sotherton, B.L. Harleian MS, 1576, fols 252–53, reproduced in Fletcher and McCullough, *Tudor Rebellions*, 147.

70. Richard Bancroft, *Daungerous Positions and Proceedings* (1593), 164.

71. Reproduced in Cosin, 40.

72. Ibid., 47, 56.

73. Ibid., 22.

74. Cosin recounting Coppinger, 41–46, 56; Booty, p.300. On the religious anomalies of Hacket's career, see Walsham, 'Frantic Hacket', 38–45.

75. Hans Hut, *On the Mystery of Baptism*, in Baylor, *Radical Reformation*, 165. See likewise 156–58, 164–65, 169–70.

76. Baylor, ibid., xxiii.

77. Kenyon MSS, 609.

78. Perusal of the Hacket materials suggests four further parallels with *2 Henry VI* which turn out, however, to be non-evidentiary. Like Arthington on Hacket ("We two are messengers from heaven, who have a good Captaine to guide us"[Cosin, 42; see also 47,58]), Shakespeare styles Cade "captain" ("your captain is brave and vows reformation: 4.2.57): but the term is common Elizabethan vernacular, and is much used of Cade in Halls' Chronicle. Cosin calls Hacket illiterate and opposed to books (21, 22, 46), but this is unproven, a possible government slur, and a fact that Hacket's Angels were not likely to have made public. The accusation of lechery and intended commonality of wives in Cosin p.43, 'echoed' in the play at 4.7.111–15, seems likewise formulaic libel, and conveniently links Hacket explicitly with John of Leiden's Munster (Cosin, 91). That the followers of both Hacket and Cade's massacre like butchers (Cosin 57, *2 Henry VI* 4.3.1–5) merely draws on cliché.

79. Cosin, 56.

80. In the months before the rising, Coppinger had made contact, mainly by letter, with a large number of Puritan leaders, including Thomas Cartwight, Walter Travers, Stephen Egerton, Job Throckmorton, Nicholas Fuller, Peter Wentworth, Edward Phillips, John Penry, John Udall, and William Charke— most of whom cautioned or rebuffed him, many doubting his mental stability: Bauckham, *Tudor Apocalypse*, 192–94; Walsham, 'Frantic Hacket', 32–38.

81. *Homily Against Disobedience*, 226.

82. See Kristen Poole, 'Facing Puritanism: Falstaff, Martin Marprelate and the Grotesque Puritan' in *Shakespeare and Carnival: After Bakhtin* ed. Ronald Knowles (New York: St. Martin's, 1998), 97–122.

83. Critical consensus dates Munday's original of *Sir Thomas More* to circa 1592–94 (as reflecting anti-alien tensions in London in that period), and Tilney's veto on its performance, certain diplomatic additions notwithstanding, to shortly afterwards (see Vittorio Gabrieli and Giorgio Melchiori,

editors of the *Revels* edition, Manchester U P, 1990, 11–12, 26–29). Controversy persists, however, as to when the additions widely ascribed to Shakespeare (Addition II, Hand D) were written: prior to Tilney's prohibition, according to Gabrieli and Melchiori, ibid., and also to Scott McMillan ('*The Book of Sir Thomas More*: dates and acting companies' in *Shakespeare and Sir Thomas More: Essays on the Play and its Shakespearian Interest*, ed. T.H. Howard-Hill, Cambridge U P, 1989, 57–76); after it, for an attempted revival of the play circa 1603–04, according to Gary Taylor's 'colloquialism-in-verse' stylometric tests (Taylor, 'The date and auspices of the additions to Sir Thomas More', in Howard-Hill, op. cit., 120–22. See also Taylor, 'The canon and chronology of Shakespeare's plays' in Stanley Wells, Gary Taylor, et al, *William Shakespeare: A Textual Companion*, Oxford, Clarendon Press, 1987, 124–25).

84. See Neal Wood, *Foundations*, 173–74.
85. See David Cressy, *Literacy and the Social order: Reading and Writing in Tudor and Stuart England* (Cambridge: Cambridge University Press, 1980): the effects of the 'education revolution' of the earlier sixteenth century meant that "The reign of Elizabeth saw a solid improvement in literacy among tradesmen and craftsmen in all parts of England," 153.
86. Article 20 of 'Kett's Demands being in Rebellion', 1549, reproduced in Fletcher and MacCullough, *Tudor Rebels*, document 17, p. 145.
87. Cressy, *Literacy and the Social Order*, 157–70.
88. Compare Greenblatt's illustrations of such depoliticising hysteria in Sidney, Spenser and others, in 'Murdering Peasants', 1–29.
89. This aspect of Cade perhaps becomes readily appreciable in performance. Apparently the 1957 production at the Old Vic in London, combining Parts One and Two, saw "many minor members of the crowd . . . turn in hugely comic performances", such that "Cade himself was obliterated in the hurly-burly." Mary Clarke, *Shakespeare at the Old Vic* (London: 1958), cit. Knowles, Third Arden ed., 9.
90. Shakespeare presents the complaint elsewhere, in Orlando, and in the behaviour of Lord in *Shrew's* Induction. In *Utopia*, Hythlodaeus had similarly complained that the sufferings of the lower classes from the system run by the rich were so unjust "that the state and condition of the laboring beasts may seem much better and wealthier" (Thomas More, *Utopia*, trans. Robinson, 142).
91. Davies, 'Popular Disorder', 244.
92. Fletcher and MacCulloch, *Tudor Rebellions*, 119, quoting Yves-Marie Bercé, tr. J. Bergin, *Revolt and Revolution in Early Modern Europe: An Essay on the History of Political Violence* (Manchester: Manchester University Press, 1987), 221.
93. Cartelli, 'Jack Cade in the Garden', 58.
94. Christopher Hill, *The Intellectual Origins of the English Revolution Revisited* (Oxford: Oxford university Press, 1997), 394–95. See also Hill, *Change and Continuity*, 185.
95. Hall, *Chronicle*, 225.
96. Andy Wood, 'Poore men woll speke', 78–80, 86. On haltered rebels see also Wood's 'Collective violence, social drama and rituals of rebellion' in *Cultures of Violence*, ed. Stuart Carroll (Basingstoke: Palgrave 2007), 105–13.
97. Ponet, *A shorte treatise of politike power*, 113–14.
98. Thomas Starkey, *A Dialogue between Pole and Lupset* ed. T. F Mayer (London: Royal Historical Society, 1989), 110–111. Discussed by Neal Wood, *Foundations*, 144–54.
99. See Neal Wood, *Foundations*, 196–97, 211.

100. Kathleen O. Irace (*Reforming the 'Bad' Quartos: Performance and Provenance of Six Shakespearean First Editions*, Newark: University of Delaware, 1994) notes the "more conventional" Cade, more vicious and corrupt, 60, 62–63; and endorses, 160, 163–65, 168–72, the view of Madeleine Doran (*'Henry VI Parts Two and Three': Their Relation to the 'Contention' and the 'True Tragedy'*, Iowa: U Iowa P, 1928, 51–53, 75–83) that the Quartos represent a memorial reconstruction abridged, perhaps for touring. All fifteen of the longest passages unique to the Folio, argues Irace, 146, "can be defended as reasonable performance cuts." For recent overviews of the complex question of Quarto-Folio relations see the excellent textual discussions by recent editors Ronald Knowles (Third Arden, 1999), 106–141 and Roger Warren (Oxford, 2002), 75–100.

101. Henry VII's seizure of power from Richard III, the defeat of the Amicable Grant in 1525, Northumberland's coup against Protector Somerset in 1549, and the overthrow of Lady Jane Grey by Mary Tudor in 1553.

102. Proclamation of July 24 1607. On this campaign, see Stirling, 'Shakespeare's Mob Scenes', passim; proclamation referred to p.225. Compare the words of the Solicitor-General at Hacket's trial, quoted in the opening of this chapter.

103. Fletcher and MacCulloch, *Tudor Rebellions*, 115–118, 123–28. On the character, and late Tudor secession from a leadership role in rebellion, of the middling sort, see particularly Andy Wood, *1549 Rebellions*, 186–207; also Andy Wood, *Riot, Rebellion*, 72, 77–79; Hindle, *State and Social Change*, 231–38;

104. Andy Wood, 'Poore men woll speke', 72, 83; also Andy Wood, *1549 Rebellions*, 204—07.

105. *Calendar of State Papers, Domestic* 1591–94: 252. I take the quotation from Carroll, *Fat King*, 144, who cites it, however, only in consideration of contemporary allegations of theatres as seditious.

106. A tradition already extant in the *Homily Against Disobedience*, preaching that rebels, *per se*, are "unmeete ministers" offering "unwholsome medicine to refourme" (214), notwithstanding their early promises of "reformation" and appeals to the poor (232, 234): an official dogma Shakespeare's narrative, once again, outwardly supports.

107. On the development of radical anti-hegemonic consciousness and programmes in a number of oppositional groups and individuals during the mid-seventeenth century, see Holstun, *Ehud's Dagger*.

108. For a contemporary instance of conscious revolutionary thought in peasant culture as constrained only provisionally by tactical pragmatism, see Şcott, *Weapons of the Weak*; and Scott's *Domination and the Arts of Resistance*, particularly chapter 7.

109. James Holstun makes much this point, declaring that "Shakespeare's failure to adopt a universally sanguine view of plebeian revolt . . . suggests a rational and pragmatic response to the straitened circumstances of class conflict in the 1590s, when a sympathetic observer might advise peasants and artisans against rebelling, not out of a metaphysic of order, but out of empirical evidence that rebellion could only lead to the gibbet and further expropriation." "Damned commotion", 198.

110. Wood, *1549 Rebellions*, 151–58, 166–68, 172–75.

111. The title of the biography, *Ungentle Shakespeare: Scenes from his Life*, by Katherine Duncan-Jones (London: Arden, 2001); see particularly 262.

112. Proclamations 715 and 716 in Hughes and Larkin, *Tudor Royal Proclamations*.

113. See Breight, *Surveillance*, 85–86, 182–83. Quotation from 182.

114. Trained bands were carefully composed of more prosperous citizens ("enrol none but such as are gentlemen, yeomen, and yeomen's sons, and artificers of some haviour") than the armies of commoners sent overseas. Breight, *Surveillance*, 57–59.

115. The problem of hungry veterans would persist, despite legislation in 1593 and 1597 ordering their support through parish rates: Beier, *Masterless Men*, 95.

116. Linda Salamon, 'Vagabond veterans: the roguish company of Martin Guerre and *Henry V*' in *Rogues and Early Modern English Culture,* ed. Craig Dionne and Steve Mentz (Ann Arbor: University of Michigan 2004), 273. Compare Breight, *Surveillance*, 175–76.

117. Breight, *Surveillance*, 86.

118. Cartelli, 'Jack Cade in the Garden', 53; Phyllis Rackin, *Stages of History*, 221.

119. Paola Pugliatti, *Beggary and Theatre in Early Modern England* (Aldershot: Ashgate, 2003), 150–52, thinks Iden to echo Thomas Harman, self-glorifying exposer and tormentor of fraudulent beggars in his popular *Caveat for Common Cursitors* (1566; rpt. 1573 and 1592): for both are of modest gentry status, bragged of aiding the poor, and Harman 'betrayed' impostors to authority (cf. Cade's "Ah villain thou wilt betray me"). Both avengers, Pugliatti argues, represent "the just man". But this construction misses the play of sympathies Shakespeare generates here. Snooping, sly Harman largely worked solo, unlike Iden with his five henchmen, just as Iden's massive bulk finds no counterpart in Harman's print persona: so stage impressions would seem unpropitious to this association. At best, I think, Shakespeare's Iden embodies a class stereotype of gentry harshness into which Harman, and much else, would fit.

120. Cartelli, 'Jack Cade in the Garden', 43. Compare Greenblatt's recognition that the Cade / Iden confrontation is framed less in terms of class than of property relations: 'Murdering Peasants', 23–25. Rackin recognizes that the unpopular new *suum cuique* doctrine of ownership is being raised here, yet regards Iden, nonetheless, as "unequivocally virtuous" in Shakespeare's eyes, and she interprets Cade, conventionally, as here being "reduced to a mechanism for ideological containment" (*Stages of History,*.215–20).

121. See Tawney, *Religion and the Rise of Capitalism*, 151–54; Wood, *1549 Rebellions*, 34–37. This nakedly individualist profiteering was sometimes claimed justified by Matthew 20.15.

122. Crowley, *Informacion and Peticion*, 157. Compare Latimer: "No rich man can say before God. 'This is my own.' No, he is but an officer over it." *Sermons*, ed. Corrie, 411; cit. Wood, *1549 Rebellions*, 36.

123. Steve Hindle, 'The Political Culture of the Middling Sort in English Rural Communities c. 1550–1700' in Harris, *The Politics of the Excluded*, 141.

124. On the political realities of English Renaissance verse of happy rural retreat, see James Turner, *The Politics of Landscape* (Oxford: Blackwell, 1979), 85–185; and Chris Fitter, *Poetry, Space, Landscape: toward a New Theory* (Cambridge: Cambridge University Press, 1995), 235–66, 292–315.

125. C.S. Lewis shrewdly suggested back in 1954 that "we have an uneasy suspicion that [Iden's] 'small inheritance' includes a ruined abbey and that the very conditions he lives in may have helped to create the poor whom he relieves. The prosperity of his class depended, after all, on rising rents." *English Literature in the Sixteenth Century Excluding Drama* (1954; rpt. Oxford: Oxford UP, 1973), 59.

126. In Hall (p.224), Iden takes the "ded body" to London, rather than slinging it on a dunghill.

NOTES TO CHAPTER 4

1. Carolly Erickson, *The First Elizabeth* (1983; reprinted New York: St. Martin's, 1997 [Griffin Edition]), 196.
2. *The Copie of a Letter to the Earle of Leycester, the Second Answere made by the Queene's Majestie*, in *Elizabethan backgrounds: Historical Documents of the Age of Elizabeth I*, ed. Arthur F. Kinney (1975; repr. Hamden, CT: Archon Books, 1990), 234.
3. Cit. J. E. Neale in *Elizabeth I and her Parliaments 1584–1601* (New York: St. Martin's Press, 1957), 196. Hereafter referred to as *Parliaments*.
4. Erasmus, *Adagia*, 3.7.1 (A dung-beetle hunting an eagle).
5. On this climate of fear, see Anne Somerset, *Elizabeth I* (New York: St. Martin's Press, 1991), 405–10.
6. Cosin, *Conspiracie*, 57.
7. *Homily against Disobedience*, 227.
8. Emrys Jones, *The Origins of Shakespeare* (Oxford: Oxford University Press, 1977), 120.
9. See Wilson, *Will Power*, 23–44; debated by Patterson, *Popular Voice*, 34–38.
10. Gurr, *Shakespearean Stage*, 5–6.
11. Michael Hattaway, 'Drama and Society' in *The Cambridge Companion to English Renaissance Drama* (Cambridge: Cambridge University Press: 1990), 101; see also 92. "Intelligence" and "intelligencer" as denoting espionage were late sixteenth century coinages: Breight, *Surveillance*, 49. The former term is used by Shakespeare in *2 Henry IV*, 4.1.246; the latter in *Richard III* at 4.4.71.
12. Gurr, *Playgoing*, 141–47. Cf. also the letter from the Privy Council of 1601 complaining that actors at the Curtain "do represent upon the stage . . . some gentlemen of good desert and quality that are yet alive": cit. Gurr, *Shakespearean Stage*, 18.
13. Gurr, *Shakespearean Stage*, 22, 25, 53.
14. Cit. Clark, *English Provincial Society*, 222.
15. Wallace T. MacCaffrey, *Elizabeth I: War and Politics 1588–1603* (Princeton: Princeton University Press, 1992), ch. 7, 137–51; Conyers Read, *Lord Burghley and Queen Elizabeth* (New York: Knopf, 1960),.459.
16. MacCaffrey, *Elizabeth: War and Politics*, 143.
17. The following account is taken from MacCaffrey, ibid., pp.149–172.
18. Ibid., 154.
19. Ibid., 168.
20. Second Arden edition, ed. Andrew Cairncross (London: Methuen, 1957, corrected 1962; repr. Routledge, 1994), 105; third edition, ed. Knowles, 369–70.
21. MacCaffrey, *Elizabeth: War and Politics*, 143, 164.
22. See Hattaway's New Cambridge edition, 230–33.
23. Cairncross, second Arden ed., 131, n.46, notes this echo of the sack, but misses, however, the point of the anachronism, and also gives the wrong date for the sack. The tactic of dispersing rebels through fear of foreign invasion perhaps echoed Somerset's instruction to magistrates to attempt this in 1549: see Fletcher and MacCulloch, *Tudor Rebellions*, 11.
24. I align myself here with the majority view that *I Henry VI* was written *after* the plays called in the Folio *Henry VI Parts Two* and *Three*, being the play referred to as "hary the vj", and labelled "ne", in Henslowe's diary, March 3 1592. For discussion of the debate, see Wells and Taylor, *Textual Companion*,

217–18, and the most recent edition of the play, Arden 3, ed. Edward Burns (2000), 3–8, 69–73, both of which support this view.

25. C. S. L. Davies, 'A rose by another name' in *The Times Literary Supplement*, June 13 2008, 13–15.
26. Kenneth R. Andrews, *Elizabethan Privateering 1585–1603* (Cambridge: Cambridge UP, 1964), tables 1, 2, and 5, chapters 3 and 7 (32–52, 124–49); MacCaffrey, *Elizabeth: War and Politics*, 98, 105.
27. Andrews, *Elizabethan Privateering*, 16.
28. Ibid., 3–5.
29. Ibid., 16.
30. The "puddle and sink' reference at 4.1.72, echoing *Homily*, 225.
31. Roger Warren, editor of the Oxford edition (2002), 92, intelligently suggests that these pirates may themselves have been some of the 'ragged soldiers sent wounded home' to whom they refer: hence their savagery.
32. Peter Linebaugh and Marcus Rediker, *The Many-Headed Hydra: Sailors, Slaves, Commoners, and the Hidden History of the Revolutionary Atlantic* (Boston, Mass.:Beacon, 2000), 162–63.
33. Andrews, *Elizabethan Privateering*, 16.
34. *The Naval Tracts of Sir William Monson*, ed. M. Oppenheim (Navy Records Society, 22, 23, 43, 45, 47), 1902–14), 2.237; cit. Andrews, *Elizabethan Privateering*, 40.
35. Andrews, *Elizabethan Privateering*, 41.
36. Ibid., 42.
37. Compare *Richard III* 1.3.158–59 on "wrangling pirates" who "fall out / In sharing".
38. Andrews, *Elizabethan Privateering*, 234.
39. Line missing: "probably one indicating that the ransom demanded can never compensate for the lives lost in battle" (Norton edition footnote to line 22). The ascription of these lines variously to Whitmore or the captain changes with different editions. Exclamation point from Arden editions.
40. "Many observers of pirate life noted the carnivalesque quality" of its proclivity to banqueting, dancing and revels: Linebaugh and Rediker, *Many-Headed Hydra*, 164.
41. Compare the favourable presentation of pirate (and privateer?) in *Hamlet* and *Twelfth Night*. Hamlet refers to his pirate captors as "good fellows", admiring their business-like efficiency: "They have dealt with me like thieves of mercy. But they knew what they did: I am to do a turn for them" (4.6.23, 17–19). Antonio, who has helped ransack one of Orsino's galleys "in a sea-fight" (3.3.26), nobly risks his life to protect Sebastian, cuts an exciting martial figure at 3.4.277, and is praised even by Orsino at 5.1.45–53. Compare also the robust anti-hierarchism of the mariners who open *The Tempest*.
42. Cit. Somerset, *Elizabeth I*, 464. The Tilbury speech has been shown to be a late seventeenth century composition (see Frye, 'Myth of Elizabeth at Tilbury') and its authenticity thus suspect; yet Elizabeth's self-dramatization as lovingly devoted to England is consistent with her customary rhetoric.
43. *Calendar of State Papers, Domestic, Elizabeth*, in the Public Records Office: 12/214/61; 12/214/66; 12/215/41; cit. Bright, *Surveillance*, 176–78.
44. Hall's *Chronicle*, 216.
45. Linebaugh and Rediker, *Many-Headed Hydra*, 151.
46. Carroll, *Fat King*, 75.
47. Patricia Fumerton, *Unsettled: the Culture of Mobility and the Working Poor in Early Modern England* (Chicago: University of Chicago, 2006), 84.
48. Manning, *Village Revolts*, 318.

49. Michael Hattaway makes in his edition of the play a similar point, relating Saye's execution and Gloucester's interrogation of Simpcox to Elizabethan 'trial upon examination', introduced, he suggests, in 1581 (15–16, 32). While this looks true of the Simpcox episode, I suggest that Martial Law, with its summary execution and its terrifying high-profile incidence in 1591, is the truer parallel; and that Suffolk's execution is another case in point.

50. Andy Wood, 'Collective violence', 99–116.

51. "Rebel councils assumed the trappings of lawcourts . . . This willingness to deploy the symbolism and injunctions of authority in justification of crowd actions has been identified as one of the defining characteristics of early modern popular politics": Wood, *1549 Rebellions*, 154, 156.

52. Where, instead, a guilty conscience enters, this is explicit: see Cade at 4.7.96 ("I feel remorse").

53. Richard Woods, *Norfolke furies, and their foyle. Under Kett, their accursed Captaine* (1615; 2nd ed., London, 1623), sigs.I1–2; cit. Wood, *Riot, Rebellion*, 69.

54. *Calendar of Patent Rolls, Elizabeth I*, 5, no.1818, 1073; cit. Diarmaid MacCulloch, 'Kett's Rebellion in Context' in *Rebellion, Popular Protest and the Social Order in Early Modern England*, ed. Paul Slack (Cambridge: Cambridge University Press: 1984), 47. On the tactic of dispersing nearly all Kett's followers by promise of pardon, see MacCulloch, *The Boy King: Edward VI and the Protestant Reformation* (New York: Palgrave, 2001), 45–49.

55. Manning, *Village Revolts*, 181.

56. Andrew Hadfield has argued that this homily's arguments "should be seen as propagandist responses to a crisis rather than the statements of a reasoned and generally accepted political status quo . . . It does not follow that what was read out in church would be generally accepted as a political principle by the majority of the congregation": *Shakespeare and Renaissance Politics*, 43–44.

57. 'Homily against Disobedience', 232–33.

58. Hall, *Chronicle*, 222.

59. Cit. David Wootton, ed., *Divine Right and Democracy: an Anthology of Political Writing in Stuart England* (London: Penguin, 1986), 102–03.

60. G. Bernard, *War, Taxation and Rebellion in Early Tudor England: Henry VIII, Wolsey and the Amicable Grant of 1525* (Brighton: 1986), 111.

61. The resulting 'Midsummer riot', and the prompt closure of theatres by the Privy Council, are discussed, with conflicting interpretations, by Manning, *Village Revolts*, 207–08, Wilson, *Will Power*, 37–39, and Patterson, *Popular Voice*, 35–37.

62. Cit. Wood, *1549 Rebellions*, 22.

63. Conrad Russell, *The Crisis of Parliaments: English History 1509–1660* (Oxford: Oxford University Press, 1971), 245; Somerset, *Elizabeth I*, 465.

64. Henry Jackman, cit. Neale, *Parliaments*, 206.

65. Conyers Read, *Mr. Secretary Walsingham and the Policy of Queen Elizabeth* (London, 1967), 3.312; cit. Somerset, *Elizabeth*, 465.

66. Hall, *Chronicles*, 205, 220, 217.

67. Ibid., 208–09.

68. Somerset, *Elizabeth I*, 394–95; Manning, *Village Revolts*, 207.

69. *Theatrum Crudelitatem Haereticorum Nostri Temporis*, 1587; see Bright, *Surveillance, Militarism and Drama*, 74–76. For the suggestion that Verstigan's several critiques of England were subversively rearticulated in Marlowe's drama, see Bright, ibid., 127–167.

70. James Heath, *Torture and English Law: An Administrative and Legal History from the Plantagenets to the Stuarts* (Westport, CT: Greenwood, 1982), 109–10.

71. The language of torture intriguingly envelops the queen also, when Margaret gleefully refers to Gloucester's "maim", enduring "two pulls at once", one of them "a limb lopped off": 2.3.41–42.
72. Fletcher and MacCulloch, *Tudor Rebellions*, 11–12.
73. Ambrose, *De Officiis Ministrorum*; cit. Cohn, *Pursuit of Millennium*, 193; compare 200.
74. *Pyers Plowmans exhortation unto the lordes, knightes and burgoysses of the parlyamenthouse*, unpaginated; cit. Shagan, *Popular Politics*, 279.
75. See Ethan H. Shagan, 'Protector Somerset and the 1549 rebellions: New Sources and New Perspectives' in *English Historical Review* 114 no.36 (Feb. 1999), 34–63; variously debated and revisited by M. L. Bush, G. W. Bernard, and Ethan Shagan in *English Historical Review* 115 no.460 (Feb. 2000), 103–33.
76. Roger B. Manning, 'Violence and Social Conflict in Mid-Tudor Rebellions' in *Journal of British Studies* 16 (1977), 28.
77. Guy, *Tudor England*, 208.
78. MacCulloch, *Boy King*, 122; Wood, *1549 Risings*, 52.
79. Fletcher and MacCulloch, *Tudor Rebellions*, 67.
80. Sir John Cheke, *The Hurt of Sedition* (1549), sporadic pagination. On Cheke's ideological turnabout see Baker, *Divulging Utopia*, 115–16.
81. Whitney Jones, *Tudor Commonwealth*, 39; Aucher cit. Conyers Read, *Mr. Secretary Cecil and Queen Elizabeth* (London: 1955), 55.
82. Hugh Latimer, *Sermons*, ed. Canon Beeching, (London: Everyman, 1926), 249; cit. Whitney Jones, *Tudor Commonwealth*, 52.
83. Crowley, *The Way to Wealth* in *Select Works*, 142–43.
84. *Gorboduc, or Ferrex and Porrex*, in *Drama of the English Renaissance*, ed. Russell Fraser and Norman Rabkin (New York: Macmillan, 1976), vol. 1, 97 and 99.
85. Sir Philip Sidney, *The Countess of Pembroke's Arcadia*, ed. Maurice Evans (Harmondsworth: Penguin, 1977), 380–81. See Greenblatt's discussion of the passage in terms of problems of artistic decorum generated by the fears aroused by the German Peasant's War of 1525, in 'Murdering Peasants', 1–29.
86. Mervyn James, 'The Concept of Order and the Northern Rising 1569' in *Past and Present* 60 (1973), 61–62; Neal Wood, *Foundations*, 127–28.
87. *Bibliotheca Eliotae*, sig.A1v, 1548; an updated version of Elyot's 1538 *Dictionary*; cit. Baker, *Divulging Utopia*, 112
88. A.N. McLaren, *Political Culture in the Reign of Elizabeth I: Queen and Commonwealth 1558–1585* (Cambridge University Press, 1999), 82, 89.
89. Ibid., 86, 89. See particularly 80–90, 198–243.
90. Ibid., 232.
91. Andy Wood, *1549 Rebellions*, 176.
92. Neal Wood, *Foundations of Political Economy*, 34. See also 79, 127.
93. I take the reference from Jones, *Tudor Commonwealth*, 218, who cites G.P. Gooch, *English Democratic Ideas in the Seventeenth Century*, 2nd edn., ed. H.J. Laski (Cambridge: 1927), 52.
94. Neale, *Parliaments*, 383.
95. Holstun, 'Damned Commotion', 208.
96. On contemporary resonances of 'commonwealth' see also Andy Wood, *1549*, 143–48.
97. 'Commonwealth' was likewise the term later taken up by pirates to define their egalitarian order: see the quotation in Linebaugh and Rediker, *Many-Headed Hydra*, 164.
98. Strier, 'Faithful Servants', 104;

99. Wootton, *Divine Right and Democracy*, 40–41. On resistance theory, see also Skinner, *Foundations of Modern Political Thought*, vol. 2, 73–81, 225–38, 338–48; and Kelley, 'Ideas of Resistance before Elizabeth'.
100. Stephen Gardiner, *Concerning True Obedience*, cit. Hattaway, intro. to 2 *Henry VI*, 121.
101. Patterson, *Popular Voice*, 51.
102. Keith Wrightson, *Earthly Necessities* (New Haven: Yale University Press, 2000), 151–52.
103. Hattaway, intro. to 2 *Henry VI*, 121.
104. Bond, *Certain Sermons or Homilies*, 224.
105. Christopher Goodman, *How Superior Powers Ought to be Obeyed* (1558; New York: Facsimile Text Society, 1931), 235; cit. Kelley, 'Ideas of Resistance', 66.
106. Collinson, *Elizabethan Essays*, 45.
107. Hadfield, *Shakespeare and Renaissance Politics*, 42.
108. Ibid., 40.
109. Proclamation 738 in *Tudor Royal Proclamations*, ed. Hughes and Larkin.
110. Read, *Lord Burghley*, 469.
111. Henry violates his oath on York's succession, as do Margaret and York himself (1.1.195–202, 248–51; 1.2.15–28; 2.2.7–8); Warwick and Clarence renounce their oaths of allegiance at will (3.3.95–97, 194; 5.1.92–94); the French King reverses his promise to King Henry, and then renews it (3.3.145–48, 231–32); and the gamekeepers, "Commanded always by the greater gust", violate their allegiance oath to one monarch in obedience to another (3.1.72–97). The imitative *I Henry VI* echoes the casual disregard of solemn oath at 5.7.26–35.
112. Roger Warren, Oxford ed., 34: e.g. Hall, *Chronicle*, 209; John Foxe, *Actes and Monuments of the Martyrs* (1583), rep. in Bullough, *Narrative and Dramatic Sources*, 127.
113. *The Works of Francis Bacon*, ed. James Spedding, 14 vols., (London: Longman, 1857–74), 8.108, 143; cit. Conyers Read, *Lord Burghley and Queen Elizabeth*, 478–79.
114. McLaren, *Political Culture*, 204.
115. Hatfield MSS, cxlviii.30; cit. B.W. Beckingsale, *Burghley: Tudor Statesman* (London: St. Martin's, 1967), 217.
116. Jill Husselby, 'The Politics of Pleasure: William Cecil and Burghley House' in Pauline Croft, *Patronage, Culture and Power* (New Haven: Yale University Press, 2002), 21.
117. Felicity Heal and Clive Holmes, 'The Economic Patronage of William Cecil' in Croft, *Patronage, Culture and Power*, 199–230.
118. J. F. Merritt, 'The Cecils and Westminster 1558–1612: the Development of an Urban Base' in Croft, *Patronage, Culture and Power*, 241.
119. A. G. R. Smith, *The Anonymous Life of William Cecil, Lord Burghley* (Lampeter: Edward Mellen Press, 1990), 108; cit. Heal and Holmes, 223.
120. See Beckingsale, 195.
121. *The Anonymous Life of William Cecil*, cit. A. G. R. Smith, in 'Lord Burghley and his Household Biographers' in Croft, *Patronage, Culture and Power*, 250–51.
122. Beckingsale, *Burghley*, 241.
123. Croft, *Patronage, Culture and Power*, xi, xix. On the Cecils' prodigious architectural pace-setting, see ibid, 1–95.
124. *Mother Hubbard's Tale*, in Edmund Spenser, *Poetical Works*, ed. J.C. Smith and E. de Selincourt (London: Oxford University Press, 1912, rpt. 1969), ll.1169–72.

125. *The Anonymous Life*, 69; cit. Smith, 'Lord Burghley and his Household Biographers' in Croft, *Patronage, Culture and Power*, 256.
126. 'The Retiring Patron: William Cecil and the Cultivation of Retirement' in Croft, *Patronage, Culture and Power*, 159.
127. Read, *Lord Burghley*, 477.
128. Sutton, 'Retiring Patron', 162–71.
129. Beckingsale, *Burghley*, 193; John Clapham, *Elizabeth of England: Certain Observations concerning the Life and Reign of Queen Elizabeth*, ed. E. P. Read and Conyers Read (Philadelphia: University of Pennsylvania Press, 1951), 77, cit. Smith, 'Lord Burghley and his Household Biographers', 254.
130. Pauline Croft, 'Mildred, Lady Burghley: the Matriarch' in Croft, *Patronage, Culture and Power* 292.
131. Ibid., 290.
132. Mildred's funeral inscription, composed by Burghley, cit. ibid, 296.
133. Croft, 'Mildred', 292.
134. Ibid., 294.
135. Ibid., 295.
136. Ibid., 297.
137. Ibid., 296.
138. Croft records one payment of two hundred and fifty pounds on behalf of a suitor for a wardship: ibid., 291.
139. See colour plate II in Croft, *Patronage, Culture and Power*.
140. Paul E.J. Hammer, *The Polarisation of Elizabethan Politics: the Political Career of Robert Devereaux, 2nd Earl of Essex, 1585–97* (Cambridge: Cambridge University Press, 1999), 114, 118.
141. Public Record Office, State Papers Domestic Elizabeth 12/181/42; cit, Croft, *Patronage, Culture and Power*, 227 n. 59.
142. Annabel Patterson, *Censorship and Interpretation: the Conditions of Writing and Reading in Early Modern England* (1984; 2nd ed. Madison: University of Wisconsin, 1990), 71.
143. See Richard S. Peterson, 'Spurting Froth upon Courtiers' in *Times Literary Supplement* May 16 1997, 14–15.
144. Croft, 'Mildred, Lady Burghley', 265–300, particularly 284, 292.
145. Following Leicester's death, Knollys had married Sir Christopher Blount in 1589: but Elizabeth's wrath toward the widow of her former favourite went undiminished.
146. Robert Lacey, *Robert, Earl of Essex* (New York: Atheneum, 1971), 30–31.
147. Anthony Bacon, cit. Read, *Lord Burghley*, 479–80.
148. Read, *Lord Burghley*, 477.
149. Hammer, *Polarisation*, 100, 104, 114, 343. Burghley further rebuked Essex in 1591 for sending 'secret' letters to James I, that were, in Hammer's words, "meddling in matters concerning the succession": ibid., 91.
150. George Peele, *Eclogue Gratulatorie* (1589) in *Works*, 1.226–27; cit. Richard C. McCoy, *The Rites of Knighthood* (Berkeley and Los Angeles: University of California Press, 1989), 80.
151. Hammer, *Polarisation*, 231–34; also the same author's *Elizabeth's Wars: War, Government and Society in Tudor England 1544–1604* (London: Palgrave Macmillan, 2003), 161.
152. Sir Henry Wotton, *Reliquiae Wottoniae* (London: 1651), p.48; cit. McCoy, *Rites*, 81–82.
153. In *1 Henry IV*, the chivalric Hotspur contemptuous of the monarch, and widely recognised as an evocation of Essex at many points, will likewise claim "methinks it were an easy leap / To pluck bright honour from the pale-faced moon" (1.3.199–200).

154. McCoy, *Rites*, 84–87. For Essex's professed reconciliation in early 1592 aimed at impressing Elizabeth with his new maturity as he sought elevation to the Privy Council, see 115–17.
155. Hammer, *Polarisation*, 153–57.
156. Ibid., 157–63.

NOTES TO CHAPTER 5

1. These lines are in all the Arden editions, but missing in the Norton.
2. Keith Wrightson, 'Estates, Degrees and Sorts in Tudor and Stuart England' in *History Today* 37 (Jan. 1987), 21; Andy Wood, 'Poore Men woll speke', 74, 82.
3. Hoyle, R.W., 'Thomas Master's Narrative of the Pilgrimage of Grace', *Northern History*, 21, 1985, 72, cit. Fletcher and MacCullough, *Tudor Rebellions*, 25.
4. Norfolk Record Office, NCR 16A/4, fol.61v; cit. Andy Wood, 'Fear, hatred', 813.
5. 'Poore Men woll speke', 72–73, 83. See also Andy Wood, 'Fear, hatred', 818–19; and *1549 Rebellions*, 204–07.
6. Edward Hext, J.P., letter to Burghley of 25 September 1596, in *Tudor Economic Documents* ed. Tawney and Power, vol. 2, 339–46.
7. Cit. Andy Wood, 'Plebeian languages of deference and defiance', 81.
8. Cartelli, 'Jack Cade in the garden', 55–56.
9. Andrew Gurr, 'Shakespeare's Playhouses' in *A Companion to Shakespeare* ed. David Scott Kastan (Oxford: Blackwell, 1999), 376.
10. Howard, *Stage and Social Struggle*, 73 and chapter 4.
11. M.P. Tilley, *A Dictionary of the Proverbs in England in the Sixteenth and Seventeenth Centuries* (1950), R 144.
12. Wood, *1549 Rebellions*, 85.
13. Phrase from Irving Wardle in *The Times*, July 14 1997, reviewing Terry Hands' RSC production; cit. Hattaway in his Cambridge edition of the play (1990), 54.
14. Bridget Escolme, *Talking to the Audience* (Routledge, 2005) notes the importance of audience address, but misses original Shakespearean historical contexts and political effects, discussing deixis only in relation to modern productions, and a rather Brechtian concern for actors standing occasionally outside their role.
15. *Titus* "stands out as a radical play keen to question belief in a hereditary monarchy as the only viable form of government . . . this can be read as a courageous—or foolhardy—beginning, especially as *Titus* has no obvious sources." Hadfield, *Shakespeare and Renaissance Politics*, 127, 134.
16. Compare Bernard Spivack on the Vice's "limitless, amoral merriment, heightened by his jubilation over the success of his intrigue": *Shakespeare and the Allegory of Evil* (New York: Columbia, 1958), 195.
17. In Hall (208), the defeated armourer is not slain, but ordered to Tyburn for hanging; and it is Shakespeare's invention that makes the pirate Lieutenant a former servant of Suffolk.
18. See third Arden edition, ed. Knowles, note to this line on 221, and also its introduction 87.
19. Roger Warren, ed., the new Oxford *Henry VI Part Two* (Oxford UP, 2002), 42.
20. "*Petty*, vaulting sea" would capture perfectly the politics of the groundling swell in the queen's contemptuous eyes: compare the "ocean, overpeering of his list", in *Hamlet*'s similar lines on mutinous commoners (4.5.95).

21. There is some confusion over the SD at 121: F fails to note Salisbury's entry, and Q to note the commons'. All modern editions, however (three Ardens, the Oxford, Cambridge and Norton), have judged both to have been the case.
22. *Henry VI Part Three* 3.2.135–37, 187.
23. Compare Mary Clarke on the 1957 Old Vic production: "the scenes of human anguish . . . often roused in the audience an almost unwilling compassion." Cit. Warren, Oxford ed., 47. Also see *Richard II* 5.2.22–36, where, as York narrates the entry into London of a Richard deposed, suffering and mocked, Shakespeare again portrays a scene of livid popular scorn towards a humbled great one that seems bound to falter through compassion: "had not God, for some strong purpose steeled / The hearts of men, they must perforce have melted, / And barbarism itself have pitied him".
24. Compare Richard II's insult of "unruly jades" at 3.3.178, and compare *Shrew* 2.1.199; *King John* 2.1.385.
25. Shakespeare echoes Hall's account of parliament's proceedings here. See Thomas Cartelli, 'Suffolk and the Pirates: Disordered Relations in Shakespeare's *2 Henry VI*' in *A Companion to Shakespeare's Works: volume 2, The Histories*, ed. R. Dutton and Jean E. Howard (Oxford: Blackwell, 2003), 325–43. Cartelli, however, sees in the pirates' language only "righteousness and eloquence", "patriotically motivated disinterestedness": 332, 328.
26. A recent production captured beautifully the analogy: "what emerges on stage as the mist rises is . . . the iron-mesh cages of a slaughterhouse. Jack-booted abattoir workers loiter threateningly, the lower halves of their faces moulded into feral snouts by protective masks [as] they busy themselves sharpening knives. At a given signal, the meat-packers don top hats and coat tails and transform themselves into the nobility": Robert Shore, reviewing *Rose Rage* in the *Times Literary Supplement*, July 5 2002.
27. The drama was performed in The Rose theatre in Southwark.
28. See Margot Heinemann, 'How Brecht read Shakespeare' in *Political Shakespeare: New Essays in Cultural Materialism*, ed. Jonathan Dollimore and Alan Sinfield (Manchester: Manchester University Press, 1985), 202–230. Brecht's quotation refers to *Coriolanus*, cit. 219.
29. Also linking the two underdog combatants are: (1) the artisanal imagery of each. Peter promises to his friends, should he be killed, his apron and hammer, whilst Cade refers to doornails, to his sword as "a great pin", and to its blade as potential hobnails (2.3.78–79; 4.9.38, 26, 57). (2) Both offer a comical prayer, apparently on their knees: Peter in victory, and Cade before the fight: "I beseech God on my knees thou may'st be turned to hobnails" (2.3.99–100; 4.9.57).
30. The exception is abuse from Eleanor at 1.2.61–65.
31. This humourous deictic targeting was apparently so successful a feature of the play that *Woodstock* echoed it, as its sole moment of deixis. At 5.1.112–13, 120, the Duke awakens, his murderers at the door, yet tragi-comically reassures himself in blundering piety, "All's whist and quiet, and nothing here appears / But *the vast circuit of this empty room* . . . Lighten my fears, dear Lord" (emphasis added).
32. In the case of Falstaff, the process extends across two plays, carnival repudiation commencing in part two of *Henry IV*.
33. Bells and bonfires were associated with may-games: see Knowles' Arden edition, note to 5.1.3.
34. Compare 3.1.310–11: "Th'uncivil kerns of Ireland are in arms / And temper clay with blood of Englishmen."
35. See Q1, TLN 792; also the quarto's stage direction for "long staves" at 4.2.1 and 30.

36. On the vexed issue of putative Shakespearean revisions of his original, visible in the Quarto, see the recent summary by Warren in his Oxford edition, 87–98.

37. Following the Quarto, several modern editions have Iden exit on being knighted. This is contradicted, however, not only by the Folio—on whose authority all modern editions are generally based—but by Henry's just-given command "henceforth attend on us" (5.1.80). The Quarto has Iden exit, I suggest, probably to enable on-tour tripling of parts, the actor returning swiftly for the ensuing busy contention of peers. On Q as an abridgement-adaptation for touring, see Madeleine Doran, '*Henry VI, Parts II and III': Their Relation to the 'Contention' and the 'True Tragedy'* (Iowa City: U of Iowa, 1928).

38. On Alexander Court as commentative framing action in *Henry V*, see Chris Fitter, 'A Tale of Two Branaghs: *Henry V*, Ideology and the Mekong Agincourt' in *Shakespeare Left and Right*, ed. Ivo Kamps (Routledge, 1991), 259–76; reprinted in *Shakespeare's History Plays*, ed. R.J.C. Watt (London: Longman, 2002), 169–83.

39. On the repertoire of gestures essential to enactment in Elizabethan theatre, see Stern, *Rehearsal from Shakespeare to Sheridan*, pp.72–76. Shakespeare quotation: *Winter's Tale*, 5.2.11–12.

40. "Holy Harry": *Richard III* 4.4.25.

41. See Chris Fitter, '*Henry VI Part Two* and the Politics of Human Commonality' in *Renaissance Words and Worlds*, ed. Amlan das Gupta (Kolkata: Macmillan India, 2003), 72–95. Mistrust of the commons is continued through *3 Henry VI*: where Henry's miming indictment of them as "Commanded always by the greater gust" (3.1.83–88) reprises Cade's contempt for them as feather-light (4.7.196–97); gamekeepers and mayor of York follow a code of convenience ignoring conflicting loyalty oaths (3.1.69–97; 4.8.31); and the commons appear to back whomever is currently most powerful, forgetful of Henry's clement rule (2.6.8–10; 4.2.1–2; 4.10.7–15). A concomitant paucity of deixis in the play sustains a lucid estrangement from both commons and nobility. Richard of Gloucester's dark charisma is centralized from act three, announced through his threatful deixis at 3.2.135–95: "Many lives stand between me and home . . . I'll slay more gazers than the basilisk" etc.

42. Knowles, Arden 3, 106.

43. Similarly, the terminus of *3 Henry VI*, even as the play problematizes regal legitimacy, and satirizes divine right ideology through caustic monarchical portraitures, will prove a dissuasion from revolt: civil war is endlessly, universally ruinous. From the tension between claimant problematics and barbarization by war emerges the customary Shakespearean position: the paradox of a pessimistic deconsecrationism that is itself a tutelary intervention.

NOTES TO CHAPTER 6

1. Gurr, *Playgoing*, 46.

2. Exclamation marks added. Their curious omission, in *The Norton Shakespeare*, *The Oxford Complete Works*, and elsewhere, as if this were a composed conversation rather than a ringing exchange of cries, suggests unconscious antipathy to such underclass comedics. Where well-born Petruccio is concerned, his lines receive a sympathetic sprinkling of exclamation marks (e.g. 2.1.158, 160, 246, 299, etc).

3. Spivack, *Shakespeare and the Allegory of Evil*, 195.

4. David Scott Kastan, '"The king hath many marching in his coats", or, "What did you do during the war, daddy?"' in Ivo Kamps, *Shakespeare Left and Right* (New York: Routledge, 1991), 248.

5. Weimann, *Shakespeare and the Popular Tradition*, 73–85. Quotations from 80–81, 230. See also 212–14, 237–39.

6. Weimann, *Shakespeare and the Popular Tradition*, 84.

7. Weimann, *Shakespeare and the Popular Tradition*, 230, 237.

8. *I Henry IV* 1.2.194.

9. For these terms see *The Semiotics of Theatre and Drama* by Keir Elam (London: Methuen, 1980), 62–65.

10. Collinson, *Elizabethan Essays*, 22–23.

11. Sir Robert Naunton, cit. Kastan, 'King hath many marching in his coats', 246.

12. *The Life and Death of Jack Straw*, 1594 (London: Malone Society Reprint, 1957), 3.

13. Richard Woods, *Norfolks Furies, or A View of Ketts Campe*, B1v; cit. Patterson, *Popular Voice*, 42.

14. See Manning, *Village Revolts*, 202–03.

15. Freedman, 'Elizabethan protest', 32–33.

16. Most editors gloss "couple" to mean placing on a leash with: but the word also signified sexual coupling, as OED shows, from the fourteenth century on. And why would a lord *returning* from the hunt (one hound needs to be "breathed", another is "embossed"), command hounds now to be put on a shared leash?

17. Prosecuted in 1597 for outspoken complaint, one Mary Stracke of Hempnall, explained that though a poor woman with three children, "when she spoke for her releef . . . they saye she skoldeth": cit. Andy Wood, *1549 Rebellions*, 120. See Wood's excellent discussion on hierarchy and silence, 91–142.

18. On the scold's bridle and *Shrew*, see Lynda E. Boose, 'Scolding brides and bridling scolds: taming the woman's unruly member' in Kamps, *Materialist Shakespeare*, 239–79.

19. David Underdown, *Revel, Riot and Rebellion: Popular Politics and Culture in England 1603–1660* (Oxford: Oxford University Press, 1985), 111.

20. Alison Wall, *Power and Protest in England 1525–1640* (London: Arnold, 2000), 152, 156–57; Harris, *Politics of the Excluded*, 76–78.

21. Compare Richard's grey mirth at 4.2.65 and 4.4.176–77.

22. M.P. Tilley, *A Dictionary of the Proverbs in England in the Sixteenth and Seventeenth Centuries* (Ann Arbor: University of Michigan, 1950), S412.

23. *Shrew* criticism has hitherto divided between reading Katherine's closing speech as either insincere (winking playfulness), or as a 'positive' sincerity (enunciating her wise assimilation to healthy communal norms). Each overlooks the closing accent on cruelty, and the latter is a textualist approach missing the larger dynamic of carnival frustration. Jean E. Howard intelligently rejects both traditions as suppressing "the degree of unresolved turbulence and contradiction" rife here and in other Shakespearean comedies, producing problematisation of both this ending and of conventional comedic closure ('The difficulties of closure: an approach to the problematic in Shakespeare' in *Comedy from Shakespeare to Sheridan*, ed. A.R. Braunmuller and J.C. Bulman [Newark: University of Delaware, 1986], 113–30). My own reading of *Shrew*'s closure in 'negative' sincerity, articulating the tragic brokenness of ludic resistance and its generation of festal exasperation, is theatrically grounded yet apparently novel.

24. In the earlier play, *The Taming of a Shrew*, almost certainly not by Shakespeare but reworked by him in *The Taming of the Shrew*, the husband cries

out "Enough, sweet, the wager thou hast won". *'The Taming of A Shrew',* *being the Original of Shakespeare's 'Taming of the Shrew',* ed. F. S. Boas (London: 1908), 63, line 143.

25. Compare Shakespeare's systemic sabotage of monarchic propaganda (from the Chorus) by staged actions immediately contradicting it, as a structural principle of *Henry V:* discussed by Fitter, 'A Tale of Two Branaghs', 259–76.

26. Stern, *Rehearsal,* 88–92. The technique is further discussed in Simon Palfrey and Tiffany Stern, *Shakespeare in Parts* (Oxford University Press, 2007).

27. Quotations from Leah Marcus, 'The Shakespearean Editor as Shrew–Tamer' in *Shakespeare and Gender,* ed. Deborah E. Barker and Ivo Kamps (New York: Verso, 1995), 220, and Coppelia Kahn, *Man's Estate: Masculine Identity in Shakespeare* (Berkeley: University of California, 1981), 117. Sanitizers of the drama claim that in this play "The dangers [in patriarchy] of violence, tyranny, deadening submission, and resentment magically disappear": Marianne Novy, *Love's Argument: Gender Relations in Shakespeare* (Chapel Hill: University of North Carolina, 1984), 62.

28. Stern, *Rehearsal,* 60, 68–69, 84–88.

29. Ioppolo, *Dramatists and Their Manuscripts,* 1, 183.

30. Stern, *Rehearsal,* 49–52, 79.

31. Ibid., 50.

NOTES TO CHAPTER 7

1. *A Student's Lamentation that hath sometime been in London an Apprentice, for the rebellious tumults lately in the Citie hapning: for which five suffred death on Thursday the 24. of July last,* anonymous, 1595, C r.

2. Terry Eagleton, *Walter Benjamin: Or Toward a Revolutionary Criticism* (London: Verso: 1981), 126

3. Taylor, *Reinventing Shakespeare;* Michael Bristol, *Big-Time Shakespeare* (New York, Routledge: 1998).

4. Eagleton, *Benjamin,* 126.

5. For a sophisticated championship of the value of reading Shakespeare topically, as well as its application to three plays, see Marcus, *Puzzling Shakespeare.*

6. Jill Levenson, '"Alla stoccado carries it away": Codes of Violence in *Romeo and Juliet'* in *Shakespeare's 'Romeo and Juliet'* ed. Jay L. Halio (Newark, University of Delaware: 1995), 83–96; quotation from 86.

7. For this dating see the Oxford World's Classics edition, ed. Jill Levenson (Oxford University Press, 2000), 97, 100–101.

8. Manning, *Village Revolts,* 200, 208.

9. Indeed within the theatre itself, summer might stir the blood more excitedly, as the proportion of workers in the audience would be greater, given retirement of gentry to their estates and arrival of vacation time for students at the Inns of Court. Freedman, 'Elizabethan Protest', 34.

10. Archer, *Pursuit,* 3–4.

11. Edelman, *Brawl Ridiculous,* 35, 173.

12. "The discovery of many more riots during the early seventeenth century reflects not increasing disorder but increasing documentation." Archer, *Pursuit,* 3.

13. Manning, *Village Revolts,* 191.

14. Wilson, *Will Power,* 34–39.

15. Freedman, 'Elizabethan protest', 17–45.

16. Manning, *Village Revolts*, 208–09. On hatred of Mayor Spencer, see also Archer, *Pursuit*, 56.
17. Wilson, *Will Power*, 40.
18. M. J. Power, 'London and the Control of the 'Crisis' of the 1590s' in *History* vol.70 (1985), 371.
19. Joyce Youings, *Sixteenth Century England* (Harmondsworth, Penguin:1984), 270. Wheat prices rose from 17.61 to 36.56 shillings per quarter between 1592–94, and thence to 40.34 in 1595, and 47.61 in 1596, as R. B. Outhwaite, 'Dearth, the English Crown and the Crisis of the 1590s' in Clark, *European Crisis*, shows in his table on 28. Andrew Appleby, in *Famine in Tudor and Stuart England* (Stanford, Stanford UP: 1978), 6 details the price increases during these years of cereals eaten by the poor: rye, for instance, had risen by 1596 to 5.68 times its price in 1593.
20. Appleby, *Famine*, 138–40.
21. Manning, *Village Revolts*, 204, 315. Compare Archer, *Pursuit*, 14.
22. John Walter and Keith Wrightson, 'Dearth and the Social Order in Early Modern England' in *Rebellion, Popular Protest and the Social Order in Early Modern England* ed. Paul Slack (Cambridge University Press:1984), 108.
23. Letter of December 1596, cit. Archer, *Pursuit*, 10–11.
24. George Abbot, *An Exposition unto the Prophet Jonah* (London: 1600), 204; cit. Appleby, *Famine*, 141.
25. Outhwaite, 'Dearth', 28.
26. Clark, *English Provincial Society*, 234.
27. Clark, ibid., 233.
28. M. J. Power, 'London and the Control of the Crisis', 372–74.
29. Cit. Neale, *Parliaments*, 335. Hunger as 'cleanness of teeth' echoes, I would guess, Amos 4.6.
30. Hindle, *State and Social Change*, 149.
31. Archer, *Pursuit*, 6.
32. Manning, *Village Revolts*, 205; Archer, *Pursuit*, 6. On food riots elsewhere in England in 1595–96 see Appleby, *Famine*, 142.
33. Cit. Manning, *Village Revolts*, 205.
34. J. W. Baldwin, *Medieval Theories of the Just Price* (Philadephia: Transactions of the Philadelphia Philosophical Society, New Series, 49, Part 4, 1959). This was one of the weekly duties of Shakespeare's father as bailiff in Stratford.
35. Archer, *Pursuit*, 6.
36. Thompson, 'The Moral Economy of the English Crowd in the Eighteenth Century', *Past and Present* 50 (Feb. 1971), 76–136. Compare Buchanan Sharp, 'Popular Protest in Seventeenth Century England' in *Popular Culture in Seventeenth Century England*, ed. Barry Reay (New York: St. Martin's Press: 1985), 271–88.
37. Walter and Wrightson, 'Dearth and the Social order', 119.
38. Archer, *Pursuit*, 6–7.
39. Walter and Wrightson, 'Dearth and the Social Order', 121.
40. Manning, *Village Revolts*, 204–05, 209, 314. Erecting gallows at the gate of a hated superior, or sketching them on a libellous note, seems to have been something of a traditional plebeian recourse against notable injustice: see Wood, *1549 Rebellions*, 102, esp. note 17.
41. Manning, *Village Revolts*, 202.
42. Ibid., 207–08.
43. Manning, *Village Revolts*, 219, 201, 208. Nonetheless, and despite the Council's harsh interventions in London's self–government during the riots, many Londoners still believed (wrongly) Elizabeth herself to be distressed by

the plight of the poor. A ballad on the dearth by Thomas Delaney in 1596, for instance, was suppressed "lest it aggravate their grief and take occasion of some discontentment", for it portrayed the queen as empathizing with the hungry: Power, 'London and the Control', 380.

44. Manning, *Village Revolts*, 209–10; Archer, *Pursuit*, 1; Breight, *Surveillance*, 88.
45. Sharp, 'Popular Protest', 285–86.
46. Archer, *Pursuit*, 7.
47. Manning, *Village Revolts*, 178–85; Power, 'London and the Control', 380.
48. Archer, *Pursuit*, 8.
49. Proclamation 'Prohibiting unlawful assembly under martial law', 4 July 1595, in *Tudor Royal Proclamations*, no. 769.
50. Stone, *Crisis of the Aristocracy*, 112, 108.
51. Stone, ibid., 98, 108–09.
52. Ibid., 112–13. Compare the Crown's studied aversion of gaze from the endemic hunting disorders of the gentry and aristocracy, wreaking a havoc throughout the sixteenth and seventeenth centuries long unrecognised by historians: Roger B. Manning, *Hunters and Poachers* (Oxford: Oxford University Press, 1993).
53. Edelman, *Brawl Ridiculous*, 25–26, 35.
54. Cit. Edelman, *Brawl Ridiculous*, 174.
55. Levenson, Introduction to the Oxford *Romeo and Juliet*, 85–86.
56. Cit. Stone, *Crisis of Aristocracy*, 120.
57. Compare Levenson, Oxford ed. Introduction, 84–85.
58. Capulet reviles her also for "gadding" (4.2.17), a term of disparagement attached frequently to vagrant rogues. That this involves further proletarianisation of Juliet is uncertain, but OED suggests that 'gad' may be a back-formation from 'gadling', meaning vagrant. To OED's examples we may add "punishment . . . cannot restrain them from their gadding . . [Rogues] gad about the country using unlawful games": William Harrison, *The Description of England* (1587), ed. G. Edelen (Washington: Folger, 1994), 185–86.
59. Compare the resented cruelty of the self "engrossed" in Sonnet 133.6; also engrossment as robbery in *All's Well* 3.2.63–64.
60. Archer, *Pursuit of Stability*, 200.
61. Kahn, *Man's Estate*, 82–103; Marianne Novy, 'Violence, Love and Gender in *Romeo and Juliet*' in *Romeo and Juliet, Critical Essays* ed. John F. Andrews (New York, Garland: 1993), 359–71. More recently, Robert Appelbaum in '"Standing to the Wall": The Pressures of Masculinity in *Romeo and Juliet*' in *Shakespeare Quarterly* 48 (Fall 1997) no.3, 251–72, has sought, in ahistorical and depoliticized terms, to link the play's representation of violence to 'masculinity' as a fixed if contradictory "regime of gender performance"(254); and can thus write of "citizens harmoniously toiling under the prince's law", "within a town where history seems to have temporarily come to an end" (271).
62. Edelman, *Brawl Ridiculous*, 176.
63. The desperate idealisation of Spain we found occasionally expressed among the poor in chapter one would not have prevailed among the cross-section of commoners gathered in the public theatre.
64. This trick is described by Gurr, *Shakespearean Stage*, 182–4. Its linkage with the murder of Paris is my own.
65. Alan Dessen, *Recovering Shakespeare's Theatrical Vocabulary* (Cambridge University Press: 1995), 191, 194–95.
66. Levenson, 'Alla stoccado', 86–88, 92, 94.

67. Alan Dessen, 'Q1, *Romeo and Juliet* and Elizabethan Theatrical Vocabulary' in Halio, *Shakespeare's 'Romeo and Juliet'* , 113.

68. It may also be that the marching, drumming and masquing activities of the Montague youths, so prominent in act one scenes four and five, were designed and performed to suggest patrician counterparts to the rituals and parades of the apprentices.

69. The stage direction for 1.4 specifies, in addition to Romeo, Mercutio and Benvolio, "five or six other masquers and torchbearers". That for 3.1 stipulates "Mercutio, Benvolio and Men", with line 34 introducing "Tybalt, Petruchio and Others".

70. Power, 'London and the Control', 379.

71. *A Student's Lamentation*, Br, C2v.

72. Events surrounding 'the Midsummer Riot' of June 1592 had demonstrated an intriguingly similar opposition, I suggest, between assumed patrician orderliness and underclass riposte. Following the lethal combat between the Southwark feltmakers and the Knight Marshal's men outside the Marshalsea on June 11 1592, the Privy Council banned theatre and carnival festivities, and imposed a curfew, whilst resurrecting an archaic torchlit watch of "householders and masters of families" on the 23rd. "The peoples' revels were suppressed with a show of street theatre from the propertied class", glosses Wilson (*Will Power*, 39). In the same period, however, clothworker apprentices seized one of the Knight Marshall's men believed to have killed a rioter, and marched him to Newgate to demand justice. "Londoners", suggests Manning, "probably noted that a different standard of justice was applied" to the Marshall's men (*Village Revolts*, 208).

73. *A Student's Lamentation*, Cv.

74. *Tudor Royal Proclamations*, number 767: 'Protecting Informers'.

75. Patterson, *Popular Voice*, chapter 3.

76. *Student's Lamentation*, C3r.

77. J. Sharpe, 'Social strain', 202.

78. On 'economic ethics' see Tawney, *Religion and the Rise of Capitalism*, chapter 1, quotation from 35. "If the medieval moralist was often too naive in expecting sound practice as the result of lofty principles alone" noted Tawney, just seven years before the Wall Street Crash, "he was at least free from that not unfashionable form of credulity which expects it from their absence or from their opposite" (37).

79. Archer, *Pursuit*, 52–57. Andrew Marvell lauds the tradition when depicting Fairfax's dwelling in *Appleton House*: "A stately frontispiece of poor / Adorns without the open door" (ll.65–66).

80. Queen Mary: Carolly Erickson, *Bloody Mary: the Life of Mary Tudor* (New York: Quill, 1978), 440–43; the *Mandatum*: Mollat, *The Poor in the Middle Ages*, 49.

81. Hindle, *State and Social Change*, 147.

82. "Cato of the commonwealth": British Library, Lansdowne MS 74/42.

83. Power, 'London and the Control of the 'Crisis' of the 1590s', 376.

84. Appleby, *Famine*, 144–45; Power, 'London', 376, 385. Bishop Gervase Babington was similarly to urge (1604) the application in times of dearth and plague of the Biblical redistributivist principle of Jubilee, by which debtors were to be released, and lands sold through pressure of poverty returned to their original owners (Leviticus 25.9–55). The theme recurs through the seventeenth century among radicals and the distressed; yet there remains, as Hill comments, "much research to be done on the underground flowing of this tradition": Hill, *English Bible*, 164–67.

85. Buchanan Sharp, 'Shakespeare's *Coriolanus* and the crisis of the 1590s', in *Law and Authority in Early Modern England*, ed. Sharp and Fissel, 48.
86. 'Enforcing orders against dearth' in *Tudor Royal Proclamations* no. 784.
87. Archer, *Pursuit of Stability*, 200.
88. Summarised by Hill, *Society and Puritanism*, 222.
89. Libel at Norwich, 1595, Historical Manuscripts Commission, Salisbury MSS, vol.13, 168–69; cit. Peter Clark, 'A crisis contained?' in *European Crisis of the 1590s* ed. Clark, 44.
90. Edward Hext, letter to Burghley of 25 September 1596, in Tawney and Power, *Tudor Economic Documents*, vol. 2, 339–46.
91. Sharp, 'Shakespeare's *Coriolanus*', 49.
92. Power, 'Control', 377–80.
93. The precise social rank of Capulet (and of Montague) appears impossible to pin down. Some editors (such as Brian Gibbons in the 1980 Arden) assume Capulet to be a nobleman, and give his wife as 'Lady Capulet'. Other editions (such as the Complete Oxford and the Norton) present them as Capulet and 'Capulet's wife', denying them aristocratic status. The indeterminacy, if the arguments of this chapter are correct, is deliberate. Such ambiguity permits them to suggest in the play both the feuding nobility (in the play's presentation of violence) and the wealthy city fathers (in the feasting theme).
94. See for instance Francois Laroque's summary of the gender transposition of Romeo and Juliet, in 'Tradition and Subversion in *Romeo and Juliet*' in Halio, *Shakespeare's Romeo and Juliet*, 29–31.
95. On *Coriolanus* and the Midlands riots, see Patterson, *Popular Voice*, 120–53.
96. Shakespeare himself, one might speculate, was particularly well placed to appreciate the pathos of an independent business man humbled in his workshop by the advent of penury, the wares of his "needy shop" now "thinly scatter'd to make up a show" (5.1.42, 48). Eight years earlier, following years of apparent financial precariousness, his father had been finally expelled from the borough council, and sued, too, for his brother Henry's debts. The strain of the condition and the vulnerability of his father would not have been lost on the son.
97. Manning, *Village Riots*, 193.
98. Archer, *Pursuit*, 55.
99. The theme is briefly discussed, with no reference to Shakespeare, by Frank Whigham in *Ambition and Privilege: the Social tropes of Elizabethan Courtesy Theory* (Berkeley and Los Angeles: University of California Press, 1984), 112–116, under the heading 'The concealment of exploitation'.
100. *The Hurt of Sedition* (1549), pagination only sporadic. Cit. Baker, *Divulging Utopia*, 115.
101. Thomas Lodge, *Rosalynde*, ed. Bullough, *Narrative and Dramatic Sources*, 2.174. See likewise 179, 189, 209.
102. *Astrophil and Stella*, sonnet 39, line 3.
103. Elizabeth is quoted by Erickson, *First Elizabeth*, 399.
104. Bullough, *Narrative and Dramatic Sources*, 277–78.
105. "Censorship", notes Annabel Patterson, "encouraged the use of historical or other uninvented texts, such as translations from the classics", which not only "allowed an author to limit his authorial responsibility for the text" but paradoxically invited the reader to consider "the timeliness of the retelling of another man's story" and "the implications of the model". *Censorship and Interpretation*, 65.
106. Jean MacIntyre, *Costumes and Scripts in the Elizabethan Theatres* (Alberta, University of Alberta Press, 1992), 141–44.

107. For the Renaissance revaluation of the night as a time of fashionable and courtly beauty, see Chris Fitter, 'The Poetic Nocturne: from Ancient Motif to Renaissance Genre' in *Early Modern Literary Studies* 3.2 (September 1997), 2.1–61.
108. Manning, *Village Riots*, 208–09.
109. The illiteracy of the servant unable to read the guest list he is supposed to act upon at 1.2.56 is matched by that of the Nurse, whose illiteracy is prominently exhibited at 2.3.189–95 where it is comically contrasted with Romeo's access to letters. The literacy of Capulet, Romeo, Juliet, the Prince and the Friar is brought to our notice by their conspicuous letter reading and writing (see 4.2.1; 5.1.25; 5.2.13; 5.3.23; 5.3.285). In early modern England, of course, literacy signified a form of class privilege which could prove literally a matter of life or death: anyone found guilty of a felony could escape hanging simply by reading 'neck–verses' from the Bible. As Shakespeare has Cade and his rebels protest in *2 Henry VI*, "Because they cannot read thou hast hanged them." The medieval ecclesiastical protection, 'Benefit of Clergy', had thus become, as Christopher Hill notes, "a shield for the propertied" (*Liberty Against the Law*, 258). Again, at a time of rioting and subsequent executions, this dramatic form of protective class privilege would not go unnoticed or unresented.
110. Gurr, *Shakespearean Stage*, 86.
111. Gurr, *Playgoing*, 52. Gerald Bentley, however, records that, subsequent to the purchases of a coat–of–arms and of New Place (1596–97), he "usually appears in legal records of property transactions, especially those about Stratford, as 'William Shakespeare of Stratford upon Avon, gentleman'": *Shakespeare: A Biographical Handbook* (New Haven: Yale, 1961), 41–42. Katherine Duncan-Jones believes that, given the heraldic scandal ensuing over Shakespeare's 1596 purchase of a coat-of-arms, "it was never absolutely clear whether his inheritance of the title 'gentleman', after his father's death in 1601, was indeed sound in the view of experts in such matters". *Ungentle Shakespeare*, 97.
112. Chambers, *Elizabethan Stage*, 4:318.
113. Marcus, *Puzzling Shakespeare*, 26–27.
114. Patterson, *Censorship and Interpretation*, 71.
115. On the openness of Tudor drama to prolific political interpretation, see Bevington, *Tudor Drama and Politics*, 1–26.
116. Andy Wood finds precisely this call to class solidarity ("All comons styk ye together"), offset by "the willingness of labouring people to reveal one another's words to the authorities" in the mid-16th rebellions: *1549*, chapters 3–6; quotations 172, 214.
117. *A Student's Lamentation*, C r.
118. 'Protecting Informers' (1594) in *Tudor Royal Proclamations*, ed. Hughes and Larkin, no. 767.
119. Alvin Kernan, *Shakespeare the King's Playwright* (New Haven: Yale University Press, 1995) postulates a Shakespeare assiduously propagandist in the monarchical cause, "the leading apologist for kings in his or any other time", 95.
120. Archer, *Pursuit*, 35–37; Manning, *Village Revolts*, 207.
121. Archer, *Pursuit of Stability*, 216.
122. See for instance, Ivo Kamps, *Historiography and Ideology in Stuart Drama* (Cambridge: Cambridge University Press, 1996), which notes, 26, and illustrates *passim*, that "the seeds for confrontation" with the crown which matured in the English Revolution "had long been sown", in drama as early as Shakespeare's *Henry V*.

123. Quoted in Christopher Hill, *Change and Continuity*, 189; see also Patterson, *Popular Voice*, 39.
124. Hill, *Liberty Against the Law*, 20.

NOTES TO CHAPTER 8

1. Lord Keeper Thomas Egerton, cit. Neale, *Parliaments*, 327.
2. Francis Bacon, cit. Neale, *Parliaments*, 338.
3. Cit. Neale, *Parliaments*, 340. The speaker's identity is unknown, but Neale, 341 n.1, thinks it probably Robert Cecil.
4. Anonymous Member of Parliament (probably a lawyer, thinks Neale), cit. Neale, *Parliaments*, 340.
5. Katherine Duncan Jones, introduction to the Penguin *As You Like It* (London: 2005), xxiii.
6. Anne Barton, *Essays, Mainly Shakespearean* (Cambridge: Cambridge University Press, 1994), 99.
7. Edward Berry, *Shakespeare and the Hunt* (Cambridge: Cambridge University Press, 2001), 171.
8. "No Shakespearean text transmits more urgently the imminence of the social breakdown threatened by the conjuncture of famine and enclosure" writes Richard Wilson (*Will Power*, 65): a judgement with which (*King Lear* and *Coriolanus* aside) I concur—although my reading of *As You Like It* is otherwise diametrically opposed to Wilson's.
9. Hill, *World Turned Upside Down*, 53–54.
10. Piero Camporesi, *Bread of Dreams: Food and Fantasy in Early Modern Europe* (1980; trans. David Gentilcore, University of Chicago Press, 1989), 158. Propertied apprehension of paupers as vermin and disease bearers is discussed by Woodbridge, *Vagrancy*, 178–87, and Pugliatti, *Beggary and Theatre*, 107–17.
11. John Moore, *The Crying Sin Of England of Not Caring for the Poor* (1653), p.11; cit. Hill, *World Turned Upside Down*, 52.
12. V. Skipp, *Crisis and Development: An Ecological Case Study of the Forest of Arden 1570–1674* (Cambridge: Cambridge University Press, 1978), 18, 33, 41, 51, 68; ref. Berry, *Hunt*, 169.
13. Ann Hughes, *Politics, Society, and Civil War in Warwickshire 1620–1660* (Cambridge: Cambridge University Press, 1987), 5.
14. Underdown, *Revel*, 34.
15. Buchanan Sharp, *In Contempt of All Authority: Rural Artisans and Riot in the West of England 1586–1660* (Berkeley: University of California Press, 1980), 167, 171.
16. Nigel Nicolson and Alasdair Hawkyard, *The Counties of Britain: A Tudor Atlas by John Speed* (London: Pavilion Books, 1988), 177; cit. Berry, *Hunt*, 170.
17. Underdown, *Revel*, 108–10.
18. Shapiro, *1599*, 238.
19. Honan, *Shakespeare: A Life*, 246.
20. On Tudor penalties for vagrancy, see Beier, *Masterless Men*, 146–170. Paul Slack's appendix in *The English Poor Law* (Cambridge: Cambridge University Press, 1990) lists the changing statutory inflictions. William C. Carroll discusses these in the wider context of Tudor 'discourses of poverty' in *Fat King*, 21–69. C. S. L. Davies has argued that the slavery provisions of the 1547 act were never in fact enforced, but that much the same condition existed under different names: as when Henry VIII had condemned vagrants

to serve in "galleys, and other like vessels" in his wars. See Davies, 'Slavery and Protector Somerset: the vagrancy act of 1547' in *Economic History Review* 19 (1966), 533–49.

21. Youings, *Sixteenth Century England*, 283. The Tudors probably "planned to use the pretense of [adequate] assistance as an excuse for passing restrictive measures of social control . . . Suppression of public disorder was the major reason for Tudor concern with poverty": J. T. Kelly, *Thorns on the Tudor Rose* (Jackson: University of Mississippi, 1977), x, 56; cit. Pugliatti, *Beggary*, 36.

22. Archer, *Pursuit*, 244.

23. Manning, *Village Revolts*, 167; Hill, *Liberty Against the Law*, 52; Peter Clark, in *The English Alehouse*, 129, agrees with the figure of 80,000. The number of vagrants expanded in periods of economic distress and military campaigns. See also Beier, *Masterless Men*, 14–16, and Carroll, *Fat King*, 31–32. In London's Bridewell prison in the 1560s, only 16 per cent of the inmates had been convicted for vagrancy, but by 1600–01 the figure had climbed to 62 per cent: Paul Slack, *Poverty and Policy in Tudor and Stuart England* (London: Longman, 1988), 93.

24. Beier, *Masterless Men*, 161.

25. J. A. Sharpe, *Crime in Early Modern England 1550–1750* (London: Longman, 1999), 146.

26. Simon Schama, *Landscape and Memory* (New York: Knopf, 1995), 154.

27. Youings, *Sixteenth Century England*, 299.

28. Sir Edwin Sandys, writing in January 1620: in *The Records of the Virginia company of London*, ed. Susan M. Kingsbury, 4 vols, (Washington, D.C.: U.S. Government Printing Office, 1933), 3.259; cit. Carroll, *Fat King*, 61.

29. See Christopher Hill, 'William Perkins and the Poor' in *Puritanism and Revolution*, 212–33; also 'Pottage for Freeborn Englishmen: Attitudes to Wage-Labour' in Hill's *Change and Continuity*, 219–238; and Hill's *Liberty Against the Law*, esp. 47–70; Youings, *Sixteenth Century England*, 298–303.

30. Hirst, *Authority and Conflict*, 15.

31. Christopher Hill, 'Pottage for freeborn Englishmen', 223, quoting D. Ogg, *England in the Reign of Charles II* (Oxford, 1955), 1.55.

32. "The concept of the freeman, owing no obligation, not even deference, to an overlord is one of the most important if intangible legacies of medieval peasants to the modern world": Hilton, *Bond Men Made Free*, 235. On early modern resentment of landless wage labour see particularly Hill, 'Pottage for Freeborn Englishmen'. Winstanley noted the depth of political despair imposed by wage-labour: "the poor see, if they fight and should conquer the [foreign] enemy, yet either they or their children are like to be slaves still, for the gentry will have all . . . For they [the poor] say, we can as well live under a foreign enemy working for day wages as under our own brethren, with whom we ought to have equal freedom by the law of righteousness." Gerrard Winstanley, *An Appeale to all Englishmen* (1650), broadside, in G.H. Sabine, *Writings of Gerrard Winstanley* (Ithaca: Cornell University Press, 1941), 414.

33. John Earle, *Microcosmography; or a Piece of the World Discovered"* (1628) in *Essays and Characters*, ed. Philip Bliss (London, 1811) , 203; cit. Carroll, *Fat King*, 214.

34. Cit. Chambers, *Elizabethan Stage*, 4.270. Pugliatti discovers that "performers of various kinds" had been periodically lumped together with vagrants in English punitive legislation dating back to 1284: *Beggary and Theatre*, pp.2–3, 36–51. Players were not, however (in Tudor times at least) in practice

subjected to the terrible penalties actually meted out to vagrants, but were fined lightly or even packed off with a caution: Pugliatti, *Beggary*, 4–5.

35. Hill, 'Pottage for freeborn Englishmen', 224. "Is it no more than an innocent trope", wonders Woodbridge, "that speakers of epilogues, who address audiences on behalf of actors and playwrights, often position themselves as *beggars* for applause?" *Vagrancy*, 262.

36. Thomas Lodge, *Rosalynde: Euphues Golden Legacie*, ed. Geoffrey Bullough, *Narrative and Dramatic Sources of Shakespeare* (New York: Columbia, 1958), 2.191.

37. Renato Poggioli, 'The Oaten Flute' in *Harvard Library Bulletin* 11 (1957), 181.

38. Slack, *English Poor Law*, 45.

39. Archer, *Pursuit*, 183.

40. Lodge, *Rosalynde*, ed. Bullough, 2.189.

41. Lady-in-Waiting Elizabeth Vernon had been banished from court in 1598 for secretly marrying Southampton, and sent, heavily pregnant, to the Fleet prison. Essex was banished from court, for his conduct in Ireland, from October 1 1599. Popular fury following his initial confinement in York House produced a spate of libels, and Cecil no longer dared go out without bodyguards. The government broke up Essex's household and dispersed his 160 servants in early December 1599 (G. B. Harrison, *Life and Death of Robert Devereux* [New York: Holt 1937], 254): an action at which Duke Frederick's seizure of Oliver's household at 3.1.9–12 possibly hints.

42. A convenient gathering of such texts is Gamini Salgado's *Cony-Catchers and Bawdy Baskets* (Harmondsworth: Penguin, 1972). For widespread belief that the homeless bloodied or mutilated themselves and their children to win sympathy when begging, see Carroll, *Fat King*, pp. 48–51, 193. Pugliatti, *Beggary*, 102–05, records kindred instances from contemporary Italy and France. For the counter-factual topos romanticising the free and merry beggar, see Carroll, *Fat King*, 63–67, 181–82, 209–15; Woodbridge, *Vagrancy*, 239–48.

43. Woodbridge, *Vagrancy*, 41–43.

44. "Scelerous secrets" quotation from Thomas Harman, *A Caveat for Common Cursitors* in *Cony-Catchers*, 81–82. Pugliatti, *Beggary and Theatre*, 125–30, distinguishes between the early rogue literature of Awdeley and Harman, largely focused on rural settings and underclass rogues, and the late Elizabethan cony-catching works, mainly featuring more prosperous types in the urban world; but Dekker hybridizes these streams.

45. See the rather credulous introduction by Arthur F. Kinney, in his *Rogues, Vagabonds and Sturdy Beggars* (Amherst, 1973). Even Beier, rightly scornful of rogue literature's fantastical exaggerations, subscribed to its myth of 'Pedlar's French', a secret language of criminal vagrancy used to exclude other's understanding (*Masterless Men*, 123–26). Piero Camporesi writes "The history of 'false beggars' is substantially literary, and therefore fantastic, highly unreal, tendentious and classist": *Il libro dei vagabondi* (Torino: Einaudi, 1973), clxxix, cited and translated by Pugliatti, *Vagrancy*, 136; compare Woodbridge, *Vagrancy*, 39–79. See also the shrewd chapters on Harman in Carroll, *Fat King*, 1996), 70–96, and by Beier in *Rogues and Early Modern English Culture*, ed. Craig Dionne and Steve Mentz (Ann Arbor: University of Massachusetts, 2004). Most writers in the latter anthology are sceptical of the existence of clandestine rogue discourse.

46. Woodbridge, *Vagrancy*, 9–10, 64–65.

47. Woodbridge, *Vagrancy*, 80–148. Stephen Greenblatt had remarked in 1988 in *Shakespearean Negotiations* (Berkeley and Los Angeles, University of California Press), 50, that these works have "the air of a jest book".

48. Carroll similarly notes the scapegoating action here. "Vagrants were . . . considered a physical threat, as well as a philosophical one, because their very nature was to cross boundaries, to transgress categories of all kinds . . . disrupting an older cosmic system of order and hierarchy" (*Fat King*, 6). For varied readings of the rogue construct as mediation of capitalism's impact on early modern London see the essays by Woodbridge, Bix, Fumerton, and Mentz, in Dionne and Mentz, *Rogues*.

49. J. A. Sharpe notes "Many of the ideas that crytallized in the rogue pamphlets as the genre developed were commonplaces of governmental thinking": *Crime in Early Modern England, 1550–1750* (London: Longman, 1999) 235.

50. Carroll, *Fat King*, 47.

51. As Marx noted of the Poor Laws "the agricultural people, first forcibly expropriated from the soil, [were] driven from their homes, turned into vagabonds, and then whipped, branded, tortured by laws grotesquely terrible, into the discipline necessary for the wage system." *Capital*, ed. Dona Torr (New York: International Publishers, 1939), 761; cit. Hill, *Puritanism and Revolution*, 221. Compare Tawney: "As far as the able-bodied are concerned the Poor Law is in origin a measure of social police. Relief is thrown in as a makeweight, because by the end of the sixteenth century our statesmen have discovered that when economic pressure reaches a certain point they cannot control men without it." R.H. Tawney, *The Agrarian Problem in the Sixteenth Century* (London: Longmans, 1912), 272.

52. The earliest English rogue book, Robert Copland's *Highway to the Spital-house*, 1536, took the fictitious, cheery-toned form of a verse dialogue with a Spital-house porter who equated the institution with Hell. It may have been stimulated by a pandemic of plague in 1535, and it coincided, as Woodbridge notes, with "the heyday of the Henrician jestbooks" (*Vagrancy*, 19, 101–02). Gilbert Walker's *Manifest Detection of the Most Vile and Detestable Diceplay*, 1552, had focused well-to-do con-men in prosperous urban settings: the cony-catcher subgenre being quite distinct in conventions and foci from the rogue literature of the tramp: Pugliatti, *Beggary*, 125–30.

53. Linda Salamon, 'Vagabond Veterans', in *Rogues*, ed. Dionne and Mentz, 270.

54. Pugliatti, *Beggary*, 133.

55. "Extend your hand, do not withdraw it. We are not the examiners of people's lives", cit. Pugliatti, 17.

56. Geremek, *Poverty*, 17.

57. "God has always looked with favour upon the poor, and condemned the rich", cit. ibid., 22.

58. Quoted in Mollat, *Poor in the Middle Ages*, 22.

59. "Without things, without hope, without faith, without seat": Michael Dalton in *The Countrey Justice* in 1618. Published 1635, 123; cit. Pugliatti, 19.

60. Paola Pugliatti, *Beggary and Theatre*, 21–22.

61. Pugliatti, *Beggary and Theatre*, 18; see also 36–38. Where England would become unique in Europe was "the national level of its poor relief; elsewhere most such programs were municipal": Woodbridge, *Vagrancy*, 153.

62. Crowley, *Select Works*, 16.

63. Bishop Ridley, letter to William Cecil, in Tawney and Power, *Tudor Economic Documents*, 2.312.

64. Cit. Carroll, *Fat King*, 27.

65. Cit. Pugliatti, *Beggary*, 61.

66. Puritanism was not uniformly anti-humanitarian. Philip Stubbes, for instance, in 1583 had lamented of vagrancy attitudes that "If we give them

a piece of brown bread, a mess of porridge (nay, the stocks and prison, with whipping cheer now and then is the best portion of alms which many gentlemen give) at our doors, it is counted meritorious." *The Anatomy of Abuses in England*, ed. F.J. Furnivall (London: N. Trubner, 1877–79), 59.

67. For Perkins, see Hill, 'Perkins and the Poor' in *Puritanism and Revolution*, esp. 227–28. Richard Baxter, *Chapters from a Christian Directory*, written in the 1640s (London: 1925), 69; cit. Hill, *World Turned Upside Down*, 330.

68. *Tudor Royal Proclamations*, ed. Hughes and Larkin, no. 796.

69. Quoted by Hill, *Puritanism and Revolution*, 219.

70. Cit. Neale, *Parliaments*, 347.

71. See Ibid., 349–50, 366–67.

72. Anon., *A Declaration of the Grounds and Reasons why we the Poor Inhabitants* etc., cit. Christopher Hill, *Winstanley: The Law of Freedom* (Harmondsworth: Penguin, 1973), 25.

73. The 1598 Act for the Punishment of Rogues, Vagabonds and Sturdy Beggars repealed the penalties for vagrancy of ear-boring, ear-removal and slavery, retaining mere whippings and incarceration; yet it embodied the insensate Tudor bias which assumed the unemployed, in a time of acute unemployment, to be reprobate shirkers.

74. Thomas Stanley, *Stanleye's Remedy, or The Way how to Reform Wandring Beggers, Theeves, High Way Robbers and Pick Pockets* (1646), 5; cit. Pugliatti, *Beggary*, 38.

75. Hill, *Puritanism and Revolution*, 228.

76. Edward Hext, letter to Burghley of September 1596, in John Strype, *Annals of the Reformation . . . during Queen Elizabeth's Happy Reign*, 4 vols., (Oxford: 1824), 4.406, cit. Hill, *Puritanism and Revolution*, 228. Compare Hill, *World Turned Upside Down*, 40, 44.

77. Beier, *Masterless Men*, 147; Woodbridge notes that officers in contemporary Paris and Amsterdam attempting pauper arrests could be violently resisted by locals, scandalised by the sin of chasing away God's poor. *Vagrancy*, 53, 36 note 5.

78. Thomas More, *Utopia*, Robinson trans., 31; Wood, *1549 Rebellions*, 103; also 123, 148–49.

79. Manning, *Village Revolts*, 26. Shakespeare, I suspect, would agree with James Holstun's remark, meditating literature, class and the historiography of early modern England, that Karl Marx's term for the foundational process of early capitalism as "primitive accumulation" (*ursprungliche Akkumulation*) is a mystifying misnomer: "A better term for this process might be *original division* or *expropriation* or *theft*." *Ehud's Dagger*, 115.

80. Hughes and Larkin, *Tudor Royal Proclamations*, proclamation 800.

81. The 1597 Act for the Relief of the Poor admitted the problem of seamen and soldiers "lawfully lycensed" in discharge, yet without the means to make their way home: Tawney and Power, *Tudor Economic Documents*, 2.353. Peter Clark records that in October 1599, on one day alone, "almost a hundred troops landed at Dover from Flushing and proceeded to tramp and possibly steal their way across the county": *English Provincial Society*, 235.

82. Breight, *Surveillance*, 185; also 122, 175–76.

83. By contrast with Orlando's sword-wielding surprise of the Duke and his men ("Forbear and eat no more!"), Lodge's Rosader, sword in sheath, had approached with consummate courtesy: "Whatsoere thou bee that art master of these lustie squiers, I salute thee as graciously, as a man in extreame distresse may." The Duke perceives at once "so proper a Gentleman in so bitter

a passion". Lodge thus bypasses any suggestion of rude vagrant violence, even though the close of Rosader's ornately courteous speech includes the stirring "If thou refuse this, as a niggard of thy cates, I will have amongst you with my sword; for rather will I die valiantly, than perish with so cowardly an extreame". As Adam and his master fall to their food, Lodge terms them "hungrie squires", thus underlining a safe class parity among all involved (*Rosalynde*, 196–97).

84. On punishing sexual delinquency in the poor, see Hindle, *State and Social Change*, 160, 185–88.

85. For the text of the decree, see *A Transcript of the Registers of the Company of Stationers of London*, 5 vols. (London: 1875–94), vol. 3, 67 and 316.

86. Cyndia Clegg, *Press Censorship in Elizabethan England* (Cambridge: Cambridge University Press: 1997), 217.

87. Clegg, *Press Censorship*, 198–217. Clegg is overturning judgements such as those of Lynda Boose, for whom the burning "marks the entrance of vernacular pornography into England": 'The 1599 Bishops' Ban, Elizabethan Pornography, and the Sexualization of the Jacobean stage' in Burt and Archer, *Enclosure Acts*, 185–200.

88. On Shakespeare's theatrical puncturings of Essex, see Fitter, 'Historicizing Shakespeare's *Richard II*'.

89. Charles Nicholl, *The Reckoning: the Murder of Christopher Marlowe* (London: Picador, 1992), 72–76.

90. Chris Fitter, 'The Slain Deer and Political Imperium: *As You Like It* and Andrew Marvell's 'Nymph Complaining for the Death of her Fawn'" in *Journal of English and Germanic Philology* April 1999, 193–218. A number of curious particulars about the "bankrupt" and "sequestered" creature in the passage, abandoned by a "velvet friend", and thereafter spurned by "fat and greasy burghers", suggest the career and current plight of Thomas Nashe: who though formerly a friend of Archbishop Whitgift, was worst hit by the prohibition on satires—all his works were to be seized and banned, as anything written by him thereafter—and was also abandoned by London's citizens, as he had complained in *Lenten Stuff*, published that year.

91. MacCulloch, *The Reformation*, 376.

92. Juliet Dusinberre in her 3rd Arden edition (2006) 6–7, 37–42 claims that a manuscript epilogue addressing the queen, found in 1972, is probably by Shakespeare, and perhaps concluded a court performance of *As You Like It*. There is no direct evidence for either proposition. If the play's character merited court approval, why was it stayed in the Stationer's Register in August 1600?

93. Critical distinction is sometimes made between Jaques as satirist, and Touchstone as clown or fool. Yet as Bednarz notes, Touchstone's comedic range encompasses all three types. Indeed "The scope of his satire . . . is remarkably comprehensive." James Bednarz, *Shakespeare and the Poets' War* (New York: Columbia, 2001), 112.

94. Recent suppression of views went beyond the Bishops' Ban. At the closing of the 1598 parliament, Speaker Yelverton's claimed that in the world's highest Commonwealth "the subjects had their freedom of discourse and their liberty of liking in establishing the laws that should govern them." Yet in the ceremony of royal assent, Elizabeth, in granite mode, vetoed no less than twelve of the forty-three bills to which parliament had taken "liberty of liking". Neale, *Parliaments*, 364–67.

95. Fitter, 'The Slain Deer and Political Imperium', 201–02.

NOTES TO CHAPTER 9

1. Barber, *Shakespeare's Festive Comedy*; M.M. Bakhtin, *Rabelais and His World*, trans. Helen Iswolsky (1968; rpt. Bloomington: Indiana University Press, 1984). Richard Wilson aligns the transgressive carnivalesque energies of *As You Like It* with "the felonies associated with forest rioters", and popular ritual with specifically criminal activities such as poaching. 'Like the Old Robin Hood: *As You Like It* and the Enclosure Riots' in *Will Power*, 63–82, quotation from 76. For a critique of the conflations and anachronisms in Wilson's essay see Andrew Barnaby, 'The Political Conscious of Shakespeare's *As You Like It* in *Studies in English Literature* 36 (1996), 373–95.

2. Goldie, 'The Unacknowledged Republic' in Harris, *Politics of the Excluded*; quotation from 182.

3. Archer, *Pursuit*, 94.

4. Christopher Hill, *Society and Puritanism in Pre-Revolutionary England* (London: Secker and Warburg, 1964), 122, 119.

5. Guy, *Tudor England*, 220.

6. Slack suggests that the major reason for the emergence in this period of so large and complex a poor relief system in England, by contrast with Scotland and Wales, was precisely the remarkable executive power of "the English civil parish" with its "collective activity, political participation at the most local level": Slack, *English Poor Law*, 48–50.

7. Hindle, 'Political Culture of the Middling Sort', 137.

8. Hill, *Society and Puritanism*, 374.

9. Hindle, *State and Social Change*, 229.

10. So great was underclass resentment in these increasingly polarised local conditions that "by the 1590s, within the south of England, the plebeian language of class shifted in its emphasis, increasingly blaming wealthier farmers for social ills, rather than (as in the 1530s and 1540s), the gentry". Andy Wood, 'Fear, hatred, and the hidden injuries of class', 818. See also Wood, *1549 Rebellions*, 204–07.

11. Hindle, *State and Social Change*, chapter 7; quotations from 177–78.

12. On the "striking" use of circuit charges and articles of inquiry in this time of "acute governmental anxiety', see Hindle, *State and Social Change*, 6–7.

13. Archer, *Pursuit*, 92–93)

14. Underdown, *Revel*, 94.

15. Max Weber, *The Protestant Ethic and the Spirit of Capitalism*, English trans. (London: 1930).

16. For a detailed local study see Keith Wrightson and D. Levine, *Poverty and Piety in an English Village: Terling, 1525–1700* (1979; 2nd ed. Cambridge University Press, 1995).

17. Underdown, *Revel*, 52.

18. Hindle, *State and Social Change*, 181.

19. Hindle, *State and Social Change*, 177.

20. Hill, *Society and Puritanism*, 152.

21. Peter Burke, *Popular Culture in Early Modern Europe* (1978; rpt.Aldershot: Ashgate, 1999), 212.

22. Hill, *Society and Puritanism*, 152–53.

23. Underdown, *Revel*, 63.

24. Shapiro, *1599*, 240.

25. Underdown, *Revel*, 56–57.

26. For theorisation of ideological process at any point into residual, dominant and emergent formations see Raymond Williams, *Marxism and Literature* (Oxford: Oxford University Press, 1997), 121–27.

27. Hindle, *State and Social Change*, 57.

28. Underdown, *Revel*, 40.
29. Archer, *Pursuit*, 96, 93.
30. Hill, *Society and Puritanism*, 368.
31. Archer, *Pursuit*, 94.
32. Clark, *English Provincial Society*, 249. See esp. 155–57. Compare Hindle on the 'culture of discipline' forged in the 1590s: *State and Social Change*, 177.
33. Underdown, *Revel*, 53–54, 59. On sixteenth-century reform of popular culture see also Burke, *Popular Culture*, 207–34.
34. Hindle, *State and Social Change*, 237.
35. Underdown, *Revel*, 64–72.
36. Hill, *Society and Puritanism*, 375.
37. Underdown, *Revel*, 40.
38. See Peter Stallybrass, '"Wee feaste in our defense": patrician carnival in early modern England and Robert Herricks' *Hesperides*' in *Renaissance Historicism: Selections from English Literary Renaissance* ed. Arthur F. Kinney and Dan Collins (Amherst: University of Massachusetts, 1987), 348–66.
39. Hill, *Society and Puritanism*, 229. Chapter seven of this book, 'The poor and the parish', remains rich and suggestive reading.
40. Hindle, *State and Social Change*, 177, 179, 187.
41. Ibid., 179–80.
42. Hill, *Society and Puritanism*, 364.
43. David Cressy, 'Mocking the clergy: wars of words in parish and pulpit' in *Travesties and Transgressions in Tudor and Stuart England* (Oxford: Oxford University Press, 2000), 142, 144. Cressy declares that the mutual revilements of pulpit and certain parisioners were merely "*ad hominem* rather than *ad clerum*" (138), yet our sketchy knowledge of many of the church court cases he discusses precludes such certainty, and there seems no reason why circumstantial conflicts over fees and tithes may not have reflected, indeed consolidated, underlying anticlericalism. Cressy's own allusions to divisive social conditions, quoted above, suggest anti-clericalism per se.
44. Hill, *Society and Puritanism*, 156–57, 367–68; Underdown, *Revel*, 60.
45. Cressy, 'Mocking the clergy', 148.
46. Eric Carlson, 'The origin, function, and status of the office of churchwarden', in *The World of Rural Dissenters 1520–1725* ed. Margaret Spufford (Cambridge: Cambridge University Press, 1995), 164–207.
47. Hill, *Society and Puritanism*, 372; quotation from Carlson, 'Churchwarden', 194.
48. Underdown, *Revel*, 31–32.
49. Carlson, 'Churchwarden', 174; Underdown, *Revel*, 59. Moral lapses might also be prosecuted in the quarter-sessions and assize courts.
50. In these culture wars, in some places outside London churchwardens chose not to present church absentees to church courts. "It was very tempting to report *omnia bene* in order to defend the community's liberty against the inquisitorial central power": Hill, *Society and Puritanism,* 337; compare Carlson, 'Churchwarden', 172–74, 200–06.
51. 39 Elizabeth, c.3; reprod. in Tawney and Power, *Tudor Economic Documents*, 2.346–47.
52. The Churchwarden was to be assisted in his work as Overseer of the Poor by four other Overseers, these others appointed by two Justices, according to the new Act. Slack, *English Poor Law*, 52–53.
53. Slack, *Poverty and Policy*, 65–66.
54. Steve Hindle, *On the Parish? The Micro-Politics of Poor Relief in England c.1550–1750* (Oxford: Clarendon Press, 2004), 1–95, 146–49. Statistics from 4 and 13.
55. Sharpe, 'People and the Law', 256.

56. Archer, *Pursuit*, 97–98.
57. Beier, *Masterless Men*, 156; Slack, *English Poor Law*, 53.
58. Beier, *Masterless Men*, 157. "Overseers were authorized to pry, with demeaning thoroughness, into poor people's lives": Woodbridge, *Vagrancy*, 275.
59. John Downame, *The Plea of the Poor; Or, A Treatise of Beneficence and Alms-Deeds*, 1616, 29, 31; cit. Woodbridge, *Vagrancy*, 72.
60. Cit. Hindle, *On the Parish?*, 257–58.
61. Beier, *Masterless Men*, 158.
62. Hindle, *On the Parish?*, 148–49, 318–21.
63. Hill, *Society and Puritanism*, 263–64, 266.
64. Hill, ibid., 255–58. Hill's excellent chapter, 'The Bawdy Courts' is pp.254–94.
65. Quoted in Hill, *Society and Puritanism*, 275.
66. Martin Ingram, *Church Courts, Sex and Marriage, 1570–1640* (Cambridge: Cambridge University Press, 1987), 6. Ingram disputes some of Hill's conclusions about these courts (7–12), noting that some of the ire towards them derived from Puritans, who thought them insufficiently severe, and from lawyers in the common law courts, whose jurisdiction overlapped with that of the ecclesiastical courts. Yet Ingram's serene report that the courts enjoyed widespread support, since "the overall standard was perfectly reasonable and there are only occasional signs of administrative lapses" (67) is at odds with the record of parliamentary protest.
67. Hill, *Society and Puritanism*, 262.
68. Hill, ibid., 271.
69. Ibid., 271–72, 263.
70. Neale, *Parliaments*, 357.
71. Ibid., 394.
72. Hindle, 'Political Culture of the Middling Sort', 143; Ingram, *Church Courts*, 214–15.
73. Hill, *Liberty Against the Law*, 202.
74. Ibid., 202–03.
75. *A Collection of Certaine Sclaunderous Articles Given Out by the Bisshops* (London: 1590), quoted in Hill, *Liberty Against the Law*, 201.
76. Hill, *Liberty against the Law*, 80 and 203.
77. B.J. Sokol, *Shakespeare and Tolerance* (Cambridge University Press: 2008), 66–68, 105.
78. Hill, *Society and Puritanism*, 272.
79. Ingram, *Church Courts*, 134, 215–16.
80. Hill suggests in fact (though for reasons relating more to developments in Puritanism) that "the fin de siècle is as important in the religious history of England as historians are coming to think it is in the political." *Society and Puritanism*, 436.
81. Quoted in ibid., 275.
82. The walls' height is taken from *The Design of the Globe*, Andrew Gurr, Ronnie Mulryne and Margaret Shewring (London: International Globe Centre, 1995), 99.
83. We need, as Charles Nicholl suggests, to multiply by five hundred to gain an approximate contemporary equivalence to Elizabethan prices: *The Reckoning*, 1.
84. Keith Thomas, *Man and the Natural World: Changing Attitudes in England 1500–1800* (London: Allen Lane, 1983), 103–04.
85. Thomas More, *Utopia*, trans. Robinson, 142.
86. *Calendar of State Papers Domestic, 1595–97*, 317.

87. Montrose notes that other Shakespearean discontented younger brothers include Duke Frederick, Richard of Gloucester, Claudius, and Antonio (in *The Tempest*): 'Place of a Brother', 53.

88. Hill, *English Bible*, 211–212.

89. Montrose, 'Place of a Brother', p.45.

90. Katherine Duncan-Jones, introduction to Penguin *As You Like It*, xxi–xxii.

91. George Bernard Shaw, quoted in Shapiro, *1599*, 212, who does not reference the observation.

92. Richard Wilson, it is true, refers to Orlando's "combination of rebelliousness and conservatism", yet he misconstrues Orlando as simply a Robin Hood stereotype. Quoting Eric Hobsbawm's definition of the 'social bandit'— "His role is that of a champion, the righter of wrongs, the bringer of justice and social equality. His relation with the peasants is one of solidarity and identity"—Wilson judges this to be "an identikit picture of Orlando"; and he goes on to associate Orlando with the Midland rioters. *Will Power*, 69, 77.

93. On the evidence for the adoption of this motto by the new playhouse see Richard Dutton, '*Hamlet, An Apology for Actors*, and the Sign of the Globe' in *Shakespeare Studies* 41 (1989), 35–44.

94. The punctuation of these lines varies from edition to edition. I have given more exclamation marks than usual, to highlight the melodramatically exclamatory tone I read here.

95. Mark Burnett, *Masters and Servants in English Renaissance Drama and Culture* (New York: St. Martin's, 1997), 83; Shapiro, *1599*, 220.

96. Lawrence Stone, *The Family, Sex and Marriage in England 1500–1800* (Harmondsworth: Penguin 1977), 120.

97. D. M. Metcalf, cit. Alan Brissenden, Oxford Classics edition, 1993, note to 2.3.39.

98. Always eye-catching, the action occasionally works to other effect than a privilege-flaunting tantalization. When Titus in dementia gives money to a clown, of all people, as payment for bearing his letter to the emperor, the effect is presumably the pathos of a great man brought low (*Titus Andronicus*, 4.3.103). Gloucester's purse-giving to Poor Tom at 4.1.63 ("Here, take this purse") enacts that new-found principle of succouring the poor on which his ensuing speech insists ("So distribution should undo excess", line 69). When later, preparing for his suicidal leap from Dover Cliff, Gloucester gives Tom "another purse; in it a jewel / Well worth a poor man's taking" (*King Lear*, 4.6.28–29), the impact seems to heighten the miraculism of a great nobleman proving solidarity with the outcast. And notably, at Dover Cliff, we are not shown that jewel.

99. D.V. Glass and D. E. C. Eversley, eds., *Population in History: Essays in Historical Demography* (London: 1965), 207, 212.

100. Manning, *Village Revolts*, 191–93.

101. Beier, *Masterless Men*, 54.

102. Susan Brigden, 'Youth and the English Reformation' *in Rebellion, Popular Protest and the Social Order in Early Modern England*, ed. Paul Slack (Cambridge: Cambridge University Press, 1984), 88.

103. Manning, *Village Revolts*, 193.

104. Keith Wrightson, 'Alehouses, order and reformation in rural England' in *Popular Culture and Class Conflict 1590–1914*, ed. Eileen Yeo and Stephen Yeo (Sussex: Harvester, 1981), 18.

105. Wrightson, 'Alehouses', 16–17.

106. *Rosalynde*, 192, 195, 220.

107. Stone, *Family, Sex and Marriage*, 116–120.

108. Archer, *Pursuit*, 217–18.
109. John Dod and Robert Cleaver, *A Plain and Familiar Exposition of the Ten Commandements*, 1603 (1662 edition, 199); cit. Hill, *Society and Puritanism*, 237. Compare Crowley: "These idle bellies will devour all that we shall get by our sore labour in our youth, and when we shall be old and impotent, then shall [we] be driven to beg." *The Way to Wealth* (1551), in *Selected Works*, 133.
110. Terry Eagleton, *The Ideology of the Aesthetic* (Oxford: Blackwell, 1990) 41; *Ideology: An Introduction* (London: Verso 1991), 20.
111. "The remembrance of their poor, indigent, and beggarly old age killeth them up. For their daily wages is so little that it will not suffice for the same day, much less it yieldeth any overplus that may daily be laid up for the relief of old age . . . an unjust and unkind public weal . . . when they be oppressed with old age and sickness . . . recompenseth and acquitteth them most unkindly with miserable death": *Utopia*, Robinson trans., 142–43.
112. The double standard is exposed from the outset in Shakespeare's career, when Adriana laments that "A wretched soul, bruised with adversity, / We bid be quiet when we hear it cry. / But were we burdened with like weight of pain, / As much or more we should ourselves complain", yet instantly proves merciless to her servant's suffering outcry—"Back, slave, or I will break thy pate across". *Comedy of Errors*, 2.1.34–36, 77.
113. Tawney and Power, *Tudor Economic Documents*, 2.348.
114. Neale, *Parliaments*, 398. The bill was defeated, by one vote. Sir Walter Raleigh, opposing the bill, deplored "what quarrelling and danger may happen, besides giving authority to a mean churchwarden!"Cit. Raleigh Trevelyan, *Sir Walter Raleigh* (New York: Henry Holt, 2002), 345.
115. These circumstances are normally related by critics (only) to *Coriolanus*. See for instance the introduction by R. B. Parker to *Coriolanus* (Oxford University Press, 1994), 40.
116. Hill, *Society and Puritanism*, 375. See also ibid 250 on later Leveller pressure to redirect embezzled charitable funds to the poor. Hill quotes a John Davenant character in *News from Plymouth* who boasts of building himself a house on misappropriated income when a Collector for the Poor.
117. Agnes Latham registers perplexity in her Arden edition (1975; rpt. 1984), Appendix A, 132–33. Alan Dessen has noted that the visibility to the audience of the groaning table would condition audience sympathy for Adam and Orlando, but has neither explored the politics of this perception, nor perceived the targeting effect of Orlando's obliviousness to the board: 'Shakespeare and the Theatrical Conventions of his Time' in *Cambridge Companion to Shakespeare Studies*, ed. Stanley Wells (Cambridge University Press: 1986), 98.
118. Behind the question on familiarity with church bells may lie not only the general Elizabethan notion that heath and forest areas fostered pagan levels of religious ignorance (see Thomas, *Religion and the Decline of Magic*, 195), but the Puritan condemnation by Perkins and others of vagrants as 'beasts' beyond the covenant, since they were not churchgoing (see Hill, *Puritanism and Revolution*, 223–226 and *Liberty Against the Law*, 50–51). Rendering Orlando's Perkinsesque assumption here both socially imperceptive and deictically comical, Shakespeare seems to be countering, once more, authoritarian Puritan ideology.
119. Shakespeare's manipulation of sympathy for sturdy beggars through presentation of Orlando and Adam may be compared with his treatment of tinkers and pedlars: the latter duo generally figured, as Carroll demonstrates, as "petty criminals and inveterate frauds . . . like their cousins the Dommerar

and Abraham Man" (*Fat King*, 162). Yet as Carroll persuasively argues, in Snout the Tinker (*A Midsummer Night's Dream*) that figure is revalued as one of "genial warmth", whilst Christopher Sly, by birth a pedlar and profession a tinker (*Shrew*) is shown to be graphically devoid of the crafty roleplaying powers for which these figures are customarily denounced. Carroll, *Fat King*, 163–67.

120. Sharp, *In Contempt of All Authority*, 164.

121. Fascinatingly, it was precisely through the market place in woodland-pasture regions that many later Tudor women may have gained "an unusual degree of independence", think some historians. Dairy farm wives were responsible for both producing and marketing butter and cheese: and this period saw expansion of the market economy and of the proportion of land devoted to dairy farming: Underdown, 'The taming of the scold', 135–36. Shakespeare's association here of robustly assertive females with woodland market and tavern may thus stand, perhaps, as one more testimonial to his keen sociological instincts.

122. Hindle, *State and Social Change*, 62.

123. Hindle, *On the Parish?*, 38–42.

124. Bakhtin, *Rabelais and His World*, 5.

125. Berry, *Shakespeare and the Hunt*, 167.

126. Hill, *World Turned Upside Down*, 40.

127. Compare Jaques' use of 'wind' in deictic mockery of the free audience, who blow on whom they please, at 2.7.48–49.

128. Henslowe lists "two mossy banks" among his own stage properties (*Henslowe's Diary*, ed. R. A. Foakes and R. T. Rickert [London: 1961], 320), but there is no suggestion of these in *As You Like It*, or even of a stage tree. When Rosalind and Celia overhear Silvius and Phebe, they do not appear to be hiding behind a tree, or anything else rural. "O come let us remove" is all Rosalind bids Celia and Corin, 3.4.52.

129. The Globe opened in 1599, probably between June and September. Andrew Gurr (*The Shakespearean Playing Companies* [Oxford: Oxford University Press, 1996], 291) thinks *As You Like It* "almost certainly the first play Shakespeare wrote for the Globe", with *Henry V* belonging to the pre-Globe months of 1599. Editor Michael Hattaway believes that "*As You Like It* could well have been the first play performed at the company's new playhouse" (New Cambridge edition, 63). Dissenters include Bednarz, *Poet's War*, 267–68, who places the play between January and March 1600.

130. Taylor, *Reinventing Shakespeare*, 326.

131. Bakhtin, *Rabelais and his World*, 6.

132. Barbara Ehrenreich brilliantly discusses modern loss of practices of 'collective joy' and the communal spirit, contrasting with these with the lineage of exultant group-mergings in primitive, classical and medieval societies, in *Dancing in the Streets: A History of Collective Joy* (New York: Metropolitan, 2006).

133. "Festivities involving dancing were naturally especially popular among young people, for whom they provided convenient courting opportunities": Underdown, *Revel*, 46. Burke notes that "Weddings often took place during Carnival, and mock weddings were a popular form of game": Burke, *Popular Culture*, 186.

134. Marjorie Garber, 'The education of Orlando' in *Comedy from Shakespeare to Sheridan* ed. A.R. Braunmuller and J.C. Bulman (Newark: University of Delaware, 1986), 102–112; Shapiro, *1599*, 204–11.

135. "Far from creating a godly commonwealth", observes historian Steve Hindle, "the reformation of manners frequently brought authority into contempt,

and often foundered to 'a chorus of mocking laughter.'" *State and Social Change*, 232.

136. Gurr, *Playgoing*, 151.
137. Gurr, *Shakespearian Playing Companies*, 293–94.
138. The surviving cast-list for this play, opening in 1598, derives from Jonson's 1616 folio.
139. Gurr, *Playgoing*, 151.
140. Ibid., 158–59.
141. Manning, *Hunters and Poachers*, 153, 218–19, 235.
142. Ibid., 182–83.
143. Ibid., 145–46.
144. Fitter, 'Slain Deer', 193–218.
145. Manning, *Hunters and Poachers*, 77, 166–67; Manning, *Village Revolts*, 295.
146. Fitter, 'Slain Deer', 206.
147. Manning, *Hunters and Poachers*, 40.
148. Indeed as Michael Hattaway records in his New Cambridge note to 4.2., p.169, this scene may echo the poaching scene in a recent Robin Hood play, "the hunting scene in Chettle and Munday's *Death of Robert Earl of Huntingdon (1598)* in which Friar Tuck enters dancing 'carrying a stag's head.'" Edward Berry however sees a suggestion of "such folk traditions as the Plough Plays", in which the Fool led a procession (*Shakespeare and the Hunt*, 183–84): one more instance, I think, of the designed carnival-saturation of the drama.
149. Fitter, 'Slain Deer', 205, 207.
150. Public Records Office, Court of Star Chamber, 5/A12/38; cit. Manning, *Village Revolts*, 296.
151. Beatrice Gottlieb, *The Family in the Western World: from the Black Death to the Industrial Age* (Oxford: Oxford University Press, 1993), 68–71.
152. Alan Haynes, *Untamed Desire: Sex in Elizabethan England* (Mechanicsburg, PA: Stackpole,1997), 8.
153. A. Gilby, *A Pleasaunte dialogue betwene a Soldier of Berwicke and an English chaplaine* (1581), cit. Hill, *Society and Puritanism*, 277.
154. Cit. Hill, *Society and Puritanism*, 277.
155. *As You Like It*, New Cambridge edition, 2000, 72.
156. Martext may indeed evoke (Martin) Marprelate; and Kemp, singled out for attack by the Martinists in 1589, excelled in impious counterblast in his adored, signature jigs. Thus, in this taunting romp, Shakespeare may, as Dusinberre puts it, "allow his clown a reprise of his best gag against a theatre-hating sect." Third Arden, appendix 2, 365–67.
157. David Cressy, 'Mocking the clergy: wars of words in parish and pulpit' in *Travesties*, 143.
158. Compare the association of "fantastical" in *Henry V* with Whitsun morris-dances at 2.4.25–27; also its association with banqueting in *Much Ado* at 2.3.19, and with mad tricks in *Measure for Measure* 3.1.340.
159. It might be objected that Martext, as a Puritan, cannot be an Anglican minister. Yet what Shakespeare manages to indict here is the church *position* on marriage. To the preacher who insists that the wedding is not "lawful" unless the bride be ritually "given", Touchstone sings "I will not to wedding with thee." Jaques on the other hand indicts Martext for lack of professionalism. Martext is thus assaulted, as it were, from both Left and Right. The Shakespearean ambiguity about Martext's exact relation to the Church of England is appropriate: 'vestry values' were simultaneously those of church authority, and where festivity was concerned, of marked Puritanical affinity.

160. Hattaway, Cambridge edition, 30.
161. *Diagnostic and Statistical Manual of Mental Disorders*, 4th edition (Washington, DC: American Psychiatric Association, 1994), 339–45.
162. The DSM further differentiates between Bipolar I, Bipolar II and Mixed Episodes, but the divergences here bear essentially simply on questions of time (frequency of occurrences and length of duration): nuances for which Renaissance drama, with its imprecise and often contradictory time-schemes, is obviously little concerned.
163. For an excellent and recent survey of this 'poetomachia' see Bednarz, *Shakespeare and the Poets' War*. Jaques is sometimes seen to embody the entire 1590s fashion for satire, evoking not only Jonson but Nashe, Hall, Guilpin, Marston, and others (Bednarz, 108–11). Dusinberre, however, thinks that Jaques may represent Thomas Lodge: 3rd Arden, 80–83.
164. See Bednarz, *Poets' War*, 113–14. Shakespearian "festive comedy functioned to undo the dictatorial poet who would attempt to constrain its liberty" (18).

NOTES TO CHAPTER 10

1. Nicholas Hytner, 'Behold the Swelling Scene' in *Times Literary Supplement*, November 1 2002, 20–22.
2. Montrose, 'The place of a brother', 39, 66. Montrose's later volume *The Purpose of Playing* amends the situation in regards to *A Midsummer Night's Dream*; though he confines to the close of a long footnote the apt recognition that "it is characteristic of Shakespeare to refuse the paradigm of a final reconciliation, conversion, or inclusion, or to grant it in such a way as to problematize or to delegitimate it" (187 n.87).
3. Jean E. Howard, 'The New Historicism in Renaissance studies' in *Renaissance Historicism: Selections from English Literary Renaissance*, ed. A. Kinney and D. Collins (Amherst: University of Massachusetts Press, 1987), 24.
4. Critics positing the play's conformity to the generic laws of romantic comedy may be assisted by tone-deafness. Anne Barton thus reads the drama as "tonally even". *Essays, Mainly Shakespearean*, 99.
5. 2nd Arden edition, 126, note on 5.4.106.
6. New Cambridge edition of 2000, 192, note to 5.4.92 SD.
7. Hattaway perceptively notes in his edition, 42, that Hymen may be "in a bit of a huff, miffed at being upstaged by Rosalind, who seems to have sorted out things fairly adequately herself".
8. Recent productions in England, those of 1994 and 1998, for instance, were able to double Adam and Hymen. See Hattaway, New Cambridge edition, 45, 61.
9. For Barton, the conclusion of *As You Like It*, like those of preceding Shakespearean comedies, "demonstrates Shakespeare's faith in comedy resolutions. It is a triumph of form". *Essays, Mainly Shakespearean*, 103, 112.
10. Compare Howard on Shakespeare's problematisation of comedy's adequacy to truth by refusing harmonious closures: 'The difficulties of closure', 113–30.
11. *Romeo and Juliet*, 3.3.91
12. Dollimore, *Radical Tragedy*, chapters 5 and 12–14.
13. *The Countess of Pembroke's Arcadia*, ed. Maurice Evans (Harmondsworth: Penguin, 1977), 846.
14. Phrase from Raymond Williams, *Country and the City*, 54.

15. *Ben Jonson*, Ed. C.H. Herford and P. and E. Simpson, 11 vols., (Oxford: Clarendon, 1925–52), 3.602.
16. Stephen Orgel 'Making Greatness Familiar' in *Pageantry in the Shakespearean Theater* ed. David Bergeron (Athens, GA: University of Georgia, 1985), 23.
17. The effect is made possible, even familiar, by the model of reality intrinsic to the new professional theatres: a world epistemologically 'horizontal' in its humanist concentration on political issues, material interests, social intrigue, 'Tacitean' self-determination, and physical pleasures, rather than being oriented to the vertical axis of metaphysical being and afterlife. Montrose argues gracefully that the *theatrum mundi* of Elizabethan playhouses "represented a profound challenge to traditional modes of thinking—not only to particular orthodox beliefs and opinions but also to the dominant paradigm of agency and authority . . . they presented an alternative framework, a dramatistic or theatrical world picture . . . a new kind of social and cognitive space." *Purpose of Playing*, 209–10.
18. Joan Thirsk, 'Younger sons in the seventeenth century' in *History* (London) 54 (1969), 360, quoted in Montrose, 'Place of a Brother', 45.
19. Auden, however, is sketching an antithesis between Western literature's "dream pictures of the Happy Place", not between political idealities. W. H. Auden, 'Dingley Dell and the Fleet', in *The Dyer's Hand and Other Essays* (London: Faber, 1975), 407–28.
20. Peter Erickson, *Patriarchal Structures in Shakespeare's Drama* (Berkeley and Los Angeles: University of California, 1985), 23. Such thinking builds upon Barber's view of a conservatism intrinsic to comic form, since the 'Saturnalian pattern' allows only temporary escape into festivity, "a misrule that implied rule": Barber, *Shakespeare's Festive Comedy*, 10.
21. Historians have shown that ideal patriarchal domination was often falsified in reality. "In practice, the balance of authority between husbands and wives varied considerably. Equally it is plain that strong, active, able wives were often prized, despite the fact the behaviour of such wives was unlikely to conform exactly to the stereotype of female virtue." Martin Ingram, 'Ridings, rough music, and the "reform of popular culture" in Early Modern England' in *Past and Present* 105 (November 1984), 98.
22. Underdown, 'Taming of the Scold', 136.
23. Gurr, *Playgoing*, 63.
24. Recent decades have seen such thinking challenged as literary criticism's 'heterosexist' insensitivity to alleged disruption by same-sex erotics: the Celia-Rosalind intimacies, for instance, the 'Ganymede'-Orlando flirtation, and Rosalind's exposure of her boy-actor status in the epilogue. There is a certain irony to such perspective as a putative gay emphasis in today's politics, when lesbians and homosexuals across the West are endeavouring not to invalidate marriage as a trap sprung by the repressive state, but to extend it to themselves: a point which perhaps should modify the regular hostility displayed to *As You Like It*'s marital resolution by progressive critics of various camps. Bruce R. Smith declares of Rosalind "he remains teasingly androgynous to the end", and that through "his pose as androgynous flirt [Shakespeare] invites us to take with us as we leave the theatre some of the liminal [i.e. same-sex] freedom we allowed ourselves during the play" (*Homosexual Desire in Shakespeare's England: A Cultural Poetics*, 1991; rpt. Chicago University Press, 1994, 155). Valerie Traub, *Desire and Anxiety: Circulations of Sexuality in Shakespearean Drama* (London: Routledge, 1992), and also Phyllis Rackin, 'Androgyny, mimesis, and the marriage of the boy heroine' in *PMLA* 102 (1987) 29–41 similarly view androgyny in the play as

disruptive of heterosexual love. In my own view, constructions of Rosalind as an essentially androgynous or bisexual figure centralise what is glancingly marginal, if intended at all. Orlando is not tongue-tied with 'Ganymede', for instance, as he had been with the person he desired (Rosalind as woman); nor, as editor Hattaway observes, does he evince any "hint of being attracted to a feminised male" (New Cambridge edition, 36). Rosalind's several allusions to herself as 'really' a woman preserve that identity uppermost in our minds; and as to her actuality as a boy actor, the efficacy of female roles such as Cleopatra and Lady Macbeth depended on the ability to keep such conventions invisible. Although it is, as Hattaway suggests, "impossible and wrong to fix one tone for the performance of much of the dialogue between the lovers" (40), I suggest that the supposed shattering of the epilogue's heterosexual closure by Rosalind's disclosure that 'she' is a boy in fact overlooks the logic of the intense sexual ambiguity of boys in that period. 'Heterosexuality' and 'homosexuality' are of course Victorian constructions, foreign to the plasticity of early modern libido, and boys were sexually attractive to both men and women; the very word 'maid' could denote an attractive and virginal young male. It follows that when Rosalind momentarily enunciates her status as a boy, she is not disrupting male desire for the female so much as presenting the object of male sexual desire as simultaneously a female and a female equivalent. Since an attractive boy was (in this case strikingly) a feminised male, Rosalind effectively is extending the category of the feminine rather than establishing an alternative to male desire for the female. Another way of putting this is to say that the epilogue's effect of a sudden whiff of forbidden fruit, rather than billowing forth a new character (Rosalind the androgynous), simply attaches to Rosalind-the-woman, sturdily established across five acts. Rosalind *qua woman* is as such sexier, saucier, smacking once again of official transgression: a kind of female-plus, distilling in her ambiguity a richer sexual perfume—advertising what Jean E. Howard calls "the contamination of sexual kinds and the multiplication of erotic possibility". On the other hand, this whole avenue of exploration may be a red herring. The main point of her (briefly) letting slip her gender mask ("If I were a woman") may be to underline the sustained brilliance of her acting—an entirely appropriate gesture as she solicits applause for the fiction, and disproves the feigned mediocrity of the performance ("[I] cannot insinuate with you in the behalf of a good play", 205–06). David Cressy likewise disagrees sharply with critics arguing for substantive homoerotic significance to cross-dressing, theatrical and otherwise. "Transvestite plotting toys with the conventions of gender distinction but does not profoundly interrogate them" ('Gender trouble and Cross-dressing in Early Modern England' in *Journal of British Studies* 35 (4) [Chicago, 1996], 458.) See also his *Travesties and Transgressions in Tudor and Stuart England* (Oxford: Oxford University Press, 2000) 92.

25. Erickson conversely sees the epilogue as the final stage of phasing out threatening female energy. "Rosalind is no-one to be frightened of since, as the Epilogue insists, she is male after all." The Epilogue thus preserves "on stage the image of male ties in their pure form with women absent" (34–35). Leaving aside the oddity of perceiving in the image of a sexually teasing boy in drag "male ties in their pure form", this perspective overlooks the way that Rosalind remains substantially in female character to the very end (flirting on, and closing with a curtsy), and it misses the complicating impact of coquette bisexuality here—hardly a final buttress of patriarchal order. Erickson, like so many critics who find their preconceptions of a conservative Shakespeare unravelled by the plays themselves, is defensively reduced to "I think there

are limits to Shakespeare's critical awareness in this pay" (36). By contrast, Dusinberre (3rd Arden, 13) reads the drama's destabilization of gender as "a vision of liberty."

26. Even with carnival, however, as Natalie Zemon Davis points out, "Comic and festive inversion could *undermine* as well as reinforce": *Society and Culture in Early Modern France*, 131.

27. Thomas Becon, *The Christian State of Matrimony*, 1546, quoted in Lisa Picard, *Elizabeth's London* (London: Weidenfeld and Nicolson, 2003), 177; original page unspecified.

28. Gurr, *Playgoing*, 147–53, quotation from 149.

29. Haynes, *Untam'd Desire*, 8. The court case struggled on until 1601, when judgement was given against the parents.

30. Neale, *Parliaments*, 356–57. The queen intervened to scotch this bill, as encroaching on royal prerogative as Supreme Head of the Church.

31. Lawrence Stone, 'The peer and the alderman's daughter' in *History Today* 11.1 (Jan. 1961), 48–55.

32. "Some chaplains in England in the seventeenth century were still not under episcopal jurisdiction, so places like Lincoln's Inn, the Southwark Mint, and Newgate Prison were known to offer possibilities to eloping couples." Gottlieb, *Family in the Western World*, 86.

33. Jurgen Habermas, *The Structural Transformation of the Public Sphere: an Inquiry into a Category of Bourgeois Society* (1962; trans. Thomas Burger, Cambridge, MA: MIT Press, 1989).

34. Norbrook, *Writing the English Republic*, 13.

35. Norbrook, *Poetry and Politics*, 190.

36. Norbrook, *Penguin Book of Renaissance Verse 1509–1659*, with editing by H.R. Woudhuysen (London: Penguin, 1992) 24.

37. Norbrook, *Poetry and Politics*, 287.

38. Habermas, *Public Sphere*, considers but dismisses Elizabethan and Stuart drama as precursors of the public sphere: many of the Globe's commoners were "a lumpen proletariat always ready for a spectacle" (38–39), and the very notion of "public opinion", allegedly, was absent from Shakespeare's plays (90).

39. Compare Hindle, *State and Social Change*, 235.

40. Gurr, *Shakespearean Stage*, 212.

41. Whilst not referring to the concept of a public sphere, Andrew Gurr writes similarly that "The part played by the different playhouse repertoires in the history of English society at this time will probably never be known with much precision, but since it was the only major medium for social intercommunication, the only existing form of journalism and the only occasion that existed for the gathering of large numbers of people other than for sermons and executions, it was certainly not cast in a minor role." *Playgoing*, 113–14.

42. Quotation, describing calendar festivity, from Underdown, *Revel*, 94.

NOTES TO CHAPTER 11

1. Wood, *1549 Rebellions*, 251.

2. The phrase "derision medicinable" is from *Troilus and Cressida*, 3.3.44. Note that Shakespeare never directly presents divine right claims except to debunk them. Carlisle's gorgeous affirmations in *Richard II* are at once undone by the materialist ease with which the monarch of the moment is overthrown, and claims that "you have but mistook me all this while." King

Claudius' pontification on the protective divinity that doth hedge a king (*Hamlet*, 4.5.120–22) is comically self-refuting, since it proceeds from a regicide. Falstaff's jest on natural recognition of a prince "by instinct" (*I Henry IV* 2.5.246–51) places monarchic distinctiveness in the realm of the ludicrous.

3. Sharpe, 'Social strain and social dislocation', 204–05.
4. Divided underclass attitudes toward the value of rebellion are likewise evident in the 'memories' of Kett's rebellion in the later century, retrieved by Andy Wood: *1549 Rebellions*, chapter 6.
5. The quotation comes one of the most brilliant critiques we have of the subversion / containment model, Holstun's third chapter in *Ehud's Dagger*, 76.
6. "I believe that the system of meanings and values which a capitalist system has generated has to be defeated in general and in detail by the most sustained kinds of intellectual and educational work . . . the task of a successful socialist movement will be one of feeling and imagination quite as much as one of fact and organisation." Raymond Williams, cited in *Raymond Williams: Critical Perspectives*, ed. Terry Eagleton (Boston: Northeastern University Press, 1989), 107.
7. The question then arises of why compassionate Shakespeare apparently gave no assistance, when elderly, to the citizens of Stratford in combatting William Combe's local enclosures in 1614–15, actually cutting instead a private deal with the encloser for personal reimbursement of losses in the value of his tithe-interests. (Samuel Schoenbaum, *William Shakespeare: A Compact Documentary Life* [Oxford: Oxford University Press, 1977], 281–85.) Given scant and ambiguous documentary survivals, the issue is enigmatic and perhaps unresolvable, but one clue is the formidable influence of the two enclosers. William Combe got away with his illegality, Chief Justice Coke declining in 1616 to punish him—since Combe was by then high sheriff (Mark Eccles, *Shakespeare in Warwickshire* [Madison: University of Wisconsin Press, 1961], 138). Combe's partner, Arthur Mainwaring, was steward to the Lord Chancellor himself, the Earl of Ellesmere. Shakespeare, given the place of these two men, and that deep scepticism about justice which we have seen his plays embody, may well have judged—accurately—that resistance was doomed, and that there was therefore no more to be done than safeguarding the interests of his own family. Such scepticism would doubtless have been reinforced back in 1601–02, when his friend, Richard Quiney, had as bailiff opposed Sir Edward Greville's enclosures and been subsequently murdered in a brawl by Greville's men. Greville prevented his men from receiving punishment (Eccles, 97–99). The mentality was widespread: Ethan Shagan's account of the Reformation, for instance, records a kindred instance of defeatist opportunism, where a devout Catholic, horrified by dissolution of the local abbey, resolves "Might I not as well as others have some profit of the spoil of the abbey? For I did see all would away." (*Popular Politics*, 163.)
8. The First Folio's frontispiece and title page would abstain, anomalously, from emblemata and Greco-Roman quotation. Producing "the type of directness associated with popular materials", their plainness posed no barrier to the unlearned. Marcus, *Puzzling Shakespeare*, 19–22.
9. Peltonen, 'Political rhetoric', 241.
10. Franco Moretti, 'The great eclipse: tragic form as the deconsecration of sovereignty' in *Shakespearean Tragedy*, ed. John Drakakis (London: Longman, 1992), 46.
11. For an early chapter of this work in progress, see Fitter, 'Historicizing Shakespeare's *Richard II*: current events and the sabotage of Essex'.

Bibliography

Anderson, Linda. *A Place in the Story: Servants and Service in Shakespeare's Plays*. Newark: University of Delaware Press, 2005.

Anderson, Perry. *Lineages of the Absolutist State*. London: Verso, 1979.

Anderson, Perry. 'The notion of bourgeois revolution'. In *English Questions*, 105–18. London: Verso, 1992.

Anderson, Perry. 'Civil war, global distemper'. In *Spectrum: from Right to Left in the World of Ideas*, 232–276. London: Verso, 2005.

Andrews, Kenneth R. *Elizabethan Privateering 1585–1603*. Cambridge: Cambridge University Press, 1964.

Appelbaum, Robert. '"Standing to the Wall": The Pressures of Masculinity in *Romeo and Juliet*'. In *Shakespeare Quarterly* 48 (Fall 1997) no. 3, 251–72.

Appleby, Andrew. *Famine in Tudor and Stuart England*. Palo Alto: Stanford University Press, 1978.

Archer, Ian. *The Pursuit of Stability: Social Relations in Elizabethan London*. Cambridge: Cambridge University Press, 1991.

Aristotle, *The Politics*. Translated by T. A. Sinclair and T. J. Saunders. Harmondsworth: Penguin, 1981.

Armitage, D., Condren, C., and Fitzmaurice, A. eds. *Shakespeare and Early Modern Political Thought*. Cambridge: Cambridge University Press, 2009.

Arnold, Oliver. *The Third Citizen: Shakespeare's Theatre and the Early Modern House of Commons*. Baltimore: Johns Hopkins, 2007.

Avila, Charles. *Ownership: Early Christian Teaching*. Maryknoll, NY: Orbis, 1983.

Baker, David. *Divulging Utopia: Radical Humanism in Sixteenth Century England*. Amherst: University of Massachusetts, 1999.

Bakhtin, M. M. *Rabelais and His World*, trans. Helen Iswolsky. 1968; rpt. Bloomington: Indiana University Press, 1984.

Barber, C. L. *Shakespeare's Festive Comedy*. Princeton: Princeton University Press, 1972.

Barton, Anne. *Essays, Mainly Shakespearean*. Cambridge: Cambridge University Press, 1994.

Bauckham, Richard. *Tudor Apocalypse*. Appleford, Oxfordshire: Sutton Courtenay Press, 1979.

Baylor, Michael G. Editor and translator, *The Radical Reformation*. Cambridge: Cambridge University Press, 1991.

Beckingsale, B. W. *Burghley: Tudor Statesman*. London: St. Martin's, 1967.

Bednarz, James. *Shakespeare and the Poets' War*. New York: Columbia, 2001.

Beier, A. L. *Masterless Men: the Vagrancy Problem in England 1560–1640*. London: Methuen, 1985.

Bentley, Gerald. *Shakespeare: A Biographical Handbook*. New Haven: Yale, 1961.

Berry, Edward. *Shakespeare and the Hunt*. Cambridge: Cambridge University Press, 2001.

Bevington, David. *Tudor Drama and Politics*. Cambridge, MA: Harvard University Press, 1968.

Bond, Ronald B., ed. *Certain Sermons or Homilies: A Critical Edition*. Toronto: University of Toronto, 1987.

Boose, Lynda E. 'Scolding brides and bridling scolds: taming the woman's unruly member'. In Kamps, *Materialist Shakespeare*, 239–79.

Boose, Lynda. 'The 1599 Bishops' Ban, Elizabethan Pornography, and the Sexualization of the Jacobean stage'. In Burt and Archer, *Enclosure Acts*, 185–200.

Booty, John. 'Tumult in Cheapside: the Hacket conspiracy'. In *Historical Magazine of the Protestant Episcopal Church*. Austin, Texas. 42 (1973), 293–317.

Breight, Curtis C. 'Duelling ceremonies: the strange case of William Hacket, Elizabethan Messiah'. In *Journal of Medieval and Renaissance Studies* vol. 19, 1 (1989), 35–67.

Breight, Curtis C. *Surveillance, Militarism and Drama in the Elizabethan Era*. New York: St. Martin's, 1996.

Brigden, Susan. 'Youth and the English Reformation'. In *Rebellion, Popular Protest and the Social Order in Early Modern England*, ed. Paul Slack, 77–107. Cambridge: Cambridge University Press, 1984.

Brissenden, Alan. *As You Like It*. Oxford: Oxford University Press (World's Classics), 1993.

Bristol, Michael. *Carnival and Theater: Plebeian Culture and the Structure of Authority in Renaissance England*. New York: Methuen, 1985.

Brown, Peter. *The World of Late Antiquity*. New York: Norton, 1989.

Bullough, Geoffrey. *Narrative and Dramatic Sources of Shakespeare*. London: Routledge and Kegan Paul, 1960, 3 vols.

Burke, Peter. *Popular Culture in Early Modern Europe*. 1978; rpt. Aldershot: Ashgate, 1999.

Burnett, Mark. *Masters and Servants in English Renaissance Drama and Culture*. New York: St. Martin's, 1997.

Burt, Richard and Archer, J. M. *Enclosure Acts: Sexuality, Property, and Culture in Early Modern England* (Ithaca: Cornell, 1994).

Butler, Martin. *Theatre and Crisis 1632–42*. Cambridge, 1984.

Cairncross, Andrew. *King Henry VI Part Two*, second Arden edition. London: Methuen, 1957, corrected 1962; repr. Routledge, 1994.

Caldwell, Ellen C. 'Jack Cade and Shakespeare's *Henry VI Part Two*' in *Studies in Philology* 92.1 (1995): 18–79.

Carey, John. *John Donne, Life, Mind and Art*. London: Faber, 1981.

Carlson, Eric. 'The origin, function, and status of the office of churchwarden'. In *The World of Rural Dissenters 1520–1725* ed. Margaret Spufford, 164–207. Cambridge: Cambridge University Press, 1995.

Carroll, William. *Fat King, Lean Beggar: Representations of Poverty in the Age of Shakespeare*. Ithaca: Cornell University Press, 1996.

Cartelli, Thomas. *Marlowe, Shakespeare, and the Economy of Theatrical Experience*. Philadelphia: University of Pennsylvania, 1991.

Cartelli, Thomas. 'Jack Cade in the Garden' in *Enclosure Acts: Sexuality, Property, and Culture in Early Modern England* ed. Richard Burt and John Michael Archer, 48–67. Ithaca: Cornell University Press, 1994.

Cartelli, Thomas. 'Suffolk and the Pirates: Disordered Relations in Shakespeare's *2 Henry VI*'. In *A Companion to Shakespeare's Works: volume 2, The Histories*, ed. R. Dutton and Jean E. Howard, 325–43. Oxford: Blackwell, 2003.

Chambers, E. K. *The Elizabethan Stage*. 4 vols. Oxford: Clarendon, 1923.

Clark, Peter. *English Provincial Society from the Reformation to the Revolution: Religion, Politics and Society in Kent 1500–1640*. Hassocks, Sussex: Harvester, 1977.

Clark, Peter. *The English Alehouse: A Social History 1200–1830*. London: Longman, 1983.

Clark, Peter, editor. The *European Crisis of the 1590s*. London: Allen and Unwin, 1985.

Clegg, Cynthia. *Press Censorship in Elizabethan England*. Cambridge: Cambridge University Press, 1997.

Cohen, Walter. *Drama of a Nation: Public Theater in Renaissance England and Spain*. Ithaca: Cornell University Press, 1985.

Cohn, Norman. *The Pursuit of the Millennium*. St Albans: Paladin, 1970.

Collinson, Patrick. *The Elizabethan Puritan Movement*. Berkeley and Los Angeles: University of California Press, 1967.

Collinson, Patrick. *Elizabethan Essays*. London: Hambledon, 1994.

Conti, V. 'The mechanization of virtue'. In *Republicanism: A Shared European Heritage* ed. Martin van Gelderen and Quentin Skinner, vol. 2, 73–83 . Cambridge: Cambridge University Press, 2002.

Cook, Ann Jenalie. *The Privileged Playgoers of Shakespeare's London*. Princeton: Princeton University Press, 1981.

Cosin, Richard. *Conspiracie for Pretended Reformation*. 1592.

Cressy, David. *Literacy and the Social order: Reading and Writing in Tudor and Stuart England*. Cambridge: Cambridge University Press, 1980.

Cressy, David. 'Gender trouble and Cross-dressing in Early Modern England'. In *Journal of British Studies* 35. 4 (1996), 438–65.

Cressy, David. *Travesties and Transgressions in Tudor and Stuart England*. Oxford: Oxford University Press, 2000.

Croft, Pauline, ed., *Patronage, Culture and Power: The Early Cecils*. New Haven: Yale University Press, 2002.

Croft, Pauline. 'Mildred, Lady Burghley: the Matriarch' in Croft, *Patronage, Culture and Power*, 283–300.

Crowley, Robert. *An Infomacion and Peticion* (1548). In *Select Works of Robert Crowley*, ed. J. M. Cowper. London: Early English Texts Society,1872.

Davies, C. S. L. 'Popular Disorder' in *The European Crisis of the 1590s* ed. Peter Clark. London: Allen and Unwin, 1985.

Davies, C. S. L. 'Slavery and Protector Somerset: the vagrancy act of 1547'. In *Economic History Review* 19 (1966), 533–49.

Davies, C. S. L. 'A rose by another name'. In *The Times Literary Supplement*, June 13 2008, 13–15.

Davis, Natalie Zemon. *Society and Culture in Early Modern France*. Palo Alto: Stanford University Press, 1975.

Dessen, Alan. 'Shakespeare and the Theatrical Conventions of his Time' in *Cambridge Companion to Shakespeare Studies*, ed. Stanley Wells, 85–99. Cambridge: Cambridge University Press, 1986.

Dessen, Alan. *Recovering Shakespeare's Theatrical Vocabulary*. Cambridge: Cambridge University Press, 1995.

Dessen, Alan. 'Q1, *Romeo and Juliet* and Elizabethan Theatrical Vocabulary'. In Halio, *Shakespeare's 'Romeo and Juliet'*.

Dionne, Craig and Mentz, Steve, eds. *Rogues and Early Modern English Culture*. Ann Arbor: University of Massachusetts, 2004.

Dollimore, Jonathan. *Radical Tragedy: Religion, Ideology and Power in the Drama of Shakespeare and his Contemporaries*. Brighton: Harvester, 1984.

Doran, Madeleine. *'Henry VI Parts Two and Three': Their Relation to the 'Contention' and the 'True Tragedy'*. Iowa: University of Iowa, 1928.

314 Bibliography

Dubrow, Heather and Strier, Richard. *The Historical Renaissance*. Chicago: University of Chicago, 1988.

Duncan-Jones, Katherine. *Ungentle Shakespeare: Scenes from his Life*. London: Arden, 2001.

Dusinberre, Juliet. *Shakespeare and the Nature of Women*. 1975; 2nd ed. New York: St Martin's Press, 1996.

Dusinberre, Juliet, ed. *As You Like It*. London: Thomson (3rd Arden), 2006.

Dutton, Richard. 'Hamlet, An Apology for Actors, and the Sign of the Globe'. In *Shakespeare Studies* 41 (1989), 35–44.

Dutton, *Mastering the Revels: Regulation and Censorship of English Renaissance Drama*. Iowa: University of Iowa, 1991.

Dzelzainis, Martin. 'Shakespeare and political thought'. In Kastan, *A Companion to Shakespeare*, 100–116.

Eagleton, Terry. *Shakespeare and Society*. London: Chatto and Windus, 1970.

Eagleton, Terry. *Walter Benjamin: Or Toward a Revolutionary Criticism*. London: Verso: 1981.

Eagleton, Terry. *William Shakespeare*. Oxford: Blackwell, 1986.

Eagleton, Terry, ed. *Raymond Williams: Critical Perspectives*. Boston, MA: Northeastern University Press, 1989.

Eagleton, Terry. *The Ideology of the Aesthetic*. Oxford: Blackwell, 1990.

Eagleton, Terry. *Ideology: An Introduction*. London: Verso 1991.

Eccles, Mark. *Shakespeare in Warwickshire*. Madison: University of Wisconsin Press, 1961.

Edelman, Charles. *Brawl Ridiculous: Swordfighting in Shakespeare's Plays*. Manchester: Manchester University Press, 1992.

Elam, Keir. *The Semiotics of Theatre and Drama*. London: Methuen, 1980.

Erasmus, *Adagia*. ed. W. Barker. Toronto: University of Toronto Press, 2001.

Erickson, Carolly. *Bloody Mary: the Life of Mary Tudor*. New York: Quill, 1978.

Erickson, Carolly. *The First Elizabeth*. 1983; reprinted New York: St. Martin's, 1997 (Griffin Edition).

Erickson, Peter. *Patriarchal Structures in Shakespeare's Drama*. Berkeley and Los Angeles: University of California, 1985.

Escolme, Bridget. *Talking to the Audience: Shakespeare, Performance, Self*. New York: Routledge, 2005.

Fernandez-Armesto, Felipe. *The Spanish Armada: The Experience of War in 1588*. Oxford: Oxford University Press, 1988.

Fitter, Chris. 'A Tale of Two Branaghs: *Henry V*, Ideology and the Mekong Agincourt'. In *Shakespeare Left and Right*, ed. Ivo Kamps, 259–76. Routledge, 1991.

Fitter, Chris. *Poetry, Space, Landscape: Toward a New Theory*. Cambridge: Cambridge University Press, 1995.

Fitter Chris. 'The Poetic Nocturne: from Ancient Motif to Renaissance Genre'. In *Early Modern Literary Studies* 3.2 (September 1997), 2.1–61.

Fitter, Chris. 'The Slain Deer and Political Imperium: *As You Like It* and Andrew Marvell's "Nymph Complaining for the Death of her Fawn"'. In *Journal of English and Germanic Philology* (April 1999), 193–218.

Fitter, Chris. 'Henry VI Part Two and the Politics of Human Commonality'. In *Renaissance Words and Worlds*, ed. Amlan das Gupta, 72–95. Kolkata: Macmillan India, 2003.

Fitter, Chris. 'Historicizing Shakespeare's *Richard II*: current events and the sabotage of Essex'. In *Early Modern Literary Studies* 11.2 (September 2005), 1.1–47.

Fletcher, A. and MacCulloch, D., *Tudor Rebellions*, 4th ed. London: Longman, 1997.

Freedman, Barbara. 'Elizabethan protest, plague, and plays: rereading the "documents of social control"'. In *English Literary Renaissance* 26 (1996) Spring, 17–45.

Frye, Susan. 'The Myth of Elizabeth at Tilbury'. In *Sixteenth Century Journal* 23.1 (1992), 95–114.

Garber, Marjorie. 'The education of Orlando' in *Comedy from Shakespeare to Sheridan* ed. A.R. Braunmuller and J. C. Bulman,102–112. Newark: University of Delaware Press, 1986.

Geremek, Bronislaw. *Poverty: A History*. Translated by A. Kolakowska. Oxford: Blackwell, 1994.

Goldie, Mark. 'The unacknowledged republic: officeholding in early modern England'. In Harris, *Politics of the Excluded*.

Gottlieb, Beatrice. *The Family in the Western World: from the Black Death to the Industrial Age*. Oxford: Oxford University Press, 1993.

Greenblatt, Stephen. *Renaissance Self-Fashioning*. Chicago: University of Chicago, 1980.

Greenblatt, Stephen. *Shakespearean Negotiations*. Berkeley and Los Angeles, University of California Press, 1988.

Greenblatt, Stephen. 'Murdering peasants: status, genre and the representation of rebellion'. In *Representing the English Renaissance*, 1–29. Berkeley: University of California,1988.

Gurr, Andrew. *Playgoing in Shakespeare's London*. Cambridge: Cambridge University Press, 1987.

Gurr, Andrew. *The Shakespearean Stage*. 3rd ed., Cambridge: Cambridge University Press, 1992.

Gurr, Andrew, with Mulryne, Ronnie, and Shewring, Margaret. *The Design of the Globe*. London: International Globe Centre, 1995.

Gurr, Andrew. 'Shakespeare's Playhouses'. In Kastan, *Companion to Shakespeare*, 362–76.

Gurr, Andrew. *The Shakespearean Playing Companies*. Oxford: Oxford University Press, 1996.

Guy, John. *Tudor England*. Oxford: Oxford University Press, 1988.

Habermas, Jurgen. *The Structural Transformation of the Public Sphere: an Inquiry into a Category of Bourgeois Society*. 1962, trans. Thomas Burger. Cambridge, MA: MIT Press, 1989.

Hadfield, Andrew. *Shakespeare and Renaissance Politics*. London: Thomson, 2004.

Hadfield, Andrew. *Shakespeare and Republicanism*. Cambridge: Cambridge University Press, 2008 (corrected ed.).

Halio, Jay. Editor, *Shakespeare's 'Romeo and Juliet'*. Newark: University of Delaware Press, 1995.

Hammer, Paul E. J. *The Polarisation of Elizabethan Politics: the Political Career of Robert Devereaux, 2nd Earl of Essex, 1585–97*. Cambridge: Cambridge UP, 1999.

Hammer, Paul E. J. *Elizabeth's Wars: War, Government and Society in Tudor England 1544–1604*. London: Palgrave Macmillan, 2003.

Harbage, Alfred. *Shakespeare's Audiences*. 1941; rpt. New York: Columbia University Press, 1964.

Harris, Tim., ed. *The Politics of the Excluded, c.1500–1850*. New York: Palgrave, 2001.

Harrison, G. B. *Life and Death of Robert Devereux*. New York: Holt, 1937.

Hartley, T. E. *Proceedings in the Parliaments of Elizabeth*. London: Leicester University Press, 1995.

Hattaway, Michael. *Elizabethan Popular Theatre.* London: Routledge Kegan Paul, 1982.

Hattaway, Michael. 'Drama and Society' in *The Cambridge Companion to English Renaissance Drama,* 91–126. Cambridge: Cambridge University Press, 1990.

Hattaway, Michael. *The Second Part of Henry VI.* Cambridge: Cambridge University Press, 1991.

Hattaway, Michael. *The Third Part of Henry VI.* Cambridge: Cambridge University Press, 1993.

Hattaway, Michael, editor. *As You Like It.* Cambridge: Cambridge University Press, 2000.

Haynes, Alan. *Untamed Desire: Sex in Elizabethan England.* Mechanicsburg, PA: Stackpole, 1997.

Heal, F. and Holmes, C. *The Gentry in England and Wales 1500–1700.* Palo Alto: Stanford University Press, 1994.

Heal, Felicity and Holmes, Clive. 'The Economic Patronage of William Cecil'. In Croft, *Patronage, Culture and Power,* 199–230.

Heinemann, Margot. 'How Brecht read Shakespeare'. In *Political Shakespeare: New Essays in Cultural Materialism,* ed. Jonathan Dollimore and Alan Sinfield, 202–230. Manchester: Manchester University Press, 1985.

Helgerson, Richard. *Forms of Nationhood: the Elizabethan Writing of England.* Chicago: University of Chicago, 1992.

Hill, Christopher. *Society and Puritanism in Pre-Revolutionary England.* London: Secker and Warburg, 1964.

Hill, Christopher. *Reformation to Industrial Revolution, 1530–1780.* Harmondsworth: Penguin,1969.

Hill, Christopher. *Winstanley: The Law of Freedom.* Harmondsworth: Penguin, 1973.

Hill, Christopher. *The World Turned Upside Down.* Harmondsworth: Penguin, 1975.

Hill, Christopher. *Milton and the English Revolution.* London: Faber, 1979.

Hill, Christopher. *The Century of Revolution.* Wokingham, Berkshire: Van Nostrand Reinhold, 1980.

Hill, Christopher. *Puritanism and Revolution.* Harmondsworth: Penguin, 1986.

Hill, Christopher. *Change and Continuity in 17th Century England.* 1974; rpt. New Haven: Yale University Press, 1991.

Hill, Christopher Hill. 'The Many-Headed Monster' in *Change and Continuity in 17th Century England,* 181–204. (1991).

Hill, Christopher. *The English Bible and the Seventeenth Century Revolution.* London: Penguin, 1994.

Hill, Christopher. *Liberty Against the Law: Some Seventeenth Century Controversies.* London: Penguin, 1996.

Hill, Christopher. *The Intellectual Origins of the English Revolution Revisited.* Oxford: Oxford University Press, 1997.

Hilton, Rodney. *Class Conflict and the Crisis of Feudalism .* Revised 2nd ed. London: Verso, 1990.

Hilton, Rodney. *Bond Men Made Free: Medieval Peasant Movements and the English Rising of 1381.* London: Routledge, 2003.

Hindle, Steve. 'The Political Culture of the Middling Sort in English Rural Communities c. 1550–1700'. In Harris, *The Politics of the Excluded,* 125–52.

Hindle, Steve. *The State and Social Change in Early Modern England, 1550–1640.* Basingstoke: Palgrave, 2002.

Hindle, Steve. *On the Parish? The Micro-Politics of Poor Relief in England c.1550–1750.* Oxford: Clarendon Press, 2005.

Hirst, Derek. *Authority and Conflict 1603–1658*. Cambridge, MA: Harvard University Press, 1986.

Hobday, Charles. 'Clouted Shoon and Leather Aprons: Shakespeare and the Egalitarian Tradition'. *Renaissance and Modern Studies* vol. 23 (1979): 63–78.

Holstun, James. 'Ranting at the New Historicism' in *English Literary Renaissance* vol. 19, number 2 (1989).

Holstun, James. *Ehud's Dagger: Class Struggle in the English Revolution*. London: Verso, 2000.

Holstun, James. '"Damned Commotion": riot and rebellion in Shakespeare's histories'. In *A Companion to Shakespeare's Works, Volume 2, The Histories*, ed. Richard Dutton and Jean E. Howard, 194–219. Oxford: Blackwell, 2003.

Holstun, James. 'The Spider, the Fly, and the Commonwealth: John Heywood and Agrarian Class Struggle'. In *English Literary History* 71.1 (Spring 2004), 53–88.

Homily Against Disobedience (1570). In Bond, *Certain Sermons*, 209–259.

Honan, Park. *Shakespeare: A Life*. Oxford: Oxford University Press, 1998.

Howard, Jean E. *Shakespeare's Art of Orchestration*. Urbana: University of Illinois, 1984.

Howard, Jean E. 'The difficulties of closure: an approach to the problematic in Shakespeare'. In *Comedy from Shakespeare to Sheridan*, ed. A.R. Braunmuller and J.C. Bulman, 113–30. Newark: University of Delaware Press, 1986.

Howard, Jean E. 'The New Historicism in Renaissance studies'. In *Renaissance Historicism: Selections from English Literary Renaissance*, ed. A. Kinney and D. Collins, 3–33. Amherst: University of Massachusetts Press, 1987.

Howard, Jean E. *The Stage and Social Struggle*. London: Routledge, 1994.

Howard, Jean E. and Shershow, Scott. *Marxist Shakespeares*. New York: Routledge, 2001.

Hughes, P. L. and J. F. Larkin, J. F., eds., *Tudor Royal Proclamations*, 3 vols. New Haven: Yale University Press, 1969.

Husselby, Jill. 'The Politics of Pleasure: William Cecil and Burghley House'. In Croft, *Patronage, Culture and Power*, 21–46.

Hytner, Nicholas. 'Behold the Swelling Scene'. In *Times Literary Supplement*, November 1 2002, 20–22.

Ingram, Martin. 'Ridings, rough music, and the "reform of popular culture" in Early Modern England' in *Past and Present* 105 (November 1984), 79–113.

Ingram, Martin. *Church Courts, Sex and Marriage, 1570–1640*. Cambridge: Cambridge University Press, 1987.

Ioppolo, Grace. *Dramatists and Their Manuscripts in the Age of Shakespeare, Jonson and Heywood*. New York: Routledge, 2006.

Irace, Kathleen O. *Reforming the 'Bad' Quartos: Performance and Provenance of Six Shakespearean First Editions*. Newark: University of Delaware Press, 1994.

James, Mervyn. *Society, Politics and Culture: Studies in Early Modern England*. Cambridge: Cambridge University Press, 1986.

Jardine, Lisa. *Still Harping on Daughters*. New York: Columbia University Press, 1989.

Jardine, Lisa. *Reading Shakespeare Historically*. New York: Routledge, 1996.

Jones, Emrys. *The Origins of Shakespeare*. Oxford: Oxford University Press, 1977.

Jones, Whitney R. *The Tudor Commonwealth 1529–1559*. London: Athlone, 1970.

Kahn, Coppelia. *Man's Estate: Masculine Identity in Shakespeare*. Berkeley: University of California, 1981.

Kamps, Ivo. *Shakespeare Left and Right*. London: Routledge, 1991.

Kamps, Ivo. *Materialist Shakespeare*. London: Verso, 1995.

Kamps, Ivo. *Historiography and Ideology in Stuart Drama*. Cambridge: Cambridge University Press, 1996.

Kastan, David Scott. '"The king hath many marching in his coats", or, "What did you do during the war, daddy?"' In Kamps, *Shakespeare Left and Right*, 241–58.

Kastan, David Scott. *A Companion to Shakespeare*. Oxford: Blackwell, 1999.

Kelley, Donald R. 'Ideas of resistance before Elizabeth'. In *The Historical Renaissance* ed. Dubrow and Strier, 48–76.

Kenyon, Lord, Manuscripts of. Historical Manuscripts Commission, 14th Report, Appendix, Part IV, 608–09.

Kahn, Coppelia. *Man's Estate*. Berkeley: University of California Press, 1981.

Kernan, Alvin. *Shakespeare the King's Playwright*. New Haven: Yale University Press, 1995.

Kiernan, Victor. *Shakespeare Poet and Citizen*. London: Verso, 1993.

Knowles, Ronald, ed. *Shakespeare and Carnival: After Bakhtin*. New York: St Martin's, 1998.

Knowles, Ronald. *King Henry VI Part II*, third Arden edition. Walton-on-Thames: Thomas Nelson, 1999.

Kott, Jan. *Shakespeare our Contemporary*. Translated by B. Taborski. London: Methuen, revised edition, 1967.

Lacey, Robert. *Robert, Earl of Essex*. New York: Atheneum, 1971.

Lake, Peter. 'Religious identities in Shakespeare's England'. In *A Companion to Shakespeare,* ed. David Scott Kastan. Oxford: Blackwell, 1999, 59–67.

Laroque, Francois. *Shakespeare's Festive World: Elizabethan Seasonal Entertainment and the Professional Stage*. Cambridge: Cambridge University Press, 1991.

Laroque, Francois. 'Tradition and Subversion in *Romeo and Juliet*'. In Halio, *Shakespeare's Romeo and Juliet*.

Latham, Agnes, editor. *As You Like It*. London: Methuen (Arden)1975.

Latimer, Hugh. *Sermons of Hugh Latimer, sometime Bishop of Worcester, Martyr (1555)* ed. G. E. Corrie. Cambridge: 1844.

Leahy, William. *Elizabethan Triumphal Processions*. London: Ashgate, 2005.

Lenz, Joseph. 'Base trade: theater as prostitution' in *English Literary History* 60.4 (1993).

Levenson, Jill. '"Alla stoccado carries it away": Codes of Violence in *Romeo and Juliet*'. In Halio, *Shakespeare's 'Romeo and Juliet'*, 83–96.

Levenson, Jill, editor. *Romeo and Juliet*. Oxford: Oxford University Press, 2000.

Levin, Harry. *The Myth of the Golden Age in the Renaissance*. Oxford: Oxford University Press, 1969.

Lewis, C. S. *English Literature in the Sixteenth Century Excluding Drama*. 1954; rpt. Oxford: Oxford University Press, 1973.

Linebaugh, Peter and Rediker, Marcus. *The Many-Headed Hydra: Sailors, Slaves, Commoners, and the Hidden History of the Revolutionary Atlantic*. Boston, MA: Beacon, 2000.

Longstaffe, Stephen. '"A Short Report and Not Otherwise": Jack Cade in *2 Henry VI*' in *Shakespeare and Carnival: After Bakhtin* ed. Ronald Knowles, 13–35. New York: St. Martin's Press, 1998.

Lovejoy, A. O. 'The communism of St. Ambrose'. In *Essays in the History of Ideas*. Baltimore: Johns Hopkins, 1948.

MacCaffrey, Wallace. *Elizabeth I: War and Politics 1588–1603*. Princeton: Princeton University Press, 1992.

MacCulloch, Diarmaid. 'Kett's Rebellion in Context'. In *Rebellion, Popular Protest and the Social Order in Early Modern England*, ed. Paul Slack, 39–62. Cambridge: Cambridge University Press, 1984.

MacCulloch, Diarmaid. *The Boy King: Edward VI and the Protestant Reformation*. New York: Palgrave, 2001.

MacCulloch, Diarmaid. *The Reformation*. London: Viking, 2003.

MacIntyre, Jean. *Costumes and Scripts in the Elizabethan Theatres*. Alberta: University of Alberta Press, 1992.

Manning, Roger B. 'Violence and Social Conflict in Mid-Tudor Rebellions'. In *Journal of British Studies* 16 (1977).

Manning, Roger B. *Village Revolts: Social Protest and Popular Disturbances in England, 1509–1640*. Oxford: Clarendon, 1988.

Manning, Roger B. *Hunters and Poachers*. Oxford: Oxford University Press, 1993.

Marcus, Leah. *Puzzling Shakespeare: Local Reading and its Discontents*. Berkeley and Los Angeles: University of California, 1988.

Marcus, Leah. 'The Shakespearean Editor as Shrew-Tamer'. In *Shakespeare and Gender*, ed. Deborah E. Barker and Ivo Kamps, 214–34. New York: Verso, 1995.

Marx, Karl. *Capital*, ed. Dona Torr. New York: International Publishers, 1939.

McCoy, Richard C. *The Rites of Knighthood*. Berkeley and Los Angeles: University of California Press, 1989.

McLaren, A.N. *Political Culture in the Reign of Elizabeth I: Queen and Commonwealth 1558–1585*. Cambridge: Cambridge University Press, 1999.

McMillan, Scott. '*The Book of Sir Thomas More*: dates and acting companies'. In *Shakespeare and Sir Thomas More: Essays on the Play and its Shakespearian Interest*, ed. T.H. Howard-Hill, 57–76. Cambridge: Cambridge University Press, 1989.

Merritt, J. F. 'The Cecils and Westminster 1558–1612: the Development of an Urban Base'. In Croft, *Patronage, Culture and Power*.

Milward, Peter. *Shakespeare's Religious Background*. Chicago: Loyola University Press, 1973.

Milward, Peter. *The Catholicism of Shakespeare's Plays*. Southampton: Saint Austin, 1997.

Mollat, Michel. *The Poor in the Middle Ages*. Translated by Arthur Goldhammer. New Haven: Yale, 1986.

Montrose, Louis. 'The place of a brother in *As You Like It*: Social Process and Comic Form'. In Kamps, *Materialist Shakespeare*, 39–70.

Montrose, Louis. *The Purpose of Playing*. Chicago: University of Chicago, 1996.

More, Thomas. *Utopia*, translated by Ralph Robinson (1551). New York: Barnes and Noble, 2005.

Moretti, Franco. 'The great eclipse: tragic form as the deconsecration of sovereignty'. In *Shakespearean Tragedy*, ed. John Drakakis, 45–84. London: Longman, 1992.

Mullaney, Steven. *The Place of the Stage*. Ann Arbor: University of Michigan, 1995.

Neale, J. E. *Elizabeth I and her Parliaments 1584–1601*. New York: St. Martin's Press, 1957.

Nicholl, Charles. *The Reckoning: the Murder of Christopher Marlowe*. London: Picador, 1992.

Norbrook, David. *Poetry and Politics in the English Renaissance*. London: Routledge and Kegan Paul, 1984.

Norbrook, David. 'Life and Death of Renaissance Man'. In *Raritan*, vol.8, issue 4 (Spring 1989), 89–110.

Norbrook, David, ed. *The Penguin Book of Renaissance Verse 1509–1659*. London: Allen Lane Penguin, 1992.

Norbrook, David. *Writing the English Republic*. Cambridge: Cambridge University Press, 1999.

Novy, Marianne. *Love's Argument: Gender Relations in Shakespeare*. Chapel Hill: University of North Carolina Press, 1984.

Novy, Marianne. 'Violence, Love and Gender in *Romeo and Juliet*'. In *Romeo and Juliet, Critical Essays* ed. John F. Andrews, 359–71. New York, Garland: 1993.

Orgel, Stephen. 'Making Greatness Familiar'. In *Pageantry in the Shakespearean Theater* ed. David Bergeron, 19–25. Athens, GA: University of Georgia, 1985.

Outhwaite, R. B. 'Dearth, the English Crown and the Crisis of the 1590s'. In Clark, *European Crisis*.

Patrides, C. A. 'The beast with many heads: Renaissance views of the multitude'. In *Shakespeare Quarterly* 16, no.2 (1965), 241–46.

Patterson, Annabel. *Censorship and Interpretation: the Conditions of Writing and Reading in Early Modern England*. 1984; 2nd ed. Madison: University of Wisconsin, 1990.

Patterson, Annabel. *Shakespeare and the Popular Voice*. Oxford: Basil Blackwell, 1989.

Peltonen, Markku. *Classical Humanism and Republicanism 1570–1640*. Cambridge: Cambridge University Press, 1995.

Peltonen, Markku. 'Political rhetoric and citizenship in *Coriolanus*'. In Armitage, *Shakespeare and Early Modern Political Thought*, 234–52.

Picard, Lisa. *Elizabeth's London*. London: Weidenfeld and Nicolson, 2003.

Pocock, J. G. A. *The Machiavellian Moment*. Princeton: Princeton University Press, 1975.

Poggioli, Renato. 'The Oaten Flute'. In *Harvard Library Bulletin* 11 (1957), 147–84.

Ponet, John. *A Shorte Treatise of Politike Power* (1556). In Winthrop Hudson, ed. *John Ponet: Advocate of Limited Monarchy*. Chicago: University of Chicago Press, 1942.

Poole, Kristen. 'Facing Puritanism: Falstaff, Martin Marprelate and the Grotesque Puritan'. In Knowles, *Shakespeare and Carnival*, 97–122.

Power, M. J. 'London and the Control of the 'Crisis' of the 1590s'. In *History* vol. 70 (1985).

Pugliatti, Paolo. '"More than history can pattern": the Jack Cade rebellion in Shakespeare's *2 Henry VI*'. In *Journal of Medieval and Renaissance Studies* 22.3 (Fall 1992).

Pugliatti, Paola. *Beggary and Theatre in Early Modern England*. Aldershot: Ashgate, 2003.

Questier, Michael. 'Elizabeth and the Catholics'. In *Catholics and the 'Protestant Nation'* ed. Ethan Shagan. Manchester: Manchester University Press, 2005.

Rackin, Phyllis. 'Androgyny, mimesis, and the marriage of the boy heroine'. In *PMLA* 102 (1987) 29–41.

Rackin, Phyllis. *Stages of History: Shakespeare's English Chronicles*. Ithaca: Cornell University Press, 1990.

Rastell, John. *Gentleness and Nobility*. In *Three Rastell Plays*, ed. Richard Axton. Cambridge: Cambridge University Press, 1979.

Read, Conyers. *Mr. Secretary Cecil and Queen Elizabeth*. London: 1955.

Read, Conyers. *Lord Burghley and Queen Elizabeth*. New York: Knopf, 1960.

Rossiter, A.P. *Angel With Horns: Fifteen Essays on Shakespeare*. 1961; rpt. London, 1989.

Rovine, Harvey. *Silence in Shakespeare: Drama, Power, and Gender.* Ann Arbor: UMI Research Press, 1987.

Russell, Conrad. *The Crisis of Parliaments: English History 1509–1660.* Oxford: Oxford University Press, 1971.

Sacks, David Harris. 'Political Culture'. In Kastan, *Companion to Shakespeare,* 117–36.

Sainte Croix, G. E.M. de. *The Class Struggle in the Ancient Greek World.* Ithaca: Cornell, 1981.

Salamon, Linda. 'Vagabond veterans: the roguish company of Martin Guerre and *Henry V'.* In *Rogues and Early Modern English Culture,* ed. Craig Dionne and Steve Mentz, 261–93. Ann Arbor: University of Michigan, 2004.

Salgado, Gamini. *Cony-Catchers and Bawdy Baskets.* Harmondsworth: Penguin, 1972.

Schama, Simon. *Landscape and Memory.* New York: Knopf, 1995.

Schoenbaum, Samuel. *William Shakespeare: A Compact Documentary Life.* Oxford: Oxford University Press, 1977.

Scott, James C. *Weapons of the Weak: Everyday Forms of Peasant Resistance.* New Haven: Yale University Press, 1985.

Scott, James C. *Domination and the Arts of Resistance.* New Haven: Yale University Press, 1990.

Shagan, Ethan. 'Protector Somerset and the 1549 rebellions: new sources and new perspectives'. In *English Historical Review* 114 no.36 (Feb. 1999), 34–63.

Shagan, Ethan. *Popular Politics and the English Reformation.* Cambridge: Cambridge University Press, 2003.

Shaheen, Naseeb. *Biblical References in Shakespeare's History Plays.* Newark: University of Delaware Press, 1989.

Shapiro, James. *A Year in the Life of Shakespeare: 1599.* New York: Harper Collins, 2005.

Sharp, Buchanan. *In Contempt of All Authority: Rural Artisans and Riot in the West of England 1586–1660.* Berkeley: University of California Press, 1980.

Sharp, Buchanan. 'Popular Protest in Seventeenth Century England' in *Popular Culture in Seventeenth Century England,* ed. Barry Reay, 271–88. New York: St. Martin's Press, 1985.

Sharp, Buchanan. 'Shakespeare's *Coriolanus* and the crisis of the 1590s'. In *Law and Authority in Early Modern England,* ed. Buchanan Sharp and Mark Fissel, 27–63. Newark: University of Delaware Press, 2007.

Sharpe, J. A. 'The people and the law'. In *Popular Culture in Seventeenth Century England ,* ed. B. Reay, 244–70. New York: St. Martin's Press, 1985.

Sharpe, Jim. 'Social strain and social dislocation, 1585–1603' . In *The Reign of Elizabeth I: Court and Culture in the Last Decade,* ed. John Guy. Cambridge: Cambridge University Press, 1995.

Sharpe, J. A. *Crime in Early Modern England 1550–1750.* London: Longman, 1999.

Shuger, Debora. 'Subversive fathers and suffering subjects: Shakespeare and Christianity'. In *Religion, Literature and Politics in Post-Reformation England,* ed. Donna Hamilton and Richard Strier. Cambridge: Cambridge University Press, 1996.

Skinner, Quentin. *Foundations of Modern Political Thought,* 2 vols. Cambridge: Cambridge University Press, 1978.

Slack, Paul. *Poverty and Policy in Tudor and Stuart England.* London: Longman, 1988.

Slack, Paul. *The English Poor Law.* Cambridge: Cambridge University Press, 1990.

Slater, Ann Pasternak. *Shakespeare the Director*. Brighton: Harvester, 1982.

Smith, A. G. R. 'Lord Burghley and his Household Biographers'. In Croft, *Patronage, Culture and Power*.

Smith, Bruce R. *Homosexual Desire in Shakespeare's England: A Cultural Poetics*. 1991; rpt. Chicago: University of Chicago Press, 1994.

Sokol, B.J. *Shakespeare and Tolerance*. Cambridge: Cambridge University Press, 2008.

Somerset, Anne. *Elizabeth I*. New York: St. Martin's Press, 1991.

Spivack, Bernard. *Shakespeare and the Allegory of Evil*. New York: Columbia, 1958.

Stallybrass, Peter. '"Wee feaste in our defense": patrician carnival in early modern England and Robert Herrick's *Hesperides*'. In *Renaissance Historicism: Selections from English Literary Renaissance* ed. Arthur F. Kinney and Dan Collins, 348–66. Amherst: University of Massachusetts, 1987.

Starkey, Thomas. *Dialogue between Pole and Lupset* ed. T. F Mayer. London: Royal Historical Society, 1989.

Stern, Tiffany. *Rehearsal from Shakespeare to Sheridan*. Oxford: Oxford University Press, 2000.

Stirling, Brents. 'Shakespeare's mob scenes: a reinterpretation'. *The Huntingdon Library Quarterly* 3, (May 1945): 213–40.

Stone, Lawrence. 'The peer and the alderman's daughter'. In *History Today* 11.1 (Jan. 1961), 48–55.

Stone, Lawrence Stone. *The Crisis of the Aristocracy, 1558–1641*. Oxford: Oxford University Press, 1967.

Stone, Lawrence. *The Causes of the English Revolution, 1529–1642*. London: Routledge and Kegan Paul, 1972.

Stone, Lawrence. *The Family, Sex and Marriage in England 1500–1800*. Harmondsworth: Penguin, 1977.

Strier, Richard. 'Faithful Servants: Shakespeare's Praise of Disobedience'. In *The Historical Renaissance* ed. H. Dubrow and R. Strier, 119–20.

Sutton, James. 'The Retiring Patron: William Cecil and the Cultivation of Retirement'. In Croft, *Patronage, Culture and Power*, 159–79.

Taylor, Gary. *Reinventing Shakespeare: A Cultural History from the Restoration to the Present*. Oxford: Oxford University Press, 1989.

Tawney, R.H. *The Agrarian Problem in the Sixteenth Century*. London: Longmans, 1912.

Tawney, R. H. *Religion and the Rise of Capitalism*. 1922; rpt. Harmondsworth: Penguin, 1980.

Tawney, R.H., and Power, Eileen. *Tudor Historical Documents*. 1924; rpt. London: Longmans, 1953.

Te Brake, Wayne. *Shaping History: Ordinary People in European Politics 1500–1700*. Berkeley: University of California, 1998.

Te Brake, William. A *Plague of Insurrection: Popular Politics and Peasant Revolt in Flanders, 1323–1328*. Philadelphia: University of Pennsylvania, 1993.

Thomas, Keith. *Religion and the Decline of Magic*. 1971; rep. Harmondsworth, Peregrine: 1978.

Thomas, Keith. *Man and the Natural World: Changing Attitudes in England 1500–1800*. London: Allen Lane, 1983.

Thompson, E. P. 'The Moral Economy of the English Crowd in the Eighteenth Century'. In *Past and Present* 50 (Feb. 1971), 76–136.

Thomson, Peter. *Shakespeare's Professional Career*. Cambridge: Canto, 1994.

Traub, Valerie. *Desire and Anxiety: Circulations of Sexuality in Shakespearean Drama*. London: Routledge, 1992.

Trevelyan, Raleigh. *Sir Walter Raleigh*. New York: Henry Holt, 2002.

Underdown, David. *Revel, Riot and Rebellion: Popular Politics and Culture in England 1603–1660.* Oxford: Oxford University Press, 1985.

Underdown, David. 'The taming of the scold: the enforcement of patriarchal authority in early modern England'. In *Order and Disorder in Early Modern England,* ed. A. Fletcher and J. Stevenson. Cambridge: Cambridge University Press, 1985.

Underdown, David. *A Freeborn People: Politics and the Nation in Seventeenth Century England.* Oxford: Oxford University Press, 1996.

Wall, Alison. *Power and Protest in England 1525–1640.* London: Arnold, 2000.

Walsham, Alexandra. 'Frantic Hacket: Prophecy, Sorcery, and the Elizabethan Puritan Movement' in *History Journal* 41.1 (1998), 26–66.

Walter, John and Slack, Paul. 'Dearth and the Social Order in Early Modern England'. In *Rebellion, Popular Protest and the Social Order in Early Modern England* ed. Paul Slack, 108–28. Cambridge: Cambridge University Press, 1984.

Warren, Roger, editor. *Henry VI Part Two.* Oxford: Oxford University Press, 2002.

Weber, Max. *The Protestant Ethic and the Spirit of Capitalism.* Trans. Talcott Parsons. London: Allen and Unwin, 1930.

Weimann, Robert. *Shakespeare and the Popular Tradition in the Theater.* Baltimore: Johns Hopkins,1978.

Wells, Stanley and Taylor, Gary. *William Shakespeare: A Textual Companion.* Oxford: Clarendon Press, 1987.

Whigham, Frank. *Ambition and Privilege: the Social tropes of Elizabethan Courtesy Theory.* Berkeley and Los Angeles: University of California Press, 1984.

Wikander, M. H. *Princes to Act: Royal Audience and Royal Performance 1578–1792.* Baltimore: Johns Hopkins, 1993.

Williams, Raymond. *The Country and the City.* Oxford: Oxford University Press, 1973.

Williams, Raymond. *Marxism and Literature.* Oxford: Oxford University Press, 1997.

Wilson, Ian. *Shakespeare: the Evidence.* New York: St. Martin's Griffin, 1993.

Wilson, John Dover. *The Essential Shakespeare: A Biographical Adventure.* Cambridge: Cambridge University Press, 1932.

Wilson, Richard. *Will Power: Essays on Shakespearean Authority.* Detroit: Wayne State University Press, 1993.

Wilson, Richard. *Secret Shakespeare.* Manchester: Manchester University Press, 2004.

Winstanley, Gerrard. *Writings of Gerard Winstanley,* ed. G. H. Sabine. Ithaca: Cornell University Press, 1941.

Wood, Andy. 'Poore Men woll speke one daye: Plebeian Languages of Deference and Defiance in England c. 1520–1640'. In Harris, *Politics of the Excluded.*

Wood, Andy. *Riot, Rebellion and Popular Politics in Early Modern England* (Basingstoke: Palgrave, 2002.

Wood, Andy. 'Fear, Hatred and the Hidden Injuries of Class in Early Modern England'. *Journal of Social History* Spring 2006.

Wood, Andy. *The 1549 Rebellions and the Making of Early Modern England.* Cambridge: Cambridge University Press, 2007.

Wood, Andy. 'Collective violence, social drama and rituals of rebellion'. In *Cultures of Violence,* ed. Stuart Carroll, 105–13. Basingstoke: Palgrave 2007.

Wood, Ellen Meiksins. *Citizens to Lords: A Social History of Western Political Thought from Antiquity to the Middle Ages.* London: Verso, 2008.

Wood, Neal. *Foundations of Political Economy: Some Early Tudor Views on State and Society.* Berkeley: University of California Press, 1994.

Woodbridge, Linda. *Vagrancy, Homelessness and English Renaissance Literature.* Urbana: University of Illinois Press, 2001.

Wootton, David, ed., *Divine Right and Democracy: an Anthology of Political Writing in Stuart England.* London: Penguin, 1986.

Wrightson, Keith. 'Estates, Degrees and Sorts in Tudor and Stuart England'. In *History Today* 37 (Jan. 1987) 17–22.

Wrightson, Keith. 'Alehouses, order and reformation in rural England'. In *Popular Culture and Class Conflict 1590–1914*, ed. Eileen Yeo and Stephen Yeo, 1–27. Sussex: Harvester, 1981.

Wrightson, Keith. *Earthly Necessities: Economic Lives in Early Modern Britain.* New Haven: Yale University Press, 2000.

Wrightson, Keith. *English Society 1580–1680*, 2nd ed. New Brunswick: Rutgers University Press, 2003.

Youings, Joyce. *Sixteenth Century England.* Harmondsworth, Penguin:1984.

Index